CGS

COMPUTER ANIMATION SERIES

Nadia Magnenat Thalmann
Daniel Thalmann (Eds.)

Creating and Animating the Virtual World

With 131 Figures, Including 69 in Color

Springer-Verlag Tokyo Berlin Heidelberg New York
London Paris Hong Kong Barcelona

Prof. Nadia Magnenat Thalmann
MIRALab, Centre Universitaire d'Informatique
University of Geneva
12, rue du Lac
CH-1207 Geneva
Switzerland

Prof. Daniel Thalmann
Computer Graphics Lab.
Swiss Federal Institute of Technology
CH-1015 Lausanne
Switzerland

Cover picture:
Design: Arghyro Paouri
Artistic and technical directors: Nadia Magnenat Thalmann and Daniel Thalmann
Copyright: MIRALab, University of Geneva and Computer Graphics Lab., Swiss Federal Institute of Technology 1992

ISBN-13:978-4-431-68188-5 e-ISBN-13:978-4-431-68186-1
DOI: 10.1007/978-4-431-68186-1

Softcover reprint of the hardcover 1st edition 1992

Preface

This book contains several invited papers and a selection of research papers submitted to Computer Animation '92, the fourth international workshop on Computer Animation, which was held in Geneva on May 20-22. This workshop, now an annual event, has been organized by the Computer Graphics Society, the University of Geneva, and the Swiss Federal Institute of Technology in Lausanne. During the international workshop on Computer Animation '92, the fifth Computer-generated Film Festival of Geneva, was held.

The book presents original research results and applications experience in various areas of computer animation. This year most papers are related to physics-based animation, human animation, and geometric modelling for animation.

NADIA MAGNENAT THALMANN
DANIEL THALMANN

Table of Contents

Part I: Physics-based Animation

Part II: Human animation

Part III: Path Planning and Motion Control

Part IV: Geometric Models

Part V: Languages and Systems

Part I
Physics-Based Animation

The Control of Hovering Flight for Computer Animation

David R. Haumann and Jessica K. Hodgins

Abstract: By combining control mechanisms and physically-based models of articulated, rigid body systems, we hope to simplify the task of generating realistic articulated motion for computer animations. As an example of this approach, we have developed a control system and a physically-realistic model to animate the hovering flight of a hummingbird. The computer model of the bird is based on the physical parameters of hummingbirds reported in the biomechanics literature. The animator specifies the desired location of the bird and the control system manipulates the model so that the aerodynamic forces acting on the wings propel the bird to satisfy that goal.
Keywords: Animation, Simulation, Aerodynamics, Control Theory, Motion Design.
CR Categories I.3.5, I.3.7, I.6.3, J.5.

INTRODUCTION

One of the open problems in three-dimensional computer animation is how the motion of objects through space can be easily and accurately controlled. With traditional keyframe animation, the generation of animation is limited by the ability of the artist and by the time available to keyframe each moving element. The burden of specifying the motion grows as the number of moving elements in the scene increases. One solution to this problem is the simulation of physically-based models. With simulation techniques, naive users can automatically generate realistic motion. Instead of controlling the positions of objects directly, the animator describes the physical properties of the objects and the environmental influences that act on the object over time. For example, a physically-based animation of leaves blowing in the wind requires the animator to specify the physical properties of the leaves. The motion is controlled by scripting how the wind blows over time (see [Wejchert 1991]). The advantage of physically-based motion is that, given a properly constructed model, the generated motion appears natural and realistic.

Physically-based models are now a widely accepted method for obtaining realistic motion in computer animation. This technique is particularly effective when applied to "passive" objects: inanimate objects such as leaves and teapots that lack muscles or motors to generate purposeful motion of their own. The animation of "active" objects like people, animals, vehicles and robots requires the specification of the forces that their muscles or motors should generate. Due to the large number of degrees of freedom in all but simple systems, manually specifying the forces required to make an object move (to walk, for example) would be overwhelming. If physically-based techniques are to be successfully used by animators for motion generation, then control systems must be designed to help control the motion.

Control systems provide algorithms that use information about the state of the object and the environment to compute joint torques required to move the object in the way the user specified. The control system can be viewed as the "brain" of the actor that an animator directs. The animator says "exit stage right" and the "brain" translates that into a walk that moves the actor offstage. The control system hides the low-level details of muscle contraction and joint rotations from the animator, allowing him or her to concentrate on the more global animation design questions such as "who should move where and when." By combining control systems with physically-based models, we hope to simplify the animator's control task while obtaining natural-looking, physically-realistic motion.

To animate an active object, we first need to build a computer model that represents the relevant physical properties of the object. In the case of a bird, we are concerned with the body and wings, their masses, moments of inertias, aerodynamic properties, and the geometry of joints and links that represent the underlying skeletal structure. We then design a control system that applies torques to the joints in the model. The torques are computed based on the position and velocity of the bird and its wings and the goals of the animator. When the torques are applied to the model, they simulate the action of the wing muscles. Animations are produced by setting horizontal and vertical position goals for the bird and recording the resulting motion. Figure 1 shows how a control system is combined with a physically-based model to animate an active system.

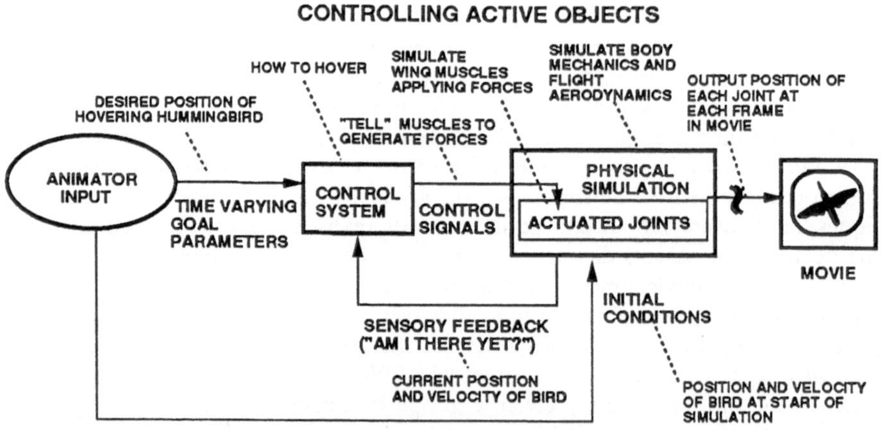

Figure 1. Active control. The addition of a control system to the physically-based model isolates the animator from the low-level details of how the model should move and simplifies the control task for active objects.

Background: The animation of self-propelled systems has been studied by several researchers interested in legged locomotion. Girard used pseudo-inverse control to describe body postures that, when interpolated and constrained by trajectory dynamics, generated realistic dancing and running gaits of bipeds and quadrupeds [Girard 1987]. Bruderlin and Calvert investigated biped walking using a system that combines high-level goal-directed control with a simplified dynamic simulation [Bruderlin 1989].

Raibert and Hodgins modeled the running and jumping of biped and quadruped robots and a kangaroo, using a "springy" leg model and principles developed for the control of legged robots [Raibert 1991]. McKenna described a model for controlling a virtual insect using forward dynamics [McKenna 1990]. Non-legged locomotion has also been investigated: Miller animated the locomotion of snakes and worms by using a mass-spring system in which he modified the spring tensions over time [Miller 1988].

Our approach to the generation of motion for animation is similar to that of [Bruderlin 1989], [Raibert 1991] and [McKenna 1990] in that we construct a control system that isolates the user from the low-level details of the underlying model. Although the specifics of leg control and ground interactions do not apply to the control of flight, [Raibert 1991] presents useful ideas for the design of control systems. They suggest taking advantage of the natural symmetries inherent in the system, and decomposing the control into separate parts. For example, a single wing generates a torque that tends to rotate the body. However, because the pair of wings flap in phase, these torques cancel, resulting in a stable hovering motion. We divide hovering flight into three main areas of control: the flap cycle, the angle of the wing with respect to the relative wind (angle of attack) and control of horizontal and vertical position.

Reynolds produced a remarkable animation of birds by using simple rules to describe large scale flocking behavior [Reynolds 1987]. The motion of the individual birds within the flock was kinematic and the flapping motion was keyframed. Amkraut animated a flock of flying birds in a film entitled "Eurhythmy" [Amkraut 1989b]. She used force fields to control the flock formation and to avoid collisions between birds. The flapping motion of the individual birds was procedurally generated based upon the speed and orientation of the bird [Amkraut 1989a]. In contrast to Reynolds and Amkraut, we focus our attention on generating physically-realistic motion for a single bird. Eventually, it should be possible to apply techniques like theirs to many physically-realistic models to generate flocking.

The control system for hummingbird hovering described in this paper was designed by hand and required significant physical intuition about the problem. Others have begun to address the question of automatic generation of control systems in the context of optimization problems and optimal control theory [Witkin 1988], [van de Panne 1990]. These approaches offer the potential of great generality but have yet to be applied to complex systems where the growth of the search space may prove to be a problem.

HUMMINGBIRD HOVERING

Because of their ability to fly backwards, upside-down and to hover motionless in the air for relatively long periods of time, hummingbirds (order Apodiformes, sub-order Trochili) have acquired a well-deserved reputation for superb aerobatics. The aerobatic capabilities of hummingbirds are due to unique adaptations in their structure and metabolism.

Hovering flight requires a higher output of energy than forward flapping flight. During forward flight the body has kinetic energy relative to the still air and this stored energy may be converted to lift by the wings even when they are not flapping. In contrast, the only source of lift during hovering is flapping. Because they are small, hovering hummingbirds have the highest energy output per unit weight of any warm-blooded animal; ten times that of a man running nine miles an hour [Greenwalt 1960]. The energy reserves that support this level of activity are fed by a diet consisting mainly of sugars (from nectar) and conserved during times of inactivity by a comatose form of sleep.

Like other birds, the skeletal structure of the hummingbird wing is analogous to the human bone-joint structure and consists of a hand, wrist, forearm, elbow, upper arm and shoulder (see Figure 2). The "primaries" or principal flight feathers grow from the hand. When compared with other birds, the hummingbird hand is oversized, making up the largest portion of the wing. The oversized sternum accommodates large wing muscles that account for a relatively high percentage of the body weight (25-30%) when compared with other birds (15-25%) [Greenwalt 1960].

When hovering, most birds articulate at the elbow and wrist, folding the wing to reduce drag during the upstroke. No lift is generated during the upstroke. The hummingbird elbow and wrist joints are permanently fused in a folded position and the shoulder joint is free to rotate in all directions. This combination of wing rigidity and shoulder joint flexibility allows the hummingbird to generate lift during the upstroke by turning its wing upside down so a positive angle of attack is maintained.

The hummingbird hovering model we used is based largely upon the research presented in [Weis-Fogh 1972]. He analyzed hovering flight to derive quantitative estimates of the force and power consumed during hovering. He used the Glittering-Throated Emerald (Amazilia Fimbriata Fluviatilis) native to South America for his analysis. Data from the analysis is shown in Table 1.

COMPUTER MODEL OF A HUMMINGBIRD

The computer model we constructed made several simplifications to the analysis presented by [Weis-Fogh 1972]. We have restricted the number of degrees of freedom in the model to five and have ignored some aerodynamic effects. The motion of the body is restricted to three degrees of freedom; it is free to move only in a single plane perpendicular to the ground. When the hummingbird model is oriented with its tail pointing down, it can move left or right, up or down and rotate about its abdomen (see Figure 3). The wing is restricted to two degrees of freedom: the stroke angle (wing flapping) and the angle of attack. The flap cycle of the wings is restricted to a plane that contains the shoulder joints and lies perpendicular to the central axis (running head to tail) of the body (see Figure 4 and Figure 5). The stroke angle is measured in this plane. We refer to this plane as the "stroke" plane. The angle of attack is the angle the wing surface makes relative to the air flow (see Figure 7).

The wingtip trace of the hummingbird is a figure eight lying on its side; the wingtip sweeps down from head to tail during both the upstroke and the downstroke, and returns by rapidly sweeping towards the head at the end of the strokes (see Figure 5). It is believed that the rapid upsweep action is an adaptation that allows the proper angle of attack to be achieved almost instantly to avoid loss of lift when the wing reverses direction ([Weis-Fogh 1972]). Since this simulation model is primarily concerned with the control issues in hovering flight, and not the aerodynamics of hovering, we chose to ignore the details of flapping that may be related to unsteady aerodynamic effects. The analysis presented by [Weis-Fogh 1972] showed that steady-state aerodynamics was sufficient to produce the lift required to maintain hovering. Steady-state aerodynamics provides a conservative analysis since the inclusion of unsteady effects would increase the lifting capability of the model.

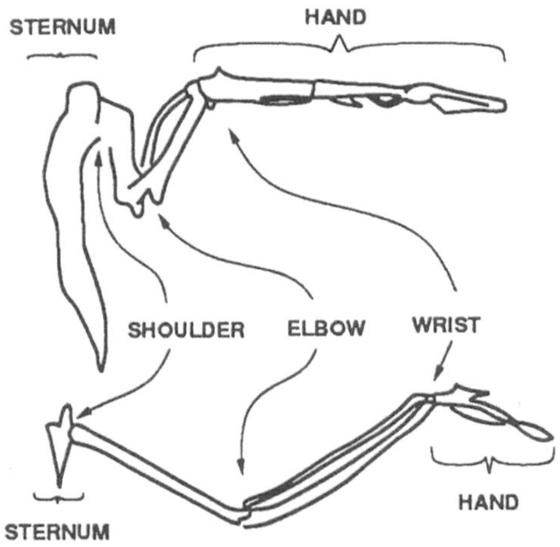

Figure 2. Skeletal structure of hummingbird compared to pelican. The skeletal structure of the hummingbird (top) differs from other birds such as the pelican (below, scaled to show both at the same length). The hummingbird wing is almost all hand, and the elbow and wrist joints are fused in a folded position. (Adapted from [Greenwalt 1960]).

Table 1. Hummingbird Physical Properties from [Weis-Fogh 1972] for Amazilia fimbriata fluviatilis:

total mass	5.1 g
single wing mass	0.1545 g
body mass	4.791 g
single wing length (shoulder to tip)	5.85 cm
single wing area	8.5 square cm
wing stroke (flap) frequency	35 hz
single wing stroke (flap) amplitude	1.05 rad (60 deg)

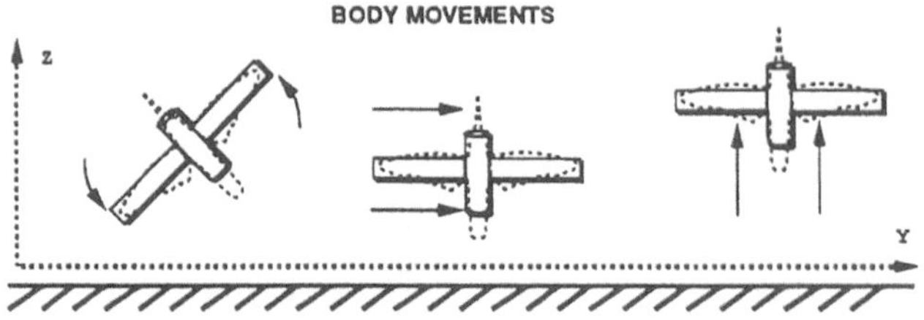

Figure 3. Degrees of freedom in computer model of hummingbird body. The body is restricted to three degrees of freedom: translating and rotating within a plane perpendicular to the ground. Wings flap about the bird's central (Z) axis, moving into and out of the plane.

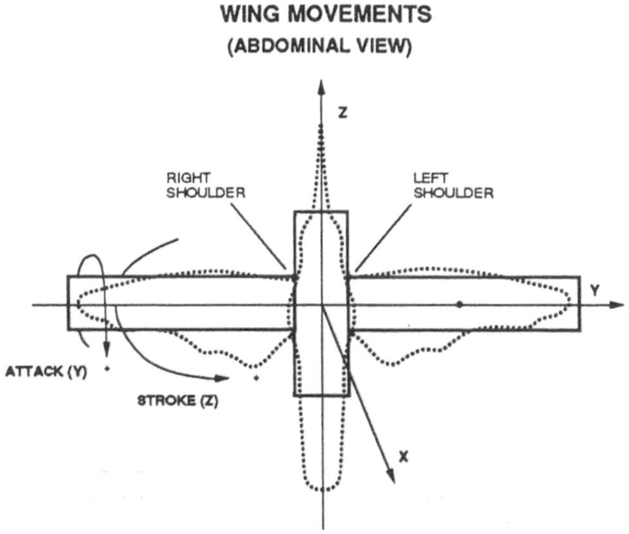

Figure 4. Degrees of freedom in computer model of hummingbird wing. The computer model restricts the wing motion to two degrees of rotational freedom about the shoulder joint: "flapping" about the Z-axis and "twisting" about the long (Y) axis. The "twisting" is used to set the proper angle the wing makes with respect to the relative wind (the angle of attack, see Figure 7).

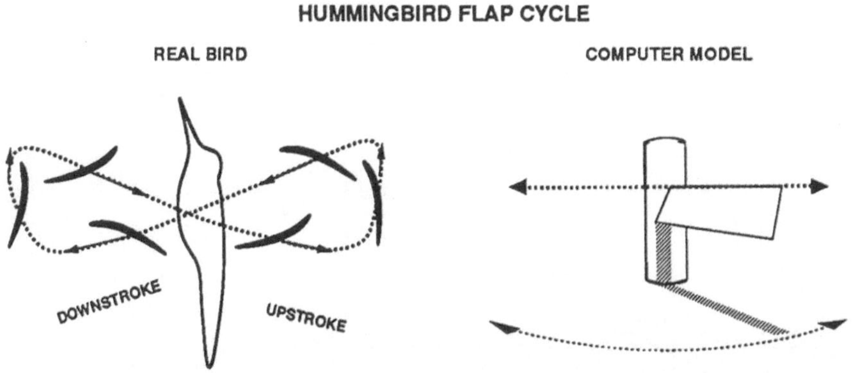

Figure 5. Stroke pattern in the hummingbird flap cycle. The wingtip path of a real bird (left) during the flap cycle resembles a figure eight (shown by dotted line, greatly exaggerated). The rapid wing twist and up sweep at the extremes of the stroke may be adaptations to avoid loss of lift. The computer model (right) ignores these adaptations and flattens the stroke to a plane so that the wingtip path is a horizontal line.

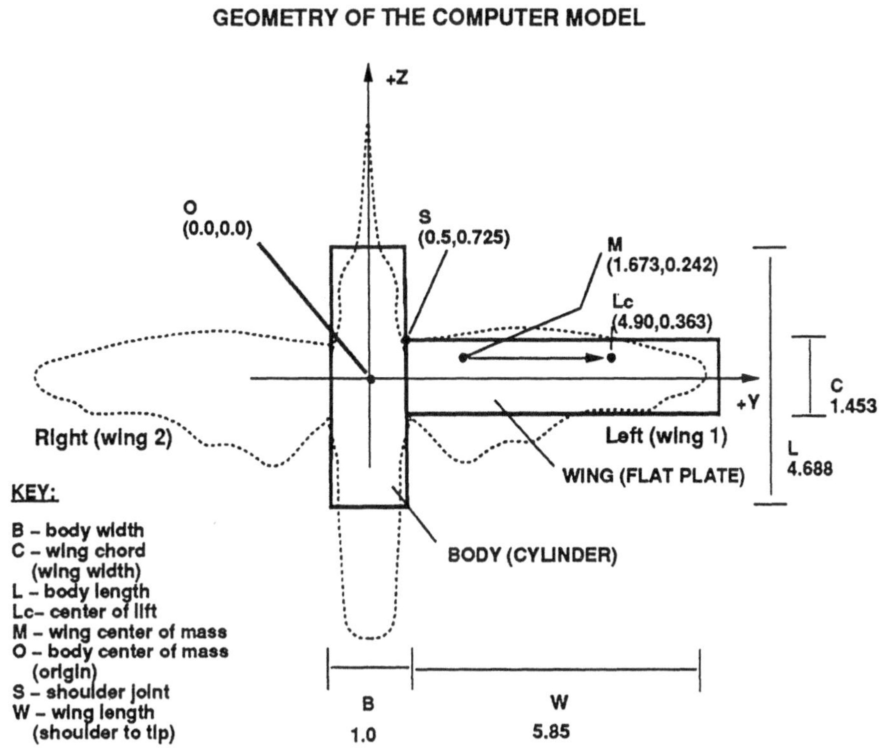

Figure 6. Detailed geometry of computer model. All measurements are in centimeters.

The body of the bird is modeled as a cylinder of uniform density, with the same mass as the body of the actual hummingbird. The size of the model encloses the bird body and head but not the beak or tail feathers. We assume, in the absence of specific data, that the mass and moments of the beak and tail feathers are negligible (see Figure 6). The wing is modeled as a thin flat rectangular plate. Its length (from shoulder to tip) and area match those of the tabulated data, but the width is constant. In estimating the moments of inertia of the wing, the density distribution along the long axis of the wing was matched to data supplied by [Weis-Fogh 1972]. The mass per unit area distribution along the short axis (leading to trailing edge) of the computer wing was modeled as a wedge shaped distribution, highest at the leading edge and falling off linearly to zero at the trailing edge.

Aerodynamics: Due to the aspect ratio and the high angle of attack, Weis-Fogh concludes that the hummingbird wing can be modeled as a high lift wing with aspect ratio 1:6 as described in [Prandtl 1934]. A table of lift and drag coefficients for this wing is shown in Figure 8. These coefficients are used to calculate the lifting force that acts perpendicular to the air flow over the wing, and the drag force that works parallel to it. Throughout these calculations, we have assumed that the wing velocity relative to the air is entirely due to its flapping motion in the stroke plane. We do not add in wind components that would be contributed by the motion of the stroke plane itself (as the bird travels towards a goal), since such motion is small when compared to the speed of

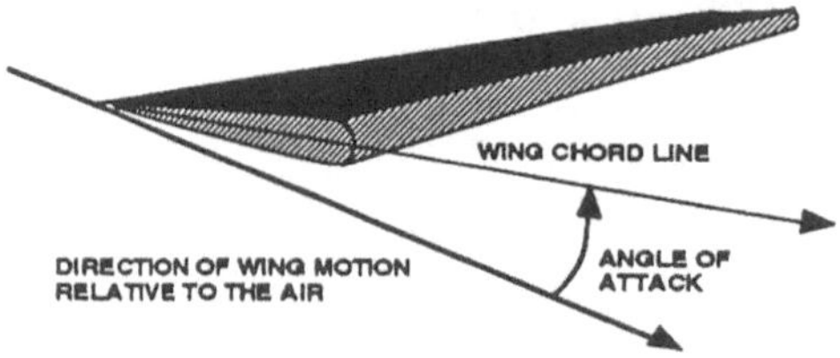

Figure 7. The angle of attack. The angle of attack is defined to be the angle between the relative wind due to the motion of the wing through the air and the chord line of the wing.

the wings flapping. This aerodynamic model would need to be revised to handle high speed forward flight.

The magnitude of the lifting force on the wing is computed using the standard equation for lift:

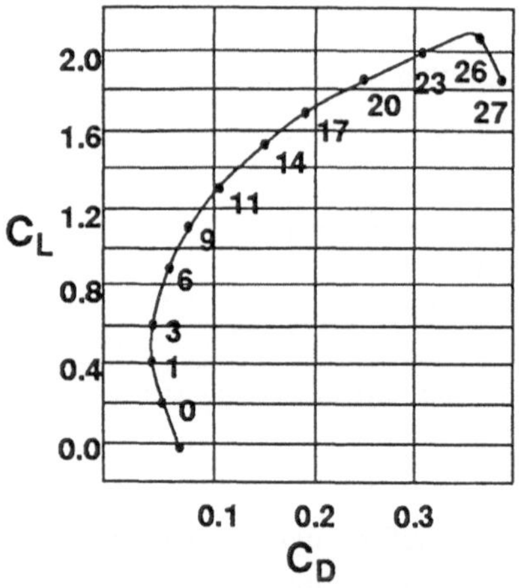

Figure 8. Polar diagram. Wing coefficients of lift and drag for the high lift wing that best matches the aerodynamic properties of the hummingbird's wing [Weis-Fogh 1972]. The dots represent different angles of attack in degrees. Increasing the angle of attack increases the lifting coefficient until the wing stalls (peak at upper right). (Adapted from [Prandtl 1934], figure 99.)

$$F_L = \frac{1}{2} \rho A C_L v^2$$

where F_L is the lifting force generated, ρ is the density of air, A is the wing area, C_L is the coefficient of lift and v is the velocity of the air over the wing. Since the velocity varies with the distance from the center of rotation of the wing, the lift force must be integrated over the radius of rotation of the wing:

$$F_L = \int_{r_0}^{r_1} \frac{1}{2} \rho C_L \, \omega^2 r^2 c \, dr = C_L \, \omega^2 (\frac{1}{2} \rho c \int_{r_0}^{r_1} r^2 \, dr) = C_L \, \omega^2 \, \beta_L$$

where the velocity is replaced by the product of angular velocity, ω, and the distance from the rotation center, r; and the area is replaced by the product of the chord width (width of the wing) c, and the radius differential, dr. Given a fixed geometry where r_0 is zero, and r_1 is the length of the wing, the definite integral for the force depends only upon C_L and ω, and can be reduced to the final form shown. Using an air density of 1.23 g/cc, we compute $\beta_L = .0594$g-cm. The magnitude of the drag force F_D is computed by substituting the coefficient of drag, (C_D), for the coefficient of lift (C_L) in the above equations.

We also need to determine the point on the wing where the lift force is to be applied; i.e. the center of lift, L_C. The location of this point along the long axis (length) of the wing is calculated by solving the integral

$$L_C = \frac{1}{F_L} \int_{r_0}^{r_1} r\, dF$$

where

$$dF = \frac{1}{2} \rho C_L\, \omega^2 r^2 c\, dr,$$

and

$$F_L = C_L\, \omega^2\, \beta_L.$$

Substituting for dF and F_L, we see that the $C_L\, \omega^2$ terms cancel yielding a constant value:

$$L_C = \frac{1}{C_L\, \omega^2\, \beta_L} \int_{r_0}^{r_1} \frac{1}{2} \rho C_L\, \omega^2 r^3 c\, dr = \frac{\rho c}{2\beta_L} \int_{r_0}^{r_1} r^3\, dr\,.$$

For the hummingbird model L_C is 4.4cm from the rotation center. Although the exact location of the center of lift along the short axis of the wing varies with angle of attack, we assume it is constant following an empirical rule suggested by [Alexander 1983], which places it one quarter of the chord length from the leading edge of the wing.

THE CONTROL MODEL

The basic primitives used in our control model are proportional-derivatives servos. These are critically damped oscillators or mass/spring/damper systems, in which the spring is fixed at one end and attached to the mass at the other. Such systems satisfy the equation:

$$m\ddot{x} + b\dot{x} + k(x - x_D) = 0$$

where m is the mass of the system, x is the current position of the mass, x_D is the equilibrium position of the mass, $\dot{x}$ and $\ddot{x}$ are the velocity and acceleration of the mass, $k(\geq 0)$ is the spring constant, and $b(\geq 0)$ is the damping coefficient. A critically damped system is one which satisfies

$$k = \frac{b^2}{4m}$$

and is one that when disturbed will most rapidly return to equilibrium [Marion 1970].

Such an oscillator acts to control the position of the mass in that if the end of the spring is moved to a new location, the mass will follow so as to again be in equilibrium. The inputs to the servo are the location of the mass, (x), a "goal" or "set point" value, (x_D), and the velocity between them, $(\dot{x})$. The output of the servo is the desired force $b\dot{x} + k(x - x_D)$.

Any deviation of the current state x from the set point x_D results in a signal that can be used to restore the current state to the set point. The signal can be used as input to other servos in the system, or it can be used to actuate "muscles" or "motors" to generate forces. For example, if the current shoulder stroke joint position is less than its set point, the servo will cause a positive torque to be applied to the joint to move it back towards the set point. The velocity damping term reduces the torque applied to the joint once movement towards the set point is underway.

The Flap Cycle: According to [Greenwalt 1960], the flapping frequency of a hummingbird rarely varies and [Hertel 1966] has confirmed that the flapping is very nearly sinusoidal. Therefore, we control the flap cycle by connecting the output of a sine generator to the input of a servo that controls the stroke of the wing (see Figure 9). The frequency of this generator is 35 cycles per second [Greenwalt 1962] for a bird of the size of our model. The servo generates torques about the stroke axis of the shoulder joint. Since the set point is changing sinusoidally, this servo causes the wings to flap.

Greenwalt observed that when more lift was required the amplitude of the flapping (not the frequency) increased accordingly. Our model modulates the amplitude of the sine generator according to the lift requirements.

The Angle of Attack: The angle of attack is defined as the angle formed by the chord (a line connecting the leading and trailing edge of the wing cross section) and the velocity of the wing relative to the air (Figure 7). Considering only the wing motion within the stroke plane (neglecting the global motion of the bird) the angle of attack is the angle between the wing and the stroke plane itself. Weis-Fogh [Weis-Fogh 1972] analyzed data supplied by Hertel [Hertel 1966] and found that the average angle of attack was 23 degrees. To maintain this angle of attack, a proportional-derivative servo compares the desired angle of attack to the current angle of attack, and generates torques to correct any differences. During the downstroke, the set point is 23 degrees. To invert the wing for the upstroke, we substitute the supplementary value ($180 - 23 = 157$ degrees) for this set point. Because the wing takes time to rotate about its angle of attack axis, the control system performs this substitution before the downstroke is completed.

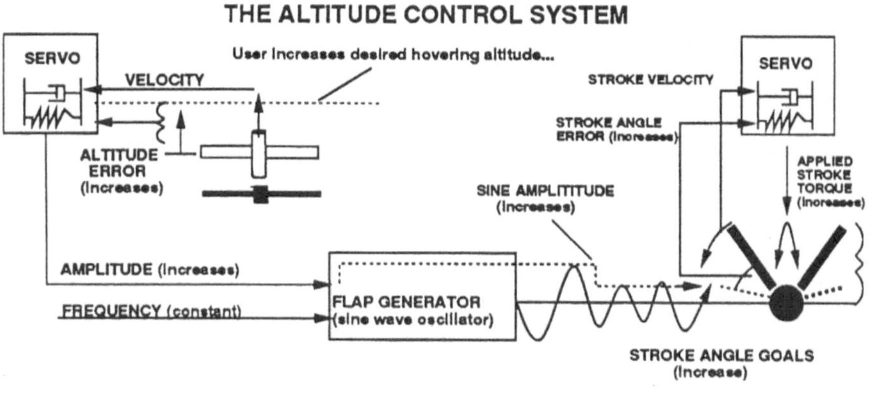

Figure 9. Schematic diagram of the operation of a portion of the control system. If the user increases the desired hovering altitude, the error between the current altitude and the desired altitude will cause a servo to increase the amplitude of the flap sinewave generator. This affects the strength of the flapping by increasing the error between the desired and current stroke positions of the wing, resulting in greater torques at the shoulder joint, higher wing speed, and greater lift from the wings.

Control of Altitude: Control of hovering altitude is achieved by monitoring the current and desired altitudes and modulating the amplitude of the stroke generator that controls the flap cycle. Since the equilibrium position of the flap cycle generates exactly enough aerodynamic lift (when integrated over a complete cycle) to counteract the pull of gravity, an increase or decrease in the amplitude will cause the bird to climb or descend. Figure 10 shows the altitude of the bird in response to changes in the altitude set point. Figure 11 shows how the amplitude of the flap cycle changes when the bird descends.

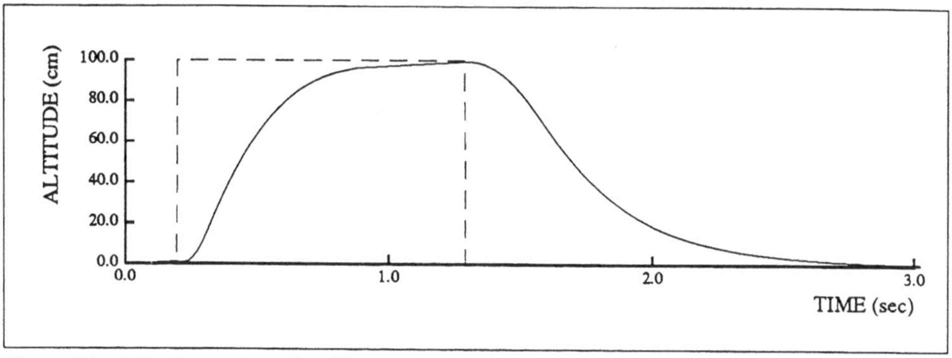

Figure 10. Altitude vs. time plot. The graph shows the altitude (centimeters) of the hummingbird over time (seconds). The dotted line represents the altitude "goal" position.

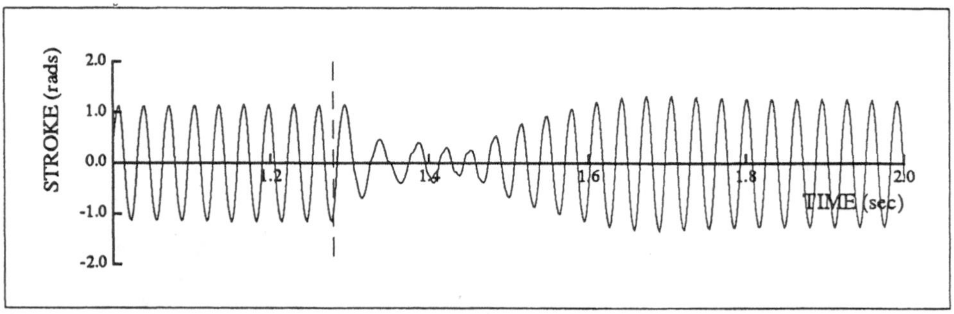

Figure 11. Stroke angle vs. time plot. The graph shows the stroke angle (radians) of the hummingbird shoulder when the altitude goal was changed from 100.0 back to 0.0 centimeters at time = 1.28 (indicated by the dotted line). The stroke amplitude is reduced so that the bird acquires a downward velocity. Once the velocity is sufficient and the goal is near, the amplitude increases to break the descent.

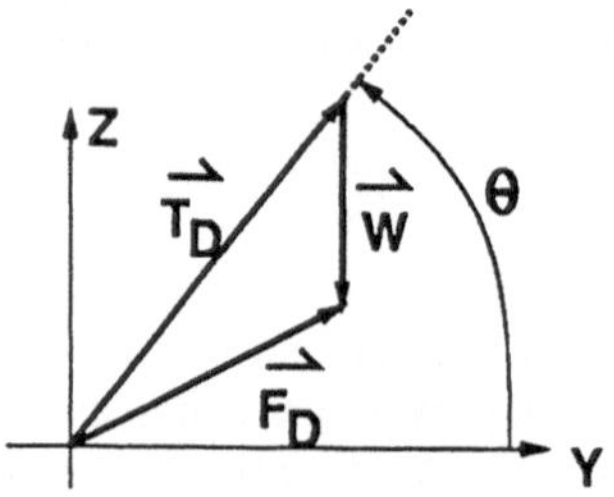

Figure 12. Computing the desired roll angle. Generating velocities with a horizontal component requires that the bird have a non-vertical roll angle. The roll angle is determined by solving the vector equation as shown.

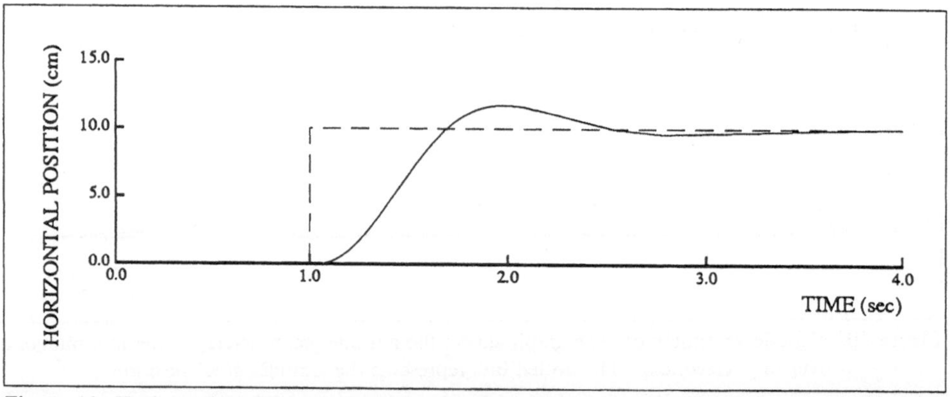

Figure 13. Horizontal position vs. time plot. The graph shows the horizontal position of the bird as it moves to a new goal position. The dashed line shows the goal position.

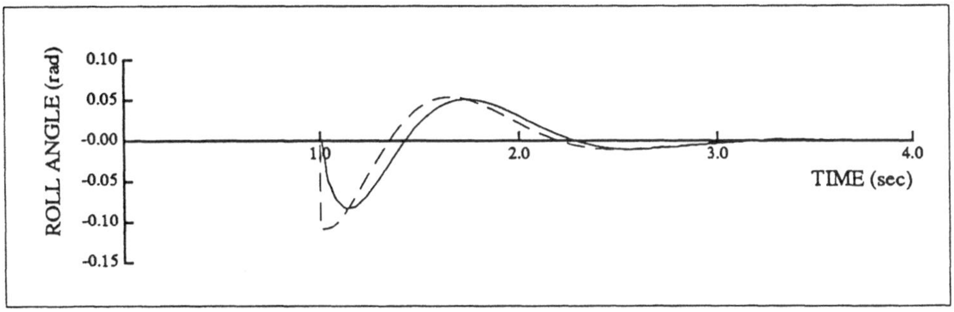

Figure 14. Roll angle vs. time plot. The graph shows the roll angle of the bird as it moves to a new goal position. To generate a positive horizontal velocity the bird rolls in the negative direction. The bird rolls in the positive direction to reduce the horizontal velocity as the bird nears the goal. As the bird reaches the desired horizontal position, the bird rolls back to vertical.

Control of Horizontal Position: The control algorithm for horizontal position is similar to the one used for altitude. A servo compares the desired horizontal position with the current horizontal position and generates a "throttle" signal that modulates the horizontal thrust produced by the bird. The difficulty in controlling horizontal position is that the current bird model can generate thrust only in a direction parallel to its central (long) body axis (running from tail to head). In order to generate horizontal components the model must be rolled about the $\underline{x}$-axis. The desired roll angle is determined by solving the vector equation $\bar{F}_D = \bar{T}_D + \bar{W}$ for $\bar{T}_D$, where $\bar{F}_D$ is the net force in the desired direction of acceleration, $\bar{T}_D$ is the desired thrust, and $\bar{W}$ is the force due to gravity (see Figure 12).

Rolling is given top priority when allocating the limited resource of thrust because the correct roll angle must be reached before any horizontal goals can be achieved. Rolling is implemented by thrust differentials produced by the wings; greater thrust on one side will cause the bird to turn towards the opposite side. If the thrust differential needed for rolling is greater than or equal to the maximum differential, then all available thrust is used in turning. If this is not the case, then the remainder can be used to generate a component in the desired direction, but only if the current roll angle is close to the desired roll angle. An example of horizontal position control is shown in Figure 13 and Figure 14.

A schematic of the control mechanism is shown in Figure 15. Competition between the horizontal and vertical goals for the available wing thrust is mediated to determine a thrust differential between the wings, causing the bird to roll. If the current roll direction is correct, the differential will be zero and both wings will provide equal thrust. The thrust produced by each wing is controlled by varying the amplitude of the flap cycle.

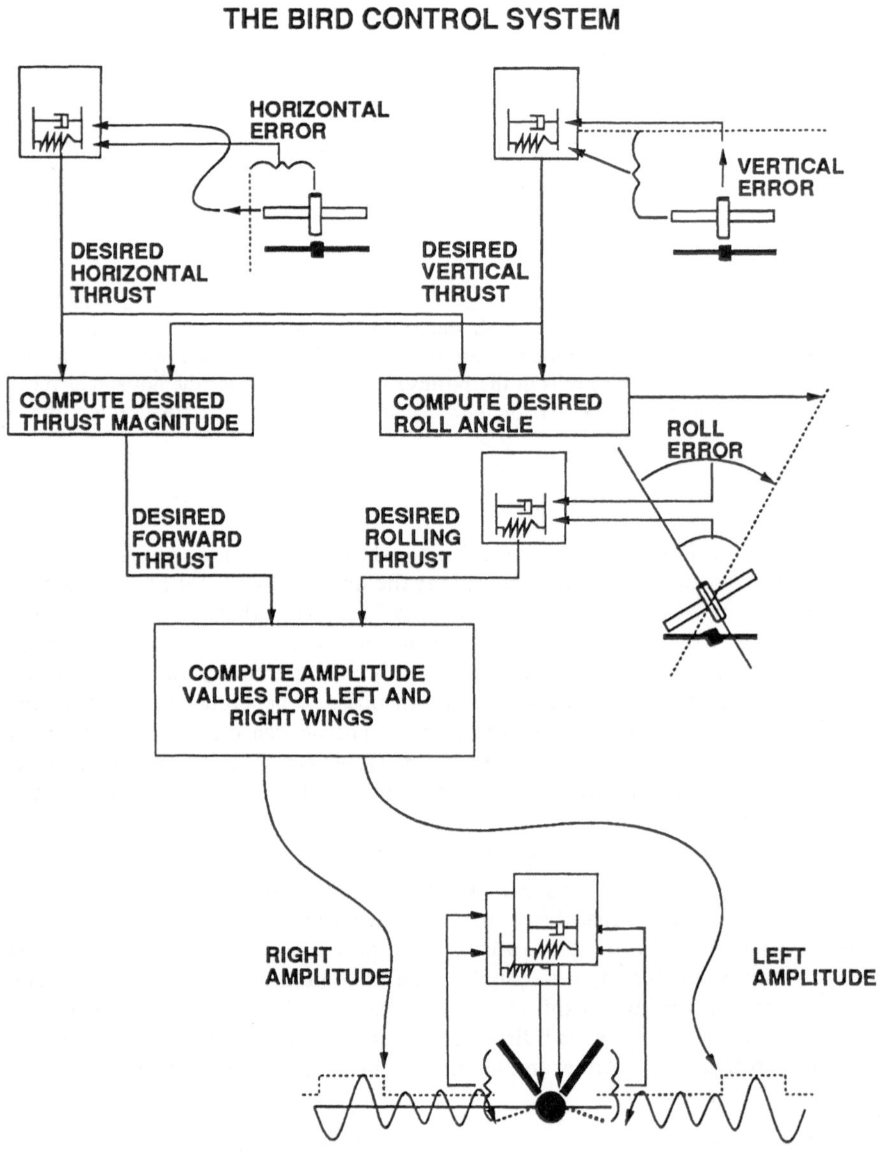

Figure 15. Schematic diagram of the control system. Horizontal and vertical errors between the current and the desired "goal" position determine the rolling and forward thrusts. These are converted into wing flap amplitude values. Differences between the left and the right flap amplitudes cause the bird to roll.

DISCUSSION

We have described one solution to the problem of generating realistic animation: physically-based models that move under the direction of control algorithms, environmental forces and high-level commands from the animator. As an example of this approach, we have automated the generation of a particular motion (hovering) for a specific character (the hummingbird). Other examples of this approach include control of legged robots and a kangaroo ([Raibert 1991], [Raibert 1992]) and control of a juggler and a unicyclist [Hodgins 1992].

Control algorithms allow users to direct the motion of physically-based models by setting high-level goals. With animations such as this one, animators can generate motion more quickly and easily than with traditional computer keyframe techniques. The cost of this ease of use is that the animator no longer has control of the low-level details of the motion. This control could be restored by allowing the animator to edit the motion curves after they have been generated. The animation would provide a first cut at the motion which the animator would then adjust to meet his or her vision of the personality and emotions of the character. Control could also be restored by refining the control algorithms to include parameters that influence the style of the motion more directly.

Animators need not understand the physics of the model in order to use such an animation; however, the designer of the control system must have considerable physical intuition about the problem. The development of this physical intuition takes time and the development of the control system usually progresses in stages. For the hummingbird model, the stroke oscillation control was designed first, then the angle of attack, and finally the hovering position behavior.

The cost of developing a controlled animation suggests that completed models should be stored in a library of motion behaviors for future use. The controlled models could be used repeatedly to generate motion for different applications in animation, multi-media and virtual reality. If the control mechanisms are robust, the models can produce appropriate motion behaviors for a variety of story-telling or interactive situations. Hopefully, this generality will offset the initial effort of developing the model.

By basing our simulation on the analysis presented in [Weis Fogh 1972b], we can visualize how such a bird might be able to fly. Although the model is simple, it captures some of the characteristics of the hovering and altitude-seeking behaviors exhibited by real hummingbirds. The model is correct in that the physical properties such as mass and moments of inertia match those of the real bird. However, describing the physics correctly is not enough to guarantee natural motion. The control algorithms must also be constructed in such a way that they mimic the controlled behaviors observed in the real system. In the hummingbird, for example, increases in the net lift are achieved by increasing the stroke amplitude. But for some aspects of hovering flight, we have very little data regarding the actual control mechanisms and so we are reduced to experimentation to find what "looks" right. This kind of research cannot confirm the existence of the "true" control mechanism, but it can provide confirming evidence for a hypothesis. It also suggests that control system design may be a new creative space available for artistic exploration.

ACKNOWLEDGEMENTS

Thanks to Alan Norton for launching the joint project on animation control with MIT. Thanks to the MIT Leg Lab for loaning us the simulation environment that was used to construct this model and especially to Marc Raibert for his expertise, contagious enthusiasm, and ice cream (but hold the sushi). Paula Sweeney provided invaluable assistance in implementing the simulation code. Al Khorasani implemented the graphical interface.

REFERENCES

[**Alexander 1983**] Alexander, R., "Animal Mechanics", Blackwell Scientific Publications, Boston. (1983)

[**Amkraut 1989a**] Amkraut S., "Flock: A Behavioral Model for Computer Animation", Masters Thesis, Art Education, The Ohio State University. (1989)

[**Amkraut 1989b**] Amkraut S., Girard, M., "Eurhythmy", SIGGRAPH Video Review Issue 52, Selection #8 (1989) (Video supplement to Computer Graphics)

[**Bruderlin 1989**] Bruderlin, A., Calvert, T. W., "Goal-Directed Dynamic Animation of Human Walking", Computer Graphics, V23 N3, July 1989 (SIGGRAPH Proceedings), p233-242.

[**Girard 1987**] Girard, M., "Interactive Design of 3D Computer-Animated Legged Animal Motion", IEEE Computer Graphics and Animation, June, 1987: 39-51.

[**Greenwalt 1960**] Greenwalt, C. H., "Hummingbirds" Doubleday, New York (1960)

[**Greenwalt 1962**] Greenwalt, C. H., "Dimensional Relationships for Flying Animals", Smithson. Misc. Collns, 144 (2) p1-46. (1962)

[**Hertel 1966**] Hertel, H., "Structure, Form and Movement", Reinhold, New York. (1966)

[**Hodgins 1992**] Hodgins, J. K., Sweeney, P. K., Lawrence, D. G. 1992. "Generating Natural-Looking Motion for Computer Animation", Proceedings of Graphics Interface '92. In press.

[**Marion 1970**] Marion, J., "Classical Dynamics of Particles and Systems", Academic Press, New York, (1970)

[**McKenna 1990**] McKenna, M., Zeltzer, D., "Dynamic Simulation of Autonomous Legged Locomotion", Computer Graphics V24 N4, August 1990 (SIGGRAPH Proceedings) p29-38.

[**Miller 1988**] Miller, G. S. P., "The Motion Dynamics of Snakes and Worms," Computer Graphics V22 N4 August 1988 (SIGGRAPH Proceedings) p169-178.

[**Prandtl 1934**] Prandtl, L., Tietjens, O. G., "Applied Hydro- and Aeromechanics", McGraw-Hill. New York, (1934).

[**Raibert 1991**] Raibert, M. H., Hodgins, J. K., "Animation of Dynamic Legged Locomotion" Computer Graphics, V25 N4, July 1991 (SIGGRAPH Proceedings) p349-358.

[**Raibert 1992**] Raibert, M. H., Hodgins, J. K., Playter, R. R., Ringrose, R. P. "Animation of Maneuvers: Jumps, Somersaults, and Gait Transitions", Proceedings of Imagina, 1992.

[**Reynolds 1987**] Reynolds C., "Flocks, Herds, and Schools: A Distributed Behavioral Model" Computer Graphics, V21 N4, July 1987 (SIGGRAPH Proceedings) p25-34.

[**van de Panne 1990**] van de Panne M., Fiume, E., Vranesic, Z., "Reusable Motion Synthesis Using State-Space Controllers", Computer Graphics V24 N4, July 1990 (SIGGRAPH Proceedings) p225-234.

[**Weis-Fogh 1972**] Weis-Fogh, T., "Energetics of Hovering Flight in Hummingbirds and Drosophila", Journal of Experimental Biology, V56, 1972 p79-104.

[**Wejchert 1991**] Wejchert, J., Haumann, D., "Animation Aerodynamics", Computer Graphics, V25 N4, July 1991 (SIGGRAPH Proceedings) p19-22.

[**Witkin 1988**] Witkin, A., Kass, M., "Spacetime Constraints", Computer Graphics, V22 N4, July 1988 (SIGGRAPH Proceedings) p159-168.

David R. Haumann is currently a Research Staff Member at IBM T. J. Watson Research Center in Yorktown Heights, N.Y. He received his Ph.D. in Computer Science at The Ohio State University in 1989, and his B.S. in Applied Mathematics from Brown University in 1977. His experience in computer graphics spans the fields of radiation treatment planning, flight simulation and commercial computer animation production. His research interests include computer graphics, animation and physically-based modeling. He co-produced the award winning films "Dynamic Simulations of Flexible Objects", "Balloon Guy" and "Leaf Magic", and contributed to several others, including "Broken Heart" and "Dirty Power". David is a member of Phi Kappa Phi Honor Society, ACM (SIGGRAPH) and IEEE.
Address: IBM T.J. Watson Research Center, POB 704, Yorktown Heights, New York 10598 USA.

Jessica Hodgins received a B.A. degree in Mathematics from Yale University in 1981, and a Ph.D. from Carnegie Mellon University in 1989. Her Ph.D. thesis, "Legged Robots on Rough Terrain: Experiments in Adjusting Step Length," explored algorithms which allowed a two-legged running machine to place its feet on chosen footholds while maintaining balanced running. Hodgins is currently a member of the Animation and Image Synthesis Group at the IBM Thomas J. Watson Research Center. She is studying the application of control algorithms to physically accurate models for the production of realistic animations of dynamic motor tasks.
Address: IBM T.J. Watson Research Center, POB 704, Yorktown Heights, New York 10598 USA.

Inverse Problems in Computer Graphics

MICHAEL KASS

ABSTRACT

Most traditional computations in computer graphics can be posed as forward problems: given the value of **x**, compute the value of some function $f(\mathbf{x})$. Increasingly, however, important computer graphics computations involve inverse problems: given the value of a function $f(\mathbf{x})$, compute **x**. Inverse problems tend to be much more difficult than forward problems, and their solution requires methods which are unfamiliar to many computer graphics practitioners. An awareness of when they arise and how they can be solved is of substantial value in a wide variety of computer graphics applications.

Key Words: Inverse problems, reparameterization, constraints, optimization.

I. INTRODUCTION

Traditional computer graphics computations in modeling, animation and rendering are primarily *forward* computations -- they can be described as the result of computing a (possibly vector-valued) function f on an input vector **x**. The position of a point on a spline surface, for example, is given by a function of its u and v parameters and the positions of its control points. If the surface is animated, the position of the control points may be given by a different function, often a spline function of time. When the point is projected onto the image plane, its 2D position is given by a function of its 3D position and the viewing matrix. When it comes time to render the point, its color is usually given by a function of the surface normal, albedo, the lighting parameters, etc.

While many important computer graphics problems can be solved with forward computation, an increasingly important set of problems involve *inverse* computations where we are given the value of the function $f(\mathbf{x})$ and need to find the value of **x**. If we know how to compute the inverse function directly, the problem is easy. Most of the time, however, there is no simple computable expression for the inverse and we must resort to one of a collection of numerical methods suitable for inverse problems. If the original function is many-to-one, we have to deal with the fact that at some points there will be no inverse, and at other points, the inverse will be ambiguous.

Inverse problems arise in diverse areas of computer graphics. Among these, one area which gives rise to inverse problems particularly frequently is the area of model fitting. When computer graphics models are used to fit measured real-world data, it is often impossible to measure the model parameters directly from the data. Instead, we typically know some function of the model parameters which should match the data. Inverting this function for the given data yields the desired model parameters. Typical sources of data include images from cameras and volume data from medical scans.

When the data comes from still or moving images, model fitting falls on the boundary between computer graphics and computer vision. That inverse problems arise frequently on the boundary is largely because computer graphics and computer vision can be regarded as nearly inverse disciplines (e.g. [1; 2]). Computer graphics is concerned with going from a description of a scene to one or more images of it, while computer vision is concerned with reversing that process: going from one or more images back to a description.

A second area of computer graphics which frequently gives rise to inverse problems is the area of control. In control problems, we have a set of model parameters we are able to modify, and we would like to adjust them to achieve some desired effect. If the parameters are well-chosen, this process may be very easy. In many cases, however, adjusting the parameters to achieve a desired effect can be extremely difficult, particularly when there are a large number of parameters which interact in complicated ways. Making the model easy enough to control may require a new parameterization.

In some cases, it is possible to reparameterize a model by expressing the original parameters $\mathbf{x}$ as a function $\mathbf{g}$ of the new parameters $\mathbf{z}$. Then the reparameterization can be accomplished in a purely forward manner by composing the functions and computing $f(\mathbf{g}(\mathbf{z}))$. In many cases, however, a suitable function $\mathbf{g}$ is not available directly, and we must resort to inverse methods. If we can express the desired behavior as the minimum of an objective function $E(\mathbf{x})$, then we can adjust the parameter vector $\mathbf{x}$ using an inverse method so that the objective function is minimized. Similarly, if we can express a constraint among the parameters by an equation $c(\mathbf{x}) = 0$, then we can adjust the parameters within the constraints by using inverse methods.

Whether they arise from model fitting, control, or some other area of computer graphics, inverse problems require very different methods from the usual forward computations. In section 2, we discuss the relevance of optimization for inverse problems. In section 3, we consider a set of inverse problems in curve modeling which illustrate the basic issues. Then we examine surface models in section 4 and camera models in section 5. Finally, in section 6, we consider the problem of controlling articulated models.

2. OPTIMIZATION

If we know absolutely nothing about a given function f except how to compute it, then the only way to compute its inverse is to scan the domain of f exhaustively until we find an $\mathbf{x}$ such that $f(\mathbf{x})$ has the desired value. Fortunately, most inverse problems of importance in computer graphics are posed with somewhat more information. For example, we usually know that f is smooth (at least differentiable) and we very often can evaluate its derivatives. If we also have an approximate guess for the inverse, we can use that as a starting point for local optimization. Suppose we are given $f(\mathbf{x}) = y$ and we want to find $\mathbf{x}$. If we minimize the function

$$E = (f(\mathbf{x}) - y)^2 \qquad \text{(eq. 1)}$$

and find an x such that $E = 0$, we know we have inverted f for that value of y. A variety of optimization methods are possible if we have enough rough information about the inverse that a suitable starting value is available[3]. A nice property of eq. 1 is that if no inverse exists, it finds a locally optimal estimate in the least-squares sense.

Even if the forward function is one-to-one and an inverse exists for the given value of y, there can be several local minima in the objective function of eq. 1. If the forward function is many-to-one, there may be several global minima as well. Choosing among these and avoiding the unwanted local minima can be a very difficult task. It may not even be possible to express the "correct" inverse in objective terms.

Unlike those which arise in many other disciplines, optimization problems in computer graphics usually have visual representations. As a result, we can often resort to interactive optimization, where a user can watch the visual representation and guide the system towards the desired local minimum. As computers have gotten more powerful, this has become an increasingly practical technique in the last few years.

In order to perform an optimization interactively, it is important to present the optimization in a way which is visually understandable to the user. For example, instead of taking the largest possible step at each opportunity, it is important to maintain continuity from step to step. One effective way of doing this is to cast the optimization as a differential equation:

$$\partial \mathbf{x}/\partial t = -\mathbf{k}\cdot\ \partial E/\partial \mathbf{x} \qquad \text{(eq. 2)}$$

This first-order differential equation guides the system towards the nearest local minimum with velocity proportional to the slope of the energy surface. If we think of E as an energy function, then its derivatives are forces, so eq. 2 describes Aristotelian dynamics: $f = mv$ where **k** is a matrix which determines the masses of the individual parameters. Unlike Newtonian dynamics described by the law f=ma, Aristotelian dynamics is always critically damped and has no inertia, so it is much better suited to optimization problems.

In order to guide the optimization towards the desired local minimum, we can supply the user with interactive methods of applying forces on the system and modify the differential equation to add in the effect of these forces:

$$\partial \mathbf{x}/\partial t = -\mathbf{k}\cdot\ \partial E/\partial \mathbf{x} + \mathbf{F}_{user} \qquad \text{(eq. 3)}$$

The user forces can come from imaginary springs, guiding energy potentials or an application specific source.

3. CURVES

The ordinary cubic splines used commonly in computer graphics are often derived by analogy to thin wooden or metal splines bent by draftsmen into curves. Physical splines minimize their bending energy subject to the positional constraints of the lead weights or "ducks" which constrain them to pass through certain positions, so their behavior is easily described as an inverse problem. Points along the curve move such that the gradient of the energy is zero. In two dimensions, if $x(s)$ and $y(s)$ are the parametric representation of a spline curve, the bending energy is approximately (e.g. [4; 5])

$$E = \int (d^2x/ds^2)^2 + (d^2y/ds^2)^2\ ds. \qquad \text{(eq. 4)}$$

We can calculate the energy in a forward manner using eq. 4 if we know the shape of the curve, but if we want to calculate the shape of the curve from knowledge about the energy, we have an inverse problem.

It is easy to show that the energy function of eq. 4 is minimized between constrained points by the familiar piecewise cubic polynomials on which most computer graphics splines are based (e.g. [4]). As a result, the inverse problem can be turned into a forward problem. The coefficients of the cubics are specified by some user interaction and then the resulting cubics are evaluated in a forward manner to yield points along the curve. For this particular problem, the inverse has a simple symbolic representation which makes it possible to evaluate points on the curve and manipulate them with just forward computation.

Even among piecewise cubics, there are a variety of different parameterizations which have proven useful. B-splines, Bezier splines, Catmull-Rom splines and Beta splines are examples of reparameterizations of the basic piecewise cubics. Each has its own particular properties and distinctive feel to the user. In their normal use, these reparameterizations can all be evaluated with just forward computation.

If second order continuity is desired and the spline has to interpolate a set of known points, then forward computation does not suffice. Instead there are a set of simultaneous constraints to be solved. This problem arises, for example, in B-spline based modelers that need to interpolate a set of measured data points. Fortunately, the simultaneous constraints are linear, so they can be solved very easily. Here, the inverse problem can be solved by inverting a matrix (although the linear system can be solved most efficiently without ever actually forming the inverse matrix).

In order to experiment with a variety of inverse problems, an interactive system called GO[6] (**G**raphical **O**ptimizer) was developed at Apple Computer. GO is a graphical programming environment for expressing and solving numerical optimization problems which is particularly suited to problems that arise in computer graphics. Mathematical functions are graphically represented as boxes on the screen with vector or scalar inputs and outputs. The user constructs the function to be optimized by creating boxes and connecting together their inputs and outputs. The optimization is performed very efficiently using a sparse-Hessian Newton iteration and compile-time symbolic differentiation.

Any function-box input which is not connected to the output of another box is potentially a state variable for optimization unless the user chooses to "freeze" it. Frozen inputs are displayed in blue and are not allowed to change during the optimization. The objective function for optimization is specified by choosing one or more output nodes. The chosen outputs are displayed in green and summed to create the objective function.

Figure 1a shows GO being used to minimize the energy function in eq. 4. The selector box contains a set of 100 samples of a curve in the plane. Successive points along that curve are used to approximate the second derivative by the formula *dxx = (a+b-2c)/h^2*. The Dot box computes the dot product of the second derivative approximation with itself, yielding the integrand of eq. 4. The TOpt box computes the integral of this quantity over time, the parameter of the curve. The user has chosen to freeze five points in the selector box with particular values input by hand. Subject to its inability to change the positions of these points, GO optimizes the objective function to create the natural spline curve shown in figure 1a. The Curve, Circle and Sel Copy boxes specify the visualization of the curve with circles drawn around the frozen points.

In the example of figure 1a, GO optimizes its objective function numerically without making use of the fact that the optimum is a piecewise cubic. Its input is just a finite-difference statement of the problem from first principles. Nonetheless, using sparse matrix methods, GO computes the minimum in linear time.

Since the minimum of eq. 4. is well known to be a piecewise cubic, there is no practical reason to compute it from first principles. If the energy function is modified slightly, however, the analytic techniques used to derive the forward computations for splines no longer work. For example, consider the energy function:

$$E = \int (d^2x/ds^2)^2 + (d^2y/ds^2)^2 + k\left|(x, y) - (x_0, y_0)\right|^{-1} ds. \qquad \text{(eq. 5)}$$

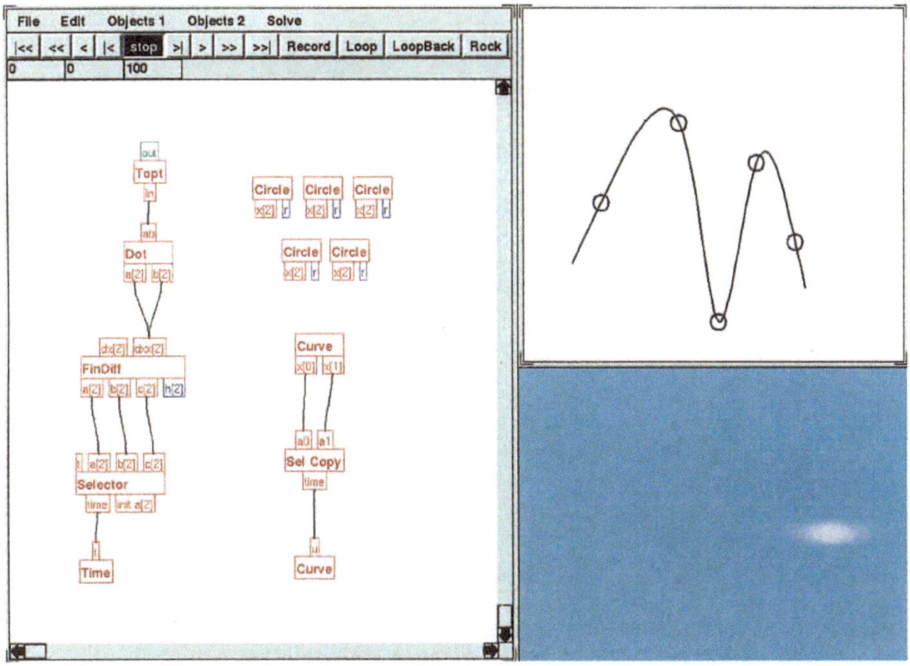

Figure 1a: GO used to minimize the energy of a natural spline from first principles.

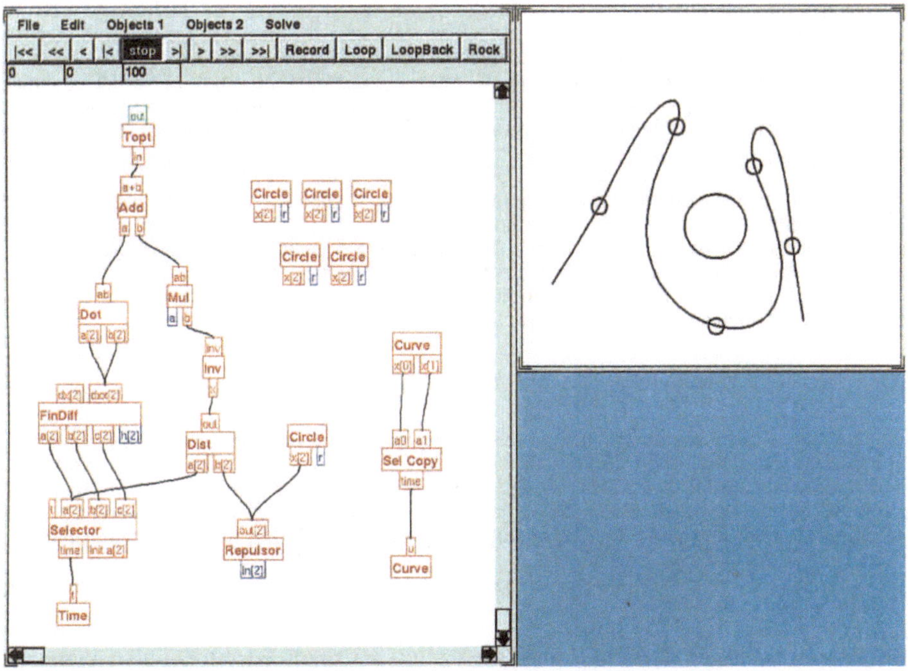

Figure 1b: The minimization of figure 1a modified to include a 1/r repulsor.

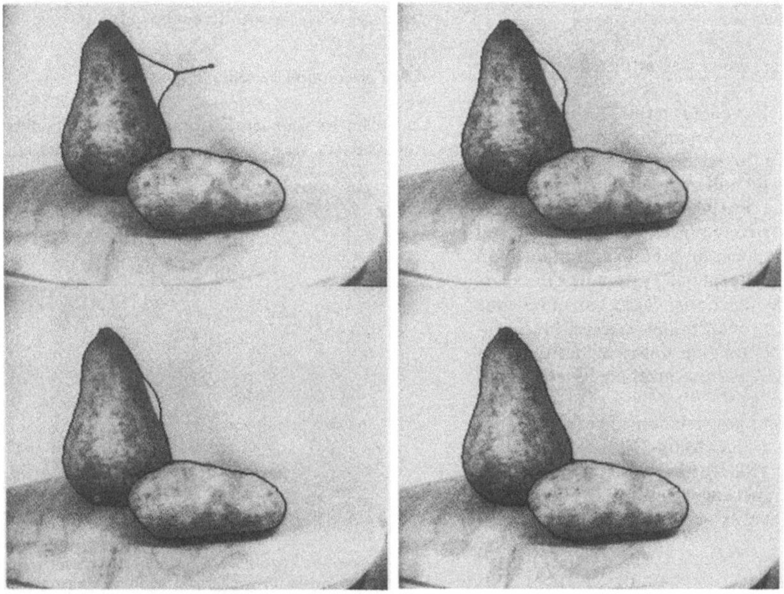

Figure 2: Two edge-seeking snakes on a pear and potato. Upper left: The user has pulled one of the snakes away from the edge of the pear. Others: After the user lets go, the snake snaps back to the edge of the pear.

The energy function of eq. 4 has been modified by the addition of a $1/r$ repulsive potential which pushes the curve away from the center of the potential. In a sense, this produces a reparameterization of the curve since its shape now depends on the origin of the repulsive potential. With this change, the minimum energy curve is no longer a piecewise cubic, so the forward methods used with the energy of eq. 4 are not applicable. Instead, we must use general optimization methods for this energy function. Figure 1b shows how GO can be used to calculate the minimum energy configuration. The box labelled "repulsor" contains the origin of the $1/r$ potential. Note that the repulsor provides a different type of control of the curve than the typical spline knots. The curve loops around staying away from the center of the potential as if avoiding an obstacle.

Another small modification of the energy function of eq. 4 allows a curve to be used for model fitting. Suppose we have a digitized monochrome image I(x,y) that has been captured from a camera or scanner, and we wish to match the curve to the edge of an object seen in the image. One way to do this is to take the ordinary spline energy function and add a term which pulls the curve towards regions of high contrast in the image. If we measure contrast with the image intensity gradient, then a suitable energy function is[7]

$$E = \int (d^2 x / ds^2)^2 + (d^2 y / ds^2)^2 - k |\nabla I(x, y)|^2 ds. \qquad \text{(eq. 6)}$$

Figure 2 shows the above energy being interactively minimized on a photograph of a potato and a pear. The user pulls on the curve with a simulated spring. As soon as the spring is released, the curve attaches itself to the nearest edge. Since there are many possible edges in the photograph, the interactive optimization allows the user to pick the intended one by creating a starting condition near the intended edge and manipulating the curve during the optimization process.

Interactive curve models which minimize energy functions closely related to eq. 6 have come to be known as "snakes."

Curve modeling brings up many of the important aspects of inverse problems in computer graphics. The original problem statement for physical splines is an inverse problem. Nonetheless, it is solvable in a forward manner under some conditions. Even so, the forward computation allows a variety of different parameterizations which have a very important effect on the user experience of controlling the splines. If we adjust the problem conditions slightly, the purely forward method fails and the solution requires a simple inverse computation: solving a tridiagonal linear system. Changing the energy function slightly brings us into the realm of nonlinear optimization and a full inverse formulation. The full inverse formulation makes it possible to do interactive model-fitting.

4. SURFACES

Surface modeling brings up issues very similar to curve modeling, but since surface computations are much more computationally demanding, even more efforts are made to rely on forward computation. A very widely used method is to construct tensor-product surfaces from standard spline curves. The resulting surfaces can be computed in a forward manner. Tensor-product B splines, for example, are very popular in free-form surface design.

As in curve design, if we restrict ourselves to forward computation, we are limited in the surface behavior we can create. Control of the surfaces can be modified by changing the parameterization, but only if we can express the reparameterization as a forward function. If we are willing to accept inverse computation, however, the range of possible surface behavior we can create is a great deal wider. The computational cost is greater, but so are the possible rewards.

In analogy to the draftsman's spline, we can begin with surfaces whose behavior is modeled on that of a thin metal plate under elastic deformation. The basic energy function for a thin plate can be written

$$\mathbf{r}(u, v) = (x(u, v), y(u, v), z(u, v))$$
$$E = \int |\mathbf{r}_{uu}|^2 \, ds + 2|\mathbf{r}_{uv}|^2 + |\mathbf{r}_{vv}|^2 \, du \, dv \qquad \text{(eq. 7)}$$

As with the curves in section 3, we can then modify this basic behavior with the addition of new terms in the energy function. The additional terms give the surface a preference for certain types of shapes which can be chosen for their importance in a specific domain.

A particularly interesting type of surface we can create with inverse computation is a symmetry-seeking surface[8]. We begin with an elastic surface described by the energy of eq. 7. and turn it into a tube by joining two opposite edges. Then we add an elastic curve for the symmetry axis constructed according to a 3D analog of the energy in eq. 4. Finally, we add an energy function which introduces a coupling force between the cylinder and the axis which tries to keep the elastic cylinder as symmetric as possible around the axis.

The result is an odd kind of non-physical material which responds somewhat like clay on a potter's wheel. Wherever the model is pushed inward towards the axis, it will tend to contract radially. When pulled outward from the axis, the tube will tend to expand radially. Unlike clay on a potter's wheel, however, the symmetry-seeking material can have an arbitrarily bent axis. In contrast to generalized cylinder models (e.g. [9]), the symmetry-seeking material expresses a preference for symmetric configurations, but can be pulled away from symmetric configurations when sufficient force is applied.

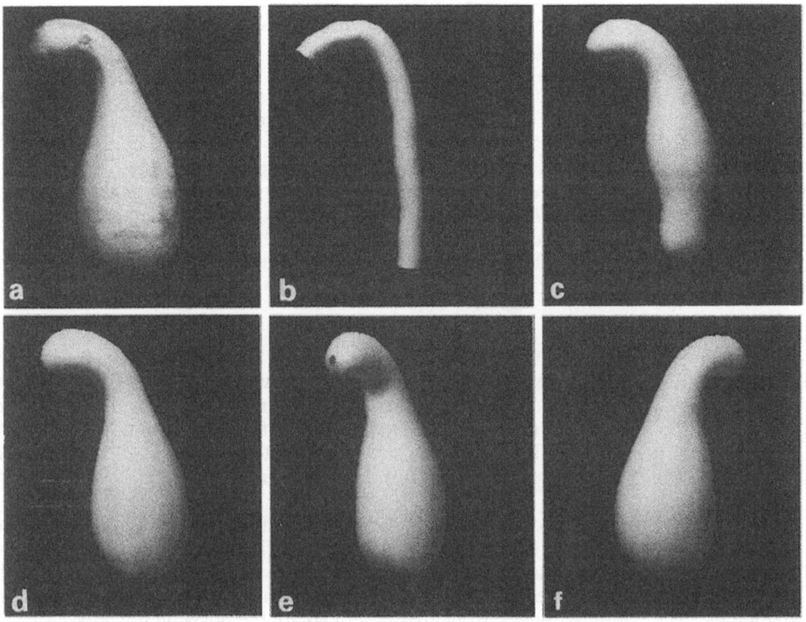

Figure 3: Model fitting of a squash. (a) Squash photograph. Selected frames from an animation sequence are shown: (b) Initial state of th 3D model, (c) Intermediate shape during model fitting, (d) Final model. (e,f) Model rotating rigidly in space.

In figure 3, the symmetry-seeking material has been used to fit a nearly symmetric surface to the silhouette of a squash. Figure 3a shows a photograph of a real squash, and 3b shows a starting point for solving the inverse problem. In addition to the basic symmetry-seeking energy function, the surface in figure 3 was given an energy term which pulls points along its silhouette towards areas of high contrast in the image[8; 10]. As a result, the surface adjusts itself until its silhouette matches the silhouette of the original image, while maintaining the greatest possible smoothness and symmetry. Complex behavior of this type is difficult, if not impossible to achieve without inverse methods.

5. CAMERAS

Traditional camera models in computer graphics are forward models. The user typically specifies a point to look from, a point to look at, an amount of twist and the field of view. Once the camera is specified, the camera matrix is constructed and an image of the model is rendered. The forward camera model maps from camera parameters to the positions of objects. If the user wants an object to be in a particular position in the image, he has an inverse problem, but in most available computer graphics systems, he usually has to try to modify the forward camera parameters by trial and error until the objects are appropriately positioned. To avoid these difficulties, Blinn[11] presented a special-purpose inverse camera model suitable for limited positional constraints. Recently, Drucker et. al[12] and Gleicher and Witkin[13] have investigated inverse camera models using more general inverse techniques.

Figure 4 shows how GO can be applied to an inverse camera problem which occured while trying to automatically rotoscope some movement for the purpose of facial animation[14]. A performer moved around with a series of ultraviolet reflective spots on his face and a set of four spots on a piece of cardboard rigidly connected to his head. When video-taped in ultraviolet light, the spots were very easy to track automatically. For the purpose of the full facial animation, the positions of all the dots were used, but for our purposes, we will consider the problem of computing the transformation from the head coordinate system to the camera screen based on the screen-space projections of the four dots on the piece of cardboard. This problem has been previously addressed with optimization by means of special-purpose code[15; 16]. Figure 4 shows its implementation with GO.

In this problem, we are given the 3D positions of four dots in a reference frame fixed on the piece of cardboard. For convenience, we can chose the reference frame so that the four points form a unit square centered on the origin in the x-y plane. We are also given the 2D positions of the same dots in the image plane. What we would like to find is the set of camera parameters which correspond to this projection. There are seven relevant camera parameters (3 rotation, 3 translation and the field-of view of the camera) and eight measured pieces of data (the x,y positions of the 4 dots), so there is hope of being able to recover the camera transformation.

The expression of this problem in GO initially seems odd to many people, because at the bottom of figure 4 we start with the unknowns: the rotation matrix, the translation vector and the field of view, *s*. This is in contrast to more familiar methods of forward problems where one typically starts with the knowns. The boxes at the bottom represent hypothesized values for the rotation, translation and field of view. We then express a set of constraints on these hypothesized values and let the optimizer solve for them.

There are four boxes labelled xyz1 through xyz4 which hold the 3D positions of the dots in the reference frame on the piece of cardboard. These are frozen, because they are given in the problem specification. The four boxes labelled uv1 through uv4 hold the measured 2D positions of the dots on the camera screen. These are similarly frozen because they represent measured data. The boxes labelled "Viewing Xform" compute the transformation of the known 3D points given the hypothesized camera parameters. The points transformed into 2D are then subtracted from the measured 2D points and the result squared by the Eq2d function block. Thus each Eq2d function block will have an output value of zero if and only if the hypothesized transformation of the correspondng 3D point brings it into the measured 2D position. There is one further constraint on the problem which is that the rotation matrix should be orthogonal. This is handled by the Ortho3d function block which computes the function $|A\,A^T - I|^2$ which vanishes if and only if the matrix is orthogonal.

As expressed in figure 4, the inverse camera problem involves 13 state variables (the 9 elements of the rotation matrix, the 3 in the translation vector and the field of view). As a result, the Newton iterations involve a 13 by 13 matrix and the solution is much slower than it needs to be. A more efficient implementation of the inverse would use quaternions[17] for the rotation and therefore reduce the number of state variables in the optimization to 8. The presentation of figure 3 was chosen for pedagogical clarity.

6. ARTICULATED MODELS

Perhaps the canonical example of an inverse problem in computer graphics is *inverse kinematics*. With ordinary articulated models, we have a forward function which allows us to compute where the pieces are from the joint angles and the origin of the body. The position of the finger or the foot, for example, is usually a complex non-linear function of the joint angles. If we want to take the articulated model and place its foot on the ground, or its finger on a table, we are faced with an inverse problem. Since the problem is generally underconstrained, it is important to use up the redundant degrees of freedom in a sensible way. One way to do this is to simulate what would happen if we physically pulled the foot down to the ground, or pulled the finger over to

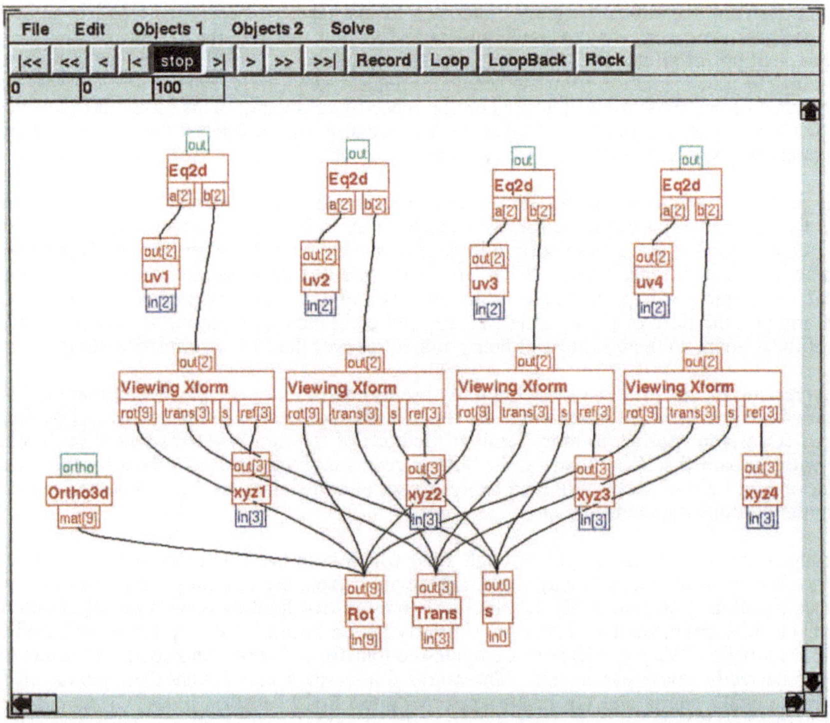

Figure 4: GO used to recover camera parameters from the projections of 4 known points.

the table.

Since inverse kinematics is concerned only with positioning a figure, rather than specifying its motion, the Aristotelian dynamics formulation of eq. 2 is very appropriate. The main special issue is determining a suitable mass matrix **k**. To achieve an intuitive, physically-based method for specifying the underconstrained behavior, we can model the articulated figure as being composed of a series of mass points. If we let $\mathbf{r}_i$ be the vector position of the *i*th mass point, and m_i its mass, then we should use the Jacobian matrix **J** to convert the masses of the individual mass points into the generalized masses which appear in **k**:

$$\mathbf{J}_i = \partial \mathbf{r}_i / \partial \mathbf{x}$$
$$\mathbf{k} = \sum_i m_i \mathbf{J}_i \mathbf{J}_i^T \qquad \text{(eq. 8)}$$

With this mass matrix, the motion of an articulated figure when pulled to a given position using eq. 1 and eq. 2 is as if it is critically damped at the joints.

A very important set of inverse problems arise in goal-directed control of physically-based models. In ordinary physically-based modeling, integration of the Newtonian equations of motion gives the parameters of the model over time as a function of the initial conditions and the forces exerted on the model. This forward-based simulation is suitable for many purposes, but articulated figures are notoriously hard to control. Specifying the joint torques and other forces required to create pleasing motion is extremely difficult.

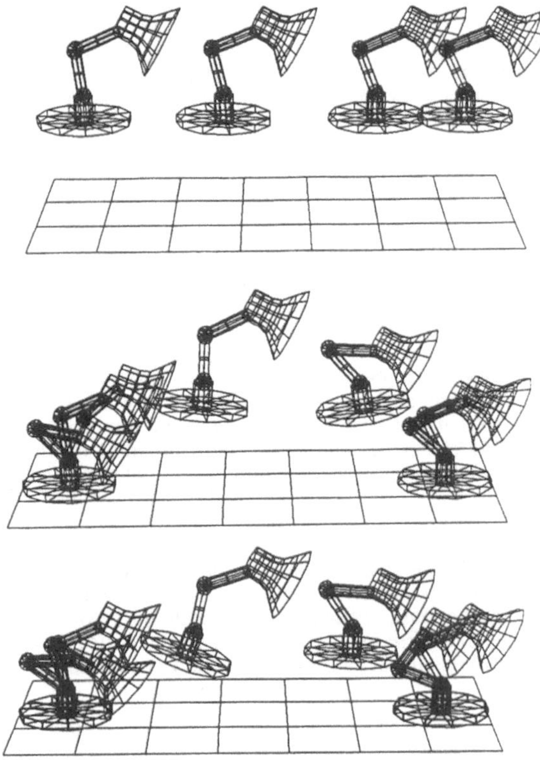

Fig 5: Spacetime animation of jumping lamp. Top: Starting motion supplied by a user. Middle: Jump after optimization. Bottom: Same jump with the mass of the base doubled.

In order to address these difficulties, Witkin and Kass[18] introduced an inverse method for physically-based control called spacetime constraints. The technique combines physical constraints on the motion and goals specified by the animator into a single constrained optimization. In the course of solving the optimization, the spacetime constraint method computes the forces necessary to achieve the goals in a physically realistic manner. Subject to the physical and goal constraints, the spacetime method allows the rest of the motion to be specified by an optimization criterion. For typical character animation, where graceful, natural-looking motion is important, this criterion might involve minimizing work.

Figure 5 shows the spacetime method being used to animate a simple jumping desk lamp inspired by the Pixar film "Luxo Jr."[19] The lamp is composed of four links and has an angular muscle at each joint. It is constrained to obey Newtonian physics, to begin and end at rest, and to have its base on the floor at specified positions at the beginning and end of the jump. Subject to these constraints, the mean-square power output of the lamp's muscles is minimized. The top of figure 5 shows the initial path supplied by a user where the lamp flies above the floor. This keyframed motion was used merely as a starting point for the constrained optimization procedure. The results after the optimization are shown in the middle of figure 5 where the lamp makes a physically realistic jump from one point to another.

The lamp anticipates its jump by squashing down. It then stretches out as it leaps and squashes down again as it lands. After it lands, the lamp follows through by continuing to move forward. Anticipation, squash, stretch and follow-through are techniques of traditional cartoon animation[20]. In key-framed computer animation, these techniques have to be carefully introduced by the animator[21]. Using spacetime constraints, they arise automatically because of the physical structure of the problem. In order to jump without using excessive force, the lamp has to anticipate and squash down. The force to propel it into the air is supplied by stretching out. The impact force makes the lamp squash down when it lands, and its momentum causes the follow-through.

The bottom of figure 5 shows a slight variation of the basic jump where the mass of the base has been doubled and the optimization run again. Note that the base lags behind the rest of the lamp. This is in conformity with another principle of traditional animation[21]: heavier parts of an object drag further behind. Once again, this results simply from the physical constraints. In order to make the base look heavier, the spacetime constraints animator has only to increase its simulated weight. By contrast, with key-frame animation, all the key-frames might requre subtle modifications in order to change the apparent weight. With a forward dynamic simulation, it would be easy to change the weight, but then the goal state would not be achieved. Only an inverse method such as spacetime constraints can allow a user to adjust the problem parameters while maintaining physically-correct motion and achieving a set of motion goals.

7. CONCLUSION

Inverse problems are a great deal more challenging than forward problems. They require more computation and much more complex numerical methods than forward methods. Over- and under-constrained situations always pose difficulties. Nonetheless, with the availability of increasingly powerful computers, inverse methods have become important in computer graphics because they allow new and valuable behavior for a wide variety of models.

REFERENCES

[1] Poggio, T., Torre, V. and Koch, C. "Computational Vision and Regularization Theory," Nature **317**, 1985 p. 314-319.

[2] Witkin, A., Kass, M., Terzopoulos, D. and Barr, A. "Linking Perception and Graphics: Modeling with Dynamic Constraints," in Barlow, Blakemore and Weston Smith, eds., *Images and Understanding*, Cambridge University Press, 1990.

[3] Gill, P., Murray, W. and Wright, M., *Practical Optimization*, Academic Press, 1981.

[4] Rogers, D. and Adams, J., *Mathematical Elements for Computer Graphics*, McGraw Hill, 1976.

[5] Faux, I., and Pratt, M., *Computational Geometry for Design and Manufacture*, Ellis Horwood, 1979.

[6] Kass, M., "GO: A Graphical Optimizer," ACM Siggraph '91 Course notes, *Course 23: An Introduction to Physically Based Modeling*, 1991.

[7] Kass, M., Witkin, A. and Terzopoulos, D. "Snakes: Active Contour Models," *International Journal of Computer Vision* **1**, 1988 p. 321-331.

[8] Terzopoulos, D., Witkin, A. and Kass, M., "Symmetry-Seeking Models and 3D Object Reconstruction," *International Journal of Computer Vision* **1** 1988 p. 211-221.

[9] Agin, G. and Binford, T. "Computer Descriptions of Curved Objects," *Proc. Third Int. Joint Conf. on Artificial Intelligence*, 1973, p. 629-635.

[10] Terzopoulos, D., Witkin, A. and Kass, M. "Constraints on Deformable Models: Recovering 3D Shape and Nonrigid Motion," Artificial Intelligence 36, 1988 p. 91-123.

[11] Blinn, J. "Where am I? What am I looking at?," *IEEE Computer Graphics and Applications*, p. 76-81, July 1988.

[12] Drucker, S., Galyean, T. and Zeltzer, D. "CINEMA: A System for Procedural Camera Movements," *Proc. of the 1992 Symposium on Interactive Computer Graphics*, to appear, 1992.

[13] Gleicher, M. and Witkin, A. "Through-the-Lens Camera Control," to appear.

[14] Williams, L., "Performance-Driven Facial Animation," Proc. Siggraph '90, 1990, p. 235-242.

[15] Lowe, D., "Solving for the Parameters of Object Models from Image Descriptions," *Proc. Image Understanding Workshop*, April 1980, p. 121-127.

[16] Gennery, D., "Stero Camera Calibration," *Proc. Image Understanding Workshop*, April 1980, p. 201-208.

[17] Shoemake, K. "Animating Rotations with Quaternion Curves,"*Computer Graphics* 19 (3) p. 245-254, July 1985 (Proc. Siggraph '85).

[18] Witkin, A. and Kass, M. "Spacetime Constraints," *Computer Graphics* 22(4) August, 1988 p. 159-168 (Proc. Siggraph '88).

[19] Pixar, *Luxo Jr.*, (film), 1986.

[20] Thomas, F. and Johnston, O., *Disney Animation--The Ilusion of Life,* Abbeville Press, New York, 1981.

[21] Lasseter, J., "Principles of traditional animation applied to 3D computer animation," *Computer Graphics* **21** (4) (1987) p. 35-44 (Proc. SIGGRAPH-87).

Michael Kass is a staff research scientist with the Advanced Technology Group of Apple Computer. He received a B.A. in artificial intelligence from Princeton University, an M.S. in computer science from M.I.T. and a PhD. in electrical engineering from Stanford University. He has received numerous prizes and awards for his papers and animations including the Grand Prix Pixel INA from Imagina in 1991 for *Splash Dance*, an animation of fluid movement. Before joining Apple Computer in 1988, he worked at Schlumberger Palo Alto Research in the field of computer graphics and computer vision. His current research focus is on the use of physical simulation in computer graphics.

Address: Apple Computer, 20525 Mariani Ave.,
Cupertino, CA 95014 USA.
email: kass@apple.com

NPSNET: Physically-Based Modeling Enhancements to an Object File Format

MICHAEL J. ZYDA, JAMES G. MONAHAN, and DAVID R. PRATT

ABSTRACT

The Naval Postgraduate School (NPS) has actively explored the design and implementation of real-time three-dimensional simulators on low-cost, readily accessible graphics workstations. Many of the simulator platforms have had tremendous success due to the fact that a common object format was used. Prototyping time is dramatically reduced when the tedious and often repetitious task of object design is replaced with the simpler task of modifying an existing object description file. The current level of support that the NPS Object File Format (NPSOFF) provides is descriptions for lights, lighting, material characteristics, the expected graphics drawing primitives (lines, polygons, surfaces,...), and provisions for texturing and special lighting effects (spotlights, decaling,...). The objectives of this work are the enhancement of the basic NPSOFF structure with information necessary for accurate physically-based rendering in real-time; to construct a library of functions specifying an object's physical properties and the internal/external forces controlling the object and to develop a tool to rapidly design and test an object's dynamic characteristics.

1. THE BASIC OBJECT FILE FORMAT

In the past, the various areas of real-time, three-dimensional (3D) visual simulator research at NPS have had specific scope and purpose for a unique vehicle platform (Zyda 1991c). The visual simulators developed in the Graphics and Video Laboratory include the FOG-M missile simulator, the VEH vehicle simulator, the Airborne Remotely Operated Device (AROD), the Moving Platform Simulator series (MPS-1, MPS-2 and MPS-3), and the High Resolution Digital Terrain Model (HRDTM) system. Simulation design and implementation techniques optimized the technology of workstations in use. Advances in workstation hardware and software have always lead to more accurate simulations with each successive generation. An area of concern was to prevent an iconoclastic attitude between existing simulation projects and to facilitate the rapid prototyping of new simulator platforms. It soon became evident that future simulator development would demand a more unified protocol for object/scene description, rendering, and manipulation.

Advances in hardware capabilities such as lighting and texturing were painfully absent from these early simulations. There was no ability to quickly modify and port various objects between platforms; object renderings and control modifications were tedious for the platform's author let alone a follow-on design team. The NPSOFF initial research was designed to solve these problems by introducing an editable ASCII file with the information necessary to render an object along with various support routines to show, manipulate and save NPSOFF objects (Zyda 1991a, Zyda 1991b).

The version 1.0 NPSOFF consisted of lights, light model, material (color) and drawing subprimitive (lines, polygons, surfaces) definition tokens along with some administrative tokens for file maintenance and readability. The rendering of an object was accomplished in 3 steps: 1) pre-render parsing of the ASCII file into a dynamically allocated structure of object definition opcodes, 2) pre-render definition of lights and light models, 3) traversing the opcode list, drawing only the graphic primitives and selecting the "currently active" light, light model or material definition. Step 3 is the only one required each time through the display loop.

2. ADDITIONS TO THE BASIC OBJECT FILE FORMAT

Further enhancements to NPSOFF included tokens to select textures, decaling, 2-sided lighting, spotlights and other rendering attributes. While current NPSOFF objects *looked* just like the real world objects that they were simulating, unfortunately, many of the NPSOFF object simulations did not *behave* realistically. As each NPSOFF object was nothing more than a description of its "skin", it was usually animated by implicitly specifying changes in linear position/velocity and orientation. NPSOFF objects could quite literally become "...faster than a speeding bullet, more powerful than a locomotive..." and defy many more laws of physics that we implicitly, if not explicitly, understand.

3. INCORPORATING PHYSICAL REALISM

More recent research at NPS, specifically the Autonomous Underwater Vehicle (AUV), has taken a current NPSOFF submarine object and animated it under the constraints of accurate hydrodynamic laws of motion (Jurewicz 1989). The result is an amazingly realistic, both visually and physically, simulation of one specific NPSOFF object. A small drawback of the AUV simulation is that the physically-based modeling (PBM) representation of the dynamics is hardcoded. Adding/adjusting the AUV's dynamics is not a simple task, and the integration of a physically different submarine model would require software maintenance by a knowledgeable AUV programmer.

4. RELATED WORK

4.1 bolio

bolio is an integrated graphical simulation platform developed by David Zeltzer et al at MIT's Media Lab (Brett 1987, Sturman 1989, Zeltzer 1989). The project's goal has been to provide an environment that animates objects governed by a network of constraints (dynamic and kinematic). The bolio file format is similar in nature to NPSOFF in that the top level file contains ASCII keyword/value pairs specifying object characteristics. While bolio identifies additional binary data structure files, NPSOFF remains completely ASCII. The product development at NPS is almost exclusively experimental research and it was felt that a 100% human readable file format was needed during platform prototyping. When the final project design has been accepted, each NPSOFF file can be converted into binary to reduce I/O.

While bolio has demonstrated exceptional realism with the constraint-based movement of a *few articulated bodies*, the NPSOFF and the NPS simulation network (NPSNET) programs have been more concerned with the real-time animation of a *legion of 3D icons* (Zyda 1991c). Only with recent advances in workstation hardware has there been a capability to render a multitude of minimally articulated vehicles, in real-time. The vehicular nature of most NPSNET objects has lead toward a more interactive form of object-control, rather than bolio's use of kinematically specified task-level manipulations. Also, the constraints in NPSOFF are used more as a specification of an object's *physical capabilities*, rather than a notation for an object's *desired behavior.*

4.2 Virya

Virya is a graphical editor for specifying an articulated object's motion-control characteristics, designed by Jane Wilhelm's group at UCSC (Wilhelms 1986, Wilhelms 1987). A user can assign to each body's degree of freedom (DOF), one or more controlling functions (forces or torques vs. time or positions vs. time). These functions can exist in one of many control states such as position or dynamics control, frozen or relaxed. The control functions are cubic spline curves delineated by control points maintained in an ASCII file format.

4.3 Notion

Additional motion control work by Jane Wilhelm's group describes a technique that allows a user to depict an object's behavior based on internal sensors (provocation detectors), effectors (propulsion mechanisms) and mappings (connections and nodes) between them (Wilhelms 1990). Connections provide data transfer/modification from sensors to effectors, while nodes permit multiple connections from many sources of input/output. This technique has been demonstrated with an interactive, workstation-based system called Notion which allows a user to specify and view an object's behavior-derived motion.

4.4 Dynamic Constraints

Barzel and Barr present an approach to controlling rigid bodies with dynamic constraints (Barr 1987, Barzel 1988a, Barzel 1988b). These constraints are instanced and then sustained throughout the animation using inverse dynamics. The resultant "constraint" forces determine the object's motion. Rather than construct "constraining" forces, we are more interested in specifying "controlling" forces, similar to Barzel/Barr's use of external forces to guide objects prior to constraint initiation.

This paper describes an approach for enhancements to NPSOFF which bestows an object with physical characteristics and provides mechanisms to govern the object's motion given a list of known internal and external forces acting on the object. We have developed a rudimentary algorithm for the automatic maintenance of multiple objects' current placement and orientation in real time. Using a tool developed at NPS called the NPSOFF Mover Tool, a designer can view NPSOFF objects from all perspectives, including those from an object's point of view. After a set of forces is added and adjusted in location/affect, the designer is then able to "test-drive" an object to verify its force characteristics. Constraints on the force actuators and object movement are easily added or changed. The modified NPSOFF object is saved back to a file and is ready for integration into any simulation utilizing the NPSOFF library of object and force functions.

The following sections describe: basic dynamics theory for object animation, the use of a layered approach to the creation and application of force definitions, force control and action control in NPSOFF, the capabilities and performance of the NPSOFF Mover Tool development and testing simulator. The final section concludes with a description of future work to increase the accuracy and realism of the physically-based modeling while lowering the final complexity of user-specified object movement.

5. THE DYNAMICS OF OBJECT ANIMATION

The use of dynamics in rigid-body simulations requires a delicate understanding and balancing of geometric and algorithmic complexities. If we are interested in modeling the precise physical interactions of simple objects, we can afford the computational expense of dynamics simulation. Increasing an object's structural complexity and having it interact with a greater number of peer objects, strains many dynamics algorithms to the point where they are unusable for real-time simulation. It is clear that the use of dynamics to simulate Newtonian mechanics is essential for most forms of motion (ballistic, robotic, ambulatory and piloted). The following sections attempt to provide broad insight into simplifying the task of dynamics integration. Additional amplification is available in two exceptional references, Jane Wilhelm's dynamics tutorial (Wilhelms 1988) and Goldstein's mechanics theory text (Goldstein 1980).

6. NON-DEFORMING FORCES

6.1 Initial Conditions

The object's current position and orientation are calculated based on a set of current initial conditions:

$$\left[p_{x_0}, p_{y_0}, p_{z_0}\right] \qquad \text{(position)}$$

$$\left[\theta_{x_0}, \theta_{y_0}, \theta_{z_0}\right] \qquad \text{(orientation)}$$

$$\left[\frac{\delta}{\delta t}(p_{x_0}), \frac{\delta}{\delta t}(p_{y_0}), \frac{\delta}{\delta t}(p_{z_0})\right] \qquad \text{(linear velocity)}$$

$$\left[\frac{\delta}{\delta t}(\theta_{x_0}), \frac{\delta}{\delta t}(\theta_{y_0}), \frac{\delta}{\delta t}(\theta_{z_0})\right] \qquad \text{(angular velocity)}$$

and initial time t_0.

Often, the initial velocity values are not needed as most objects begin life motionless. Nevertheless, the ability to create an object, such as an airplane, in all phases of its movement description requires a provision for non-zero initial velocities.

7. NEWTON'S LAWS

$F_{xyz} = m \times a_{xyz}$ or simply "A given force acting on a given mass will accelerate it." More specifically,

$$F_{xyz} = m \times \frac{\delta^2}{\delta t^2}(p_{xyz})$$

$$T_{xyz} = m \times \frac{\delta^2}{\delta t^2}(\theta_{xyz})$$

where

F_{xyz}	= the net force directed at the object's center of mass.
T_{xyz}	= the net torque directed at the object's center of mass.
m	= object mass.

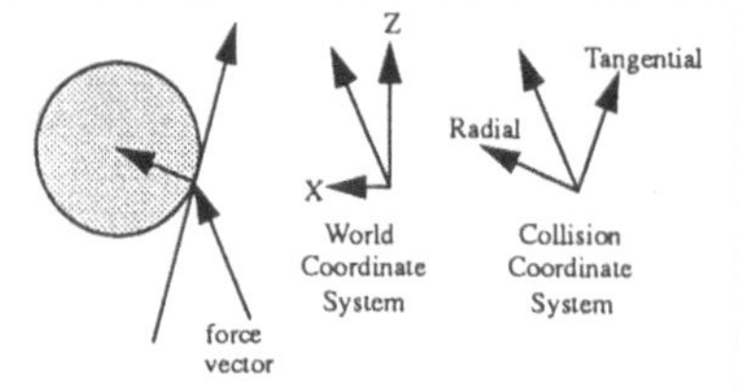

Figure 1 Force Components

$\delta^2/\delta t^2(p_{xyz})$ = linear acceleration component.

$\delta^2/\delta t^2(\theta_{xyz})$ = angular acceleration component.

8. LOCAL FRAME OF REFERENCE

Each non-deforming force vector is converted into two collision coordinate system vectors; one that affects a torque (tangential) and one that affects a translation (radial) in each of the XY, YZ and XZ planes respectively (Figure 1). Since each component of the movement force 6-vector (three tangential forces and three radial forces) is mutually exclusive, they are summed to generate a *cumulative* object frame movement force 6-vector.

The movement force 6-vector specifies an object-frame acceleration 6-vector (the three tangential force components create three rotation acceleration components as the remaining three radial force components create three translational accelerations). For example, in the XZ plane, only the X and Z components create linear motion and torque about the Y axis. Each force adds its effects to the object's six object frame of reference accelerations along and around each of the three object's axes. An object-frame velocity 6-vector is calculated using constant acceleration over the integration time interval δt. Both 6-vectors are then mapped into their world frame counterpart 6-vectors. These world frame accelerations and velocity 6-vectors are then used in a modified Euler integration (Spiegal 1988).

$$\frac{\delta}{\delta t}(Fp_{xyz}) = \frac{\delta}{\delta t}(Ip_{xyz}) + \left(\frac{\delta^2}{\delta t^2}(Ip_{xyz}) \times \delta t\right)$$

$$\frac{\delta}{\delta t}(F\theta_{xyz}) = \frac{\delta}{\delta t}(I\theta_{xyz}) + \left(\frac{\delta^2}{\delta t^2}(I\theta_{xyz}) \times \delta t\right)$$

These two equations calculate final linear/angular velocities, given current velocities and accelerations over a time interval δt.

$$Fp_{xyz} = Ip_{xyz} + \left(\frac{\delta}{\delta t}(Fp_{xyz}) \times \delta t\right) + \left(0.5 \times \frac{\delta^2}{\delta t^2}(p_{xyz}) \times (\delta t)^2\right)$$

$$F\theta_{xyz} = I p_{xyz} + \left(\frac{\delta}{\delta t}(F\theta_{xyz}) \times \delta t\right) + \left(0.5 \times \frac{\delta^2}{\delta t^2}(\theta_{xyz}) \times (\delta t)^2\right)$$

These two equations calculate final linear/angular positions, given current positions/velocities and predicted velocity averages at sample time.

where

$\delta/\delta t(Fp_{xyz})$	= final linear velocity component
$\delta/\delta t(F\theta_{xyz})$	= final angular velocity component
Fp_{xyz}	= final position component
Ip_{xyz}	= initial position component
$F\theta_{xyz}$	= final orientation component
$I\theta_{xyz}$	= initial orientation component
δt	= time interval since last integration

The modified Euler method was selected for its simplicity and iterative speed. Each object's force list is updated once per rendering loop, therefore nullifying the additional precision provided by second order and higher methods of integration. Obviously, Euler's method will lose accuracy as each object is subjected to rapidly changing forces. A future implementation will sample the force updates in parallel, track the relative changes in linear/angular accelerations and switch to a higher order integration method, such as Runge-Kutta, under a rapidly moving scenario.

Each global force (such as gravity) affects the object at its center of mass causing only linear acceleration. Since the movement does not involve rotations, it can be added after the net effect of all local forces is determined.

9. DEFORMING FORCES

A deforming force affects the object in one of three ways. Each polygon in the object has an associated *break* and *bend threshold* token specified in newtons/meter^2. Using the relationship that a force dissipates its kinetic energy inversely over the square of the distance from the force origin to the polygon, a dissipated force per unit polygon surface area value is calculated. If the force is strong enough to break the polygon, the original polygon token is removed from the object token list and replaced with a list of smaller triangular polygonal shard tokens (Figure 2). Triangles are used to guarantee planar polygons.

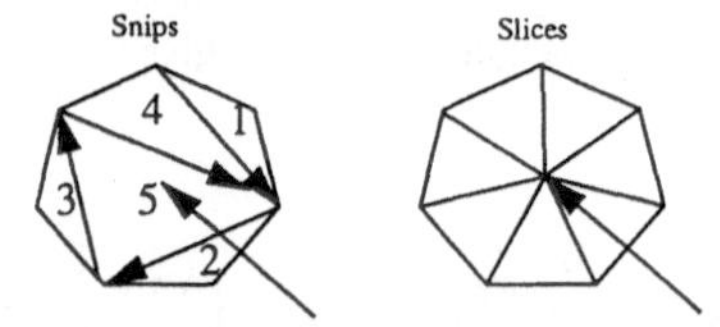

Figure 2 Breaking Force

The shards are initially determined by "snipping" off the corners of a multi-sided convex polygon, thus spiraling inward until the remaining quadrangle is divided in two. The rationale is to 1) prevent identical "pizza slice" shards as explosions are rarely symmetrical and 2) generate (*n-2*) versus *n* fragments from an *n*-sided polygon. Any remaining shards are broken along their hypotenuse, as needed.

If the force is only strong enough to bend the polygon, the polygon token is removed from the object token list and replaced with a new bendable polygon that tracks a moving point of bending force impact (Figure 3). The bending force is modeled using Hooke's Law and a spherical spring that seeks to return the moving vertex back to the polygon's actual point of impact.

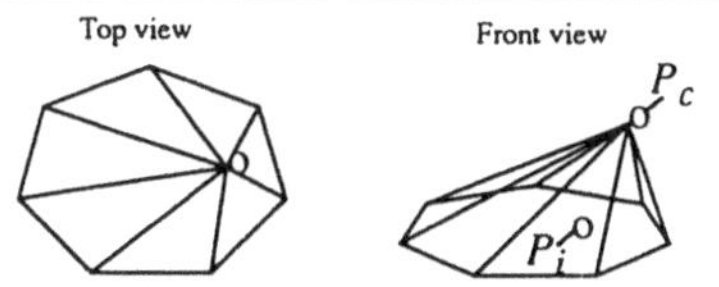

Figure 3 Bending Force

$$F_{xyz} = -(k_s \times \Delta p_{xyz} + k_d \times \Delta v_{xyz})$$

where

Pi	= initial point of bending force impact.
Pc	= current point of bending force impact.
F_{xyz}	= linear bending component.
k_s	= spring constant.
k_d	= damping constant.
Δp_{xyz}	= difference between the position components of the initial and current points of impact.
Δv_{xyz}	= difference between the velocity components of the initial and current points of impact.

If the force is neither strong enough to break or bend a polygon, then it may only push a polygonal shard.

10. A LAYERED APPROACH

The initial objective of our work was to provide a structured mechanism for object behavior control that would allow varying degrees of *user* and *designer* involvement with the simulation. The end user is concerned with realism: visual accuracy and similarity of interface (i.e *look* and *feel*). The simulated object's appearance and movement must closely resemble its real world counterpart. Objects that instantly accelerate to highly unnatural velocities provide a temporary sensation of giddiness, bordering upon the comical. A lack of expected visual clues from the objects' Newtonian interactions, such as the lack of gravity effects, reduces the allure of the virtual reality. A similar degradation in simulator immersion is also evident when the user is expected to identify and interface with an inordinate number of forces, which are manipulating several objects.

11. METHOD

The desired implementation would allow the art design team to create a specific object hierarchy with realistic shape, colorings and positioning data. The engineering section would then add the subobject physical attributes (mass, center of mass and object elasticity) and affecting force descriptions (force position, or point of affect in the object's frame of reference, along with the force direction unit vector, magnitude and type of force). Reasonable defaults for omitted physical attributes are assumed and/or calculated from other specifications. The analysis team would then specify mappings between subobject movement and the forces affected by such movement. The end user is then able to control a given object in a realistic manner with realistic results by manipulating a set of *control subobjects* linked to local forces. The result is an adjustable "focus" in specifying high-level object motion in a range of control modes: directly, indirectly through local *force* control, and even more indirectly with *subobject* control.

The final objective was to design a suite of tools, so that a single user, with even a limited background in Newtonian mechanics, could rapidly design and test an object's physical characteristics.

12. DESCRIPTIONS OF EACH LAYER

Similar to Barr's view of Teleological Modeling (Barr 1988), the approach is for each layer to provide a control description to the layer below. The lowest layer consists of rendering descriptions (drawing primitives, materials and lighting controls to color their skins). The second layer consists of the object's physical characteristics and a set of force descriptions (a list of forces and their influence upon specific objects). The third layer consists of action descriptions (a mapping of an object's movements to changes in a set of force descriptions) (Figure 4).

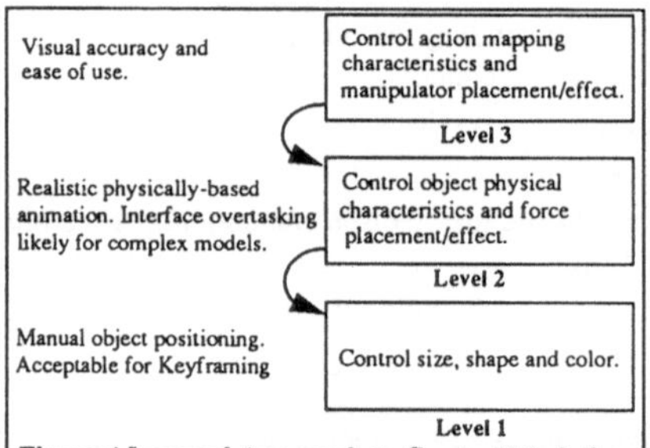

Figure 4 Layered Approach to Control Modeling

13. PRIMITIVE ADDITIONS

As described, the version 1.0 NPSOFF file supported only drawing subprimitives such as lines, polygons, and meshed surfaces. Other common generalized surface primitives (cones, cylinders, spheres and parallelepipeds) were usually calculated off-line, with their polygonal data stored into an NPSOFF file. The major disadvantage to this approach was that these NPSOFF files were extremely large and difficult to edit. As scenarios requiring different colors on a primitive were rare at best, the inclusion of a set of parametrized primitive descriptions was required. For example, a cylinder token is specified by a height, radius, and quality factor that indicates the maximum number of polygons or mesh points to use in the rendering. The advantages were automatic minimal

Table 1 UNITS OF MEASURE

Token Function	Argument Type(s)
units of dimension	char
units of force	char
units of mass	char

Table 2 FORCE CHARACTERISTICS

Token Function	Argument Type(s)
name	char
type	char
origin	float, float, float
origin constraints (low)	float, float, float
origin constraints (high)	float, float, float
direction	float, float, float
magnitude	float
magnitude constraints	float, float
asleep	yes or no

polygonal computation based on ranging data from a specified viewpoint, a simple mechanism for multiple object resolution creation and known mass/center of mass values, to name a few.

14. OBJECTS AND FORCE CONTROLS

The models in the various NPS simulators have quite an eclectic background. Some came from non-organic sites such as NASA and MIT, requiring conversion from other file formats. Many others were designed in-house and more often than not, the various models were rarely scale compatible. The first set of extensions to the NPSOFF language, (Table 1), included tokens to specify and convert between the various units of measure (Level 1).

15. OBJECT MODELING REQUIREMENTS

The next set of extensions, (Table 2), included tokens to specify the capabilities and constraints of a force acting upon an object (Level 2)The next set of extensions, (Table 3), included tokens to specify the physique, initial conditions, and motion boundary conditions of an object (Level 2). A default bounding volume is calculated as the object is read into memory. Provisions for specifying a smaller (or larger) bounding description (spherical, rectangular or ellipsoid) were added to facilitate parallel research efforts in collision detection. As much of the research at NPS involves the simulation of piloted vehicles, the inclusion of a vehicle viewpoint was a requirement.)

The concept of a "sleeping" or suspended force is to leave the force attached to the object but remove its effect. The rationale for this was for simplification during the force definition and analysis phase. A given force can be isolated by leaving it the sole "awake" or active force. The unacceptable alternative is to nullify the other forces by restricting their magnitudes and/or directions.

16. OBJECTS AND ACTION CONTROL

What we have now is a "marionette" object that is manipulated by pulling and pushing "force" strings and rods. For objects with a simple description of force effectors, this is quite acceptable as each force can be visualized as

Table 3 OBJECT CHARACTERISTICS

Token Function	Argument Type(s)
initial position	float, float, float
position constraints (low)	float, float, float
position constraints (high)	float, float, float
initial rotation	float, float, float
rotation constraints (low)	float, float, float
rotation constraints (high)	float, float, float
initial linear velocity	float, float, float
linear velocity constraints (low)	float, float, float
linear velocity constraints (high)	float, float, float
initial rotation velocity	float, float, float
angular velocity constraints (low)	float, float, float
angular velocity constraints (high)	float, float, float
mass	float
center of mass	float, float, float
elasticity	float
bounding volume radius	float
bounding volume length	float
bounding volume width	float
bounding volume height	float
viewpoint from object	float, float, float

a controlling "object" rather than a force. Realistically, most objects' movements are *described* by a complex network of forces, yet *controlled* from a small number of input sources. Level 3's objective will be to identify a small set of *control* objects and provide a mapping from their movement (translations/rotations) changes to a set of force description (origin/direction/magnitude) changes.

We will want to specify a set of *dynamic* controlling forces and then provide an abstraction for altering their effect based on user input changes. As early key-frame animation control systems identified key object positions and then interpolated the in-between positions as a function of time, so should we specify key controlling force effects and then interpolate the in-between effect components as functions of a user input position/orientation. This approach will provide for a natural migration from *simulated* input sources to *actual hardware/sensor* input sources.

For example, a jet object has three forces that describe the effects of two ailerons and one stabilizer. The action induced by their movement is controlled by one input source, the pilot's stick. The user will describe simple mappings for the stick's lateral rotation (affecting the aileron forces) and longitudinal rotation (affecting the stabilizer force). Adding additional mappings for throttle/rudder pedal positions and we will have an airplane that is fully controllable with changes in the *input device's position and rotation* (Figure 5).

As the construction of Layer 3 is part of continuing research, the following is a *specification* for a possible NPSOFF file mapping from subobject movement (translations/rotations) changes to a set of force description (origin/direction/magnitude) changes:

```
defmapping sample_map_name
 sample_object               name
 sample_force                name
 rot_to_force_origin         matrix
 rot_to_force_vector         matrix
 trans_to_force_origin       matrix
 trans_to_force_vector       matrix
defend
```

Each object and force has an initial (neutral) state specified in their respective descriptions. Each respective 3x3 matrix would transform a 3-vector (controlling object rotation and translation changes) into another 3-vector (force origin and vector incremental updates). Additional mappings would require velocity information as well.

17. THE NPSOFF MOVER TOOL

The objective of the NPSOFF Mover Tool is to provide an environment to design and test the dynamics of NPSOFF objects. An NPSOFF object without physical characteristics is read into memory from disk and the object is measured for future calculations. A default mass, mass center, elasticity and object viewpoint are calculated. The user is then able to "fine tune" any of these approximations based on known data. The user then specifies the initial values for object position, orientation and velocity. At the lowest layer of the tool's control, the user is able to continually update the object's movement by indicating the linear/angular direction and speed. This would be acceptable for specifying instances for a keyframing sequencer, but we are more interested in providing mechanisms to accelerate the object just like its real world counterpart. The mechanism of choice is a force description.

18. APPLICATION

The user controls a set of forces that are in turn, controlling the object's movement. A force is positioned around an object and its range of effect is specified. For example, our jet fighter object is re-read into the Mover Tool and the engine forces are added via a force interface (Figure 6). A separate force vector is positioned in the center of each exhaust nozzle, initially directed forward (direction of the *reactive* force) and parallel to the turbine housing, with a zero newton magnitude. The force's magnitude is constrained by a non-negative range of thrust values. The point of effect is also given a small range of values along the axis parallel to the direction of thrust to account for the change in thrust position when the engine is operated in afterburner and additional fuel is combusted behind the main combustion chamber. Similar forces are added to the wings for lift and drag forces created by the various control surfaces (flaps, ailerons, spoilers,...).

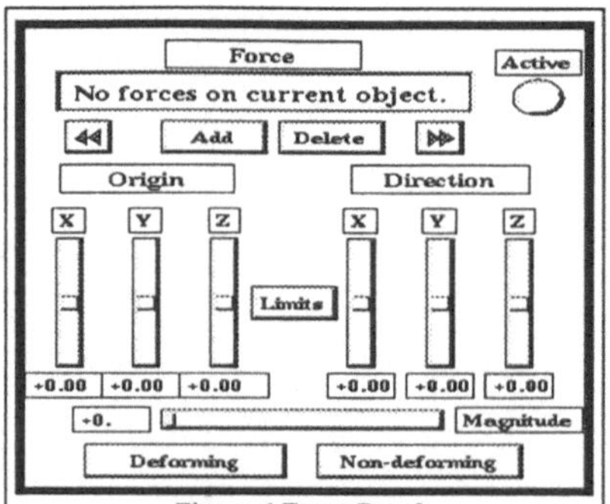

Figure 6 Force Panel

Additional pseudo forces, such as parasitic drag can be added to tune the realism. The result is a vehicle that will maneuver with amazing realism. The object can be "test flown" in isolation or with other testbed objects to verify the object's force parameters. The object is saved to a file when the desired physical model is accepted. The NPSOFF file force descriptions are always editable with any ASCII text editor.

The following is a sample NPSOFF file force description for the plane's left engine:

```
defforce left_jet_engine
 force_type                      non-deforming
 force_origin                    -4.0 0.5 -0.8
 force_origin_low                0.0 0.0 0.0
 force_origin_high               -4.5 0.5 -0.8
 force_direction                 -1.0 0.0 0.0
 force_magnitude                 8000.0
 force_magnitude_constraints     0.0 10000
 asleep                          no
defend
```

19. POSTDESIGN

The same functions that are used to animate objects in the NPSOFF Mover Tool are embedded in the NPSOFF function library. In addition to the functions that read in an object file, ready it for display, and display it each time through the display loop, are a host of new functions that: add/delete objects and forces from the animation environment, navigate the object/force lists, alter the object/force parameters, and start/stop the animation process.

20. NPSOFF FILE AND CODE INTEGRATION SAMPLE

Figure 7 is a fragment of an NPSOFF file description of an SU-25 Frogfoot Soviet ground attack aircraft. Figure 8 shows a C-code fragment that demonstrates the various phases of NPSOFF file integration with the force/object functions.

```
defunits
/* All lengths are in meters. Other length choices are available. */
dimension meters
/* All force magnitudes are in newtons. Other force choices are available.
*/
force newtons
/* All mass amounts are in kilograms. Other mass choices are available.
*/
mass kilos
defend

defphysics
/* This object's initial position is (X,Y,Z) in meters relative from the en-
vironments's center. Unless otherwise specified, all triples are X,Y,Z re-
spective. */
location 0.00 0.00 0.00

/* The object's position is constrained to a one meter level square, rela-
tive from the object's initial position. */
location_lower -1.00 -0.00 -1.00
location_upper 1.00 0.00 1.00

/* This object's initial orientation (Roll, Yaw, Pitch) in degrees. */
orientation 0.00 0.00 0.00

/* The object's orientation is unconstrained. */
orientation_lower 0.00 0.00 0.00
orientation_upper 360.00 360.00 360.00

/* The object's initial linear velocity in meters/second. */
linear 0.00 0.00 0.00

/* The object's linear velocity is constrained to: 0.00 to 1000.0 longitu-
dinal, +/- 1000.0 vertical and +/- 500.0 latitudinal. */
linear_lower 0.00 -1000.00 -500.00
linear_upper 1000.00 1000.00 500.00

/* The object's initial angular velocity in degrees per second. */
angular 0.00 0.00 0.00

/* The object's angular velocity is constrained to: +/- 10.00 longitudinal,
vertical and latitudinal. */
angular_lower -10.00 -10.00 -10.00
angular_upper 10.00 10.00 10.00

/* The object's center of mass and amount in kilos. */
mass_amount 25000.00
mass_center 0.00 0.00 0.00

/* The object's ability to absorb local forces. (0.0 is perfectly inelastic) */
elasticity 0.80

/* The dimensions of the object's bounding volume (e.g. for collision de-
tection). The volume dimensions are calculated if this data is omitted. */
bv_radius 30.00
bv_latitude 15.00
bv_longitude 20.00
bv_vertical 8.0

/* The location of the object's local viewpoint. */
setviewpoint 0.00 38.241650 0.00
defend

defforce left_jet_engine
 force_type non-deforming
 force_origin -4.0 0.5 -0.8
 force_origin_low 0.0 0.0 0.0
 force_origin_high -4.5 0.5 -0.8
 force_direction -1.0 0.0 0.0
 force_magnitude 8000.0
 force_magnitude_constraints 0.0 10000
asleep no
defend

/* Additional forces (right_engine, left_aileron,...) would follow here. */

/* The next two definitions specify a polygon lighting/shading character-
istic. */
defmaterial su25mat0
emission 0.00 0.00 0.00
ambient 0.047059 0.086275 0.047059
diffuse 0.235294 0.431373 0.235294
specular 0.00 0.00 0.00
shininess 0.00
alpha 1.00
defend
defmaterial su25mat1
emission 0.00 0.00 0.00
ambient 0.047059 0.094118 0.047059
diffuse 0.235294 0.470588 0.235294
specular 0.00 0.00 0.00
shininess 0.00
alpha 1.00
defend

/* A particular lighting/shading characteristic is activated. */
setmaterial su25mat0

/* The next definition specifies a triangular polygon. */
defpoly
/* Normal, number of vertices and vertex coordinates. */
0.875439 -0.483329 0.00
3
40.142231 6.476233 1.029732
39.087486 4.565808 -1.076130
40.142231 6.476233 -1.029732
```

Figure 7 NPSOFF File Sample

21. PERFORMANCE

The following tables are used to illustrate the cost associated with this physically-based modeling technique. All tests were performed on a Silicon Graphics 4D/240VGX workstation (single-thread). Test case group A involves a small, average and large polygon count object with small, average and large non-deforming force lists (Table 4). Test case group B involves small, average and large sets of an average polygon count object with small, aver-

```
/* Initializing the environment. */
initialize_environment();

/* Let's add gravity. */
add_global_force();
strcpy(current_global_forceptr->name,"gravity");
modify_force_origin(current_global_forceptr,0.0,1.0,0.0);
modify_force_direction(current_global_forceptr,0.0,-1.0,0.0);

/* Adding and modifying an object. */
objectptr = read_object("sample_filename");
ready_object_for_display(objectptr);
add_object_to_environment(objectptr);

/* Any characteristics (specified or not in the NPSOFF file) can be
modified. We can check if a particular object characteristic has
changed (e.g. by polling an input device), add adjust it prior to cal-
culating the objects' motion. */
modify_object_position(objectptr,px,py,pz);
modify_object_position_lower(objectptr,lx,ly,lz);
modify_object_position_upper(objectptr,ux,uy,uz);
modify_object_rotation(objectptr,rx.ry,rz);
modify_object_rotation_lower(objectptr,lx,ly,lz);
modify_object_rotation_upper(objectptr,ux,uy,uz);
modify_object_linear_velocity(objectptr,vx,vy,vz);
modify_object_linear_velocity_lower(objectptr,lx,ly,lz);
modify_object_linear_velocity_upper(objectptr,ux,uy,uz);
modify_object_angular_velocity(objectptr,vx,vy,vz);
modify_object_angular_velocity_lower(objectptr,lx,ly,lz);
modify_object_angular_velocity_upper(objectptr,ux,uy,uz);
modify_object_mass(objectptr,mass,mx,my,mz);
modify_object_bounds(objectptr,radius,latitude,longitude,vertical
);

/* If the object needs to be removed, we delete it. */
delete_object_from_environment(objectptr);

/* If we want to suspend all forces on an object, */
suspend_object(objectptr);

/* or to allow all active forces to influence an object. */
wakeup_object(objectptr);
/* Adding and modifying a force. */
add_local_force(objectptr);
/* or */
add_global_force();

/* Any characteristics (specified or not in the NPSOFF file) can be
modified. We can check if a particular force characteristic has
changed (e.g. by polling an input device), add adjust it prior to cal-
culating the objects' motion. */
modify_force_origin(forceptr,ox,oy,oz);
modify_force_origin_lower(forceptr,lx,ly,lz);
modify_force_origin_upper(forceptr,ux,uy,uz);
modify_force_direction(forceptr,ox,oy,oz);
modify_force_magnitude(forceptr,magnitude);
modify_force_magnitude_constraints(forceptr,lower,upper);
modify_force_type(forceptr,type);

/* If the force needs to be removed, */
delete_local_force(objectptr,forceptr);
/* or */
delete_global_force(forceptr);

/* If we want to suspend a force, */
suspend_force(forceptr);
/* or to re-allow this force to influence the object. */
wakeup_force(forceptr);

/* Functions are provided to update all or individual objects' phys-
ics in the environment. The update process applys applicable forc-
es, modifies velocities and updates location and orientation infor-
mation.*/
update_environment();
update_only_this_object(objectptr);

/* An object can be displayed by the environment or individually
by the user. Also a transformation matrix for the object can be re-
quested. */
display_environment()
display_only_this_object(objectptr);
objmatrixptr = object_matrix(objectptr);
```

Figure 8 NPSOFF File Integration Sample

age and large non-deforming force lists (Table 5). Test case group C involves a small, average and large polygon count object with a small deforming force list, during the explosion phase (Table 6). All numbers are in frames per second.

A note of interest in case A - the frame rate actually increases from one force to five forces and then decreases from then on. We are reclaiming idle CPU time and improving graphics-CPU overlap.

In the case of non-deforming forces, the frame rate decreases linearly with the *total number of non-deforming forces* attached to all objects, (Figures 9 and 10). In the case of deforming forces, the frame rate decreases linearly with the *number of initial polygons* in the pre-destroyed object (Figure 11).

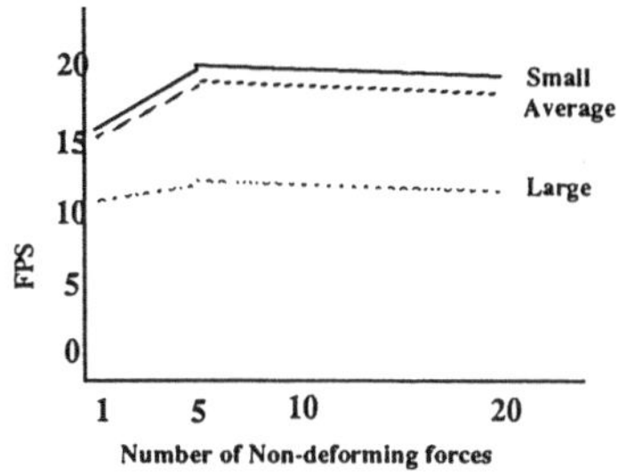

Figure 9 Object Size and Non-deforming Forces

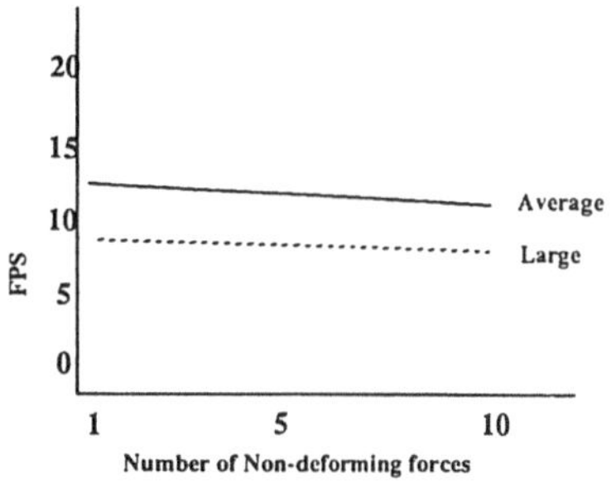

Figure 10 No. of Objects & Non-deforming Forces

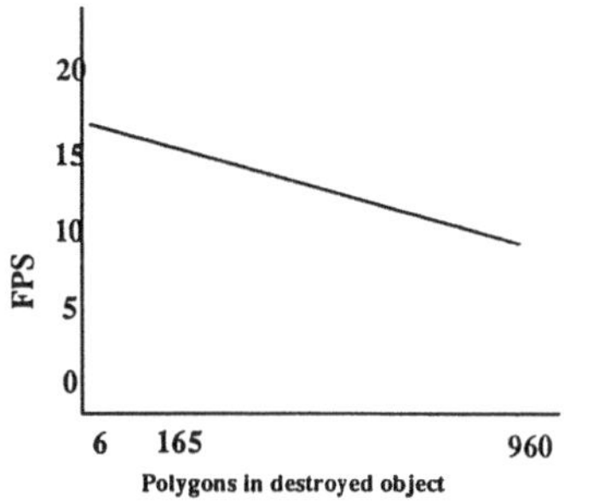

Figure 11 Object Size and Deforming Forces

22. CONCLUSIONS AND FUTURE WORK

The use of physically-based modeling is still in its infancy at NPS. Previous simulations were able to "fake" or "downplay" the expected visual clues from an object's physical interactions. As hardware and software technology afford us with greater *capability* in animation realism, we are obligated to strive for more accurate physical modeling, but not at the expense of increased *user workload* to specify and control the animation process. The extensions to NPSOFF present a simplified mechanism for building models with physical characteristics and adding controlling functions that are as complex as necessary given the current hardware support.

Future work includes the implementation of the Action Control layer using the Layer 3 specification. Generation of the mapping function matrices could be achieved quite easily by selecting the object/force pair and then taking "snapshots" of a series of object motion/force description couplings. Each coupling would then be displayed in a 2D graph (object component vs. force component) for any desired function smoothing/modification. Addition, deletion, and modification mechanisms would function similarly to identical object functions in key-framing systems. Further refinements to the integration process would include parallelization of the force sampling process and the addition of an adaptive algorithm for more accurate positioning of objects with rapidly fluctuating forces.

23. REFERENCES

Barr, A. H. (1987) "Dynamic Constraints", *ACM SIGGRAPH '87 Tutorial Notes: Topics in Physically-Based Modeling*, August 1987.

Barr, A. H. (1988) "Teleolgical Modeling", *ACM SIGGRAPH '88 Course Notes #27: Developments in Physically-Based Modeling, Section E*, August, 1988.

Barzel, R. and Barr, A. H. (1988a) "A Modeling System Based on Dynamic Constraints," *ACM SIGGRAPH '88 Conference Proceedings*, Vol 22 No 4, August 1988, pp. 179-188.

Barzel, R. and Barr, A. H. (1988b) "Controlling Rigid Bodies with Dynamic Constraints," *ACM SIGGRAPH '88 Course Notes #27: Developments in Physically-Based Modeling, Section E*, August, 1988.

Brett, C., Pieper, S., and Zeltzer, D. (1987) "Putting it all Together: An Integrated Package for Viewing and Editing 3D MicroWorlds," *Proc. 4th Usenix Computer Graphics Workshop*, October 1987.

Goldstein, H. (1980) *Classical Mechanics*, Second Edition, Addison-Wesley, Reading, MA, 1980.

Jurewicz, T. (1989) "A Real Time Autonomous Underwater Vehicle Dynamic Simulator," M.S. Thesis, Naval Postgraduate School, Monterey, CA, June 1989.

Spiegel, M. (1988) "*Applied Differential Equations, Third Edition*," Prentice Hall, Inc., Englewood Cliffs, N.J. 1988, pp. 1-26.

Sturman, D., Zeltzer, D. and Pieper, S. (1989) "The Use of Constraints in the bolio System," *ACM SIGGRAPH '89 Course Notes: Implementing and Interacting with Realtime Microworlds*, Boston, MA, July 31, 1989.

Wilhelms, J. (1986) "Virya - A motion Control Editor for Kinematic and Dynamic Animation," *Proceedings of Graphics Interface 86*, May, 1986, pp. 141-146.

Wilhelms, J. (1987) "Using Dynamic Analysis for Realistic Animation of Articulated Bodies," *IEEE Computer Graphics and Applications*, Vol 7 No 6, June 1987, pp. 12-27.

Wilhelms, J. (1988) "Dynamics for Computer Graphics: A Tutorial," *Computing Systems*, USENIX Association, Winter, 1988, pp. 63-93. also *UCSC Computer and Information Science Technical Report* UCSC-CRL-87-5.

Wilhelms, J. and Skinner, R. (1990) "An Interactive Approach to Behavior Control," *ACM SIGGRAPH '90 Course Notes: Developments in Physically-Based Modeling*, July, 1990.

Zeltzer, D., Pieper, S. and Sturman, D. (1989) "An Integrated Graphical Simulation Platform," *Proceedings of Graphics Interface 89*, June 19-23, 1989, London, Ontario, pp. 266-274.

Zyda, M. (1991a) "Book 7, Computer Graphics", *Naval Postgraduate School Course Notes CS 4470: Computer Graphics*, 2 April 1991.

Zyda, M. (1991b) "Book 9, Computer Graphics", *Naval Postgraduate School Course Notes CS 4470: Computer Graphics*, 31 May 1991.

Zyda, M. and Pratt, D. (1991c) "NPSNET: A 3D Simulator for Virtual World Exploration and Experimentation", *Society for Information Display 1991 International Symposium Digest of Technical Papers*, 31 May 1991, pp. 361-364.

Table 4 OBJECT SIZE VERSUS NUMBER OF FORCES (Frames/second)

	Small **Polygon Count** (6) Object	*Average* **Polygon** Count (165) Object	*Large* **Polygon** Count (960) Object
Single **Non-deforming** Force	17.117	16.547	11.174
Small **Set of** Non-deforming Forces (5)	20.083	18.166	11.864
Medium **Set of** Non-deforming Forces (10)	19.923	18.063	11.519
Large **Set of** Non-deforming Forces (20)	19.525	17.876	10.765

Table 5 NUMBER OF OBJECTS VERSUS NUMBER OF FORCES (Frames/second)

	Average **Number** of Objects (5)	*Large* **Number** of Objects (10)
Small **Set of** Non-deforming Forces (5)	11.861	8.441
Average **Set of** Non-deforming Forces (10)	11.525	8.179
Large **Set of** Non-deforming Forces (20)	10.935	8.025

Table 6 OBJECT SIZE VERSUS A DEFORMING FORCE (Frames/second)

	Small **Polygon** Count (6) Object	*Average* **Polygon** Count (165) Object	*Large* **Polygon** Count (960) Object
Small **Set of** **Deforming** Forces	16.535	15.493	10.454

24. ACKNOWLEDGEMENTS

We wish to acknowledge the sponsors of our efforts, in particular George Lukes of the USA Engineer Topographic Laboratories, David Neyland of DARPA/ASTO, Michael Tedeschi of the USA Test and Experimentation Command, John Maynard and Duane Gomez of the Naval Ocean Systems Center, San Diego, LTC Dennis Rochette, USA of the Headquarters Department of Army AI Center, Washington, D.C. and Carl Driskell of PM-TRADE.

Michael J. Zyda is an Associate Professor of Computer Science at the Naval Postgraduate School, Monterey, California. He has been at NPS since February of 1984. Professor Zyda was the chair of the 1990 Symposium on Interactive 3D Graphics, held at Snowbird, Utah. In addition to academic duties, Professor Zyda has consulted with over 15 different companies throughout Japan. Professor Zyda began his career in Computer Graphics in 1973 as part of an undergraduate research group, the Senses Bureau, at the University of California, San Diego. His active research centers around the production of inexpensive, real-time 3D visual simulation and virtual world systems. Professor Zyda received a BA in Bioengineering from the University of California, San Diego in La Jolla in 1976, an MS in Computer Science/Neurocybernetics from the University of Massachusetts, Amherst in 1978 and a DSc in Computer Science from Washington University, St. Louis, Missouri in 1984. Professor Zyda can be contacted at the Naval Postgraduate School, Code CS/Zk, Dept. of Computer Science, Monterey, California 93943-5100 or via electronic mail: zyda@trouble.cs.nps.navy.mil.

David R. Pratt, an Adjunct Instructor in the Department of Computer Science at the Naval Postgraduate School. Mr. Pratt is a half-time instructor, with the other half-time devoted to work on the NPSNET efforts. Mr. Pratt is also a Ph.D. student in the Department of Computer Science. He has 12 years of computer experience, with 6 1/2 of those years in the Marine Corps.

A New Method for Approximative Interactive Dynamics

ULRICH LEINER and BERNHARD PREIM

ABSTRACT

This paper presents the use of kinematics and dynamics to specify object motion in computer animation systems. To achieve real-time interactivity, objects are modeled by masspoints with connecting geometrical constraints which interact with the surrounding environment. The motion control is performed by known external forces and unknown constraint forces. The latter ones act on the masspoints in order to keep the constraints satisfied. To calculate these unknown quantities, a linear equation system is derived and then solved by an iterative algorithm for each timestep. Different examples including a three-dimensional six-body pendulum show the efficiency and accuracy of this algorithm.

Keywords: Physically Based Animation, Kinematic and Dynamic Simulation, Constraints, Real-time Interactivity

1. INTRODUCTION

Motion specification is the central task in computer animation. Using traditional keyframe animation, key events are specified as values of state variables for moved objects at selected frames. Interpolation yields the values for unspecified frames. Unfortunately, this method is both cumbersome for the animator and inaccurate from the physical point of view. Therefore, it is only suitable to model motion which is either not too complex or which needs not bear much resemblance with physical reality.

It is, however, possible to achieve more realistic motion with less specification effort, if the kinematic and dynamic properties of objects are taken into account. Using Lagrange's equation of motion

$$\frac{d}{dt}\left(\frac{\partial L}{\partial \dot{q}}\right) - \frac{\partial L}{\partial q} = Q \tag{1}$$

for the Lagrange function L, generalized coordinates q and forces Q, differential equations can be derived from the geometry and mass distribution of objects. Their solution provides a highly realistic motion, although some effects such as friction and elasticity are still neglected in most cases.

As in robotics (e.g. Pfeiffer 1987), a growing interest in dynamic simulation for computer animation has been identified (Isaacs 1987; Lee 1990; Thalmann 1989; Wilhelms 1988; Witkin 1987; Zeltzer 1985).

Derivation and solution of the dynamic equations (1) is a very complex and time consuming task which still can not be done in real-time, except for rather small problems. Real-time solutions that allow interactive manipulation of objects and motion are, however, of special importance and interest for computer animation problems. Therefore, new techniques have been developed which are especially adapted to this task.

- One basic idea is to restrict objects to masspoints, because their dynamic behavior is much easier and faster to handle (Schmitt 1990; van Overveld 1990; Witkin 1990; Witkin 1991a). Of course, this a severe restriction which causes severe physical inaccuracies, but it reduces the complexity of the problem drastically.
- A further idea is to define constraints among different bodies or masspoints (Barzel 1988; Witkin 1987; Witkin 1991b).While objects move, these constraints provoke constraint forces which are used to determine the exact motion. This technique is well known in mechanics, but here it is used in a slightly different way: Constraints determine the motion directly instead of being used to reduce the number of degrees of freedom for the masspoint-system and to transform it to generalized coordinates.

Interactive motion simulation by constraint satisfaction has been used for two main purposes: One purpose is to construct new objects, starting at a random initial state and satisfying the constraints successively over time (Barzel 1988). The other is to calculate object motion by keeping the constraints satisfied for a certain time interval (Witkin 1990).

We present an algorithm for these tasks which is new under several aspects:

- The derivation and solution of equations for the constraint satisfaction is performed with reduced calculation effort.
- The method enables approximative modeling of solid objects by a net of spacial distributed masspoints within an system for interactive dynamics.

The algorithm is applied for several examples and its accuracy is shown for a three-dimensional six-body pendulum, whose motion is calculated by the algorithm and compared to the exact solution.

2. CONSTRAINED PARTICLE DYNAMICS

Particles in 3D-space are defined by their position $p_i(t)$, their velocity $\dot{p}_i(t)$ and their masses m_i. Their motion is specified by Newton's law

$$m_i\ddot{p}_i(t) = f_i(t) \tag{2}$$

where the forces $f_i(t)$ are applied to the masspoints (Witkin 1991a). If a constant force is applied over a finite time interval δt the new position of the particle after this time will be

$$p_i(t+\delta t) = p_i(t) + \delta t\dot{p}_i(t) + \frac{\delta t^2}{2} \cdot \frac{f_i(t)}{m_i} \tag{3}$$

The definition of geometric relations among particles can be used to model kinematic or dynamic configurations. These relations can be expressed by constraint functions of equality or inequality type

$$C_j(p, \dot{p}, t) = 0 \qquad \text{or} \qquad C_j(p, \dot{p}, t) \le 0 \tag{4}$$

with p denoting the combined position vector of all masspoints. The calculations described in the following chapters will be restricted to constraints of type $C_j(p) = 0$, which is sufficient for most problems in computer animation.

All constraints of this kind can be combined to a constraint vector C

$$C(p) = 0 \tag{5}$$

For example a fixed distance c between two masspoints can be expressed as

$$C_j(p_1, p_2) = |p_1 - p_2| - c = 0 \tag{6}$$

Each constraint added to a particle system decreases the degree of freedom of the system and therefore influences its motion. To express how constraints influence the particles, Newton's law (2) and its meaning for particle positions (3) have to be extended by adding constraint dependent terms.

3. DERIVATION OF CONSTRAINT FORCE EQUATIONS

3.1 Equation of Motion for Constrained Particle Systems

The objective is to calculate the motion of a particle system $p(t)$, satisfying the constraints $C(p) = 0$. This can be achieved by integrating Newton's equations of motion (2). However, a term for unknown forces must be added corresponding to the constraints.

$$M \cdot \ddot{p}(t) = f_{ex}(t) + f_c(t) \tag{7}$$

The components of Newton's law represent:

M: diagonal massmatrix, in $\Re^3$ each mass appears three times

$\ddot{p}$: acceleration vector for the masspoints

f_{ex}: known external forces, e.g. gravity

f_c: unknown constraint forces of the system

The vector of unknown constraint forces f_c has to be determined in such a way, that the constraints $C(p) = 0$ are and stay satisfied. Therefore, they have to be derived from the constraint equation (5) and its derivatives with respect to time.

3.2 Time Derivatives used for Constraint Force Equations

Witkin, Gleicher and Welch (1990) propose to use the second time derivative $\ddot{C}(p) = 0$ to achieve an easily solvable equation system for the constraint forces. Substitution according the chain rule yields

$$\ddot{C} = DC \cdot \ddot{p} + \dot{p}^{\mathrm{T}} D^2 C \dot{p} = 0 \tag{8}$$

with the Jacobian matrix $DC = \dfrac{\partial C}{\partial q}$. Substituting $\ddot{p}$ by (7) solved for $\ddot{p}$ results in a linear equation system for f_c:

$$DC \cdot M^{-1} f_c = -\dot{p}^{\mathrm{T}} D^2 C \dot{p} - DCM^{-1} f_{ex} \tag{9}$$

For f_c the principle of virtual work can be applied. It says, that no constraint force adds or removes energy to or from the whole system. This is ensured (e.g. Kuypers 1990), if the constraint forces are orthogonal to all legal displacements which satisfy $C = 0$. These orthogonal directions form the null space complement of DC which is $DC^{\mathrm{T}} \cdot \lambda$ and each f_c must satisfy the equation

$$f_c = DC^{\mathrm{T}} \cdot \lambda \tag{10}$$

with the vector of Lagrangian multipliers λ. Substitution of this equation into the equation system (9) produces a symmetric linear equation system for the unknown forces. Its solution will be discussed in the next chapter.

3.3 Time Incremented Positions used for Constraint Force Equations

Based on an idea of van Overveld (1990), we propose an alternative approach to derive an equation system for the constraint forces. Instead of using $\ddot{C}(p) = 0$, it is demanded, that the constraints $C(p) = 0$ are still satisfied at the next time step $t + \delta t$:

$$C(p(t + \delta t)) = 0 \tag{11}$$

Using the equation for particle positions (3), this can be rewritten to

$$C(p(t + \delta t)) = C\left(p + \delta t \dot{p} + \frac{\delta t^2}{2} M^{-1} (f_{ex} + f_c)\right) = 0 \tag{12}$$

Newton's method for this nonlinear equation with respect to f_c yields

$$C\left(p + \delta t \dot{p} + \frac{\delta t^2}{2} M^{-1} f_{ex}\right) + DC \cdot \frac{\delta t^2}{2} M^{-1} f_c = 0 \tag{13}$$

and finally:

$$DCM^{-1} f_c = -\frac{2}{\delta t^2} C\left(p + \delta t \dot{p} + \frac{\delta t^2}{2} M^{-1} f_{ex}\right) \tag{14}$$

The left hand side the same term as in (9) can be found. The right hand side of (14) needs one evaluation of the constraints at the position

$$\tilde{p} = p + \delta t \dot{p} + \frac{\delta t^2}{2} M^{-1} f_{ex} \tag{15}$$

This position can be found quickly. The current position $p(t)$ and the external forces $f_{ex}(t)$ are known, a good estimate for the velocities $\dot{p}(t)$ is easily derived. A physical interpretation of this motion shows that $\tilde{p}$ is the position vector of the masspoints if their velocities are propagated without constraints under the influence of external forces only.

3.4 Comparison of the Algorithms

The left hand sides of (9) and (14) are identical. The right hand side of (14) is also very closely related to the right hand side of (9). This will be shown by the following transformations, which use Taylor-series several times:

$$\frac{2}{\delta t^2} C\left(p + \delta t \dot{p} + \frac{\delta t^2}{2} M^{-1} f_{ex}\right) = \frac{2}{\delta t^2}\left(C(p) + DCa + \frac{1}{2} a^{\mathrm{T}} D^2 C a + O(\delta t^3)\right) \tag{16}$$

with $$a = \delta t \dot{p} + \frac{\delta t^2}{2} M^{-1} f_{ex} \tag{17}$$

$$\ldots = DCM^{-1} f_{ex} + \dot{p}^{\mathrm{T}} D^2 C \dot{p} + c_1 C(p) + c_2 \dot{C}(p) + O(\delta t) \tag{18}$$

If the terms of order δt and higher are neglected, four terms remain. The first and the second are identical to the right hand side of equation (9). The remaining components - $C(p)$ and its first time derivative - can be assumed to be equal to zero, according to the conditions for the constraints mentioned at the beginning of this chapter (i.e. $C(p) = 0$ and $\dot{C}(p) = 0$). Another possible interpretation is to consider them as feedback forces, which neutralize violations of the constraints implicitly. Again these two terms can be found in a modified correction algorithm of Witkin (1990).

The main advantage of this algorithm is the minimal computational effort which is required to evaluate the right hand side of equation (14). Only one constraint evaluation is necessary per timestep. Compared with the evaluation and calculation of (9) or even (18), this is a significant advantage. If time-dependent constraints are considered, the difference between the two methods even grows. This algorithm has been proposed for and applied to specialized two-dimensional cases by van Overveld (1990). In that paper, as in others (e.g. Barzel 1988; Witkin 1987), constraint forces f_c are interpreted as virtual spring forces pulling the particle system into a legal state by satisfying all constraints.

4. SOLUTION OF CONSTRAINT FORCE EQUATIONS

The unknown constraint forces $f_c(t)$ can be derived now by solving a linear equation system. Both equations, (9) and (14), can be expressed in the form:

$$DCM^{-1} DC^{\mathrm{T}} \lambda = b \tag{19}$$

The matrix M^{-1} is diagonal, the matrix DC is sparse, i. e. most of its elements are equal to zero. There are many well known algorithms to solve such a problem, but those using the sparsity of the system are of special interest here. Witkin (1990) uses a conjugant gradient method to minimize the squared linear system, which takes advantage of the sparsity within the implementation of this algorithm.

We used the Jacobi-algorithm, an iterative method to solve this equation. It is expressed by the following iteration scheme:

$$Diag_A + A\lambda_i = b \tag{20}$$

$$\lambda_{i+1} = \lambda_i + \delta\lambda_{i+1} \tag{21}$$

with $\lambda_0 = 0$ and $Diag_A$: diagonal part of matrix A

For special types of constraints, $Diag_A$ can be expressed in closed form depending only on the masses of the involved particles. Using the resulting $\delta\lambda_{i+1}$, the constraint forces can be calculated. These are added to (15) as position corrections for a new estimate for $\tilde{p}$.This iteration scheme reduces the calculation effort in many cases significantly.

For this and similar iterative methods, convergence conditions and rates have been extensively investigated (e.g. Stoer 1978). The Jacobi-iteration converges, if and only if

$$\rho\,(I - Diag_A^{-1}A) < 1 \tag{22}$$

holds for the spectral radius ρ of the iteration matrix. Unfortunately, this is not guaranteed for all matrices which are found in the discussed problem. Nevertheless, the stability of the algorithm is significantly improved by inserting a damping factor c_3 into the correction step

$$\lambda_{i+1} = \lambda_i + c_3\delta\lambda_{i+1} \text{ with } c_3 < 1 \tag{23}$$

The correction of λ will still be in the same direction δt, but damped by c_3.

Based on these theoretical results, some questions can be answered, which were discussed by van Overveld (1990). His algorithm used this iteration scheme for some special kinds of constraints such as two point rods and three point joints:

1. Does this iteration converge in all cases? The answer is no, the criteria for the spectral radius must be satisfied. A damping value helps to enlarge the region of convergence.

2. Does a faster convergence scheme exist? The answer depends on the problem. It is clear, that examples can be constructed, which fail to converge at all. Others will be solved faster with Witkin's method and even such exist which can be most efficiently solved by a LR matrix decomposition.

3. If the iteration converges, does it always converge to the exact solution of Eulers equations? As long as a finite timestep $\delta t > 0$ exists, the accurate solution will not be achieved. With $\delta t \rightarrow 0$, however, the iteration will approach the solution according to the convergence criteria for initial value differential equations.

5. APPLICATIONS OF THE ALGORITHM

5.1 Simple Examples with Different Constraints

We introduced several special types of constraints to test the implemented algorithm:

- point-to-point constraint: A masspoint is fixed to a certain position which is either constant (nail-connection), user-guided (e.g. by mouse-pointer) or script-guided.
- rod constraint: two masspoints have constant distance which can be interpreted as a rod connection. Limited intervals for legal distances are also easy to add with only slight modification of the algorithm.
- angular constraints: Three masspoints form an angle in space, which can either be fixed or limited by an interval. Four masspoint form an angle with a well defined rotation axis.

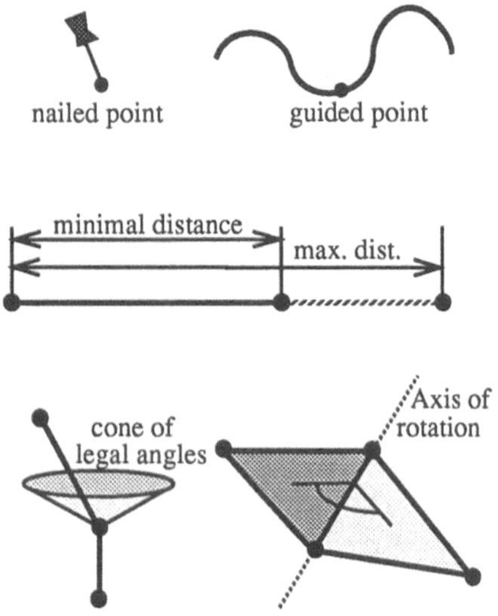

Fig.1: Different constraints

For these constraints the values for $Diag_A$ can be expressed, depending only on the masses and positions of the concerned points. It has been shown (Niemöller 1990) that several tinkertoys in a virtual three-dimensional space can be moved in real-time (see fig. 2).

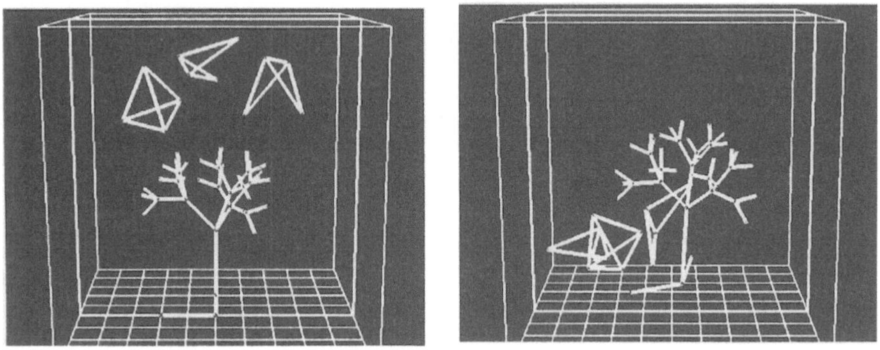

Fig.2: Several 3D objects in a virtual environment: In a arbitrary starting position (left) and after applying gravity over a certain time interval (right)

In that environment, objects can be dragged, pulled and thrown under or without influence of gravity. The short reaction time enables a framerate of about 10 to 20 frames per second (on a SG Iris 50 G with 0.7 Mflops). A simple collision detection algorithm keeps the object inside a virtual room.

5.2 Modeling Complex Objects by Networks of Masspoints

As a next step, we tried to apply the algorithm to more complex objects like multibody systems. These objects have solid bodies with mass distribution given by matrices of inertia. Existing systems (e.g. MESA VERDE (Wittenberg 1985)) to derive and solve the dynamic equations are very complex and can not be used for real-time applications.

Our objective therefore was to substitute this problem by a related but faster solvable one. We choose to build a net of masspoints which are connected by rod constraints. Their spacial distribution was used to approximate the inertias of the original bodies. To keep the model small enough, we restricted it to a maximum of 5 masspoints with 10 rods to substitute one solid 3D-body (fig. 3). Of course, this restriction does not always allow an accurate substitution, but a quite good approximation is often constructible.

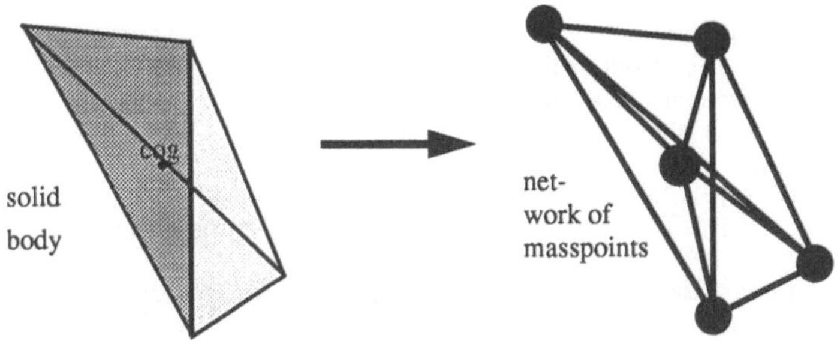

Fig. 3: Substitution of an solid object by a network of masspoints

The matrix of inertia for a multi-masspoint system has the form

$$I_{masspoints} = \sum_i m_i \begin{bmatrix} y_i^2 + z_i^2 & -x_i y_i & -x_i z_i \\ * & x_i^2 + z_i^2 & -y_i z_i \\ * & * & x_i^2 + y_i^2 \end{bmatrix} \tag{24}$$

with the masspoint coordinates (x_i, y_i, z_i) relative to their center of gravity. Therefore, a solution or an approximation of the equation

$$I_{masspoints} = I_{body} \tag{25}$$

can be used to define the location and masses of the substituting masspoints.

5.3 Results for a Multibody Pendulum

To test this idea of masspoint networks, we applied it to a 6-body pendulum in 3D-space. Each of its 5 axes of rotation is twisted by 90 degrees in relation to its predecessor (fig. 4).

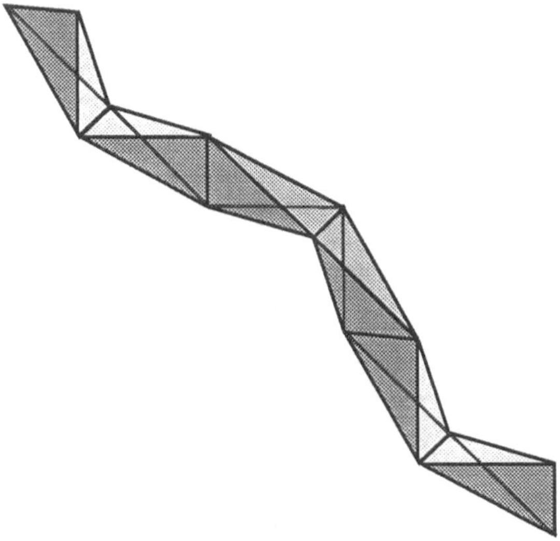

Fig. 4: A six-body pendulum with 5 axes

The masspoint system, substituting this original problem, consists of 20 masspoints with 55 rod constraints, leaving only five rotatorial degrees of freedom to the object. This corresponds exactly with the original pendulum. The masses and positions of the masspoints were chosen using equation (25) to achieve corresponding moments of inertia with the original pendulum.

For the simulation, the first body, respectively its masspoints, were fixed in space and the chain was put under influence of gravity, starting at a certain initial position. We compared the results of the masspoints-and-constraints algorithm for the five joint angles with numerical values resulting from an integration of the exact differential equation (high order Runge-Kutta integrator with variable stepsize). The results are shown in the two diagrams below. Fig. 5 shows the result of the numerical integration, fig. 6 presents the curves we achieved, by letting the masspoint network swing with the same start position.

These diagrams show a nearly perfect congruence of the exact solution with the values of the approximative model. This is especially remarkable because this problem is highly nonlinear and chaotic in its behavior as can be seen by the regular and rapid changes of the angles in the diagrams. The simulated time period depends on the scaling of the size of the pendulum. It is about 5 seconds for a one meter sized object. The time needed for the calculation was about 3 minutes on a SG 50G 0.7 Mflops workstation. Of course, this is not real-time compared to the simulation time but it shows the achievable high accuracy of the algorithm.

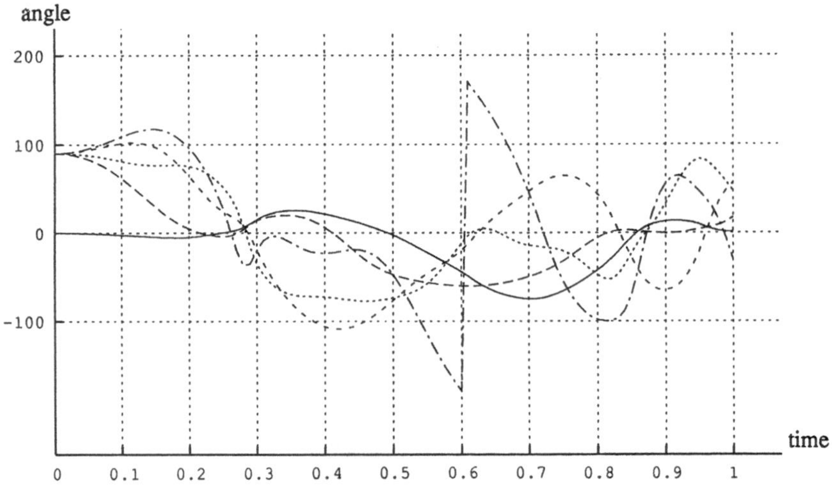

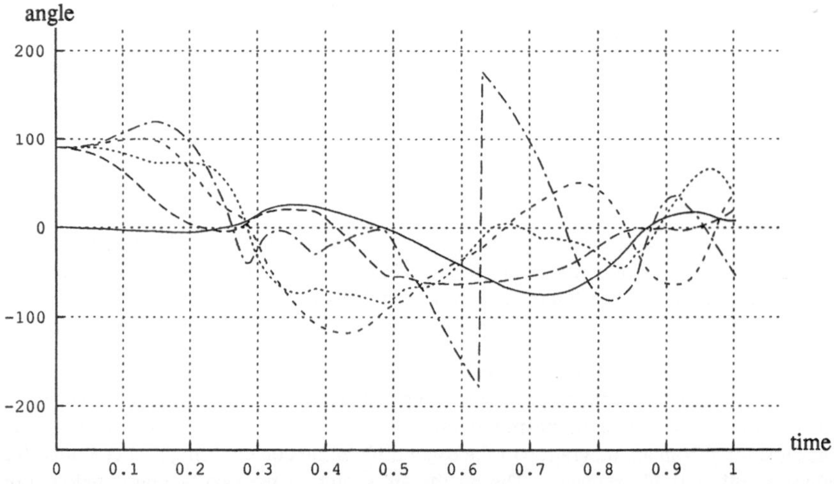

Fig. 5, 6: Exact (top) and approximated (bottom) solution for the 6-body pendulum problem

There are several parameters which influence speed and accuracy of the algorithm: maximal number of iterations for constraint satisfaction (compare chapter 4), stepsize for time increment and error tolerance for the constraints. Reducing the number of iterations and increasing the stepsize for the time increment led to much faster, but not that accurate results.

Fig. 7 shows the swinging pendulum at different timesteps. The starting position is shown in the upper left figure (a). It is followed by (b) showing the situation after 1 second, (c) after 2 seconds, (d) after 3 seconds, (e) after 4 seconds and (f) after 5 seconds. The oscillation to the right (c and d), the looping of the last link (d) and the motion back to the left (f) can be observed.

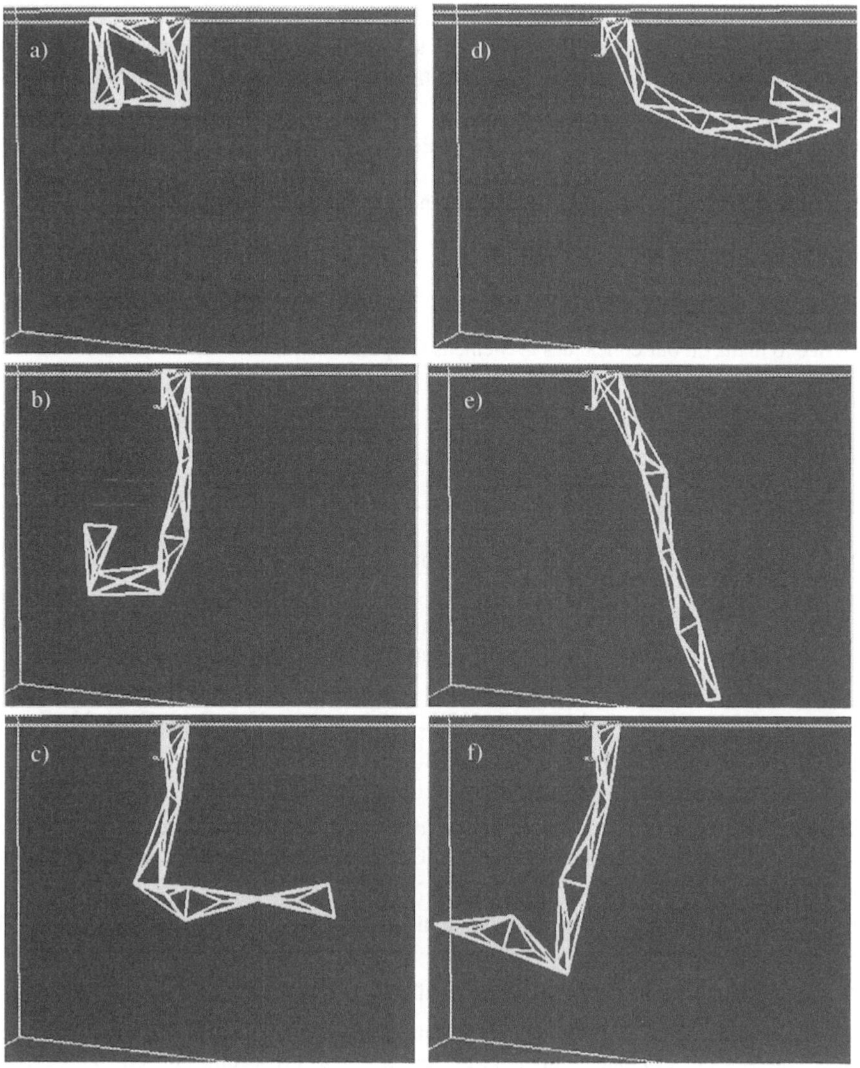

Fig. 7: Swinging multibody pendulum at different timesteps

6. CONCLUSIONS

The presented algorithm shows a new method for real-time approximative dynamics. It applicability to complex multibody problems was shown. Some answers to questions on convergence for iterative algorithms were given, while others remain currently unsolved.

There are still several open problems and questions. Can the algorithm be improved and generalized by a variable timestep size and a more sophisticated guess for the velocity $\dot{p}$? Will an adaptive damping factor accelerate the convergence? Other types of constraints have to be added as well.

The algorithm has been integrated as a simulation module into a computer animation system, supporting the motion specification for highly complex objects. Further studies and comparison of exemplary motions will to be undertaken in the future.

7. ACKNOWLEDGEMENT

We like to thank all our colleagues at Siemens Corporate Research and Development for their support and encouragement of our work.

REFERENCES

Barzel R, Barr A (1988) A Modeling System Based On Dynamic Constraints. Computer Graphics 22(4): 179-188

Isaacs P, Cohen M (1987) Controlling Dynamic Simulation with Kinematic Constraints, Behavior Functions and Inverse Dynamics. In Proceedings of 'SIGGRAPH 87' pp 215-224

Kuypers F (1990) Klassische Mechanik. VCH, Weinheim New York Basel Cambridge

Lee P, Wei S, Zhao J, Badler N (1990) Strength Guided Motion. Computer Graphics 24(4): 253-262

Niemöller M, Leiner U (1990) Approximative dynamic simulation of objects in computer animation systems. In: Proceedings of 'Computer Graphics 1990'. Blenheim Online, London, pp 229-240

van Overveld C (1990) A technique for motion specification in computer animation. The Visual Computer 6(2): 106-116

Pfeiffer F, Reithmeier E (1987) Roboterdynamik. B. G. Teubner, Stuttgart

Schmitt A, Leister W (1990) Simulation dynamischer Massenpunktsysteme und ihre Anwendung in der Computeranimation. In: Reuter A (ed) Proceedings of 'GI - 20. Jahrestagung II'. Springer, Berlin Heidelberg New York London et al., pp 559-568

Stoer J, Bulirsch R (1978) Einführung in die Numerische Mathematik. Springer, Berlin Heidelberg New York

Thalmann D (1989) Motion Control: From Keyframe to Task-Level Animation. In: Magnenat-Thalmann N, Thalmann D (eds) State-of-the-art in Computer Animation, Proceedings of 'Computer Animation 89'. Springer, Tokyo Berlin Heidelberg New York et al., pp. 3-17

Wilhelms J et al. (1988) Dynamic Animation: Interaction and Control. Visual Computer 4(6): 283-295

Wittenburg J, Wolz U (1985) MESA VERDE: Ein Computerprogramm zur Simulation der nichtlinearen Dynamik von Vielkörpersystemen. Robotersysteme 1: 7-18

Witkin A, Fleischer K, Barr A (1987) Energy Constraints On Parametrized Models. Computer Graphics 21(4): 225-232

Witkin A, Gleicher M, Welch W (1990) Interactive Dynamics. Computer Graphics 24(4)

Witkin A (1991a) Particle Systems Dynamics. In: SIGGRAPH 1991 course notes C23: An Introduction to Physically Based Modeling, pp C1-C11

Witkin A (1991b) Constraint Dynamics. In: SIGGRAPH 1991 course notes C23: An Introduction to Physically Based Modeling, pp G1-G12

Zeltzer D (1985) Towards an integrated view of 3D Computer Animation. In: Proceedings of 'Graphics Interface 85', pp 239-248

Ulrich Leiner is member of the computer animation group at Siemens Corporate Research and Development labs in Munich. He received his diploma in Mathematics from Technical University of Munich (Technische Universität München) in 1984. In 1989 he received a Ph.D. in mathematics from the same university. His thesis studied path optimization problems in robotics. His main interest includes physical simulation and behavioral animation.

Address: Siemens AG, Corporate Research and Development
Otto-Hahn-Ring 6
D-W-8000 Munich 83
e-mail: ulrich@ztivax.siemens.com

Bernhard Preim has studied Computer Science at the Technical University of Magdeburg since 1989. He worked as a summer student with the computer animation group at Siemens Research and Development labs in Munich in 1991.

Address: Technical University of Magdeburg
Institut für Simulation und Graphik
P. O. Box 124
D-O-3010 Magdeburg

Part II
Human Animation

Extraction of 3D Shapes from the Moving Human Face Using Lighting Switch Photometry

HITOSHI SAJI, HIROHISA HIOKI, YOSHIHISA SHINAGAWA, KENSYU YOSHIDA, and TOSIYASU L. KUNII

ABSTRACT

The face is the most important part of the human body and characterizes the personality and expresses the emotion. To analyze human faces, it is necessary to extract detailed facial shapes such as wrinkles. This paper introduces a new method called "Lighting Switch Photometry". This method computes the normal vector at each point that varies with time. The 3D facial shape is reconstructed from the vectors. This method enables the 3D reconstruction of complicated shapes of a moving human face.

Keywords: lighting switch photometry, photometric stereo, 3D reconstruction, detailed facial shape, moving human face

1 INTRODUCTION

The extraction of a detailed description of the human face is an important task. Up to now, many systems have been developed (Vannier, Pilgram, Bhatia and Brunsden 1991; Waters and Terzopoulos 1991) which extract human facial shapes in detail. With these systems, however, the subject must fix the face for some time interval. For this reason, if the subject moves, the shape cannot be obtained. Thus, natural expressions such as that which portray anger or happiness cannot be extracted.

On the other hand, much research on the extraction of human facial motion has been done based on tracing the motion of characteristic regions, such as the eyes, the nose and the mouth or on tracing the motion of artificial markers attached on the face (Kurihara and Arai 1991; Patterson, Litwinowicz and Greene 1991; Williams 1990). With these methods, the number of positions which can be traced are few. Hence, the other portions must be interpolated to extract the whole facial shape. Consequently fine wrinkles cannot be extracted.

Furthermore, optical flow based methods (Horn and Shunck 1981; Mase 1989) are developed recently to obtain human facial muscle movements. These methods assume that the intensity of radiance at the traced point does not change. Under this assumption, the subtle facial motion cannot be extracted. This is because the human facial muscles expand and contract in a complex manner.

This paper introduces a new method called Lighting Switch Photometry. The idea of Lighting Switch Photometry is to take the time-sequence images, from the same view point, with the scene illuminated in turn by separate light sources. The normal vector at each point on the surface is computed by measuring the intensity of radiance. The 3D shape of the face at a particular instant is then determined from these normal vectors obtained by using an iterative scheme. Even if the human face moves, the detailed facial shape such as the wrinkles on a face can be extracted by Lighting Switch Photometry.

This paper is organized as follows. Section 2 describes the basic algorithm of Lighting Switch Photometry. The 3D reconstruction algorithm is explained in section 3. The experimental results are shown in section 4. Other methods that can be integrated into Lighting Switch Photometry and that can extract facial shapes more accurately are discussed in section 5. The applications of Lighting Switch Photometry are also discussed in section 5. Finally, section 6 concludes this paper.

2 LIGHTING SWITCH PHOTOMETRY

2.1 Photometric Stereo

Lighting Switch Photometry extracts the surface normals by illuminating an animated subject in turn by separate light sources. Multiple light sources method (Photometric Stereo (Woodham 1980)) has been developed to extract surface normals of the static object. Photometric Stereo method uses the reflectance maps and assumes that the reflectance maps for an object material are lambertian. Under this assumption, this method cuts down the number of possible solutions to the normal vector computation. The algorithm of this method is described briefly.

Suppose three incident light sources S_k (k = 1,2,3) are prepared and three images are obtained by varying the light sources in turn. Each radiance at one object point is characterized as follows:

$$L_{S_1} = I_{S_1} R \cos \psi_{S_1}, \quad (1)$$
$$L_{S_2} = I_{S_2} R \cos \psi_{S_2}, \quad (2)$$
$$L_{S_3} = I_{S_3} R \cos \psi_{S_3}, \quad (3)$$

where I_{S_k} is the intensity of incident illumination of S_k, R is the reflectance factor, ψ_{S_k} is the incident angle between the ray from S_k and the normal vector at the point and L_{S_k} is the intensity of radiance. From these three equations, the normal vector at the point can be computed.

The time intervals of light switching is not under consideration in photometric stereo. For this reason, the shape of the moving object cannot be taken by the method. Lighting Switch Photometry switches the lights at constant short intervals, so that the shape of the moving object can be taken.

2.2 Algorithm

This section presents the algorithm of Lighting Switch Photometry to extract the normal vector at one subject point.
First, some assumptions are given.

- three light sources S_1,S_2,S_3 are used and switched in turn ($S_1 \rightarrow S_2 \rightarrow S_3 \rightarrow S_1 \rightarrow S_2 \rightarrow \cdots$) at short constant intervals (Δt) and no other light sources illuminate the subject (Fig. 1).
- the image projection is approximated as an orthographic projection.
- the incident rays illuminate the subject directly and uniformly.
- the intensity of each incident light is constant at all time.
- the reflectance map is lambertian.

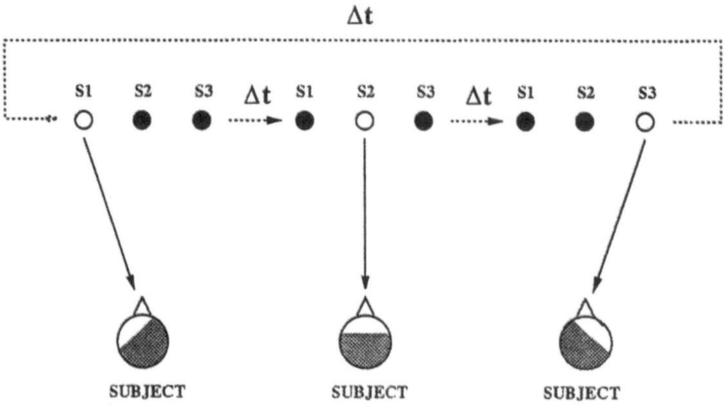

Fig. 1 Light Switching

Under these assumptions, when the subject point is illuminated by one incident light source, the normal vector at the instant is computed as follows.

We assume that the subject is illuminated by S_2 at time t. The five equations are derived.

$$L_{S_3,t-2\Delta t} = I_{S_3} R_{t-2\Delta t} \cos \psi_{S_3,t-2\Delta t}, \tag{4}$$
$$L_{S_1,t-\Delta t} = I_{S_1} R_{t-\Delta t} \cos \psi_{S_1,t-\Delta t}, \tag{5}$$
$$L_{S_2,t} = I_{S_2} R_t \cos \psi_{S_2,t}, \tag{6}$$
$$L_{S_3,t+\Delta t} = I_{S_3} R_{t+\Delta t} \cos \psi_{S_3,t+\Delta t}, \tag{7}$$
$$L_{S_1,t+2\Delta t} = I_{S_1} R_{t+2\Delta t} \cos \psi_{S_1,t+2\Delta t}, \tag{8}$$

where $I_{S_k}$is the intensity of incident illumination from S_k, $L_{S_k,t}$ is the intensity of radiance by S_k at t, R_t is the reflectance factor at t and $\psi_{S_k,t}$ is the incident angle between the ray from S_k and the normal vector at the point at t

If Δt is small,

$$\cos \psi_{S_1,t-\Delta t} = \cos(\psi_{S_1,t} - \Delta t \delta \psi), \tag{9}$$
$$\cos \psi_{S_1,t+2\Delta t} = \cos(\psi_{S_1,t} + 2\Delta t \delta \psi), \tag{10}$$

where $\delta\psi$ is constant, and

$$\cos \psi_{S_1,t-\Delta t} = \cos \psi_{S_1,t} \cos(\Delta t \delta \psi) + \sin \psi_{S_1,t} \sin(\Delta t \delta \psi) \tag{11}$$
$$\approx \cos \psi_{S_1,t} + \Delta t \delta \psi \sin \psi_{S_1,t}, \tag{12}$$
$$\cos \psi_{S_1,t+2\Delta t} = \cos \psi_{S_1,t} \cos(2\Delta t \delta \psi) - \sin \psi_{S_1,t} \sin(2\Delta t \delta \psi) \tag{13}$$
$$\approx \cos \psi_{S_1,t} - 2\Delta t \delta \psi \sin \psi_{S_1,t}. \tag{14}$$

Hence

$$\cos \psi_{S_1,t} = \frac{2 \cos \psi_{S_1,t-\Delta t} + \cos \psi_{S_1,t+2\Delta t}}{3}. \tag{15}$$

If $R_{t-2\Delta t} = R_{t-\Delta t} = R_t = R_{t+\Delta t} = R_{t+2\Delta t} = R$,

$$I_{S_1} R \cos\psi_{S_1,t} = \frac{2L_{S_1,t-\Delta t} + L_{S_1,t+2\Delta t}}{3}. \tag{16}$$

Similarly

$$I_{S_3} R \cos\psi_{S_3,t} = \frac{L_{S_3,t-2\Delta t} + 2L_{S_3,t+\Delta t}}{3}. \tag{17}$$

From three equations (6), (16) and (17), the normal vector and the reflectance factor R of the subject point at the instant t can be computed.

2.3 Accuracy Consideration

The normal vector error is caused by some sources. The most influential factor of error in Lighting Switch Photometry is the light switching time intervals. In this section, the accuracy of the computed normal vector is considered.

Suppose at time t one subject point is illuminated by the light S_2. The assumptions are the same with that described in the previous section.

First, we employ the 3D Cartesian coordinate system (Fig. 2). The origin of this coordinate system is the subject point. The direction of z-axis is aligned with the ray direction of S_2 from the subject point. The x-axis is in the plane spanned by z-axis and the ray direction of S_1-from the subject point.

Next, this Cartesian coordinate system is transformed into the polar coordinate system. The zenith angle θ is measured clockwise from the direction of z-axis and the azimuth angle ϕ is measured counterclockwise from the direction of x-axis in the plane perpendicular to the z-axis.

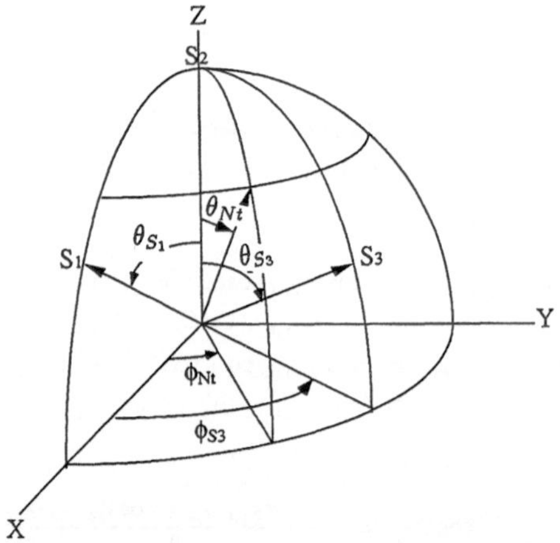

Fig. 2 The coordinate system useful for accuracy consideration

From these angles, the ray directions of light sources S_1,S_2 and S_3 are written as vectors $\mathbf{S_1}$,$\mathbf{S_2}$ and $\mathbf{S_3}$ respectively as follows:

$$\begin{aligned}\mathbf{S_1} &= (\sin\theta_{S_1}, 0, \cos\theta_{S_1}), &(18)\\ \mathbf{S_2} &= (0,0,1), &(19)\\ \mathbf{S_3} &= (\sin\theta_{S_3}\cos\phi_{S_3}, \sin\theta_{S_3}\sin\phi_{S_3}, \cos\theta_{S_3}), &(20)\end{aligned}$$

where $0 \leq \theta_{S_1}, \theta_{S_3}, \phi_{S_3} \leq \frac{\pi}{2}$.

Suppose unit normal vector $\mathbf{N}$ of the subject point at time t is:

$$\mathbf{N} = (\sin\theta_{Nt}\cos\phi_{Nt}, \sin\theta_{Nt}\sin\phi_{Nt}, \cos\theta_{Nt}), \tag{21}$$

where $0 \leq \theta_{Nt} \leq \frac{\pi}{2}$ and $-\frac{\pi}{2} + \phi_{S_3} \leq \phi_{Nt} \leq \frac{\pi}{2}$.
Obviously:

$$\theta_{Nt} = \psi_{S_2,t}, \tag{22}$$

where $\psi_{S_2,t}$ is the incident angle between the ray from S_2 and the normal vector at the subject point at t. Furthermore, for arbitrary t:

$$|\psi_{S_1,t+\Delta t} - \psi_{S_1,t}| \leq \Omega, \tag{23}$$

where $\psi_{S_1,t}$ is the incident angle between the ray from S_1 and the normal vector at the subject point at t and Ω is constant determined by the velocity and the angular velocity of the point.

If $\psi_{S_1,t-\Delta t} \leq \psi_{S_1,t+2\Delta t}$,

$$max(0, \psi_{S_1,t+2\Delta t} - 2\Omega) \leq \psi_{S_1,t} \leq min(\frac{\pi}{2}, \psi_{S_1,t-\Delta t} + \Omega). \tag{24}$$

If $\psi_{S_1,t+2\Delta t} \leq \psi_{S_1,t-\Delta t}$,

$$max(0, \psi_{S_1,t-\Delta t} - \Omega) \leq \psi_{S_1,t} \leq min(\frac{\pi}{2}, \psi_{S_1,t+2\Delta t} + 2\Omega). \tag{25}$$

In the former case,

$$\cos\alpha \leq \mathbf{N}\cdot\mathbf{S_1} \leq \cos\beta, \tag{26}$$

where $\alpha = min(\frac{\pi}{2}, \psi_{S_1,t-\Delta t} + \Omega)$ and $\beta = max(0, \psi_{S_1,t+2\Delta t} - 2\Omega)$.
That is,

$$\cos\alpha \leq \sin\theta_{S_1}\sin\theta_{Nt}\cos\phi_{Nt} + \cos\theta_{S_1}\cos\theta_{Nt} \leq \cos\beta. \tag{27}$$

From equation (22),

$$\cos\alpha \leq \sin\theta_{S_1}\sin\psi_{S_2,t}\cos\phi_{Nt} + \cos\theta_{S_1}\cos\psi_{S_2,t} \leq \cos\beta. \tag{28}$$

If $\sin\theta_{S_1}\sin\psi_{S_2,t} \neq 0$,

$$\frac{\cos\alpha - \cos\theta_{S_1}\cos\psi_{S_2,t}}{\sin\theta_{S_1}\sin\psi_{S_2,t}} \leq \cos\phi_{Nt} \leq \frac{\cos\beta - \cos\theta_{S_1}\cos\psi_{S_2,t}}{\sin\theta_{S_1}\sin\psi_{S_2,t}}. \tag{29}$$

From these equations, the accuracy of the computed normal vector can be estimated by the range of ϕ_{Nt}. That is, the range of ϕ_{Nt} becomes smaller as Ω becomes smaller and/or θ_{S_1} becomes larger. In the case of equation (25), the same estimations are also done. Furthermore, similar relations are derived between S_2 and S_3 and between S_1 and S_3. We conclude that Lighting Switch Photometry is accurate in cases where the distances between any two light sources are long and the images are taken at high speed.

3 3D RECONSTRUCTION

3.1 Overview

To extract 3D facial shapes, it is necessary to reconstruct the facial surface height from the normal vectors. The surface height means the position in the direction of the camera axis. When the data are noisy, a height value obtained at some point will depend on the integration path. It is better to find a best-fit surface Z to the given normal vector **N**. To solve this problem, the error function E is introduced:

$$E = \int\int (Z_x \cdot p + Z_y \cdot q + 1)^2 dxdy, \tag{30}$$

where $\mathbf{N} = (p, q, 1)$.
This equation means the summation of the differences between the given normal vector N and the normal vector of the reconstructed surface at each point. In this paper, we obtain the surface height that minimizes the above error function E.

3.2 Algorithm

The error function defined in equation (30) is transformed into the discrete approximation as follows:

$$E = \sum_{i,j} (\overline{X}_{i,j}\delta + Z_{i+1,j} - Z_{i,j})^2 + \sum_{i,j} (\overline{Y}_{i,j}\delta + Z_{i,j+1} - Z_{i,j})^2, \tag{31}$$

where δ is the spacing between picture cells, $\overline{X}_{i,j} = \frac{p_{i+1,j}\sqrt{p_{i,j}^2+q_{i,j}^2+1}+p_{i,j}\sqrt{p_{i+1,j}^2+q_{i+1,j}^2+1}}{\sqrt{p_{i+1,j}^2+q_{i+1,j}^2+1}+\sqrt{p_{i,j}^2+q_{i,j}^2+1}}$, $\overline{Y}_{i,j} = \frac{q_{i,j+1}\sqrt{p_{i,j}^2+q_{i,j}^2+1}+q_{i,j}\sqrt{p_{i,j+1}^2+q_{i,j+1}^2+1}}{\sqrt{p_{i,j+1}^2+q_{i,j+1}^2+1}+\sqrt{p_{i,j}^2+q_{i,j}^2+1}}$ and $N_{i,j} = (p_{i,j}, q_{i,j}, 1)$.

Differentiation this equation with respect to $Z_{i,j}$ provides the equation for the change in the errors which must be zero for ideal situations.

$$\begin{aligned}\frac{\partial E}{\partial Z_{i,j}} &= -2\overline{X}_{i,j}\delta - 2(Z_{i+1,j} - Z_{i,j}) + 2\overline{X}_{i-1,j}\delta + 2(Z_{i,j} - Z_{i-1,j}) \\ &\quad -2\overline{Y}_{i,j}\delta - 2(Z_{i,j+1} - Z_{i,J}) + 2\overline{Y}_{i,j-1}\delta + 2(Z_{i,j} - Z_{i,j-1}).\end{aligned} \tag{32}$$

This gives the following iterative equation:

$$Z_{i,j}^{k+1} = \frac{1}{4}(Z_{i+1,j}^k + Z_{i-1,j}^k + Z_{i,j-1}^k + Z_{i,j+1}^k) + A, \tag{33}$$

where k is the number of the iteration and

$$A = \frac{1}{4}(\overline{X}_{i,j}\delta - \overline{X}_{i-1,j}\delta + \overline{Y}_{i,j}\delta - \overline{Y}_{i,j-1}\delta). \tag{34}$$

On the boundary,

$$(Z_x, Z_y) \cdot \mathrm{n} = (p, q) \cdot \mathrm{n}, \tag{35}$$

where $\mathrm{n} = (-\frac{dy}{ds}, \frac{dx}{ds})$ is a normal vector to the boundary curve and s is arc-length along the boundary. The component of (Z_x, Z_y) normal to the chosen boundary curve must match the normal component of (p,q).

The boundary curve on digital images is polygonal, with horizontal and vertical segments only. On vertical segments of the boundary,

$$Z_{i+1,j} - Z_{i,j} = \overline{X}_{i,j}, \tag{36}$$

and on horizontal segments of the boundary,

$$Z_{i,j+1} - Z_{i,j} = \overline{Y}_{i,j}. \tag{37}$$

If the height at one point is fixed, the surface height at each point is computed from equations (33), (36) and (37).

4 EXPERIMENTATION

This section shows the results of the experiments in this research. The experimental process is composed of four steps (Fig. 3).

In the first step, the images of a face illuminated by three light sources in turn are taken by a video camera and are converted into the digital images by the recording apparatus. In the second step, a facial region is extracted from time sequence of three digital images (preprocessing). In the third step, the normal vectors are computed on the facial region. In the final step, the 3D shapes are reconstructed from the vectors.

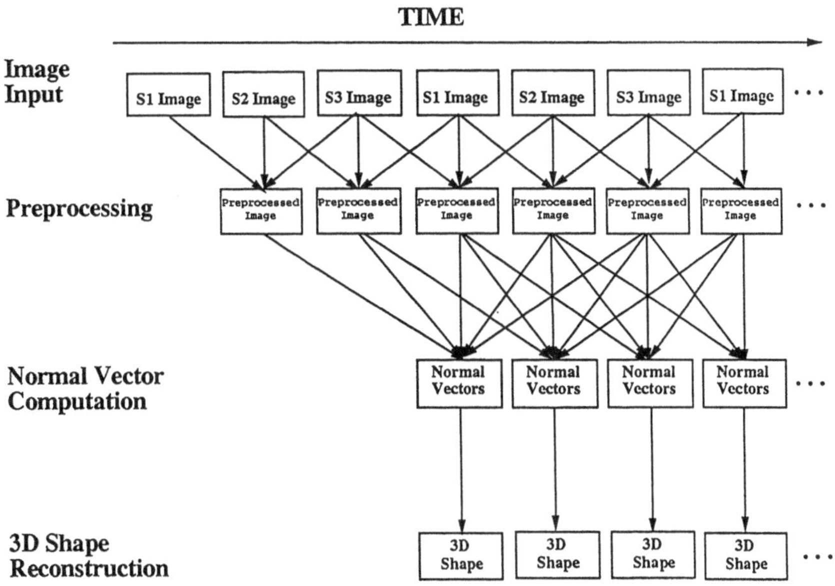

Fig. 3 Overview of the experiment

4.1 Experimental Apparatus for Taking Images

Before showing the experimental results, we describe the specifications of the experimental apparatus for Lighting Switch Photometry and the conditions required for taking images.

Three light sources (S_1, S_2, S_3) are arranged at the vertices of the regular triangle with sides $1.1(\simeq 0.635 \times 2\cos 30^\circ)$ meters. The illuminances of three light sources are 200 lux (at the distance of 3 meters from the center of the light source). To switch the incident illumination at high speed, a disc with five holes on the same radius is set in front of three lights. The holes have the same size and are arranged at the same intervals on the disc, that is, the center angle between the adjacent hole is 72°. The disc can rotate at the constant speed($\frac{4}{3}\pi$ rad/sec).

A video camera is set in front of the disc. The optical axis of the camera is aligned with the axis of rotation of the disc and the axis passes through the center of the triangle composed of three light sources perpendicularly. The distance between the video camera lens and the disc is 0.5 meters. The distance between the lens and the subject is 2.5 meters and they are approximately at the same height. The images are taken 10 frames per second using the video camera and the disc rotated by the motor. The sampled video frame is converted to the digital gray scale image (256 levels) by the general recording apparatus. The size of the digital image is 640 x 483 pixels. Fig. 4 and Fig. 5 show the details of the experimental apparatus.

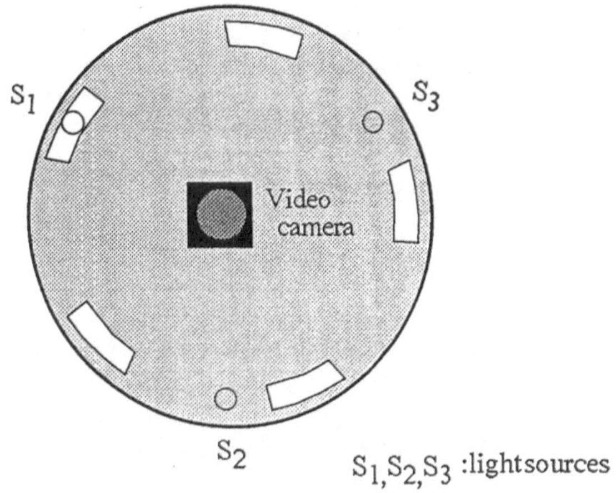

Fig. 4 The front view of the experimental apparatus

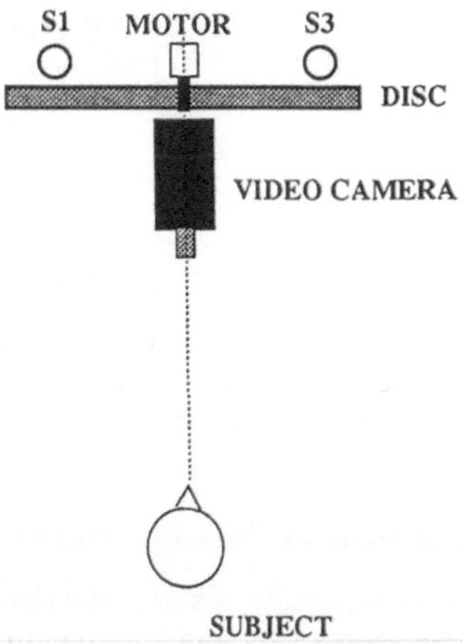

Fig. 5 The top view of the experimental apparatus

4.2 Preprocessing

It is necessary to extract the facial regions from input digital images for the following processings. In the processings, noise reduction, thresholding, and extraction of facial regions are performed. First we assume that the raw images obtained by the video camera have high contrast, and no object other than the subject is recognizable and hence a full face of the subject is visible in each image.

Noise Reduction

Since a raw image inevitably contains noise, noise reduction is essential to the image processing. Median filtering that reduces the influence of the extreme intensities in the neighbors, is widely used for noise reduction. Although the fine details of the raw image are lost slightly, the effectiveness concerning the noise reduction of the median filter is obviously visible.

Thresholding

A high contrast image can be segmented into the foreground and the background by the thresholding. We consider about the distribution of the intensity gradient magnitudes of an image to find automatically a suitable threshold level. Since the low intensity gradient regions correspond to background or the inner object regions and high intensity gradient regions correspond to the object edge regions, if the influence of the low gradient region is removed, the less biased bimodal intensity histogram is likely to obtain. The mean value of the distribution of the intensity gradient magnitudes is selected as a threshold between low gradient and high gradient. The intensity histogram is computed only in the high gradient regions. The remaining problem is to determine a suitable threshold level in this histogram. We employ the discriminant thresholding selection method(DTSM)(Otsu 1980).

Let N be the size of an L gray levels image, and n_i pixels have the intensity level i $(0 \leq i \leq L-1)$. The set of pixels is divided into two classes $C_1 : \{x \mid 0 \leq I(x) < t\}$ and $C_2 : \{x \mid t \leq I(x) \leq L-1\}$(where $I(x)$ represents the intensity of pixel x) by threshold level t. The DTSM computes the optimum threshold level T as follows.

Let the probability of the intensity level i be p_i, the mean intensity of the whole image be m, and the probability of the class C_1 and C_2 be ω_1 and ω_2 respectively, then,

$$\omega_1 = \sum_{i=0}^{t-1} p_i, \tag{38}$$

$$\omega_2 = \sum_{i=t}^{L-1} p_i, \tag{39}$$

$$\omega_1 + \omega_2 = 1. \tag{40}$$

Hence, the mean intensity of C_1 and C_2:

$$m_1 = \left(\sum_{i=0}^{t-1} i p_i\right) / \omega_1, \tag{41}$$

$$m_2 = \left(\sum_{i=t}^{L-1} i p_i\right) / \omega_2. \tag{42}$$

Note that,

$$\omega_1 m_1 + \omega_2 m_2 = m. \tag{43}$$

Now $\sigma^2(t)$ is defined as the variance between C_1 and C_2.

$$\sigma^2(t) = \omega_1(m_1 - m)^2 + \omega_2(m_2 - m)^2. \tag{44}$$

Eliminating m now gives,

$$\sigma^2(t) = \omega_1\omega_2(m_1 - m_2)^2. \tag{45}$$

The optimum threshold T is determined by,

$$\sigma^2(T) = \max_{0<i<L-1} \sigma^2(i). \tag{46}$$

Extraction of Facial Regions

The sequence of three images are used to extract the facial regions. Intuitively, within the regions in the shadows cast by the nose or the hair, the computations of the surface normal and the reflectance factor are unreliable, that is, the computations are valid only within the regions illuminated by all three incident light sources. If the motion of the face during the time taking three images is so small as to be negligible, the valuable regions can be extracted by taking the simple logical AND operation of the three images. If a pixel intensity is zero in one of three images, the values of the corresponding pixels in the other images are replaced to zero, otherwise the original values are preserved. This AND operation also helps to separate the face from the neck and the ear. When all the above processings are applied, the facial region can be found easily by object labeling. The largest object is selected as the facial region. In the following processing, we can concentrate on this region, instead of the whole image.

Fig. 6 shows the time sequence of input three images. The left figure, the middle figure and the right figure show that a face is illuminated by S_1, S_2 and S_3 respectively. Fig. 7 shows the preprocessed image.

4.3 Normal Vector Computation

To compute the normal vectors, three equations (6), (16) and (17) are applied to the time sequence of preprocessed five images. The results are the normal vectors at the instant. Fig. 8 shows the needle diagram that shows the normal vectors projected on the image plane.

4.4 3D Shape Reconstruction

Fig. 9 shows the 3D facial surface reconstructed from computed normal vectors with 3000 times iterative computations. In this figure, the detailed facial shapes such as wrinkles on the cheeks are visible. Fig. 10 shows the time sequence of 3D facial shapes.

5 DISCUSSION

This section discusses the method by which Lighting Switch Photometry can be used to extract facial shapes more accurately. This can be done for example by increasing the number of light sources and integrating the stereo method into our method. The applications of this method for human facial analysis are also discussed.

5.1 Increasing the Number of Light Sources.

Lighting Switch Photometry uses three light sources for computing normal vectors. This method assumes that the reflectance map is lambertian. To extract the facial shapes more accurately, the general reflectance map that includes specular component should be analyzed. This component varies somewhat randomly with the cleanness of the surface and it may not be easy to determine it accurately. More probably it will be sufficient to check whether significant specularity is present, so that the corresponding region of the surface can be ignored for absolute reflectance calculation. However, finding the specularity peaks can give important information on the human face such as the eyes, the teeth and the hair which cannot be extracted correctly by three light source photometry.

If four or more images corresponding to one scene are obtained using further illumination sources, more information can be obtained and the general reflectance map can be analyzed. Some methods are presented using the four or more light sources method for extracting shapes of static objects (Coleman and Jain 1982; Davies 1990). By these methods, however, much sampling time is needed to compute normal vectors at a particular instant. Hence, a higher grade video camera which can sample more frames per second than conventional ones is needed to compute accurate normal vectors of a scene from four or more images.

5.2 Integration of the Stereo Method into Lighting Switch Photometry

By Lighting Switch Photometry, the normal vector can be computed at the points where three incident light sources illuminate. It is difficult to compute the accurate normal vector at the point where the intensity of radiance is small. Hence the results of calculation are incorrect in the shadowed regions which are hidden from the illumination by other parts such as the nose and at the shadow boundaries where the real normal vectors are perpendicular to the direction of illumination of incident rays. Consequently, the normal vectors at the regions such as those near the facial contours are computed incorrectly.

A distance measurement method such as stereo method helps to solve these problems (Barnard and Fischler 1982). The stereo method can establish the correspondence at certain characteristic points and uses the geometric relation over stereo images to recover the surface depth. The depths of contour regions which have the conspicuous characteristics are measured correctly. Using the stereo method, however, a dense set of points are difficult to recover. Lighting Switch Photometry can recover the detailed local surface normals correctly.

For this reason, to combine Lighting Switch Photometry with the conventional stereo method is useful for recovering the depth and the gradient information correctly on the whole surface.

5.3 Applications of Lighting Switch Photometry

In recent years, much research has been done on the analysis of human face. There have been two main applications of human facial analysis. One is the personal identification of human faces and the other is the analysis of human expressions.

In the former case, some characteristic parameters of the face are used to identify the person (Abe, Aso and Kimura 1990; Harmon 1977). If the facial direction of subject is different from that of the stored data, the person cannot be identified correctly. Hence, the rotational invariant parameters should be used to identify the person correctly. Using Lighting Switch Photometry, the normal vectors of the face are computed. Rotational invariants such as the Gauss curvature can be computed easily from the normal vectors and hence, this method can be used to identify the person correctly.

In the latter application, the conventional methods (Ekman and Friesen 1975; Parke 1982) analyze the human facial expressions using a few features on the face such as the shapes of the eyes and the mouth. To analyze the subtle human facial expressions, however, it is necessary to extract detailed shapes such as wrinkles on the face. Lighting Switch Photometry can extract detailed shapes on human faces and recognize the subtle changes of human facial expressions.

6 CONCLUSIONS

This paper presents a new method called Lighting Switch Photometry that recovers time variant shapes of a human face. This method switches the three incident light sources at high speed and can compute a set of normal vectors aligned at the interval of a pixel size on a human face at a particular instant. The 3D surface at the instant is reconstructed from the normal vectors. The subtle changes in the facial shapes can be obtained from the sequence of 3D reconstructed surfaces. The experiments were carried out using the data of human faces. Time variant shapes of 3D faces were reconstructed from the normal vectors. Some indications were given that extend Lighting Switch Photometry to general reflectance map and integrate stereo method into Lighting Switch Photometry to enhance the accuracy of 3D reconstructed shapes. Some applications of Lighting Switch Photometry were also discussed.

ACKNOWLEDGEMENTS

We would like to express our sincere gratitude to Dr. Ichiro Hagiwara, the senior researcher, and Ms. Wakae Kozukue, the research engineer of Nissan Motor Co., LTD. for their support to this research.

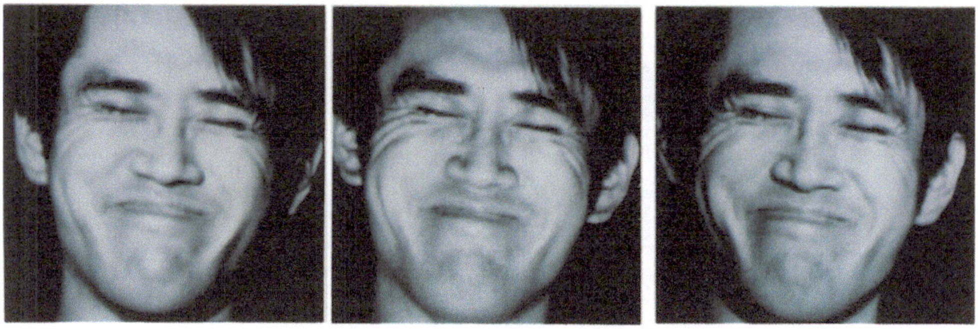

Fig. 6 The input images

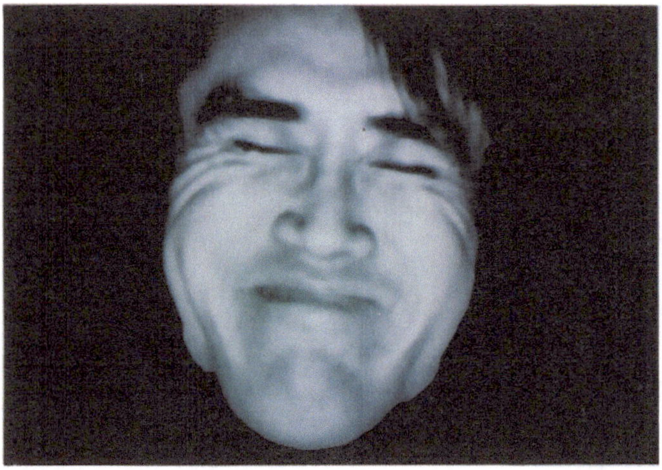

Fig. 7 The preprocessed image

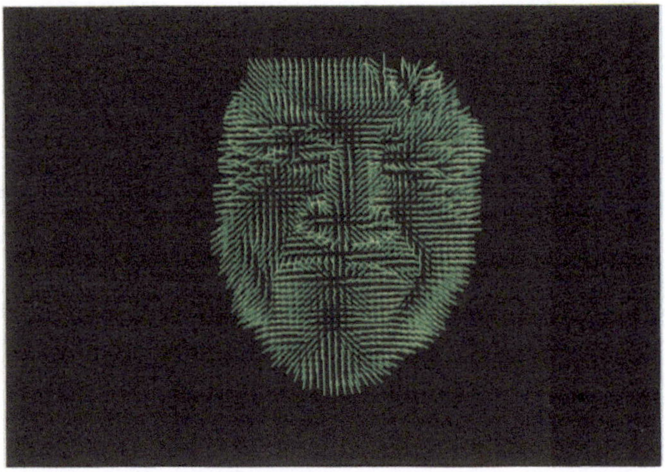

Fig. 8 The needle diagram

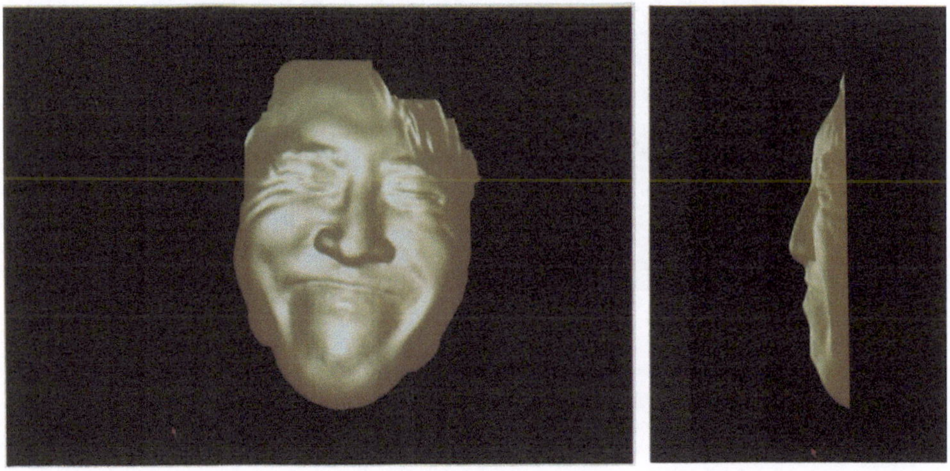

Fig. 9 The 3D facial shape

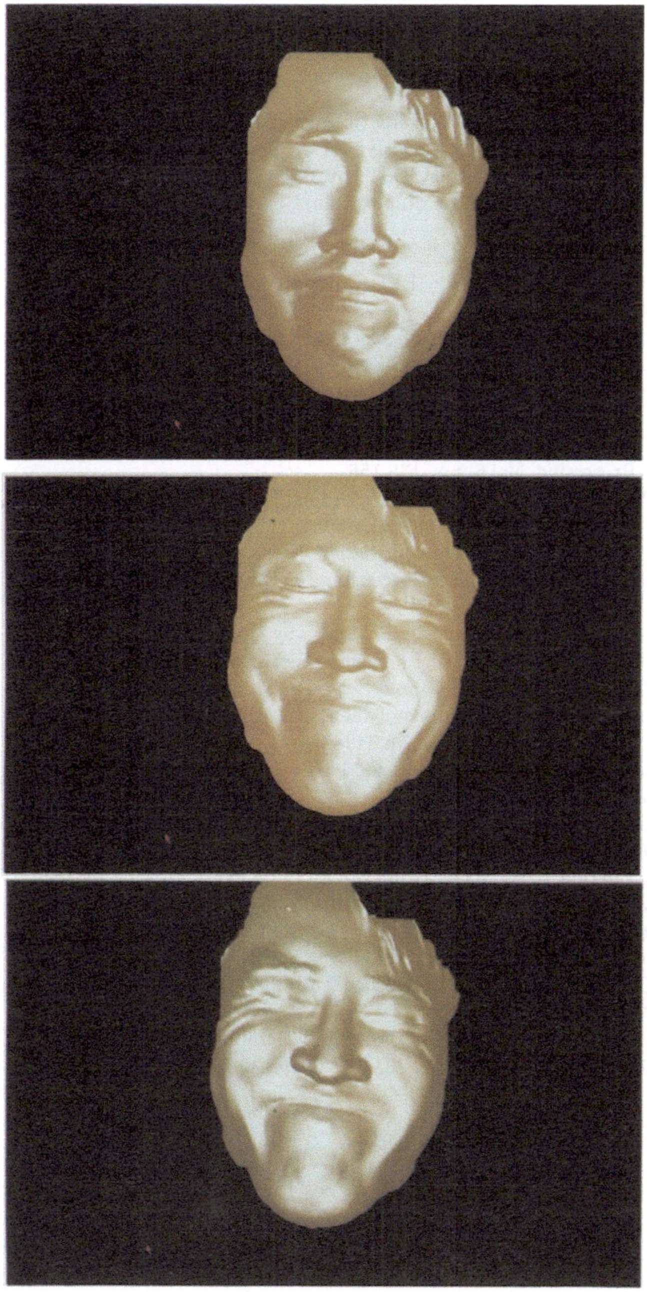

Fig. 10 The time sequence of 3D facial shapes

REFERENCES

Abe T, Aso H, Kimura M (1990) Automatic Identification of Human faces Using Profiles Extracted from 3-D Data. The Transanctions of the Institute of Electronics and Communication Engineers of Japan, Vol. J73-D-II, No.9, pp.1468-1476.

Barnard ST, Fischler MA (1982) Computational Stereo. ACM Computing Surveys, Vol.14, No.4, pp.553-572.

Coleman EN, Jain R (1982) Obtaining 3-Dimensional Shape of Textured and Specular Surfaces Using Four-Source Photometry. IEEE Computer Graphics and Image Processing, Vol.18, pp.309-328.

Davies ER (1990) Machine Vision: Theory, Algorithms, Practicalities. ACADEMIC PRESS, London San Diego New York Boston Sydney Tokyo Toronto

Ekman P, Friesen WV (1975) Unmasking The Face. Prentice-Hall, Englewood Cliffs New Jersey.

Harmon LD (1977) Automatic Recognition of Human Face Profiles, IEEE Computer Graphics and Image Processing, Vol.6, pp. 135-156.

Horn BKP, Shunck BG (1981) Determining Optical Flow, Artificial Intelligence, Vol.17, pp.185-203.

Kurihara T, Arai K (1991) A Transformation Method for Modeling and Animation of the Human Face from Photographs. Proceedings of Computer Animation '91, Springer-Verlag, pp.45-58.

Mase K (1989) Detection of Facial Muscle Motion by Optical-flow. The Institute of Electronics, Information and Communication Engineers, Technical Report, IE89-101, pp. 17-24.

Otsu N (1980) An Automatic Threshold Selection Method Based on Discriminant and Least Squares Criteria. The Transactions of the Institute of Electronics and Communication Engineers of Japan, Vol.J63-D, No.4, pp.349-356.

Parke FI (1982) Parameterized Models for Facial Animation. IEEE Computer Graphics and Applications, Vol.2, No.9, pp.61-68.

Patterson EC, Litwinowicz PC, Greene N (1991) Facial Animation by Spatial Mapping. Proceedings of Computer Animation '91, pp.31-44.

Vannier MW, Pilgram T, Bhatia G, Brunsden B (1991) Facial Surface Scanner. IEEE Computer Graphics and Applications, Vol.11, No.6, pp.72-80.

Waters K, Terzopoulos D (1991) Modelling and Animating Faces using Scanned Data. Visualization and Computer Animation, Vol.2, No.4, pp.123-128.

Williams L (1990) Performance-Driven Facial Animation. Computer Graphics, Vol.24, No.4, pp.235-242.

Woodham RJ (1980) Photometric Method for Determining Surface Orientation from Multiple Images. Optical Engineering, Vol. 19, No. 1, pp.139-144.

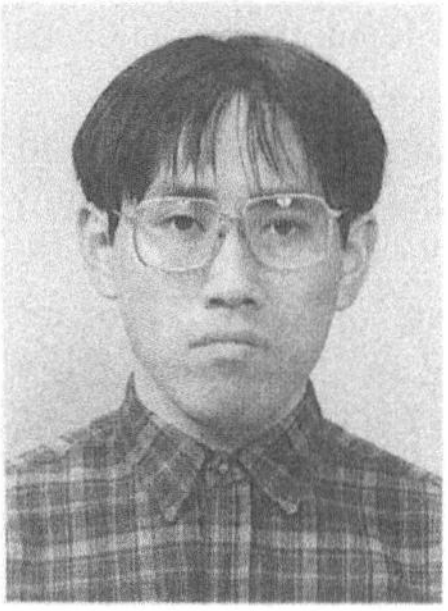

Hitoshi Saji is currently a doctoral course graduate student of the Department of Information Science of the University of Tokyo. His research interests include computer vision, computer graphics and computer animation. He received the B.E. degree in mechanical engineering and the M.Sc. degree in information science all from the University of Tokyo in 1987 and 1992 respectively. He is a student member of ACM, IEEE Computer Society and IPSJ.

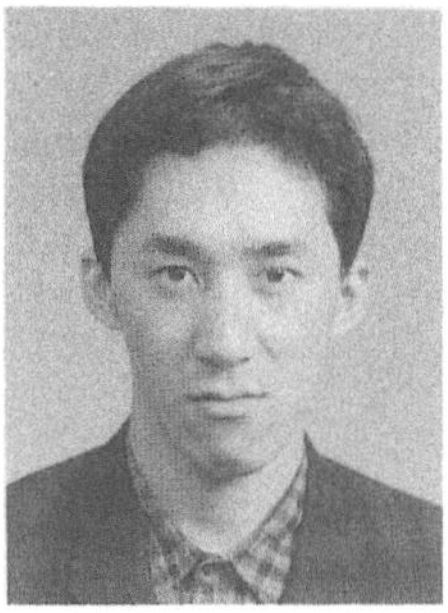

Hirohisa Hioki is currently a master course graduate student of the Department of Information Science of the University of Tokyo. His research interests include computer graphics, image processing and image recognition. He received the B.Sc. degree in information science from the University of Tokyo in 1992.

Yoshihisa Shinagawa is currently a Research Associate of the Department of Information Science of the University of Tokyo. His research interests include computer graphics and its applications. He received the B.Sc. and M.Sc. degrees in information science all from the University of Tokyo in 1987 and 1990 respectively. He is a member of ACM, IEEE Computer Society, IPSJ and IEICE.

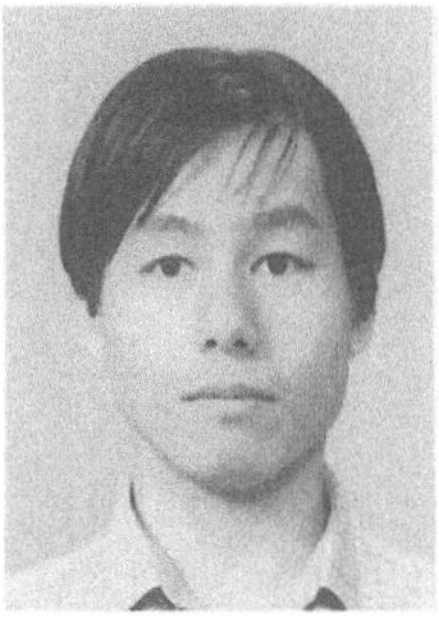

Kensyu Yoshida is currently a doctoral course graduate student of the Department of Information Science of the University of Tokyo. His research interests include computer aided geometric design, computational geometry and numerical computation. He received the B.Sc. and M.Sc. degrees in information science all from the University of Tokyo in 1990, 1992 respectively. He is a student member of ACM and IPSJ.

Tosiyasu L. Kunii is currently Professor of Information and Computer Science, the University of Tokyo.
He authored and edited more than 32 computer science books, and published more than 120 refereed academic/technical papers in computer science and applications areas.
Dr. Kunii is Founder of the Computer Graphics Society, Editor-in-Chief of *The Visual Computer: An International Journal of Computer Graphics* (Springer-Verlag), Associate Editor-in-Chief of *The Journal of Visualization and Computer Animation* (John Wiley & Sons) and on the Editorial Board of *IEEE Transactions on Knowledge and Data Engineering, VLDB Journal* and *IEEE Computer Graphics and Applications.* He is on the IFIP Modeling and Simulation Working Group, the IFIP Data Base Working Group and the IFIP Computer Graphics Working Group. He is on the board of directors of Japan Society of Sports Industry and also of Japan Society of Simulation and Gaming. He received the B.Sc., M.Sc., and D.Sc. degrees in chemistry all from the University of Tokyo in 1962, 1964, and 1967, respectively. He is a fellow of IEEE and a member of ACM, BCS, IPSJ and IEICE.

Address: Department of Information Science, Faculty of Science, the University of Tokyo, 7-3-1 Hongo, Bunkyo-Ku,Tokyo, 113 Japan

An Interactive Tool for the Design of Human Free-Walking Trajectories

LAURENT BEZAULT, RONAN BOULIC, NADIA MAGNENAT-THALMANN, and DANIEL THALMANN

ABSTRACT

This paper presents an interactive tool dedicated to the design of walking trajectories for human figures. It uses a global human free-walking model built from experimental data on a wide range of normalized velocities. This tool is particularly efficient in that the higher level of the walking model work independenly from the effective play of the low level joint trajectories by the figure. This independence is gained by means of a transfer function calibrating the figure's normalized velocity with respect to the theoretical normalized velocity. Two real-time display functionnalities greatly eases the design of trajectories in complex environments.First the current range of permitted velocities indicates the potentialities of the local dynamic of the walking behavior. Second the set of step locations shown on the desired path allows precise placement.

Keywords: Human Animation, Walking trajectory

1. INTRODUCTION

Walking is one of the key motions of human beings and as such has been extensively studied in varied fields as varied as biomechanics, robotics, ergonomics and, of course, computer animation. However, no approach provides a means for designing continuously varying walking motions with precise specification of the step locations or speed. Such capabilities are fundamental in the behavioral response of a walking human figure to its environment.

Previous work in human or animal locomotion was made mainly by (Girard and Maciejewski 1985; Girard 1987; Bruderlin et al 1989; Zeltzer 1989) and incidentally by (Calvert et al 1991, Phillips et al 1991). Until now, impressive animation sequences have been made with the system defined in (Girard 87) but without facilities for designing speed variations. A promising approach based partly on a dynamic model was described in (Bruderlin et al 1989) and integrated in (Calvert et al 1991). Nevertheless, it has a granularity of one step in speed variation and does not describe any tool to support such a requirement. Another approach comes from keyframing over constraints associated to inverse kinematic control in (Phillips et al 1991) but the realism is still limited. At last traditionnal keyframing over walking key attitude is possible but high level control over the speed is difficult (Calvert et al 1991).

For these reasons we use a functionnal model defined in (Boulic et al 1990) which is based on a large set of experimental data. The main idea of this approach is to take advantage of the intrinsic dynamics of the studied motion and extend its application context to continuously varying speed and arbitrary path on a plane. This model has been used for the kinematic control of three human figures in the computer generated film "Still Walking" with speed variations and personified gaits. In this system, the speed profile was interactively set.

The purpose of the present paper is to describe a new tool including path and speed profile design with real-time visualization of the step locations. This ability gives the animator both spatial and temporal control over the human figure's trajectory: for example, walking on the white squares of a chessboard or following stones in a Japanese garden path; the motions becomes easy to define.

We first present the main features of the walking model and the concept of the transfer function which calibrates figure velocity with respect to the theoretical velocity. Then the tool itself is detailed with special emphasis on the constrained speed profile construction and the design loop architecture. We evaluate the advantages and limitations of this approach, and end the paper with proposed future improvements.

2. WALKING MODEL

The present study uses the human free-walking model established in (Boulic et al 1990). This model is based on several experimental studies in biomechanics and provides a coherent approach to dealing with a continuously varying velocity.

2.1 Definitions

By definition, walking is a form of locomotion in which the body's center of gravity moves alternately on the right side and the left side. At all time at least one foot is in contact with the floor and, during a brief phase, both feet are in contact with this floor.

As this activity is cyclic, the model only describes the motion between two successive contacts of the left heel with the floor. It is parameterized by an associated phase variable between 0.0 and 1.0. Figure 1 shows the temporal structure of the walking cycle with the main events and duration information. Figure 2 presents the spatial parameters of the same cycle.

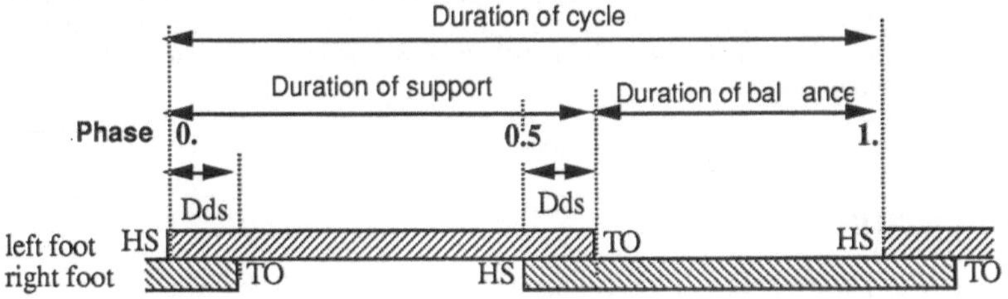

Figure 1: Temporal structure and events of the walking cycle
Dc: Duration of cycle; HS: Heel Strike ; TO: Toe Off;
Ds: Duration of support (duration of contact with the floor);
Db: Duration of balance (duration of non-contact with the floor); Dds: duration of double support

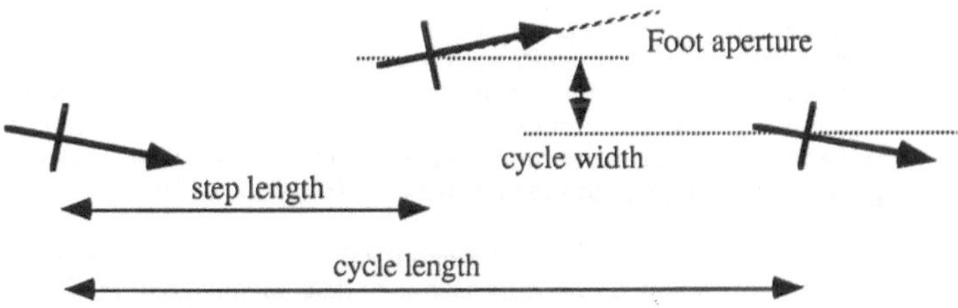

Figure 2: Spatial parameters of the walking cycle

We also denote as the *virtual floor* the plane supporting the body at the standing position. This concept is useful in controling any human figure so as to track a desired path belonging to the supporting plane. Virtual floor frame, rigidely linked to the body reference frame, is simply designated to move along the path.

2.2 Two levels structuration

Let us now define the theoretical relative velocity, noted RV, as:

$$RV = V / Ht \tag{1}$$

where :
V (m/s) is the average velocity of the body reference frame.
Ht (m) is the height of the thigh. It is the distance between the flexing axis of the thigh and the foot sole. This distance is used to normalize all the spatial parameters.

The cycle frequency, inverse of the cycle duration, is given by (from Inman 1981):

$$fc = 0.743 \sqrt{RV} \tag{2}$$

In the general case of a continuously varying velocity we evaluate the current walking phase, noted Ph, as proposed in (Boulic et al 1990) by :

$$Ph = \int fc(t)\, dt \tag{3}$$

Then

$$Ph\_\mathbf{left} = Ph \text{ modulo}[1] \tag{4}$$

$$Ph\_\mathbf{right} = (Ph + 0.5) \text{ modulo}[1] \tag{5}$$

This approach guarantees the coherence of the motion as all the low-level trajectories are parameterized by RV and Ph (see Boulic et al 1990).

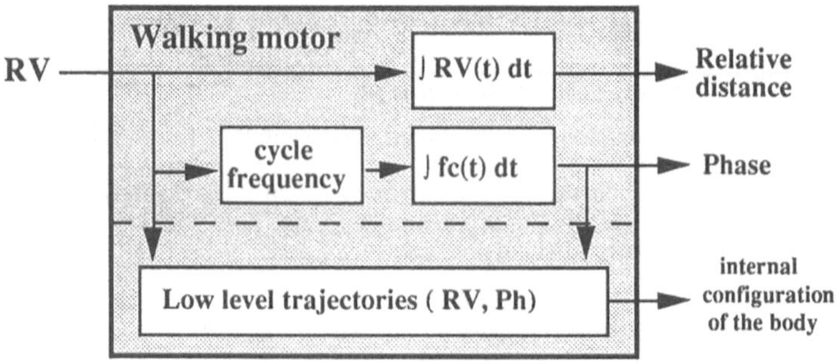

Figure 3 : The two level walking motor

We can use the model at two levels (figure 3):

- At the higher level we can generate the average temporal and normalized spatial characteristics and derive the step locations as explained further. Very few calculations are involved at this stage which makes it suitable for real-time design.
- At the lower level the parameterized trajectories update the current configuration of the specific figure. This stage is more time consuming and require a complete 3D model of the figure to play the motion. We minimize this stage by introducing the transfer function as shown in the next section.

3. HUMAN FIGURE TRANSFER FUNCTION

As the model comes from the synthesis of a great number of walking trajectories over a large set of performers, it provides a walking pattern suited for an average body structure.

When applied to a specific human figure, the body configurations generated by the model may exhibit small discrepancies in support of the virtual floor or step length. This latter problem results in a sliding impression proportionnal to the difference of the theoretical step length. For this reason, we introduce the concept of a personified velocity, noted PV, given by (Boulic et al 1990):

$$PV(RV) = fc(RV) \cdot 2 \cdot PL / Ht \tag{6}$$

Where fc is the theoretical cycle frequency given by expression (2) and PL is the personified step length measured on the 3D model of the human figure (Figure 4a).

The transfer function is the evaluation of expression (6) over the whole range of theoretical velocity RV. This evaluation is made only once and fully characterizes the human figure's free walking behavior (figure 4b). An adaptive algorithm recursively samples expression (6) until the local slope variation is under a predefined threshold. It provides a linked list of the sample points as representation of the transfer function. Given a particular RV, it is straightforward to get the associated PV by searching its bracketing sample points and making a linear interpolation. The inversion process is similar and can easily be inserted into the free-walking trajectory design as shown in the next section.

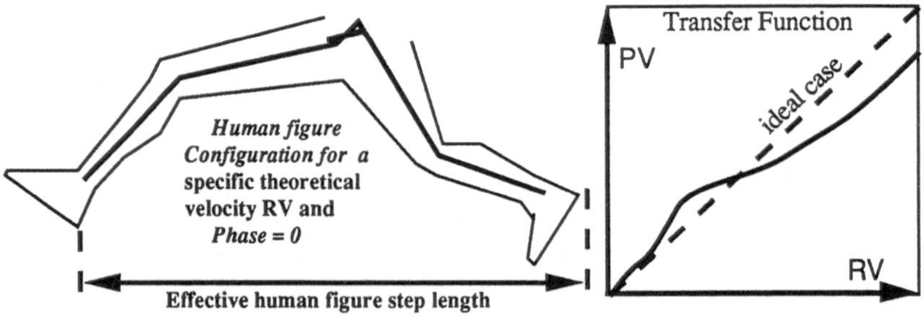

Figure 4 : (a) Evaluation of the Personified step length (b) A Transfer Function

The great advantage provided by the transfer function is the independence gained over the effective play of the low-level trajectories by the 3D model of the human figure. This functionality also greatly improves the real-time capability of the general design process.

4. THE WALKING DESIGN PROCESS

We are interested in the precise design of walking trajectories in the plane. This goal requires some ability to set spatio-temporal constraints such as a global timing and desired locations for the steps.

Such constraints can be fulfilled while working only at the higher level of the walking model with the use of the inverted transfer function.

4.1 General structure

The main principle is to separate the design of spatial and temporal characteristics. The path design takes place first, then the temporal characteristic can be constructed in the following continuous design loop.(Figure 5) :

.Constrained design of distance over time to provide personified speed.
.Translation into relative theoretical velocity with the inverted transfer function.
.Computation of the phase to determine the step instances and locations
.Visualization of the step along the path

This design architecture is important when the human figure moves in a predefined setting. Due to the real-time visualization, the user can instantaneously check the validity of step positions with regard to the setting. Following stones in a path or avoiding puddles continuously are clear examples of its usefulness In addition, temporal control provides a desired rhythm during the animation.

4.2 Path design

The path is design on a 2D layout of the scene by means of Cardinal splines. Four control points are sufficient to determine a cubic segment passing through the two middle points. The complete path is defined by a list of such control points ensuring the following characteristics:

.Passing through the control points (except the first and last ones)
.First order continuity between adjacent segments.
.Tension adjustment
.Local control

The detailed expression of this spline family is given in Appendix A.

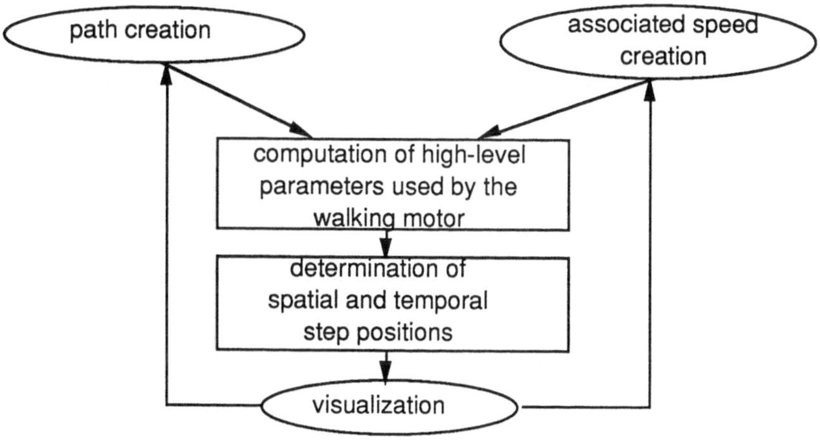

Figure 5: General design process

4.3 Path Tracking

Prior to the walking trajectory mapping, the path is transformed in a sequence of line segments using an adaptative sampling algorithm (Koparkar and Mudur 1983).

The incremental mapping process of the covered distance over the segmented path is then trivially realized by linear interpolation. The tangent is also interpolated and provides the forward direction. The resulting frame constructed with the vertical direction is assigned to the virtual floor coordinate system. This approach guarantees the coherence of floor support for any human figure.

4.4 Constrained Design of the distance over time

A execution time information (T) is important for same-stage integration of synthetic actors with other actors, moving objects, or even real video. The user defines the path with an execution time T and a temporal law which allowing the synthetic actor to finish the path at the specified instant T (first constraint). Moreover, we must consider a maximum velocity of the walker (second constraint).

If the user defines temporal law by velocity function of time, we must normalize the area covered under the function to respect these two constraints, but this could deform the previous profile wanted.

A more appropriate solution is editing the distance d(t), (a function of time). So, instead of a velocity normalization, it is sufficient to draw a curve passing through the end of the path (L) at the maximum time (T) (first constraint). The derived function d'(t) represents the velocity. For having a velocity between 0 and Vmax (our second constraint), tangents must belong to this interval. So, the principal problem is the creation of splines which need to have, at all points, tangents included in the interval.

We have implemented Hermite splines because of the local control they permit, with Hermite base functions which need the information of two control points with their tangents. For simple use, we initialize the first curve with first point (d(0)=0) and last point (d(T)=L --the first constraint imposed).

When a new control point is inserted, its tangent is defined by default with the vector v = (previous, next control points), but it could be interactively modified; it represents the walker's velocity.

4.5 Insertion of a new Control Points on d(t)

Insertion new control points deforms the d(t) profile according to the needs of animator. Therefore a modification of control point tangents locally changes the profile, and then allows us to locally obtain new values for ST_step.

To insert new control points, deform the spline between the previous and next points. Contraints imposed are :

- Increasing monotonic function
- derived restriction between [0 , Vmax]

A new control point could be inserted if we can calculate two new splines with all tangents included in [0, Vmax] (one between the previous and the inserted point, the other between the inserted and the next point). If tangents can not be include in the interval at all points of the two new splines, the new control point is not accepted. During insertion we want to visualize, at the position of the new control point, the interval of "possible tangents" which respect the constraint (Plate 1). The mathematic signification and resolution along with algorithm are detailed in Appendix B.

4.6 Step location setting methodology

The steps instant and location represent Spatial and Temporal characteristics of a step which are referred to as ST_step. The temporal characteristic is the time when the foot is upright to the body. ST_steps are visualized on Plate 2.

An adjustment of the distance over time will result in a small deformation of the speed profile and then a displacement of ST_step. Plate 3.shows an adjustement of the first control point tangent which allows us to increase the number of steps on a small curve of the associated path.The following figure (6) represents the function diagram of the interface.

5. INTEGRATION IN THE 3D ANIMATION SYSTEM

The 3D model is based on a tree hierarchy, oriented for an animation system. It is composed of various heterogenous objects, linked together by a tree framework whose root represents the principal reference of 3D space (*word reference frame).*

The basic construction entity of the tree hierarchy is denoted *3D Node*, and collects basic topological and geometrical and functional informations.

From a functionnal point of view, each 3D node is associated with complementary informations. Up to now, three internal types are defined:

- *Neutre*: default entity with invariable position in relation to father's node.
- *joint* : maintains a "one degree of freedom" local transformation.
- *free*: is a complete local transformation (orientation and position).

All other type nodes are terminal nodes (leaves):

- *Figure* : polygonal surface representation.
- *Camera* : camera information.

We have created a new terminal type of node to insert the path information in the hierarchy:

- *Path C2D* :.path information is described in a local reference. This C2D node allows positioning of the current point in relation to the local path reference. The operation of linking *word node* with *C2D node* using a *free* type node with complete transformation (figure 7), allows two styles of animation definition:
- the walker's positions is invariant with regards to *word node*, and the path moves under his feet (like a treadmill).
- the path is invariant and biped walks along it.

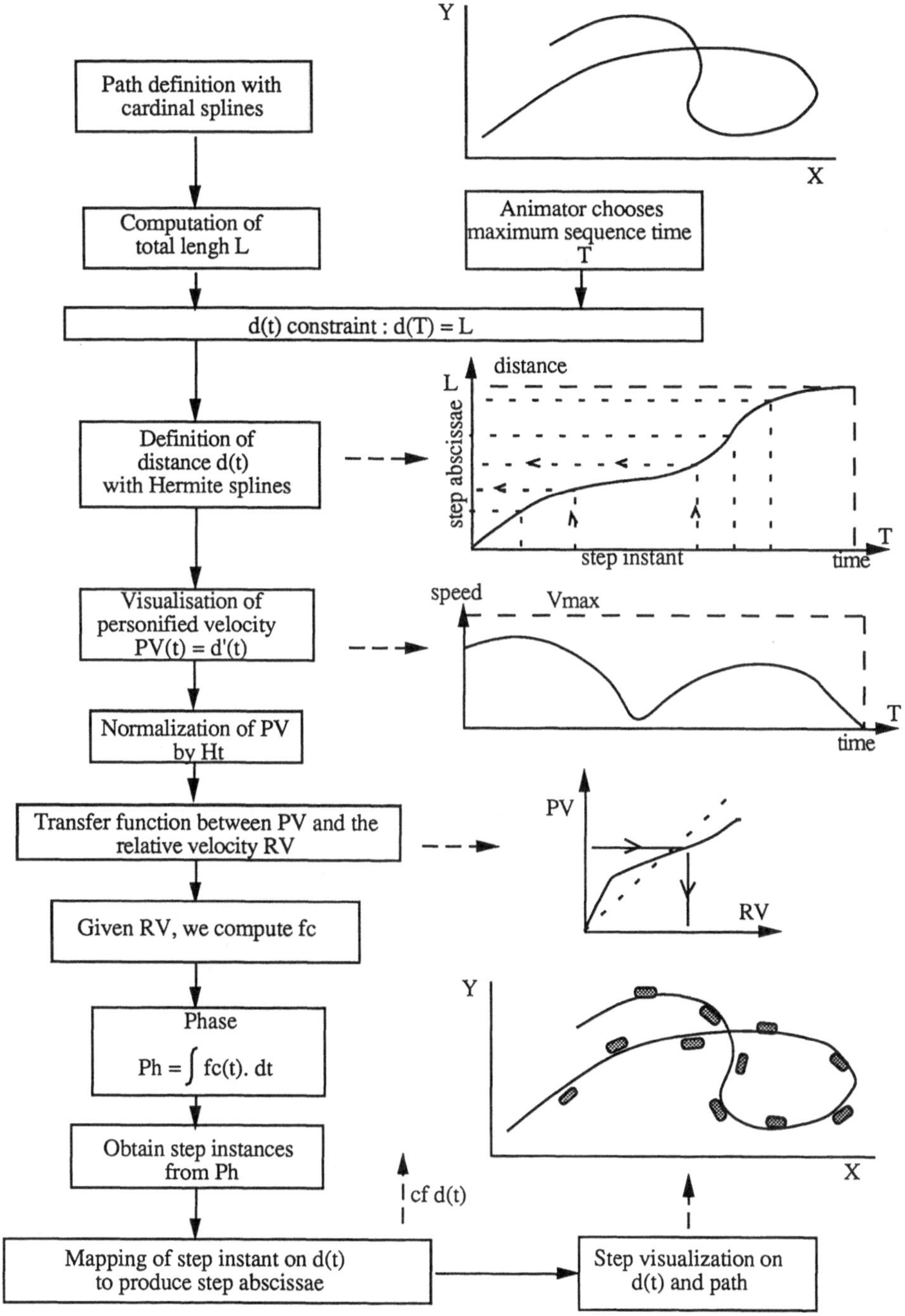

Figure 6: Function diagram of the interface

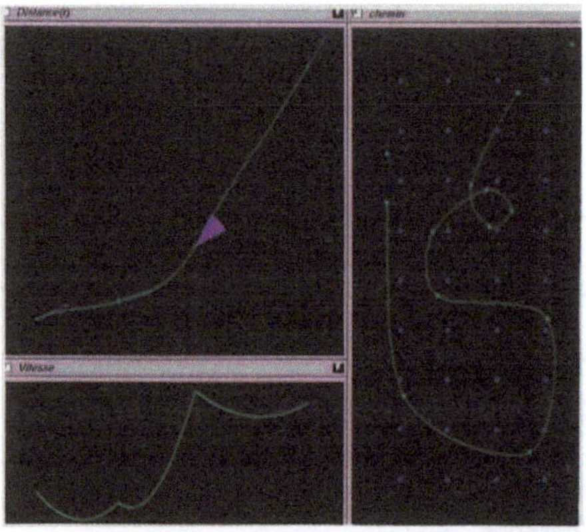

Plate 1: Creation of a path and speed profile -- upper left: distance(time), lower left: speed(time), right: path.

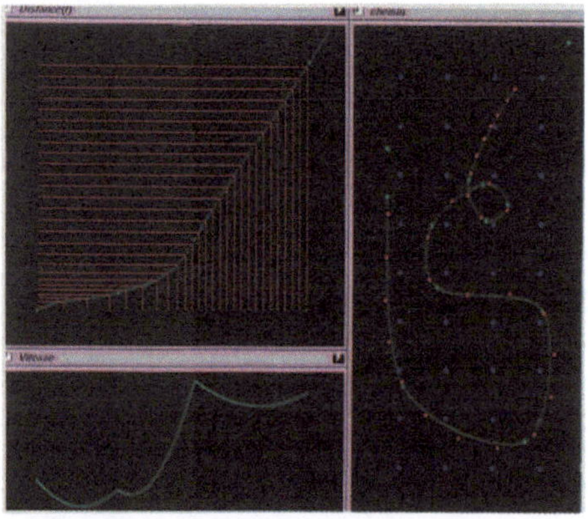

Plate 2: Visualization of step instances and location

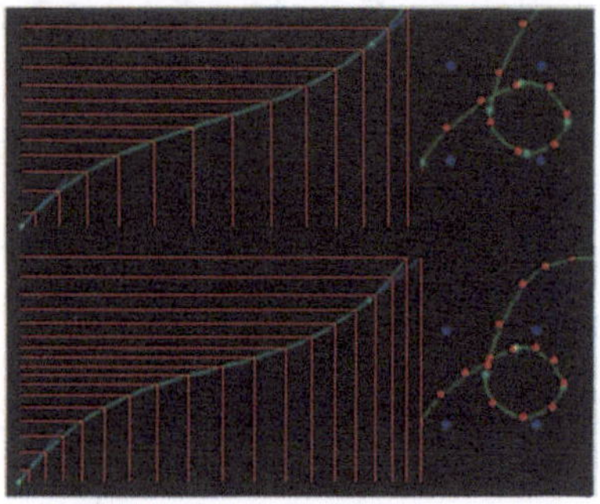

Plate 3: Modification of step instant and location by tangent adjustement

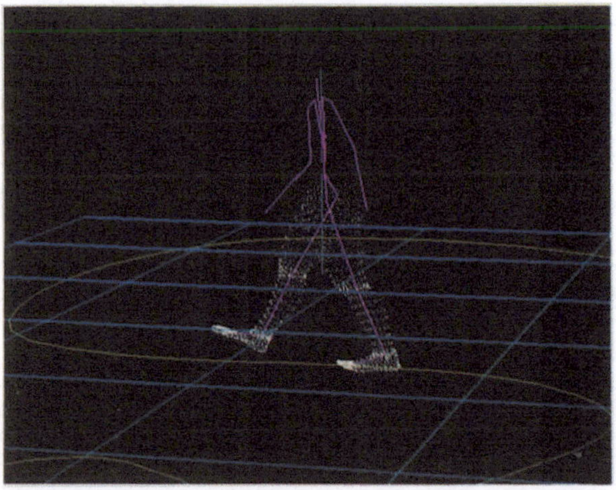

Plate 4: Real-time visualization of the walker along the path

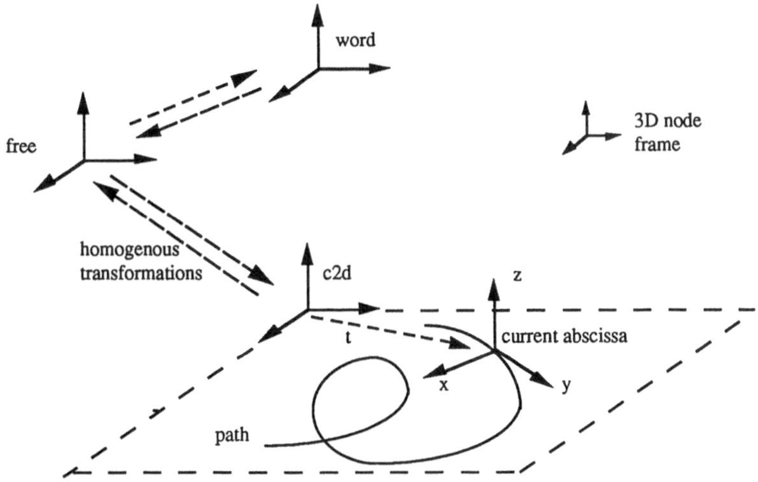

Figure 7: insertion of path information in the hierarchy:

6. EVALUATION AND RESULTS

Using this interface, we only define the high-level parameters needed by the walking motor. It creates trajectories based on mathematical parametrizations coming from biomechanical experimental data. The trajectories are realistic for a straight path.

In our case, spatial and temporal inputs define the movement of the body coordinate system. The foot coordinate system is linked to it and defines foot position during a straight walk. Rotation of the body coordinate system, so as to follow a curve in a path, includes a rotation of the entire skeleton, producing a foot sliding effect.

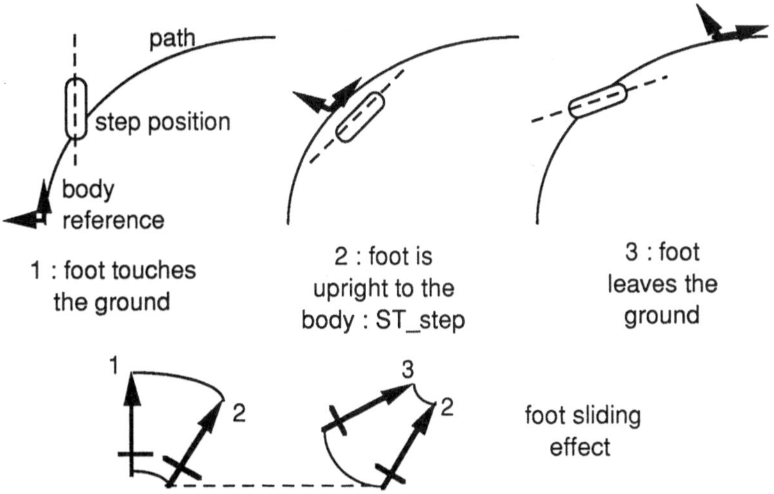

Figure 8: Foot sliding effect

Plate 5: Top view from selected positions of the sequence with realistic rendering (design Arghyro Paouri)

Plate 6: View from selected positions of the sequence with realistic rendering

Plate 7: View from selected positions of the sequence with realistic rendering

This effect can be noticed when the arc covered in one step has high curvature along . An empirical curvature limit of 60 degrees per step provides a good criteria for the design of speed profile. Over this limit the foot sliding effect becomes noticeable. A good and physically coherent behavior is to decrease the speed prior to a high-curvature segment. Moreover, during a sequence, the animation of all of the body diminishes the perception of this effect.

Plate 4 represents the real-time visualization of the walker along the path. Plates 5, 6 ,7 show five successive positions of the walker in the same sequence with realistic rendering by rayshade.

7. FUTURE IMPROVEMENTS

In the future, we will be able to implement a "system with premeditation" which will include an interactive foot orientation during an important change of direction. This little adaptation for curve motion may satisfy the animator but may be incompatible from a physical point of view.

In light of this new adpatation, ST_steps represent the times when a foot is upright to the body. At these moments, the path tangents represent the orientation along which the foot would have to be placed.

An interesting improvement could be the modification of ST_steps directly on d(t), by shifting one step abscissa along the distance axis, or respectively one step instant along the time axis. For step abscissae it could be done also along the path curve. Of the step shifting will result an iterative resolution to deform the distance curve until it respects the spatial and temporal step characteristics imposed. This method represents the automatization of the actual step modification which need to adjust the distance function.
The interface can be extended to create several paths to compare the movement of different actors. Therefore, we should draw the stage set-up on the path plan to integrate the actor in this stage and later in a live video stage. In the future, the actor could know his surroundings, pass around obstacles (Renault et al 91), and be confronted with group walking problems.

8. FUTURE WALKER INSERTION IN DIGITIZED LIVE VIDEO

Future research will focus on the insertion of the walker in live video only by designing the path inside a simple model of the real world where some special points are known in 3D.

We are currently developing an Acquisition System for Live Video Camera Position based on resolution algorithms (Bogart 91) and vision computation methods to determine, camera positions during a real stage sequence. Ideally, the position database and simple 3D world model should allow visualization of both the 2D situation plan and the vision volume of the live video camera during the path creation.

The hierarchical framework of the walking model enables the design of an extensible geometric environment. So, it should include things such as C2D, a 3D (modelization) stage, camera position and LVD frames. This new environment should allow, by matching synthetic and real camera positions, real time insertion of a synthetic actor on some frames of live video. Main problems will be the acquisition system, the calibration of the synthetic camera with regard to the real one and CPU performance in calculating walking animation during visualization.

The LVD should also interest designers for the creation of key frame sequences with the help of live video movements.

9. CONCLUSION

We have proposed a new tool for the design of human free-walking trajectories. The complete independence of this tool regarding 3D simulation of motion is gained by the use of the figure transfer function. This functionality greatly eases real-time interaction through the general design loop.
Besides the separate design of the path and the speed profile, the system continuously evaluates the validity of the speed profile and the corresponding step locations. These features help to guarantee the coherence of the final motion with some animator-defined spatio-temporal requirements and will result in easy modeling of complex walking animation.

ACKNOWLEDGEMENTS

The authors are greateful to Arghyro Paouri for the ray-casting sequences production and to Martin Werner and Prem Kalra for their help in revising this text. The research was supported by the University of Geneva and the "Fonds National Suisse de la Recherche Scientifique".

REFERENCES

Bogart R G (1991), View Correlation, Graphics Gems II, pp 181-190,ed. Arvo J, Academic Press

Boulic R, Magnenat Thalmann N, Thalmann D (1990), A Global Human Walking Model with Real-Time Kinematic Personification, Visual Computer ,Vol. 6, No 6, pp344-358

Boulic R, Renault O (1991) 3D Hierarchies for Animation, New Trends in Animation and Visualization, Wiley Professional Computing, pp 59-77

Bruderlin A, Calvert TW (1989) Goal Directed, Dynamic Animation of Human Walking, Proc. SIGGRAPH '89, Computer Graphics, Vol. 23, No3

Calvert TW, Welman C, Gaudet S, Schiphorst T, Lee C (1991) Composition of multiple figure sequences for dance and animation, The Visual Computer, Vol 7(2-3)

Girard M (1987) Interactive Design of 3D Computer-animated Legged Animal Motion, IEEE Computer Graphics and Applications, Vol.7, No6, pp.39-51

Girard M, Maciejewski AA (1985) Computational Modeling for Computer Generation of Legged Figures, Proc. SIGGRAPH '85, Computer Graphics, Vol. 19, No3, pp.263-270

Inman VT, Ralston HJ, Todd F (1981) Human Walking, Baltimore, Williams & Wilkins

Kochanek D, Bartels R (1984) Interpolating Splines with Local Tension, Continuity, and Bias Control, Computer Graphics, Volume 18, No.3.

Koparkar PA and Mudur SP (1983) A New Class of Algorithms for the Processing of Parametric Curves, Computer-aided Design, Vol.15, No1, pp.41-45

Philips C, Badler NI (1991) Interactive behaviors for bipedal articulated figures,SIGGRAPH'91, Computer Graphics, Vol 25(4)

Renault O. Magnenat Thalmann N, Thalmann D, 'A Vision-based Approach to Behavioural Animation', Visualization and Computer Animation (August 1990) 1(1):18-21.

Smith A R (1983), Lucasfilm Ltd, Spline Tutorial Notes, Technical Memo No.77, Computer Graphics Project.

Zeltzer D, Sims K (1989) A Figure Editor and Gait Controller to Task Level Animation in: Thalmann D, Magnenat-Thalmann N, Wyvill B, Zeltzer D, SIGGRAPH '88 Tutorial Notes on Synthetic Actors: the Impact of A.I. and Robotics on Animation.

APPENDIX A: Cardinal spline for editing the path

Equations are generated using hermite base functions. Required information includes the 2 points (pti, pti+1) and their tangents (tgi,tgi+1) defined by vector :

$$tgi = ß \,.\, (pti\text{-}1,\ pti+1)$$
$$tgi+1 = ß \,.\, (pti,\ pti+2)$$

ß influences tangent norms, then allows a tension adjustment.
The equation between two consecutive points has the following form :

$$C(s) = [\, s^3\ s^2\ s\ 1\,] \underbrace{\begin{bmatrix} 2 & -2 & 1 & 1 \\ -3 & 3 & -2 & -1 \\ 0 & 0 & 1 & 0 \\ 1 & 0 & 0 & 0 \end{bmatrix}}_{\text{Hermite base}} \begin{bmatrix} pti \\ pti+1 \\ tgi \\ tgi+1 \end{bmatrix}$$

with s belonging to [0,1]

APPENDIX B: Resolution of monotonic constrained spline

B.1. Mathematic signification

We want to insert a new control point Pi(ti,di,d'i) between previous point P0(0,d0,d'0) and next point P1(1,d1,d'1). Therefore, we need to find a good value of d'i which creates two acceptable splines (tangents C [0,Vmax]). Mathematically, it could be done by searching the four "extreme splines" which represent the limits of the "possible tangents" interval. They have the following characteristics:

- two extreme splines between (P0-Pi):
  - One including inflexion point A0 with null tangent for minimum velocity.
  - The second including inflexion point B0 with tangent equal to Vmax for maximum velocity.

  (P0-Pi) spline equation:

$$f0(s) = a0\, s^3 + b0\, s^2 + c0\, s + d0 \qquad s \in [0,1] \qquad \text{with}$$

$$a0 = 2d0 - 2di + d'0 + d'i$$
$$b0 = -3d0 + 3di - 2d'0 - d'i$$
$$c0 = d'0$$
$$d0 = d0$$

- two extreme splines between (Pi-P1):
  - One including inflexion point A0 with tangent equal to Vmax for maximum velocity.
  - The second including inflexion point B0 with null tangent for minimum velocity.

  (Pi-P1) spline equation:

$$f1(s) = a1\, s^3 + b1\, s^2 + c1\, s + d1 \qquad s \in [0,1] \qquad \text{with}$$

$$a1 = 2di - 2d1 + d'i + d'1$$
$$b1 = -3di + 3d1 - 2d'i - d'1$$
$$c1 = d'i$$
$$d1 = di$$

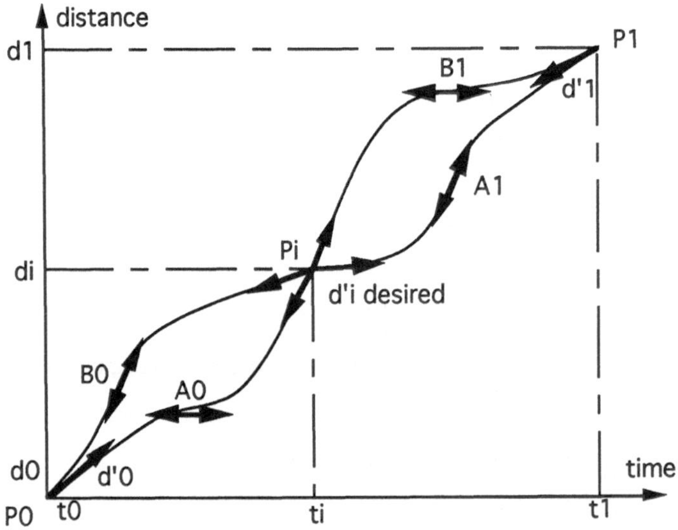

Figure 11: Validity interval of d'i defined by extreme splines

B.2. Calculated Example of Extreme Cubics Including A0

Suppose a cubic contains A0. All points are defined for $0 < si < 1$ such as:

$f''(si) = 0$ (inflexion point)
and $f'(si) = 0$ (null tangent)

using the cubic equation:

$f''(si) = 6.a0.si + 2.b0 = 0$ (4)
and $f'(si) = 3.a0.si + 2.b0.si + c0 = 0$ (5)

(4) => $si = -(1/3).(b0/a0)$

in (5): $-(b0^2 - 3.a0.c0)/3.a0 = 0$ (6)

The coefficients a0,b0,c0,d0 are calculated from d0,di,d'0,d'i [cf].
For the determination of extreme splines, d0,di,d'0 are constant and d'i is the variable.
The goal is to find the tangents d'i in Pi(ti,di) which define this cubic. We obtain it by solving (6):

In the denominator, 3.a0 :

when a0=0, the velocity, previously of second degree, becomes of first degree: the tangent at f0(s) varies monotonically between d'0 and d'iD (d'iD = d'i such as a0 = 0).

$3a0 = 3c(d0,di,d'0,d'i) = 0$
=> $3.(2d0 - 2di + d'0 + d'iD) = 0$
=> $d'iD = 2.(di-d0) - d'0$ (7)

The numerator, represents the second degree equation of d'i with coefficients fonction of (d0,d'0,di). Solving produces at most two solutions of tangent: d'a , d'b.

Studying the function (coming from (6))

$g(d'i) = -(b0^2 - 3.a0.c0)/3.a0$ => inflexion point tangent we observe a very interesting characteristic: If we classify by increasing order solutions d'iD,d'a,d'b (--> d'ß1,d'ß2,d'ß3) we always obtain the same variation table:

d'i	-inf	d'ß1	d'ß2	d'ß3	+inf
tangents sign of the inflexion point	+	−	+	−	

It signifies a simplification of the algorithm because the validity interval for A0 is simply the positive interval less than Vmax:
(U: union, I: intersection)

] -inf.,d'ß1] U [d'ß2,d'ß3] I [0,Vmax] (8)

Each equation coming from extreme splines A0,B0,A1,B1, creates an interval of this form.

During our study, we do not use the fact that s is varying only from 0 to 1 to create the cubic between two control points. Therefore to validate (8), we must intersect it with the interval defining an inflexion point on the curve when s is included in [0,1].

B.3. Determination of Tangents d'sO and d'sl so that the inflexion points are at s=0 (beginning of the spline) and,respectively s=1 (end of spline)

Suppose "si" is the value of s at the inflexion point. With equation (4) we have:

si = -b/3.a (9)
=> a<>0 --> d'iD
for si = 0 --> b = 0 --> d'sO
for si = 1 --> 3.a + b = 0 --> d'sl
with a = a0, b = b0 for A0,B0
and a = al, b = bl for A1,B1.
Studying (9), we determine the interval is :

[d'sO,d'sl] I [0,Vmax] if d'sO < d'iD < d'sl
the complementary interval of [d'sO,d'sl] on [0,Vmax], if not.

B.4. Final algorithm to calculate the interval of "possible tangents."

Convention of the algorithm diagram (figure12):
d'so : d'i such that the inflexion point is on s=0
d'sl : d'i such that the inflexion point is on s=1
d'iD : d'i such that the velocity is a one degre fonction.
IA : [d'sO,d'sl] I [0,Vmax]
IB : complementary interval of IA on [0,Vmax]
IC : tangents interval such that there is no inflexion point on the visible curve (when s is included in [0,1])
ICC : complementary interval of IC on [0,Vmax]. The visible curve has an inflexion point when d'i is included in ICC.
ICO, ICCO : IC, ICC for the spline PO - Pi
IC1, ICC1 : IC, ICC for the spline Pi - P1
ISO : tangents interval coming from the intersection of the solutions of extreme splines A0, (cf(8)), and B0
IS1 : tangents interval coming from the intersection of the solutions of extreme splines A1 and B1
ISOV : Validation of ISO on the visible curve (when s is included in [0,1])
IS1V : Validation of IS1 on the visible curve (when s is included in [0,1])
IF : Final interval. When d'i is included in IF, the constraints are respected.

∩ : Intersection
U : Union
C : Inclusion

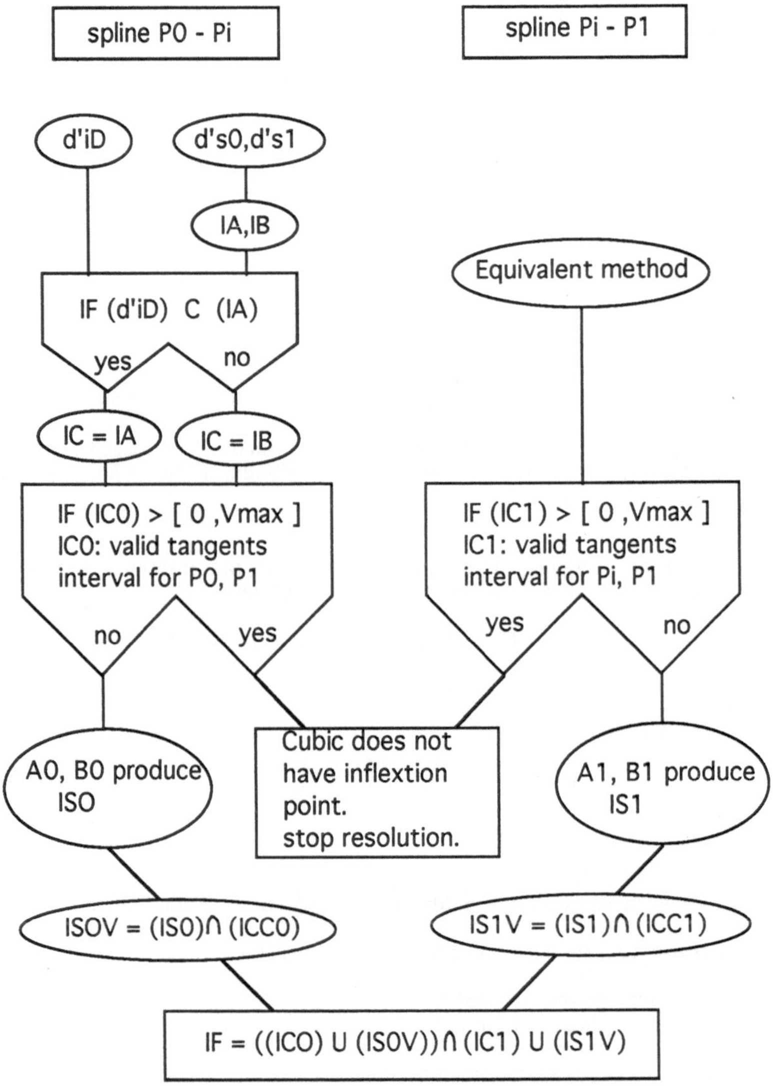

Figure 12: Algorithm to calculate the interval of "possible tangents"

Laurent Bezault is a PhD student in the Computer Graphics Lab at the University of Geneva. His research interests include 3D computer human animation and composition of synthetic and real images sequences. He received his electrical engineering diploma from the Swiss Federal Institute of Technologiy in Lausanne in 1991.

address: MIRALab, CUI, University of Geneva
12 rue du Lac, CH 1207 Geneva, Switzerland
E-mail: bezault@uni2a.unige.ch

Ronan Boulic is a senior researcher in the Computer Graphics Lab at the Swiss Federal Institute of Technology in Lausanne, Switzerland. His current research interests are 3D computer animation related to perception-action control loops and real-time man-machine interaction. He received his engineer diploma from the National Institute of Applied Sciences (INSA) of Rennes in 1983 and Computer Sciences Doctorate from the University of Rennes (France) in 1986. He spent one year as a visiting research associate at the Computer Graphics Laboratory of the University of Montreal. He contributed to the computer generated film *Still Walking* .

address: Computer Graphics Lab
Swiss Federal Institute of Technology
CH 1015 Lausanne, Switzerland
E-mail: boulic@ligsg2.epfl.ch

Nadia Magnenat Thalmann is currently full Professor of Computer Science at the University of Geneva, Switzerland and Adjunct Professor at HEC Montreal, Canada. She has served on a variety of government advisory boards and program committees in Canada. She has received several awards, including the 1985 Communications Award from the Government of Quebec. In May 1987, she was nominated woman of the year in sciences by the Montreal community. Dr. Magnenat Thalmann received a BS in psychology, an MS in biochemistry, and a Ph.D in quantum chemistry and computer graphics from the University of Geneva. She has written and edited several books and research papers in image synthesis and computer animation and was codirector of the computer-generated films *Dream Flight, Eglantine, Rendez-vous à Montréal, Galaxy Sweetheart, IAD, Flashback* and *Still Walking*. She served as chairperson of Graphics Interface '85, CGI '88, Computer Animation '89 and Computer Animation '90.

address: MIRALab, CUI, University of Geneva
12 rue du Lac, CH 1207 Geneva, Switzerland
E-mail: thalmann@uni2a.unige.ch

Daniel Thalmann is currently full Professor, Director of the Computer Graphics Laboratory and Head of the Computer Science Department at the Swiss Federal Institute of Technology in Lausanne, Switzerland. He is also adjunct Professor at the University of Montreal, Canada. He received his diploma in nuclear physics and Ph.D in Computer Science from the University of Geneva. He is coeditor-in-chief of the *Journal of Visualization and Computer Animation*, member of the editorial board of the *Visual Computer* and *the CADDM Journal* and cochairs the EUROGRAPHICS Working Group on Computer Simulation and Animation. Daniel Thalmann's research interests include 3D computer animation, image synthesis, virtual reality and scientific visualization. He has published more than 100 papers in these areas and is coauthor of several books including: *Computer Animation: Theory and Practice* and *Image Synthesis: Theory and Practice*. He is also codirector of several computer-generated films.

address: Computer Graphics Lab
Swiss Federal Institute of Technology
CH 1015 Lausanne, Switzerland

E-mail: thalmann@elma.epfl.ch

Achilles – A System for Visualizing Non Standard Human Gait

HOMERO L. PÍCCOLO, KENTARO TAKAHASHI, MARCUS G. DE AMORIM, and ANDRÉ C. DE SÁ CARNEIRO

ABSTRACT

This work presents a system for visualizing the human gait that provides facilities to compare the gait of people who have physical disabilities with the standard human walk. The system is a didactic tool to provide experience to new orthopaedists and help the clinical evaluation of a patient. It allows visualization of a defective movement through the information obtained from a set of reflexive markers. It also allows input of movement commands and visualization of the resulting effects. The control method of the articulated structure is hierarchic, allowing great flexibility and making it easier to manipulate the various joints and limbs.

Keywords : Human Movement, Articulated Figure Animation, Hierarchical Structure, Bipedal Biomechanics, Animation System.

1. INTRODUCTION

From the use of traditional techniques as key-frame (Burtnyk and Wein 1976), kinematics (Girard 1985), and dynamics (Bruderlin 1989) to new methodologies such as application of concepts of robotics (Korein and Badler 1982; Thalmann 1990), abstractions of Artificial Intelligence (Maiocchi 1991; Zeltzer 1983) and behavioral animation (Renault et al. 1990), much has being added to the field of Computer Animation. But the core of the field remains unchanged, that is the quest for a realistic synthesis of movement.

Man in movement has been the object of observation since prehistorical time. For example, the paintings of caveman with hunters running as a motif, besides various records of distinct civilizations such as Egyptians, Assyrians, Babylonians among others illustrates this concern (Gombrich 1978).

Muybridge produced in 1887 (Muybridge 1979 a; Muybridge 1979 b) photographic pictures of men and animals in motion. Braune and Fischer published a series of detailed work on human walk (including graphical analysis) from 1895 to 1904 (Braune and Fischer 1987). Since then, much has being done to unfold scientifically this field of study, the human motion.

Graphical Systems (Badler and Smoliar 1979; Badler et al. 1991; Magnenat-Thalmann and Thalmann 1985) in the last decades turned out to be a powerful tool to visualize the impact of new technologies. The synthesis and visualization of the human walk was also benefited by the advent of this tool. In all works related to synthesis of human walk, the goal to be achieved is the representation and simulation of the human walk as close to the reality as possible.

The aim of the ACHILLES system follows this trend, but differs from previous systems on the type of walk of interest. Besides the synthesis of normal walk, the systems provides facilities to visualize non-standard gait, that is the particular walk of a person with physical disability. The system also provides an user interface to input certain movement commands to be performed over the limbs, which can be applied on the human body model.

The ACHILLES system has being developed by the Computer Graphics Laboratory (Department of Computer Science - University of Brasilia) in cooperation with the Movement Laboratory (Sarah Kubitscheck Hospital - specialized in rehabilitation medicine and orthopaedics).

At the Movement Laboratory, people with physical disability are recorded while walking, and through reflexive markers, the position of the limbs are recorded and then are analized by a computational system (VICON[1]) that provides graphics of rotational angles of the various articulations in time. The data that generates these graphics constitutes one of the types of input to the ACHILLES system, that reproduces the defective movement, enabling the system to visualize the movement from new positions by a virtual camera at a desired rate of presentation. In this way, a comparison of the defective gait and the normal walk can be done, helping the clinical evaluation. The goal of the system is to colaborate in a didactic manner to the formation of an orthopaedist by providing a new tool to study the pathological gait.

2. THE MODEL OF THE HUMAN BODY AND ITS MOVEMENTS

The model of the human body constructed for the ACHILLES system follows the standard nomenclature of the human anatomy. Biomechanics concepts were used to set up a basic normative vocabulary (Hay and Reid 1982; Gowitzke and Milner 1980; Braune and Fischer 1987; Sutherland et al. 1988) throughout the work.

The structure of the human body model (Fig. 1) can be seen as a complex object with hierarchically connected parts, grouped in different logical levels.

The data structure that represents best this hierarchy is an n-ary tree, where each node has its own coordinate system. Since one node is connected with a higher level node, a propagation of a transformation that occurs in one node in relation to the universe (root node U), can be reduced to a simple task of providing an operation of generating the product of the transformation matrices corresponding to the nodes along the path that connects the node to the root node (U).

Figure 2, shows the arborescent shape of the ACHILLES human body data structure. As an example, in order to specify the adduction of one lower limb, that is the lift of one lower limb in the coronal plane, it is only necessary to adduct the thigh. Since the leg and the foot are nodes of a lower level layer, they will automatically follow the higher level node.

2.1 The Reference Planes

The planes depicted in Fig. 3, show the planes in which the movements are described. These planes of movements are common to physical therapists and physicians. Since the sagittal movement is in the direction of walk progression, a side view is the best to recognize details in this plane. Coronal movement is from side to side, and so back or front view are the recommended ones to observe the movements in

---

1 VICON is a trademark of Oxford Medlog Systems

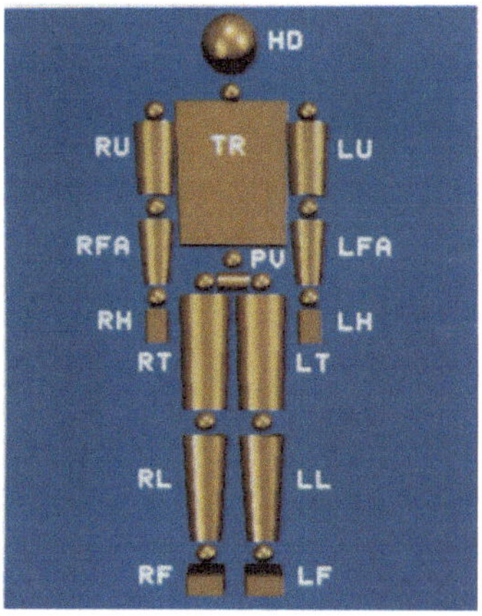

HD - head	
TR - trunk	
PV - pelvis	
RU - right upper arm	LU - left upper arm
RFA - right forearm	LFA - left forearm
RH - right hand	LH - left hand
RT - right thigh	LT - left thigh
RL - right leg	LL - left leg

Fig. 1 Human body model

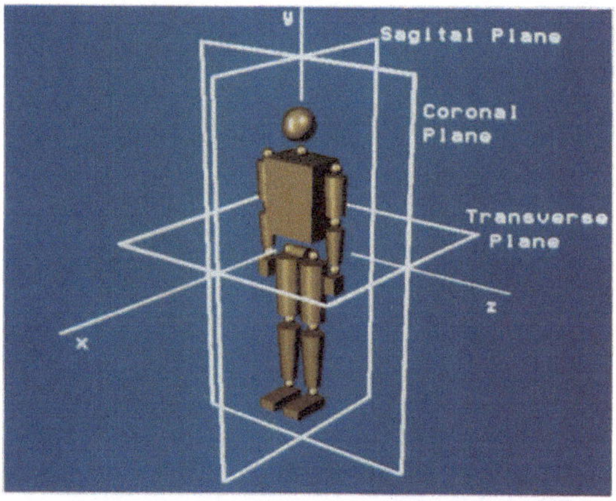

Fig. 3 Reference planes of body and coordinate system in standard anatomic position

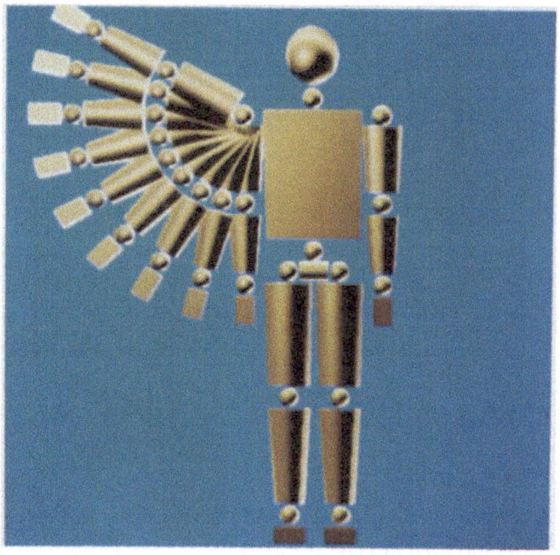

Fig. 6 Command arm-adition (right, 120°)

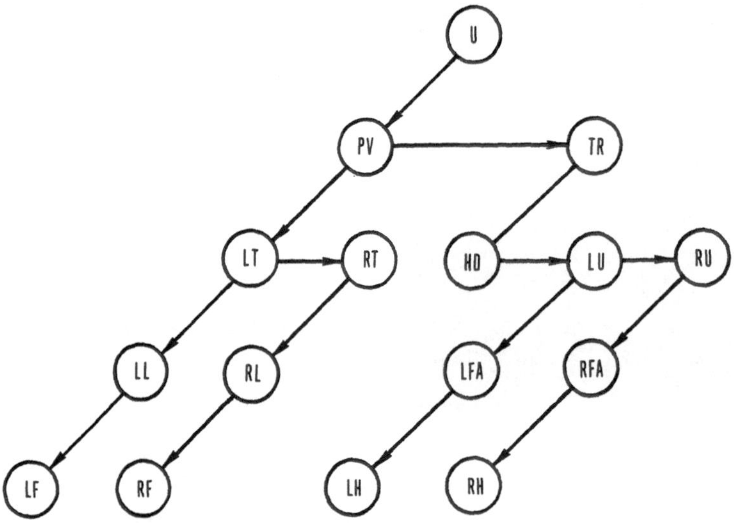

Fig. 2 Hierarchical tree of the human body model

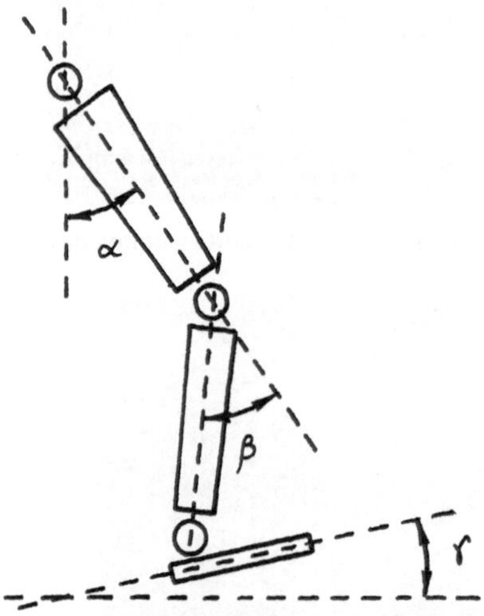

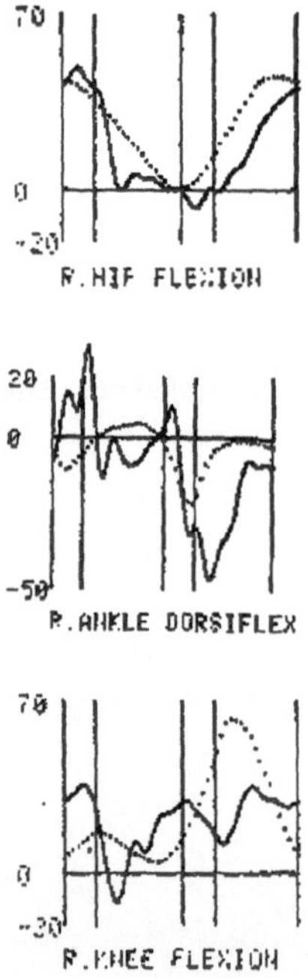

Fig. 4 (a)Rotational angles of the lower limbs in the sagital plane
(b) the graphics of angle variation (right side)

this plane. Transverse movement is about a vertical axis, and so the ideal viewpoint is from above or below the patient, these viewponts are easily accessed by a virtual camera. The possibility of positioning the virtual camera in a possibly difficult viewpoint shows one of the advantages of a computational system over the traditional approach.

2.2 The Movements

The anatomical proportions between the limbs were based on the Dempsters' work (Le Veau 1977).

In the simulation of the human walk, the following movements are considered.

a) related to the pelvis :

- a1) pelvic obliquity - rotation of the pelvis around axis X (coronal plane).
- a2)pelvic rotation - rotation of the pelvis around axis Y (transverse plane).
- a3) pelvic tilt - rotation of the pelvis around axis Z (sagittal plane).

b) related to the thigh :

- b1) hip flexion/extension - rotation of the thigh around axis Z and center of rotation settled in the joint fixed at the pelvis (sagittal plane).
- b2) femoral rotation - rotation of the thigh in the direction of the thighs' longitudinal axis (transverse plane).
- b3) hip abduction/adduction - rotation of the thigh around axis X, center of rotation located in the joint fixed at the pelvis (coronal plane). Abduction - move away from the body; Adduction - approximation related to the body.

c) related to the leg :

- c1) knee flexion/extension - rotation of the leg around axis Z, center of rotation in the joint fixed in the thigh (sagittal plane).
- c2) tibial rotation - rotation of the leg around its longitudinal axis (transverse plane).

d) related to the foot:

- d1) ankle dorsiplantar flexion - rotation of the foot around axis Z, center of rotation in the joint fixed at the leg (sagittal plane).
- d2) foot rotation - rotation of the foot in the direction of the legs' longitudinal axis (transverse plane).

In Fig. 4a are depicted : (a) the lower limbs and the angles corresponding to its movements, seen from the sagital plane. (b) the graphics of angle variation between the limbs. The exhibited movements are : hip flexion/extension (a); knee flexion/extension (b); ankle dorsiplantar flexion (g).

The graphics of the lower limb were generated by the VICON system, a comercial software developed by Oxford Medlog systems. In the graphics (Fig.4b), the bold lines are the patients data and the dotted lines are the data of a normal walk.

3. SYSTEM ARCHITECTURE

The ACHILLES system is structured over three layers of software (Fig. 5): the user interface layer, the articulation control layer and the LAFIT layer. In fact, this is a logical division, with a great degree of freedom among them, due to the easy task of changing the functionality of one layer without affecting the others.

3.1 The User Interface Layer

It is the layer in which is defined the syntax of the system's commands. This layer interacts with the user through low level commands (e.g., the rotation of the arm specified by angles and directions). This is also the layer that is used to input the data of the angle variation between the lower limbs. As an example, the command Arm-Abduction [side,angle] with parameters: side = right and angle = 120 degrees (Fig. 6), will move away the right upper arm up to 120 degrees, related to the sagital plane, independently of its position related to the coronal plane, as will be described in the next section. . Due to the hierarchical structure, the right forearm and the right hand will automatically follow the movement of the higher level limb.

3.2 The Articulation Control Layer

The control of the body movements is done by this layer. It is conducted in terms of rotational angles applied over each articulation, considering the limits of the movement of each articulation. In fact, the control of the articulations is a set of procedures that describes the movements and uses commands from the LAFIT layer.

3.2.1 The Geometric Model of an Articulation

In a great variety of cases, articulations with more than one degree of freedom can be decomposed into a sequence of articulations with one degree of freedom, which can be treated independently. This simplification will be used in the following representation. The rotational articulations (also called universal) has one or two degrees of freedom and are obtained by fixing one or two degrees of freedom.

A segment and its proximal articulations are represented by a vector on a spherical coordinate system (Fig. 7). The first two angles of the articulation are given in relation to the universal coordinate system. The angle formed between the projection of the segment in the YZ plane and axis Y is called azimuth. The angle between the segment and its projection in the YZ plane is called elevation. The third angle, the angle of longitudinal rotation is the rotational angle performed by the segment around its longitudinal axis (in this case it is the axis Y of the coordinate system solidary to the segment).

This model represents a spherical articulation divided in three rotational articulations, in which the individual alteration of one angle does not affect the angle of the other two. One observation must be made when the effect occurs in when the elevation angle surpasses 90 degrees. In this case, the projection of the segment in the YZ plane is reflected simetrically with regard to the origin. Thus, some information regarding the elevation must be recorded, to denote that the elevation is greater than 90 degrees. The angle of interest will be the one between the Y axis and the simetric vector regarding the origin of the projection of the segment in the YZ plane.

Since no articulation in the real world has a total freedom of movement, the limits of the articulation must be represented in this model. The movement limits of a certain articulation can be represented by a list of spherical angle pairs, representing vectors with origin in the center of rotation. The movement of an articulation remains restricted to the internal area of a polygon formed by the intersection points of the vectors with a sphere of unitary radius and centered around the rotation center (Korein 1982).

3.3 The LAFIT layer

LAFIT - Linguagem de Animação de Figuras Tridimensionais (Tridimensional Figure Animation language) (Piccolo et al. 1991) is basically a Pascal library that manages the animation of tridimensional figures, light sources and virtual cameras. A hierarchical structure is used to represent the limbs and its

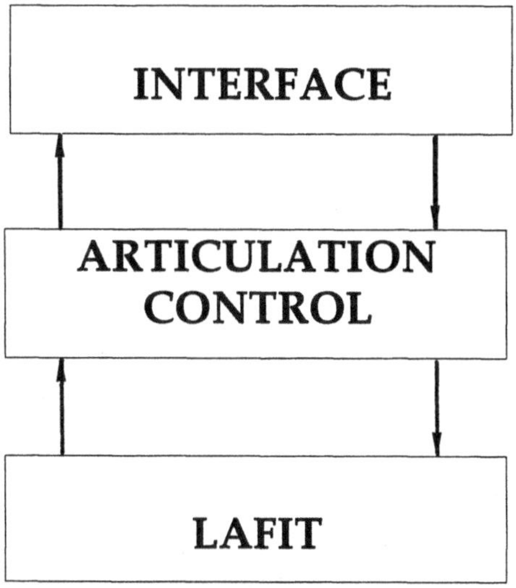

Fig. 5 Architeture of the ACHILLES system

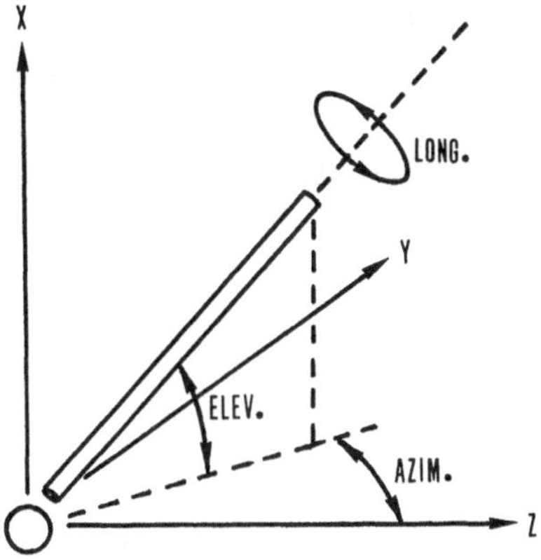

Fig. 7 Articulation model

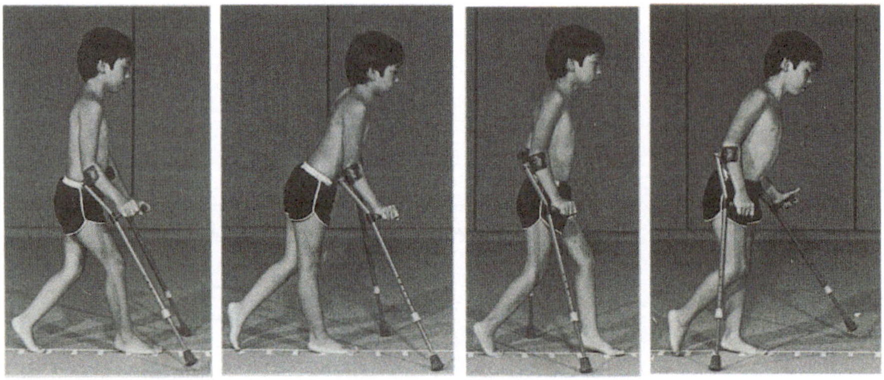

Fig. 8 The patological gait

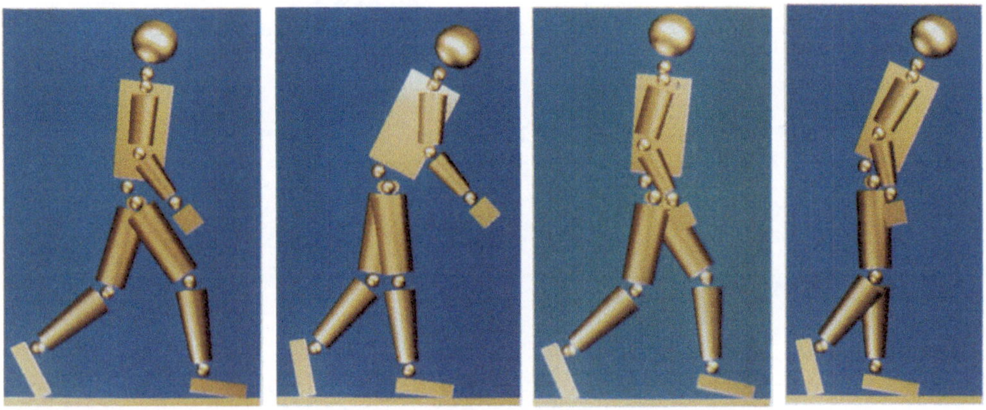

Fig. 9 The patological gait visualized by the ACHILLES system

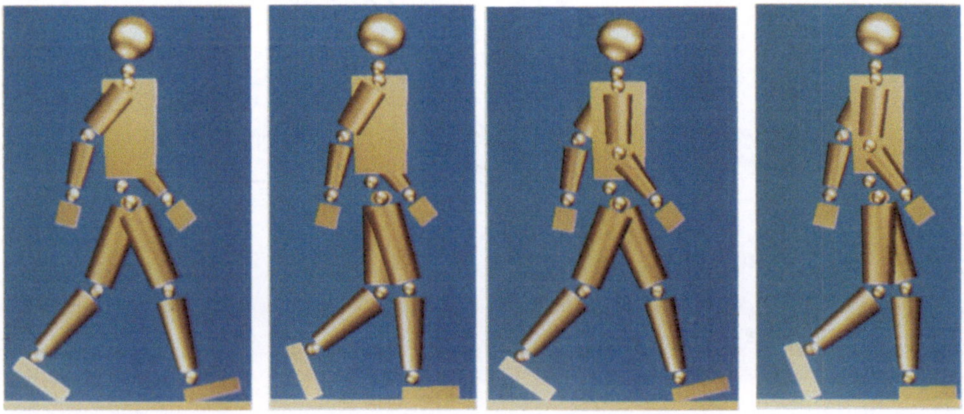

Fig. 10 The standard walk generated by ACHILLES system

relationships in order to facilitate the description of movements. This layer provides a high degree of flexibility in the animation, due to the union of procedures and control structure.

3.3.1 Control Functions

The LAFIT simulates two control structures to manage the animation sequence: the animation loop and the time block. The animation loop uses the WHILE command from Pascal; inside this loop it is defined a complete animation sequence, whose duration is previously determined. The time blocks are used to define intervals of time in which a certain sequence must occur.

4. RESULTS

To visualize the walk of a human being in the ACHILLES system it is necessary to provide information that can occur through the angular variation of the articulations.

By a set of reflexive markers along the patient body, it is possible to capture the 3D positional information. This is performed by five cameras, and once the positional information is obtained, the angular variation data are provided to the ACHILLES system. Then, the system is able to visualize the same gait, in terms of new positions and different rates of presentation.

The process of walking can be divided in phases: Development phase, Rhythmic phase and Decay phase. Development phase is characterized by a start from rest to some level of speed. The Rhythmic phase is a period of rythmic or cyclic movement at fairly average speed. Decay phase is the period of speed deceleration and stop.

The subject of interest is the Rhythmic phase, that is a sucession of cycles (walking cycles). In the walking cycle, each foot spends part of the cycle in contact with the walking surface and the remainder of the cycle in the air, moving to a new position (Inman et al. 1982; Sutherland et al. 1988). The walking cycle can be subdivided in order to identify certain events that are useful in the study of the lower limbs. In normal subjects the walking cycle begins with heel strike, continues through stance and swing phases, and ends with heel strike of the same foot.

Figure 8, shows the patient walking on a velocity of 85.59 cm/s. The duration of the walking cycle is 1.42 seconds. The presented data was generated by the VICON system.

In the following figures (Fig. 9, Fig.10) are presented some results of the ACHILLES system, according to the subdivision of the walking cycle in four events : (a) right foot strike; (b) left toe off; (c) left foot strike; (d) right toe off.

5. CONCLUDING REMARKS

The ACHILLES system is implemented on a PROCEDA 5370 workstation, and its source code is written in Pascal. The modeling of the objects has been done using a Boundary Representation (B-Rep) and the rendering of the human body model uses the normal interpolation method (Gouraud-Phong) and the Phong ilumination model (Foley et al. 1990; Rogers 1985).

There is an effort to migrate to a SUN Sparcstation 2, including the translation from Pascal to C. The interchange of information between the Computer Science Department and the Sarah Kubitscheck Hospital is recent. The ACHILLES system at the moment is an initial project being the kernel for future improvements.

Current research direction and further works in the ACHILLES system include :

- A user friendly interface for a non-LAFIT-language programmer.

- The parametrization of the limbs due to sex and age.

- The representation of anatomical defects (e.g., a shorter leg).

- Studies of the movement dynamics in order to incorporate a mechanical analysis of the walk, involving forces and torques.

- The elaboration of a model representing the neuro-muscular system of the lower limbs in order simulate the movements caused by certain damages and preview the effect of a cirurgical intervention.

ACKNOWLEDGEMENTS

We would like to express our appreciation to the following institutions and people: the Movement Laboratory (M.D. Amâncio Ramalho Jr., Alfredo Franch and José H. Cavalcante), Julio Lopes L. Filho for the excellent photographic work, Professors Fernando Albuquerque and Henrique S. Malvar for the English grammar corrections, the Desktop Publishing Team (Liana Kresch, Carlos E. Augusto, and specially Alex Meireles for doing more than his duties), Prof. Aluizio Arcela for providing the Desktop Publishing facilities, the Department of Visual Arts (Prof. Suzete Venturelli) for scanning the figures (Fig.4b), and Agnes Daldegan for her valuable comments on an early draft of this paper.

REFERENCES

Badler N.I., Smoliar S.W. (1979) Digital Representations of Human Movement. Computing Surveys, 11(1):19-38

Badler N.I., Barsky B.A., Zeltzer D. (1991) Making them Move - Mechanics, Control, and Animation of Articulated Figures. Morgan Kaufmann Publishers, Inc. San Mateo California

Braune W., Fischer O. (1987) The Human Gait. Springer Verlag, Berlin Heidelberg New York London Paris Tokyo.

Bruderlin A., Calvert T.W. (1989) Goal Directed, Dynamic Animation of Human Walking, Computer Graphics. 23(3):233-242.

Burtnyk N., Wein M. (1976) Interactive Skeleton Techniques for Enhancing Motion Dynamics in Key Frame Animation. Communications of the ACM. 19(10):564-569.

Foley J.D., Van Dam A., Feiner S.K., Hughes J.F. (1990) Computer Graphics: Principles and Practice, 2nd edition, Addison-Wesley, Reading Menlo Park New York Don Mills Wokingham Amsterdam Bonn Sydney Singapore Tokyo Madrid San Juan.

Girard M., Maciejewski A.A. (1985) Computational Modeling for Computer Generation of Legged Figures, Computer Graphics 19(3):263-270.

Gombrich E.H. (1978) The Story of Art. Phaidon Press Limited, Oxford.

Gowitzke B.A., Milner M. (1980) Understanding the Scientific Bases of Human Movement. Williams & Wilkins, Baltimore London.

Hay J.G., Reid J.G. (1982) The Anatomical And Mechanical Bases of Human Motion. Prentice-Hall, Inc., Englewoods Cliffs.

Inmann V. T., Ralston H.J., Todd F. (1982) Human Walking. Williams & Wilkins, Baltimore London.

Korein J.U., Badler N.I. (1982) Techniques for goal directed motion. IEEE Computer Graphics and Applications 2(9):71-81

Le Veau B. (1977) Willians and Lissner : Biomechanics of Human Motion. WB Saunders Co., Philadelphia London Toronto.

Piccolo H.L., Lobão A., Amorin M.G., Martinelli E. (1991) LAFIT. Proc. Compugraphics, vol.1, 163-170, Portugal.

Maiocchi R. (1991) A knowledge-Based Approach to the Synthesis of Human motion. In: Kunii T.L. (ed) Modeling in Computer Graphics. Springer Verlag, Tokyo Berlin Heidelberg New York London Paris Hong Kong Barcelona.

Magnenat-Thalmann N., Thalmann D. (1985) Computer Animation. Springer Verlag, Tokyo Berlin Heidelberg New York.

Muybridge E. (1979 a) Muybridge's Complete Human and Animal Locomotion, vol. 2, Dover Publications, Inc., New York.

Muybridge E. (1979 b) Muybridge's Complete Human and Animal Locomotion, vol. 3, Dover Publications, Inc., New York.

Renault O., Magnenat-Thalmann N., Thalmann D. (1990) A Vision-based Approach to Behavioural Animation. The Journal of Visualization and Computer Animation 1(1):18-21.

Rogers D.F. (1985) Procedural Elements for Computer Graphics, McGraw-Hill Book Co., New York St. Louis San Francisco Auckland Bogota Hamburg London Madrid Mexico Montreal New Delhi Panama Paris Sao Paulo Singapore Sydney Tokyo Toronto

Sutherland D.H., Olshen R.A., Biden E.N., Wyatt M.P. (1988) The Development of Mature Walking, Mac Keith Press, Oxford Philadelphia.

Thalmann D. (1990) Robotic Methods for task level and Behavioral Animation. In: Thalmann D. (ed) Scientific Visualization and Graphics Simulation, John Wiley and Sons.

Zeltzer D. (1983) Knowledge-based Animation, Proc. ACM SIGGRAPH/SIGART Workshop on Motion. pp. 187-192

Homero Luiz Píccolo is an assistant professor in the Department of Computer Science, University of Brasilia - UnB (Brazil). He is the director of the Computer Graphics Laboratory - LCG. Piccolo received his BS in Electrical Engineering from the University of São Paulo in 1975 and the MS from University of Brasilia in 1988. His research interests include solid modeling, rendering techniques and computer animation. He has published a dozen of academic/technical papers in the Computer Graphics field. He is a member of SIGGRAPH.

Kentaro Takahashi is a graduate student in the Department of Computer Science, UnB. Takahashi received the BS (Computer Science) in 1990 from University of Brasilia. He is a member of CGS and a student member of ACM, SIGGRAPH, SIAM and EUROGRAPHICS. His research interests include solid modeling, computer vision and computer animation.

Marcus Guilherme de Amorim is an undergraduate student in Computer Science at the UnB. Amorim will receive his BS in 1992. He is a member of SBC(Brazilian Computing Society). His research interests include animation languages and computer animation.

André Corrêa de Sá Carneiro is an undergraduate student in Computer Science at UnB. Carneiro will receive his BS in 1993. His research interests include solid modeling and computer animation.

Address : Universidade de Brasilia - UnB
Departamento de Ciência da Computação - CIC
Laboratório de Computação Gráfica (LCG)
C.P. 04640 - Campus Universitário - Asa Norte
CEP 70.910 - Brasilia - BRAZIL

E-Mails : UnB@BRFAPESP.BITNET
UnBCIC@BRFAPESP.BITNET

FAERIE: A CAD/CAM Tool for Voluntary Movement and Ergonomic Simulation

OLIVIER COPPIN and ANDRÉ CLEMENT

ABSTRACT

The purpose of this paper is to present the FAERIE project. This project is to achieve an anthropometric function capable of **simulating human behaviour** in connection with its environment. The needs in this field are analysed in order to draw the specifications of such a tool, and its interest in the field of **design assistance**. Different solutions, those studied and those accepted, are then presented. The project's progress and its prospects are mentionned. The emphasis is laid on the use of **dynamic laws** and on models developed to simulate **volontary movements.**

Keywords : CAD/CAM, Dynamic laws, Human movement, Ergonomy, Behaviour simulation.

1. INTRODUCTION

The models and developements presented in this paper are parts of the FAERIE project. The aim of this project is a CAD/CAM function of ergonomic valuation. The question is to estimate the ergonomic quality of an environment : a pilot's cockpit, a driving position, a dashboard, a working station, ... To test the environment, we use a humanoid manikin. With this manikin, the testing of accessibility, functionnality, safety and comfort of the environment is possible.

The base of FAERIE is a **dynamic simulation** module. This module allows simulation of behaviour of a manikin submitted to external actions (gravity, collision, ...). The models described in this paper are used to simulate manikin volontary movements. Because FAERIE is first developed to simulate the behaviour of a military pilot in a cockpit, the study deals mainly with problems of arm movements.

Because FAERIE is a dynamic approach, movement simulations are obtained by applying forces and torques which are the **real causes** of movement. Volontary manikin movements are achieved using articular torques. This movement definition using joint torques will allows ergonomic studies and valuations.

This dynamic option is also useful to simulate special conditions, such as crash tests, and especially to simulate movements realized under external acceleration. This last point is useful to simulate pilot's behaviour.

One of FAERIE's advantages is to be completely **integrated** in the CAD/CAM system. The FAERIE function can be used as any other CAD/CAM function during the design process.

The designer will be able to put the manikin on the seat and to simulate some fundamental pilot's movements. The designer **himself** will be able to state visually on the natural aspect of the simulated movement, because of the graphic possibilities of CAD/CAM systems. **Graphic simulation and visual estimation** are first steps of **ergonomic valuation.** Mostly, the visual estimation is adequate to define position of aircraft controls and their natural accessability.

2. CAD/CAM PROPOSAL

A lot of CAD/CAM users, having similar needs, have developed some specific tools. For a complete comparative analysis, it may be useful to refer to existing studies (Badler et al. 1979, Dooley et al. 1982). These approachs are distinguished by some fondamental choices and by possibilities which are more and less present in each developed tool.

They are usually composed of a manikin and a set of basic functions required for their use. The manikin is made of a set of segments representative of the human body segments. These segments are connected to each other by joints and they are organized as a tree.

One of the common possibilities consists of modifying the manikin by changing angular parameters value on every degree of freedom. It is then possible to distinguish between the translation/rotation of the whole manikin considered then as a no-deformable solid (6 d.o.f. of the root segment), and the deformation of the manikin, modifying articular parameters, the root remaining motionless.

The visualization tools of CAD/CAM systems procure such a comfort of analysis that the power of an ergonomic valuation function is increased. Thus, changing of viewpoint, quality of visualization (hidden lines removal, shadding, ...) and the possibilities of measuring geometric elements (distance between body parts and a hazardous area) are some other possible uses of the function.

3. MANIKIN MOVEMENTS

The ability to define a position is not sufficient to check the feasibility of an action. Some times, it is useful to check the movement by realizing the defined action. So, different tools capable of generating, automatically or imanually, some position have been developed. These positions can be applied successively to the manikin in order to form a pseudo-movement.

We can separate functions in two main categories. The first are functions including basic elements in order to reduce the number of parameter the user has to determine. The second kind of functions is based on inverse geometric methods. Because of the redundance of degrees of freedom, there is an infinite number of solutions. Thus, the user must complete the problem description by defining constraints. The computation of several configurations including constraints evolution can provide successive positions defining a pseudo-movement (Badler et al. 1987, Klein et al 1983, Zelter et al. 1982). These methods are close to robotic ones. They can't be quite satisfying for the human robot because of the problem of "natural".

Functions currently operational are limited to these possibilities. Number of geometric studies can already be done. They are nevertheless limited because of the difficulty to define an action. In some cases, the user doesn't know the right constraint to define in order to get an acceptable configuration. Finally, these functions are only geometric tools.

One type of approach to motion are analogical ones. They are used in fields such as animation (Cabezas 1989) or medicine. We can discern **rotoscopy** (Ginsberg et al. 1983) and **goniometry** (Cousins et al 1979). Quality of results obtained these ways is remarkable. Nevertheless these methods have two major disadvantages. The first of them is the necessity to use heavy and uncomfortable equipment. Another disadvantage is the need for a man to record movements and it is more restrictive. The man must be able to perform the wanted movement. In case of specific movements which require learning and training (technical motion, sports, ...) the man himself must be a specialist of the movement in order to teach it to the manikin. In the same way, dangerous movement simulations are impossible. An aircraft ejection, a car accident, every dangerous situation either for the man or for the equipment can't be simulated.

An other type of approach is based on a movement notation system. A comparison can be done with music writing. Notations look like scores where positions or displacements of segments or joints are written. Nowadays, several developments in different fields are using notational methods. These works consist on one hand in analysing movements, and on the other hand in movement generation to animate humanoid models according to given scores (Hutchinson 1970, Benesh 1956, Eshkol 1958, Strauss et al. 1977).

These techniques are interesting because they are a kind of solution to the movement specification problem. Nevertheless mastering such a system requires learning a quite complex notation system. These kinds of methods remain geometric ones.

Except for analogical techniques, movements are natural in so far as the user is able to estimate this natural in a given environment and if he masters the movement definition tool. This results in two alternatives : either the resulting movement is constrained by the used method and natural is then **included** in the method itself, or the user has a wide definition autonomy and natural is limited to his **judgment**.

4. METHODS

Methods can be classified according to the movement approach used. Thus, we can distinguish first of all **geometric** methods. These methods define a movement as a sequence of positions only geometrically specified. In the simplest methods, these positions are independent from one another. An evolution introduced continuity resulting then in path definition.

Kinematic methods distinguish themselves by notions of velocity and time. A set of configurations defined by positions and associated velocity (q_i and $\frac{dq_i}{dt}$) take the place of geometric positions. In the most advanced cases, the temporal parametrization is complete. Resulting movements are more realistic. We can naturally think of introducing the notion of acceleration in kinematic methods. These are **dynamic** methods. Methods including higher orders of derivation aren't used in practise.

With dynamic methods, a fundamental barrier is overcome. It is then possible to deal with causes of movement. The fundamental principle of dynamics expresses motion as result of forces and torques actions. We no more define movement but **causes** of motion. Even when third order terms are negligeable, the advantage of causality remains.

5. MOVEMENT PSYCHICAL ASPECT

Movement psychical aspects are the most difficult ones to isolate. This field is extremely wide. It is out of question to study in detail and to define completely human behaviour concerning volontary movements. We will restrict ourselves to the statement of some general and fundamental elements.

At the beginning of his life, a man is a baby. At this time, a man discovers the world around him. At first, this discovery is passive, but very soon, the man begans to manage interactions with his environment. It's the beginning of a very long **learning** by experience.

During his first years, the child becomes conscious of his body and he learns to move his limbs in space. Thus, gradually, the brain integrates data relating to muscle and movement co-ordination. As a little child, his movements are blunt, inaccurate and badly controlled. Gradually, he learns to master his movements. This mastery is very accurate. We all reach such a level of control that we are able to **optimize** our movements.

The first optimization is energetic. We learn to avoid useless efforts, and no to spend too much energy for a given movement. Thus we use the inertia of our arm when we want to grasp something. We know efforts to apply in order to precisely reach the thing to grasp. We don't have to stop our arm to immobilize it. Everything happens as if the arm ends its displacement with its momentum and stops itself. In fact, we use the inertia of our arm and articular friction in an optimal way.

When we decid to grasp something, we have first looked at it. Then we develop the necessary efforts to grasp it. We do this without preliminary practice. Visual inspection is enough. Our brain is able to use its knowledge to **forecast**. We know how to evaluate necessary efforts ourselves before performing the movement. The human machine is so perfect that we develop nearly optimum efforts from the first performance. Forecasting possibilities of our brain are quite asthonishing. There are these possibilities we use to grasp a moving ball for example.

Some authors have studied motion planning theories. According to Sakitt (1980) and Hogan (1985), the brain's functioning is mainly and fundamentally **associative.** The brain stores a lot of **equivalences** between hand positions (reachable points) and arm configurations obtained at the end of the reaching movement of these positions. Afterwards, when we want to reach any point, our brain uses stored associations around this point to do a kind of interpolation of the final arm configuration.

To each arm configurations is associated a muscular state of all the arm muscles. The muscular configuration is one of the brain control techniques. Mussa et al. (1988) and Flash et al. (1985) express the hypothesis the actual movement planning (producing of control orders) is done in the same space as the movement performance one : the **muscular** space.

The brain associative memory is so powerful that there is no execution feedback during motion. Movement is realized in an **open loop**. It is only when movement is completed that a checking process is engaged. If the checking procedure reveals an error, a correction is done (Green 1982).

One remarks that this schema explains relatively well our disappointement when we perform a movement under conditions other than ordinary earth gravity (weightlessness or variable acceleration). In this case, our stored associations are no longer valid. That's why we are then unskillful. We are then in the same conditions as the little child during the training phase. After a time of practise under such conditions, we are able again to find new valid associations and to be skillful (astronauts, divers, ...).

6. THE REALISM

The problem of realism is a crucial one. Every ergonomic valuation function has to deal with it. The validity of such a function is totally based first of all on natural, on the natural look of the manikin behaviour.

It is impossible to define a natural movement in absolute. Natural itself is not definable. The only approach to have is to consider a simulated movement as natural if a man performs the same movement, under the same conditions. From this point of view, natural is not measurable.

Contrary to robotics, the problem is to find, not only one manikin movement, but THE ONE which will be qualified as natural. The question is then to quantify the conformity of a movement with the natural one. Every movement quantification attempt is based on an objective function definition. This function, among others parameters, includes an achievement movement evaluation and natural representating parameters. This equational representation is of course very difficult and none of the many attempts is completely satisfying.

The most commonly gauge of natural admitted is **comfort**. The simplest methods use articular comfort areas in the same way as ergonomic tables to define the least uncomfortable posture. Other kinds of methods attempt to quntify this still indefinite notion of comfort.

One of the most commonly approved hypothesis is to have an **energetic approach** of comfort. The more energy consuming a position is, the less such a position is felt comfortable. A minimum of energetic consumption will reveal a near natural position. In case of several energetic minima, it can be necessary to include influence of other factors (obstacles, ...) to reduce the number of possible solutions. Natural then becomes dependent on external conditions. Energy taken in account here is mechanical and physiological. Muscular actions, articular energy effeciency must be modelled.

Energy consumption is also a gauge of natural of movement. We unconsciously optimize our movements to reduce energy consumption. Here arise optimization problems. The first difficulty is to define which factors have to be optimized to generate a natural movement (Wells 1988, Nelson 1983). It is a common idea that an optimized movement is the least jerky possible, in other words, the path is the smoothest possible (Morasso 1983, Hatze 1976).

The main optimization difficulty is that a movement must be optimized in its globality. Most of generative methods can only optimize movements step by step during generation. But a local optimization on each step doesn't result in a global optimization on the whole movement. It is obvious that a natural movement isn't only optimized step by step. Thus it is necessary to **optimize** the **whole movement**.

7. THE FAERIE PROJECT

Dynamic Why : As we have explained before, realism must be included in any method. This is a result of the necessity to impose as little ergonomic knowledge as possible to the function user. The idea is to submit the manikin to the fundamental law governing motion : the fundamental law of dynamics. This approach, already used in realistic animation (Whilhelms 1987) is then more useful in behaviour simulation. Man being modelled as a poly-articulated chain of solids, the goal is to model the behaviour of such a system in time, in terms of applied efforts. Behaviour realism and natural result from simulating natural and physiological laws which rule humain behaviour. Movement results from cause transformation by a physical law. If the set of causes is valid, realism is then certain.

One more interesting aspect of the dynamic approach is to be able to compute external and internal efforts applied on the manikin. The use of a physiological evaluation system will provide ergonomic data. Thus, it is possible to access mechanical and muscular human measurements. We can verify that neither body or muscular-stringy breaking limits or physiological limits (maximum muscular effort developable) are overstepped. It is possible to quantify several abstract notions such as fatigue, comfort of a position or of a movement. The utility of this ergonomic aspect alone justifies the use of a dynamic approach.

Another interest of the dynamic approach is to allow taking gravity effects in account. Gravity effects are not very important in common movements (except comfort and fatigue factors) but they are fundamental in cases of aircraft cockpit design where external accelerations from 2 to 5 g in variable directions are common.

Realization : The aim of the FAERIE project is carrying out a InteractivE, Real Time, Anthropometric and Ergonomic evaluation Function integrated in a CAD/CAM system. This function will be able to simulate the behaviour of a man in his environment. One of the contribution of this function will be the solving of physiological ergonomic problems. Zimmermann (1991) can be a useful reference for further information.

Designers are looking to check various possible interactions between a manikin and its environment. Contacts and collisions are then fundamental, but designers may also wish to visualize such manikin external action effects as holding a load or external accelerations (Zimmermann and Coppin 1990).

It is possible to discern major application types. On one hand, a real experimentation will not involve any danger or risk for the human test subject (position checking) and on the other hand, experiments are dangerous (i.e. crash tests). In first case, a human is quite satisfying. An instrumented inert manikin is necessary for dangerous experiments. Nevertheless, in this last case, only ballistic passive movements can be studied.

FAERIE allows voluontary actions simulations without using any human test subject, even if danger is obvious. Figure 1 shows FAERIE contributions according to dangerous/non dangerous applications and voluntary/passive movements classification.

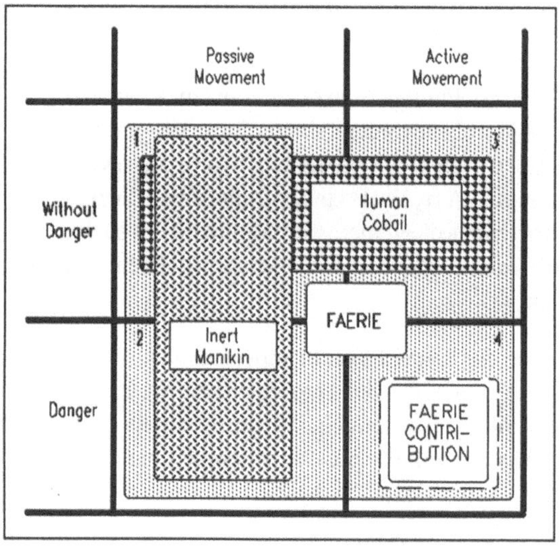

Fig 1 : FAERIE contributions

Manikins used in FAERIE are modelled as poly-articulated chains. Nowadays, manikins are made of 17 segments and 16 joints. This definition can be modified to increase model precision. An example of the manikin used is illustrated by fig 2.

Joints connecting segments to each other are modelled by knee-joints (3 d.o.f.). All joints are the same at first. Articular limits are then defined, either in order to restrict possible articular motion, or to neutralize one or more d.o.f.

Every external efforts applied on each manikin segment are introduced by defining the resulting torsor on each segment. Gravity field (constant field) can be defined in the function and any external acceleration can also be applied.

The manikin environment is mostly already defined. It's simply the numerical geometrical CAD/CAM system model. For contacts, a simple model is now used. This model is necessary to compute reaction efforts and to apply the resulting torsor to concerned manikin segments. This model is based on the spring-dumping concept. A more precise and complex model based on quantity of motion is now under development.

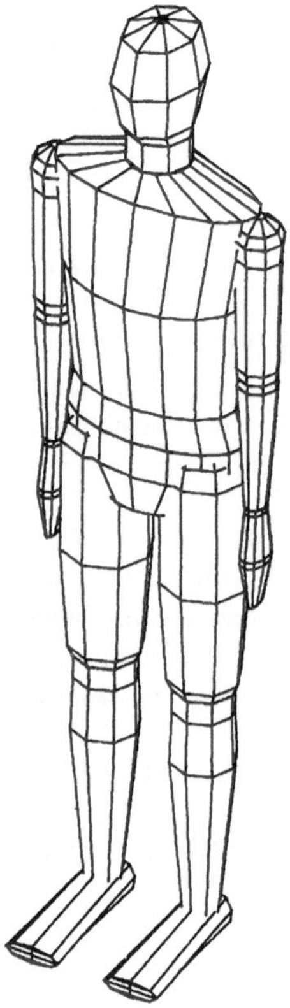

Fig 2 : Mannikin

8. MOVEMENT CLASSIFICATION - STATIC MODEL

It is nowadays impossible to build a universal movement model, usable for every kind of natural movement simulations. We propose an approach consisting in dividing the movement world in several kinds of typical movements. A typical kind of movement would include arm reaching movement of elements or commands at such a distance that the shoulder does't move. Another class would include arm movement coupled with bust movement, and so on.

Models we have developed for a few kinds of movement can be easily extended and used to the simulation of others classes. Our first aim is to deal with the case of a pilot in an aircraft cockpit. With a few kind of movement, it is possible to treat simple, but fundamental cases of cockpit design. The reachability of a control, the possiblity to pull a handle are fundamental preoccupations for designers.

The first movement simulation problem we have to face to is the determination of the movement final configuration. In general, only the goal of the movement is known, the final arm configuration being a result of the simulation. We have seen before that realism must be independent from the user. Thus, this one has not to determine himself the final arm configuration. The system must determine it automatically in the objective of realism. That's why we have developed a model we call a static muscular model. It is used to determine the entire final movement configuration.

Static Model : As we have seen before, a minimal energy consumption is our way of evaluating natural of a static configuration. The natural configuration results from muscular stretching used to hold the position and of the gravity force's action.

In a static study, only elastic muscular characteristics are useful. Our model define a pair of muscles equivalent to a real muscular system on every degree of freedom. These muscles have stiffness and slack length which are typical elastic parameters. For every movement class defined, these parameters are experimentally evaluated on a representative movement. In our field of reaching movements, several simplications can be made :

- The hand is almost always in line with the forearm.

- Shoulder and hand (so wrist) being fixed, the only remaining unknown is the elbow position. Possible elbow positions are located on a circle.

In such a case, we can reduce the problem to the shoulder joint. The wrist and the elbow joint don't have any influence on the elbow position on the circle. Thus, we only need to model the shoulder muscles and reduce parameters to 6 stiffness and 6 slack lengh.

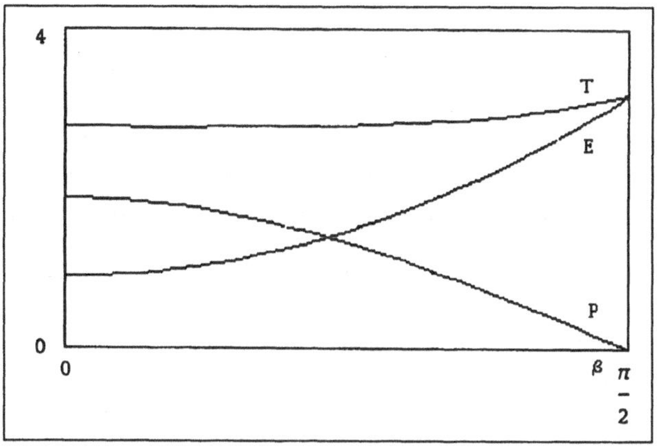

Fig 3 : Energy Evolution. P is the curve representing the potential gravity energy, E the elastic energy and T the total mechanical energy.

Figure 3 shows the evolution of mechanical gravity energy, muscular elastic energy and total mechanical energy with the elbow position on the circle. The situation parameter β is the angle defined by the plane of the arm and the forearm and the vertical plane including the center of the shoulder and center of the wrist. Total energy minimum provides natural configuration.

9. MOVEMENT MODEL

Muscles are powerful human body organs. The balance between efforts applied on a body segment and muscular forces sets the joint position related to this segment. One modifies his joints' configuration by modifying the set of muscular efforts applied.

A direction of current investigation (Hasan 1986) consists in defining a movement as a displacement of this balance. A stable position is then a degenerate movement where the equilibrium point displacement is non-existant. Thus, there is no more discontinuity between worlds of static and dynamic, between holding a position and movement. Movement is a process allowing transformation of a position into another, or in other words allowing transformation of a muscular equilibrium into another.

Elastic muscular properties are used to elaborate a joint stiffness based model. Apparent joint stiffness results of the actions of all muscles (agonists, antagonists, fixing, neutralizing) activity on this joint. We have based our model on the following equation :

$$\mu = \sigma(\theta - \theta_e) \qquad (1)$$

where μ is the joint torque, σ the apparent joint stiffness, θ the joint angle and θ_e represents the equilibrium point position.

Z. Hasan's works attempt to study and define the behaviour of the equilibrium point during an unperturbed movement. Time evolution of θ_e and σ value are determined according to global movement optimization criteria. This work has been successfully applied to one isolated degree of freedom.

We implemented this model and we use it to simulate movements of a whole human arm modelled in FAERIE with 7 degrees of freedom. The model (1) is the basis of control efforts generation used in movement simulation.

A stiffness σ is associated to each d.o.f. of each joint. For every arm movement, we have to deal with 7 stiffness, 7 equilibrium points and 7 joint angles. It results in 7 elementary joint torques. For each d.o.f., control torque is that which causes the voluntary state change of the associated component of the affected joint.

One of the Hazan's basic hypotheses is that movement will not be perturbed during its realization. This implies all other joints be motionless. For example, in case of elbow flexion, shoulder and wrist mustn't be moving. If not, (movement of several joints, interaction between segments, ...) some driving and inertia effects will perturb elbow evolution. In our case of movement of all arm segments, we have to take all these causes of perturbation in account. Torques necessary to driving and inertia effect compensation are computed all during motion and they are added to control torques. So, in the example of a shoulder movement, some compensation torques appear at the wrist and at the elbow. These torques are representative of the cohesion fixing muscles actions.

As a matter of fact, when we're performing a movement, part of the muscular effort is used to balance interference joint deformations due to other segments motion (Hollerbach et al. 1982). Control efforts are added to these efforts. Control efforts generate voluntary displacements. Holding efforts are also added to these two previous kinds of efforts. These last ones balance gravity effects. In case of unperturbed movements, the joint resulting torque applied is :

$$T_{sum} = T_{hold} + T_{inertia} + T_{control} \qquad (2)$$

If movement is perturbed, equation (2) becomes during perturbation :

$$T_{sum} = T_{hold} + T_{inertia} + T_{control} + T_{pertub} \qquad (3)$$

After perturbation, equation (2) remains valid. Control torques and inertia balancing efforts depend on the kind of perturbation (external acceleration variation, collision, ...) and how man reacts in presence of perturbation.

Model (1) provides articular control torques. Holding torques and balancing inertia effects have to be computed during mtion. This computation is easy because of the dynamic module of FAERIE.

Until now, d.o.f. are considered as mutually independent, and a joint can affect other joints only by inertia effects. In fact, there are coupling effects between d.o.f. and even between joints. These coupling effects have physiological origins (Winters et al. 1985, Wells 1988). Some muscles are fixed on three or more body segments. Some others are fixed on non-consecutive segments. A contraction of such a muscle affects more than one joint. This can have several kinds of consequences such as deformation of the "theoretiical" articular path. Some coupling actions are usually balanced by antagonist and neutralizing muscles. The actual energy consumption is then greater than what we can expect. Model (1) allows two kinds of coupling : stiffness coupling and torque coupling. In any case, coupling effect coefficients have to be defined for each kind of movement. Stiffness coupling is equivalent to the co-ordination phenomenon in complex movements. Torque coupling is due to physiology. Multi-joint muscles are almost always used in movements. Looking for natural in simulated movements implies taking coupling effects in account. Coupling effects can be written in matrix form as shown in fig 4a and fig 4b.

$$[\mu] = [\sigma].([\theta]-[\theta_e])$$

with :

$$[\sigma] = \begin{bmatrix} [\sigma_1] & [\sigma_{1/2}] & \cdots & [\sigma_{1/n}] \\ [\sigma_{2/1}] & [\sigma_2] & \cdots & [\sigma_{2/n}] \\ \cdot & \cdot & \cdots & \cdot \\ [\sigma_{n/1}] & [\sigma_{n/2}] & \cdots & [\sigma_n] \end{bmatrix} \qquad [\sigma_i] = \begin{bmatrix} \sigma_{ix} & \sigma_{ixy} & \sigma_{ixz} \\ \sigma_{iyx} & \sigma_{iy} & \sigma_{iyz} \\ \sigma_{izx} & \sigma_{izy} & \sigma_{iz} \end{bmatrix}$$

$[\sigma_i]$: segment i matrix

$[\sigma_{i/j}]$: segment i/j coupling matrix

σ_{ix}, σ_{iy}, σ_{iz} : main stiffness

σ_{ixy} : d.o.f. coupling stiffness

Fig 4a : Stiffness coupling

$$[\mu_c] = [C].[\mu]$$

with :

$$[C] = \begin{bmatrix} [C_1] & [C_{1/2}] & \cdots & [C_{1/n}] \\ [C_{2/1}] & [C_2] & \cdots & [C_{2/n}] \\ \cdot & \cdot & \cdots & \cdot \\ [C_{n/1}] & [C_{n/2}] & \cdots & [C_n] \end{bmatrix} \qquad [C_i] = \begin{bmatrix} C_{ix} & C_{ixy} & C_{ixz} \\ C_{iyx} & C_{iy} & C_{iyz} \\ C_{izx} & C_{izy} & C_{iz} \end{bmatrix}$$

$[C_i]$: segment i matrix

$[C_{i/j}]$: segment i/j coupling matrix

C_{ix}, C_{iy}, C_{iz} : main torques

C_{ixy} : d.o.f. coupling torques

Fig 4b : Torque coupling

10. RESULTS AND FUTURE WORKS

Using the FAERIE dynamic module, we can know at every simulation time every physical value of position, velocitie, acceleration and effort of each manikin segment. Figure 5a and 5b shows angular displacement of a real experimented reaching movement. Curves obtained by simulation are shown in fig 6a and 6b. The simulation has been made without joint coupling. It appears from examining curves that simulation results are satisfying : the angular evolution is quite similar in the two cases. In the simulated results, the speed is not exactly null at the end of the movement. This is due to the model used. The model used in this simulation is intentionally the simplest one. We have now developed a more complete model and the velocity is now quite null at the end of the movement.

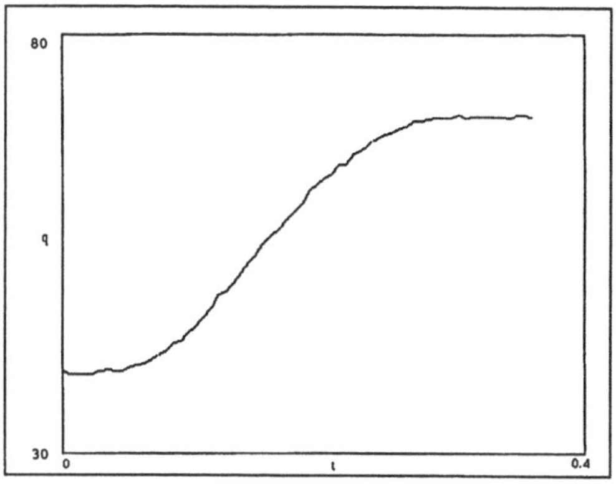

Fig 5a : Experimental results (shoulder antepulsion d.o.f.)

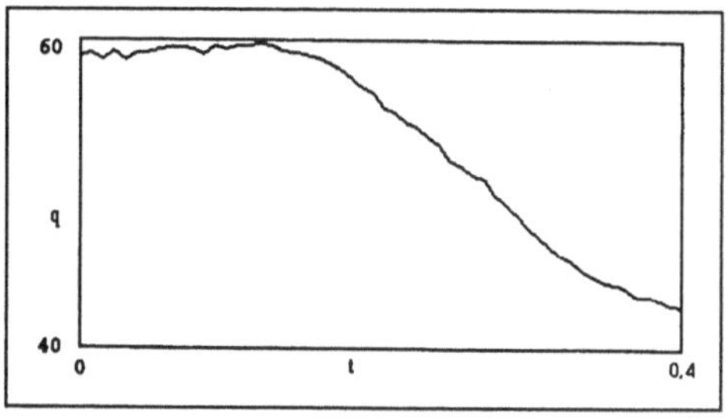

Fig 5b : Experimental results (forearm flexion d.o.f)

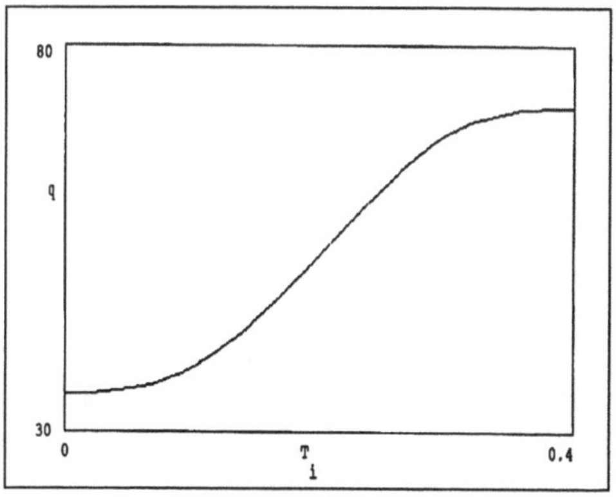

Fig 6a : Simulation results (shoulder antepulsion d.o.f.)

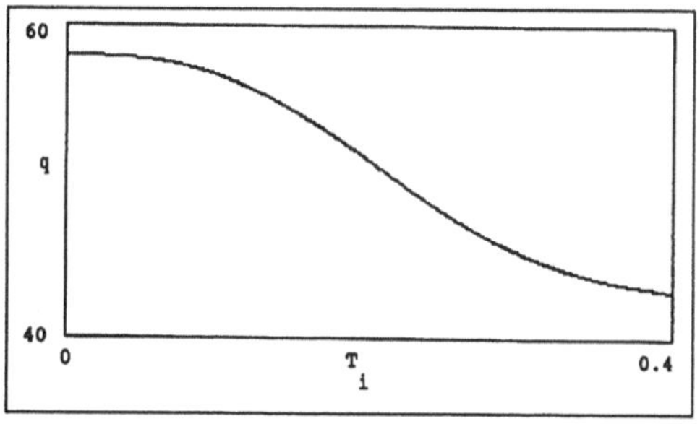

Fig 6b : Simulation results (forearm flexion d.o.f)

Differences between simulated and experimental articular paths can be observed. These differences are mainly due to joint coupling effects. These effects are now under development and they are being included in the muscular effort generation module. Nevertheless, we can note that the visual aspect of the simulation is already satisfying. Thus, FAERIE allows designers to have an initial evaluation of movement.

Simulations of movements under changing load factors are also possible. The control torque generation model is then combined with a feed-back system on the unperturbed movement. Practically, the unperturbed movement is simulated, then the perturbed movement, based on the first one. The feed-back system simulates the natural behaviour in such a case, trying to superpose the perturbed movement on the unperturbed one.

The simplest imaginable perturbation is weightlessness. The common earth gravity field (1g) is then constantly perturbed. The aim is then to simulate the behaviour of a man who isn't accustomed to the weightless state. His first reaction is to try to perform his movement as he is used to on earth. The lack of gravity causes a difference between the expected movement and the realized one. The movement is then rectified to achieve the aim. The muscular control efforts generation model allows simulation of this behaviour.

The developed models can be used in a wider field than the arm reaching movement. Physiological similarity between the arm and the leg facilitate the adaptation of this model to the leg movement case.

Parameters used in the models allow us to study movement performed under conditions other than the usual ones. It is possible to take psychological factors into account (panic, trained reflex motion, fear, tiredness, ...). In these cases, optimization criterian have to be redefined and theoretical paths aren't ruled by the same laws (Freund et al. 1978). For example, in the case of a trained reflex movement, one of the realization conditions is to speed up the limb as soon as possible and as quickly as possible. Some preliminary tests have been done using described models and results are quite promising.

The modular FAERIE structure also allows the integration of a movement planification and co-ordination module.

First level of planification is avoiding collisions and obstacles (Lecland 1991). In this field, problems are mainly due to the natural path definition difficulty depending on obstacle to avoid. With FAERIE, a complete path isn't necessary. It is enough to be able to define pass-through points. Planification consists then in hanging parts of path between pass-through points and final aim together. Muscular control generation module is then used several times between every defined points, until the aim (Flash 1985). Model modifications consist then in computing the equilibrium point path, taking into account that pass-through point velocities aren't null.

Co-ordination of simple actions is also imaginable. Thus, we can imagine the simulation of a driver who is changing gears. Co-ordination consists to define start and end time of the movements of the right hand and of the left foot.

Upper level co-ordination may also be imagined, but it implies the design of a higher level module than the muscular effort generation one. Nevertheless, the FAERIE structure easily allows such module integration. The problem is then to model the complex behaviour laws.

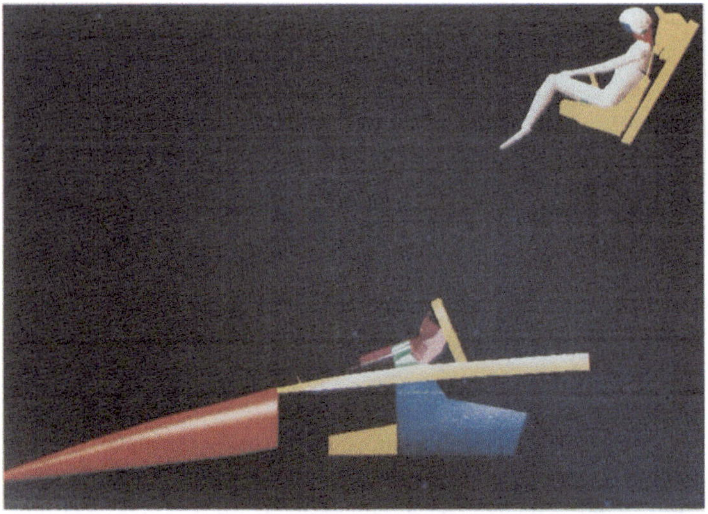

Pilot Ejection Simulation

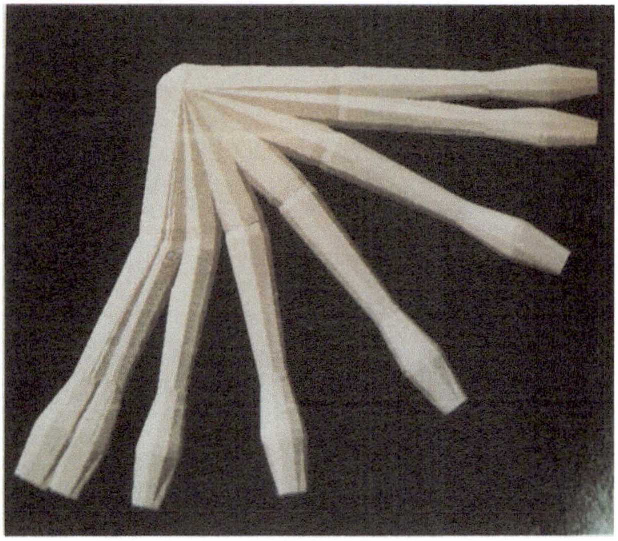

Arm Pendulation

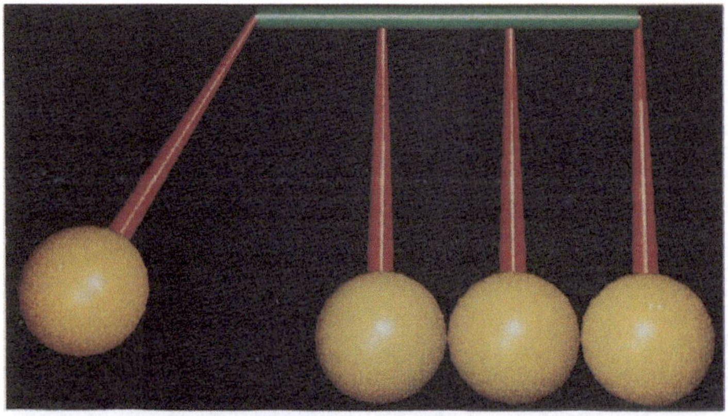

4 Balls Mobile Simulation : initial (contact model)

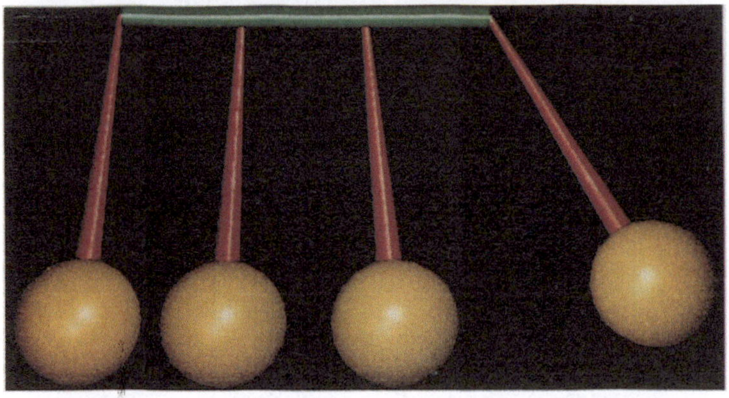

4 Balls Mobile Simulation : final

Ball Falling on ground (contact model)

ACKNOWLEDGEMENTS

Works presented in this paper are performed as a collaboration between the Laboratoire de Mécatronique of ISMCM/CESTI Saint Ouen-FRANCE, Dassault Aviation Saint Cloud-FRANCE and the Laboratoire d'Antropologie Appliquée Paris-FRANCE on a financial support of Service Technique des Programmes Aéronautiques Paris-FRANCE.

REFERENCES

N. Badler, S. Smoliar (1979) Digital Representation of Humain Movement, Computing Surveys Vol 11, No.1

N. Badler, K.H. Manoocheri, G. Walters (1987) Articulated Figure Positionning by Multiple Constraints, IEEE

R. and J. Benesh (1956) An Introduction to Benesh Dance Notation. A. and D. Black, London

R. Cabezas (1989) From Seoul To Barcelona, Computer Graphics and Animation, July 1989

S.J.Cousins, R.E. Hannah, J. Foort (1979) A Clinically Viable Electrogoniometer, 2nd Annual Int. Conf on Rehab. Eng, Atlanta, Georgia

M. Dooley (1982) Anthropomorphic Modeling Programs : a survey. Computer Graphics and Animation November 1982

N. Eshkol, R. Wachmann (1958) Movement Notation. Weidenfeld and Nicholson, London

T. Flash, N. Hogan (1985) The Co-ordination of Arm Movement : An Experimentally Confirmed Mathematical Model. J. of Neuroscience Vol 5, No 7 : 1688-1703

H.J. Freund, H.J. Büdingen (1978) The Relationship Between Speed And Amplitude of the Fastest Voluntary Contractions of Human Arm Muscles. Exp. Brain Res. 31: 1-12

C.M. Ginsberg, D. Maxwell (1983) Graphical Marionette. SIGGRAPH/SIGART Interdisciplinary Workshop in Motion : Representation and Perspective, Toronto, Canada, April 1983

E. Godaux, G. Chéron : Le mouvement. Medsi/Mc Graw Hill

P.H. Green (1982) Why Is It Easy To Control Your Arm? J. of Motor Behaviour Vol 14, No 4: 260-286

Z. Hasan (1986) Optimized Movement Trajectories And Joint Stiffness in Unperturbed, Inertially Loaded Movements. Biol. Cybern. 53: 373-382

H. Hatze (1976) The Complete Optimization of a Human Motion. Math. Bioscience 28: 99-135

N. Hogan (1985) The Mechanics of Multi-Joint Posture And Movement Control. Biol. Cybern 52: 315-331

J.M. Hollerbach, T. Flash (1982) Dynamic Interactions Between Limb Segment. Biol. Cybern 44: 67-77

A. Hutchinson (1970) Labanotation. Theatre Arts Books, New York

C.A. Klein, C.H. Huang (1983) Review of Pseudo Inverse Control For Use With Kimematically Redundant Manipulators. IEEE, Trans on System, Man and Cybernetics, Marsh/April 1983

P. Lecland (1991) Ergonomie et conception assistée par ordinateur : simulation des mouvements d'un bras anthropomorphe en présence d'obstacles. Thèse de doctorat Ecole Centrale de Paris

P. Morasso (1983) Three Dimentionam Arm Trajectories. Biol. Cybern 48: 187-194
F.A. Mussa Ivaldi, P. Morasso, R. Zaccaria : Kinematic Networks (1988) A Distributed Model. Biol. Cybern 60: 1-16
W.L. Nelson (1983) Physicals Principes for Economics of Skilled Movement. Biol. Cybern 46: 135-147
B. Sakitt (1980) A Spring Model and Equivalent Neural Network for Arm Posture Control. Biol. Cybern. 37: 227-234
G.B.Strauss, C.Wing, L. Yuen-wak (1977) Translated Excerpts of Chinese Dance Notation. Danse Research Jounal, Vol9
R.P. Wells (1988) Mechanical Energy Coast of Human Movement : An Approach To Evaluating The Transfert Possibilities. J. Biomechanics Vol 21, No 11: 955-964
J. Whilhelms (1987) Using Dynamic Analysis for Realistic Animation of Articulated Bodies, Computer Graphics and Animation, June 1987
J.M. Winters, L. Stark (1985) Analysis of Fundamental Human Movement Patterns Through the Use of In-Depth Antagonistic Muscle Models. IEEE, Trans. Biomec. Eng. BME32, N10
D. Zelter (1982) Motor Control Techniques For Figure Animation, Computer Graphics and Animation November 1982
A. Zimmermann (1991) Contribution à l'étude d'un outil d'ergonomie en environnement CFAO. Thèse de doctorat Ecole Centrale de Paris
A. Zimmermann, O. Coppin (1990) FAERIE : Vers une Fonction Anthropométrique d'Ergonomie temps Réel Interactive en CFAO. CSME Mechanical Engineering Forum, Toronto.
A. Zimmermann, O. Coppin (1990) FAERIE : Une Fonction Anthropométrique d'Ergonomie temps Réel Interactive en CFAO. Conférence ERGO'IA 90 Biarritz.

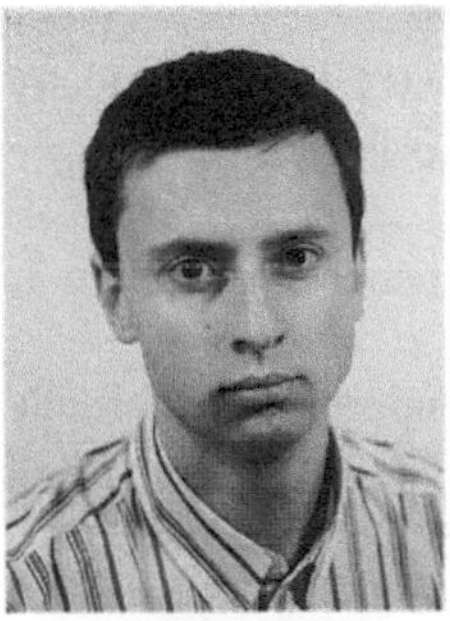

Olivier Coppin is a PHD student at Ecole Centrale des Arts et Manufactures de Paris (FRANCE). He received is D.E.A in automatics from Ecole Normale Superieure de l'Enseignement Technique de CACHAN (FRANCE) and his engineer diploma in mecanics from the Centre d'Etude Superieures des Techniques Industrielles de Saint-Ouen (FRANCE) in 1988. Since 1989 he's been working on the FAERIE project and more precisely on human behaviour simulation at the Mechatronic Laboratory of ISMCM/CESTI.
Address : Laboratoire de Mecatronique de L'ISMCM/CESTI, 3 Rue Fernand Hainaut, 93407 SAINT-OUEN CEDEX (FRANCE).

After a training in mechanics teaching at Ecole Normale Superieure de l'Enseignement Technique de CACHAN (FRANCE), Prof. André Clément worked in CAD/CAM research field. His PHD were concerning "Mechanisms Algebraic Structure in CAD/CAM Applications" and "Curves and Discrete Surfaces Generation and Control in Imprecise Mechanical Universe". He founded and he's managing the Mechatronics Laboratory of ISMCM, SAINT-OUEN (FRANCE) since 1980.
Since January 1992 he's been turning toward industrial research and is currently technical adviser attached to the general technical direction of Dassault-Systemes which develops the CAD/CAM program CATIA.
Address : Dassault-Systemes, 24-28 Avenue du Général de Gaulle - BP 310, 92156 SURESNES CEDEX (FRANCE).

Hand Motion Coding System for Algorithm Recognition and Generation

JINTAE LEE and TOSIYASU L. KUNII

ABSTRACT

The human hand is the versatile part of human limbs, that conducts not only some special action such as grasping but also very general motions such as writing and signing. A hand motion coding system for hand motion algorithm recognition and generation is introduced. The system that has been developed provides an efficient environment where a naive user without much programming knowledge can compose and code hand motion, and have the computer translate the score into an animated display of hands performing the coded motion. Fingerspelling, hand writing and directing have been generated as experiments by this system.

Keywords: hand animation, movement specification, motion coding

1. INTRODUCTION

In human animation, the complexity of motion may be arbitrarily divided into three parts: facial, hand and body animation. A great deal of attention has been devoted to facial animation and body animation, but very few scientific papers are dedicated to animating hands. The two major problems that must be addressed in producing realistic human hand animation are related to hand modelling and hand motion specification. In hand animation, most of the research has been centered around the modelling aspect. Three specific attempts are those by Catmull, Badler, and Thalmann(Catmull 1972; Badler 1982; Thalmann 1988). Thalmann presented algorithms that compute deformation of the hands and also dealt with hand grasping(Thalmann 1988). A human hand is the versatile part of human limbs, that conducts not only some special action such as grasping but also very general motions such as writing and signing. This research is aiming at the development of a hand motion coding system for hand motion algorithm recognition and generation.

The discussion in this paper is organized as follows. The next section presents the requirements for the hand motion coding system. Section 3 explains the components of HAND, the hand motion coding system that has been developed for this requirements, and the summarization of notational system. Section 4 shows some results of experiments. Section 5 concludes this paper.

2. REQUIREMENTS FOR HAND MOTION CODING SYSTEM

The movement data of objects is often available in the form of very large and complex visual information. We recognize 4D algorithms from this visual information and code them into an analyzable form. The coded algorithm may be analyzed and refined to capture expert skills in a course of action. If we improve the algorithms, it leads to improved skills(Kunii, 1992).

Then what are the requirements for a good coding system? Musical score gives an insight into the design of an ideal motion coding system. Current musical scores can support musicians in three kinds of processes satisfactorily. Initially, when a composer or a player comes up with a musical idea, he represents his idea in musical notations on a score(*coding*). Then he reviews the score and refines it over time until he gets a satisfiable score(*refinement*). The final score is performed as music by a player(*performance*). It is in this way that musicians make use of musical scores.

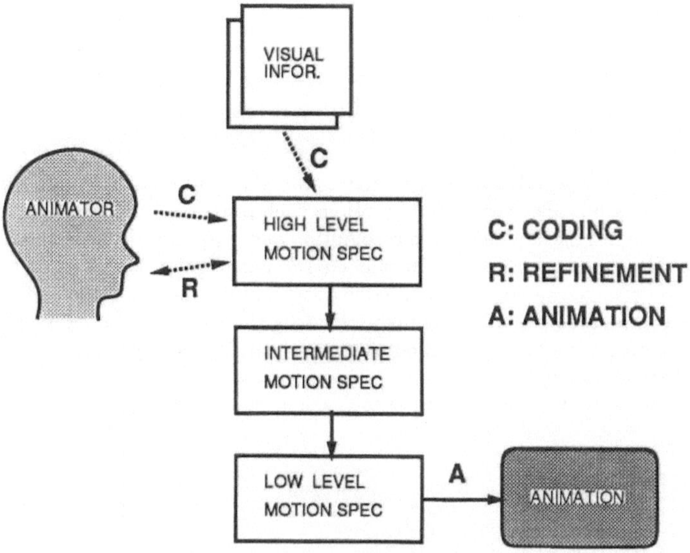

Fig. 1. The composition model of hand motion coding system

There are many similiarities between the way a musician composes music and the way an animator codes movement. We designed our coding system so that it may support the user in his *coding, refinement* and *animation* of hand motion as much as possible. The model of our hand motion coding system, the composition model, is shown in figure 1. Film or videotape can help an animator code hand motion. Or an animator may use his own imagination to code and refine hand motion. Then the computer can generate animation from the coded motion specification. The specification becomes hierarchical to make it possible for the computer to process the low level specification interpreted from the higher level specifications.

The hierarchical structure of specification is also an important tool for learning and problem solving. The casual or novice user, unfamiliar with the details of the underlying structure may observe and interact with the animation, while the sophisticated user will be able to analyze the simulation to find which factors gave rise to a given phenomena. Providing the means to move smoothly between levels can allow the novice to become expert as he gains confidence in understanding a computational model at each level. In the hierarchy of movement specification, the low level is a complete realization of the composition as a fully rendered animation. It comprises detailed geometric instructions for each limb segment. These instructions may be accessible to the animator especially for "fine tuning". Because the high level specification is an abstracted form, the specification becomes more concrete as details are added and the process moves to lower levels. The intermediate level should fill the gap between the two extreme levels. The detail explanation of our coding system is discussed in next section.

3. DESIGN OF HAND

Figure 2 shows the components of HAND(Hand Animation Notator and Displayer) system. The whole process may be divided into two stages: *coding stage* in which a user creates a score using the H-editor on the screen, and *animation stage* in which hand animation is generated by interpreting the corresponding score.

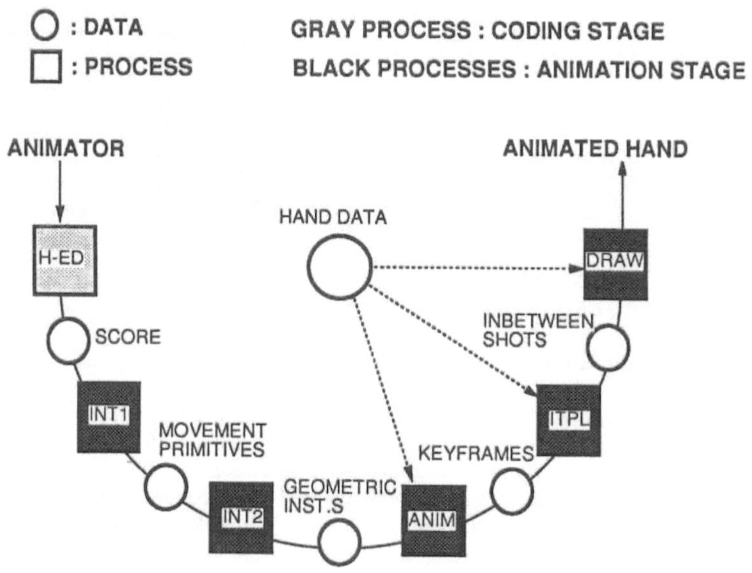

Fig. 2. Components of HAND

3.1 Modellization

The human hand is structured in three levels: the bone, the net of the muscles and the deformable and continuous skin. The bones linked at the joints do not change in size, and they serve as constraints to the control points of the deformations on the skin. When the fingers are bent, deformation occurs in the surfaces on the bone. The type of data and level of detail included in a human hand model is dictated by its purpose. The model developed here is to serve as a graphical tool for real-time human hand simulation, and an aid to assessment of hand motion coding. We have tried to achieve a balance between realism and accuracy on one hand and conceptual simplicity and adequate performance on the other.

The hand model used in our study has a two level structure, i.e skeleton and simplified surfaces. The hand skeleton used contains 20 rigid segments and 16 joints, shown in figure 3. The size of the hand segments may be varied individually or collectively, either in accordance with specific hand data or population percentiles. On our simplified surfaces, the deformations of the hands are omitted except the great muscle inflation at the interdigital cleft between the metacarpals of the thumb and the index. Either the skeleton or the surfaces or both may be displayed depending on user requirements for speed vs. realism(Fig. 4).

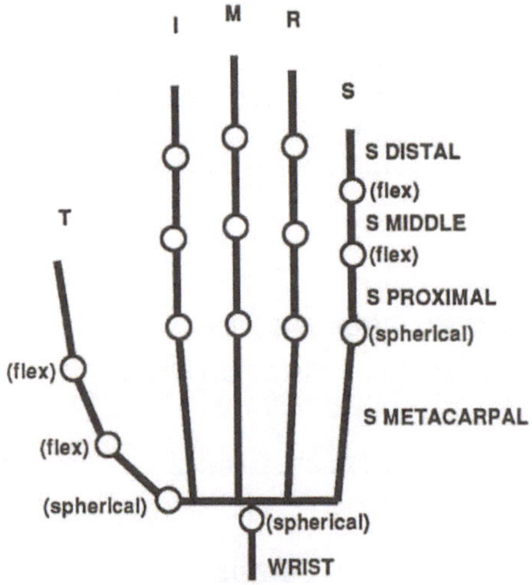

Fig. 3. Hand Model

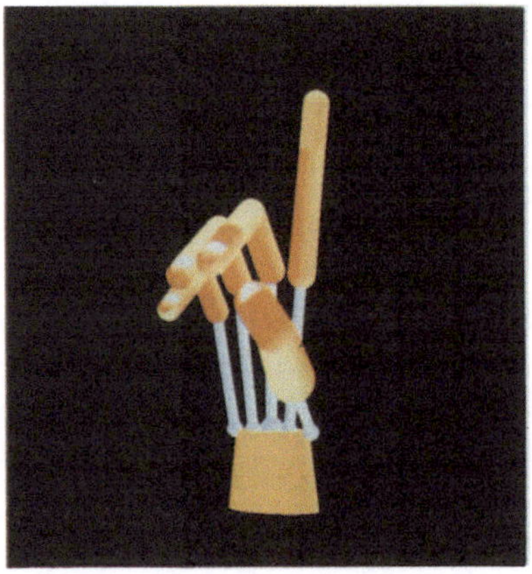

Fig. 4. Skeleton and simplified surfaces

3.2 Motion Specification

The notation-based approach is chosen for hand motion coding in our system. Notational approaches are not new to the movement specification; they were used for recording dance as early as 1920's(Hutchinson 1970) and many computer scientists have been developing computer-based systems to edit or interpret them(Badler 1979; Calvert 1978; Savage 1977). Their application to hand animation, however, has not been exploited. The following are at least three points significant in our notational system design.

1. The notational system is simple and intuitive enough to faciliate *coding, refinement*, and *animation* processes. Although a number of movement notation systems have been invented, many of them are not in substantial use because they are too complex to master.

2. The task of making a score is made easy by the support of an intelligent notation editor. The animator is able to test the score as well as enter, update and save it. Writing scores is one of the most time-consuming and laborious tasks. Our own experience has shown that more than half of the animation development time is spent for refinement of motion specification.

3. The human hand often contacts objects with grasping or moving. The notational description is inadequate in defining objects. In our study, objects are defined by high level programs and these are combined with notational descriptions in an orderly way.

We call the unit of an animation description as a *score*. A *score* is composed of sequences of *scenes* and *statements*. The statements are high level program modules, and the scenes are bundles of hand motions described by notation. A *scene* is divided into (key) *frames* that are considered as key picture units. Figure 5 shows the organization and an example of a score.

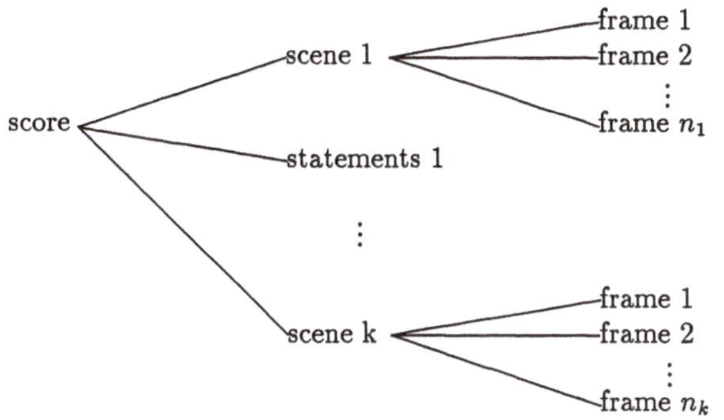


```
define-obj(ball);
scene(grasp-ball);
grasp-obj(ball);
scene(draw-ball);
moving-obj(ball,v);
scene(sec-motion);
/*arguments of
scene are seq.s
of frames repre-
sented by Hand-
notation */
```

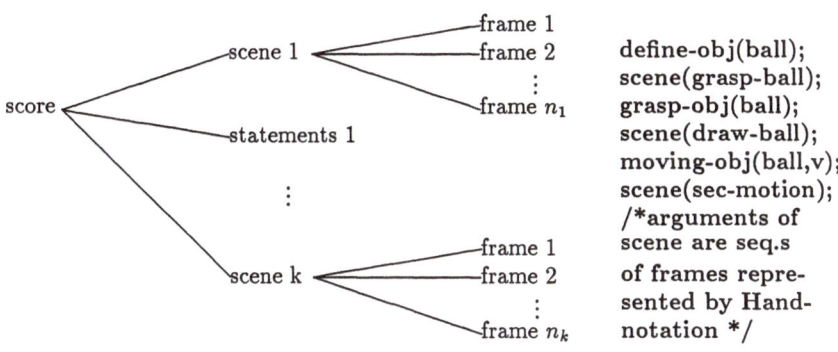

Fig. 5. Organization of a score

3.3 Handnotation

Handnotation is a notational system specially designed for hand shape description. Elements composing a hand motion are 1)hand configuration, 2)orientation, 3)location, and 4)duration time. Configuration is described by the bending states of fingers. Orientation is indicated by the directions of the fingers(strictly, by the direction of the metacarpal bone of the middle finger) and the palm.

Figure 6 is a representative sample of the notation; it is written on staves read from the top to the bottom. A stave represents motions of a hand. The staves are divided into measures that we call frames. The frames are numbered for correlation with corresponding frames of other staves. Each frame is divided into fields within which the elementary motion symbols are written. Figure 7 shows some of the basic Handnotation symbols. All the symbols are designed to help *coding* and *refinement* process of the user as much as possible.

As Handnotation is a high level specification, each and every joint is not counted as data element at this level. In principle, if the user wants to specify the angle of a specific joint that can not be specified by Handnotation, he must go down to a lower level specification.

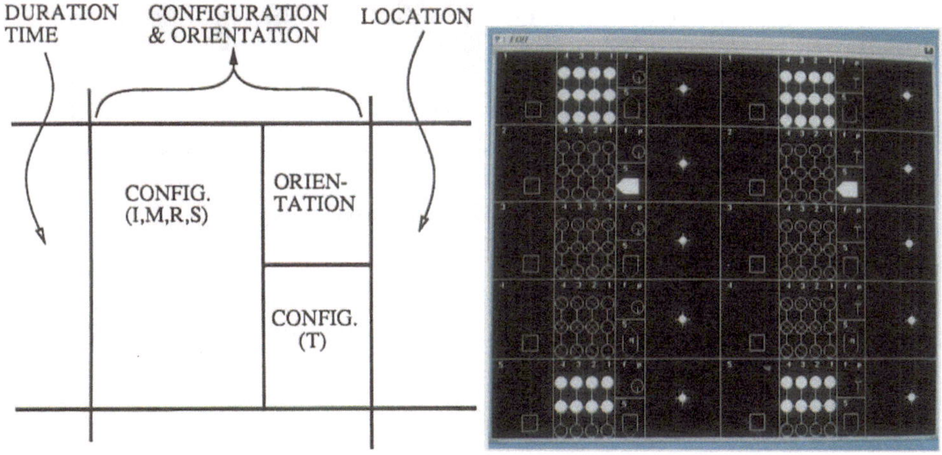

Fig. 6. Example of Handnotation

Hand configuration is represented by the bending states of the thumb and the other four fingers indicated by the bending symbols.

4 FINGERS CONFIGURATION

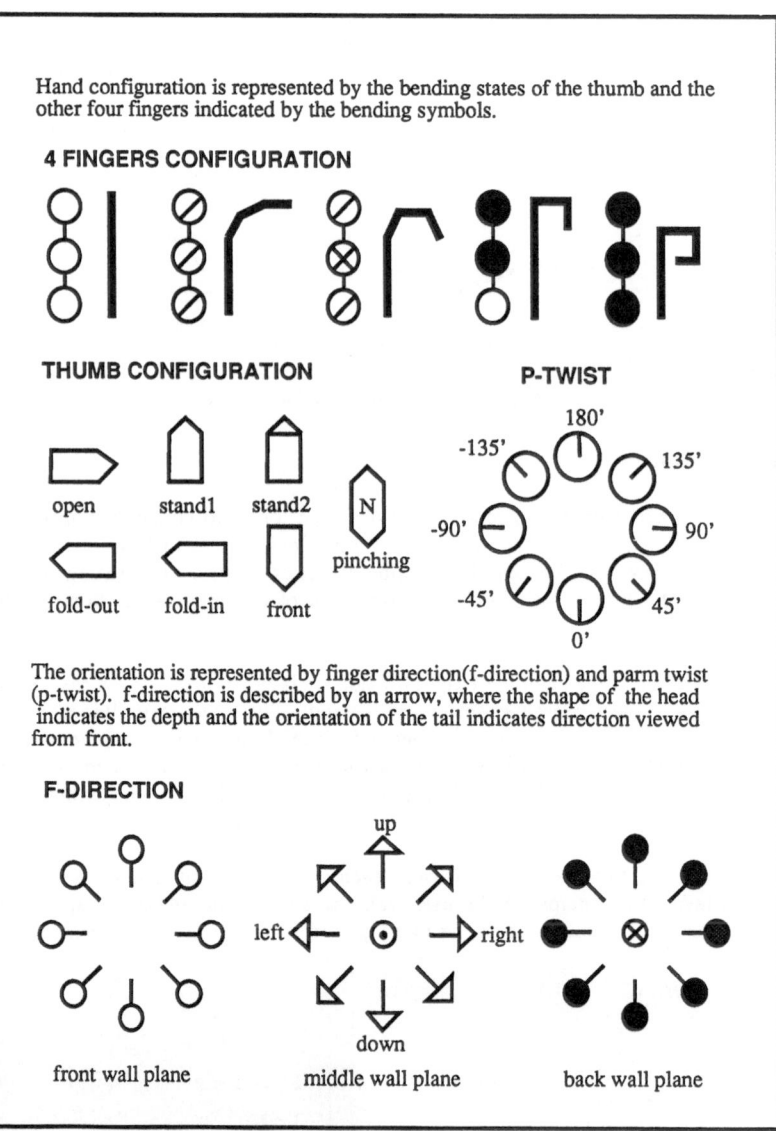

THUMB CONFIGURATION **P-TWIST**

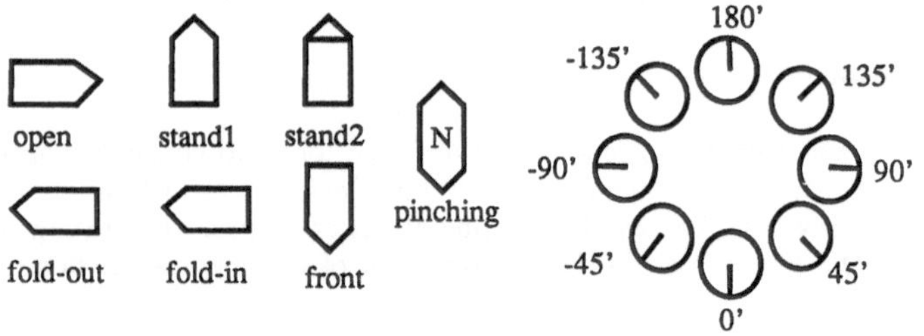

The orientation is represented by finger direction(f-direction) and parm twist (p-twist). f-direction is described by an arrow, where the shape of the head indicates the depth and the orientation of the tail indicates direction viewed from front.

F-DIRECTION

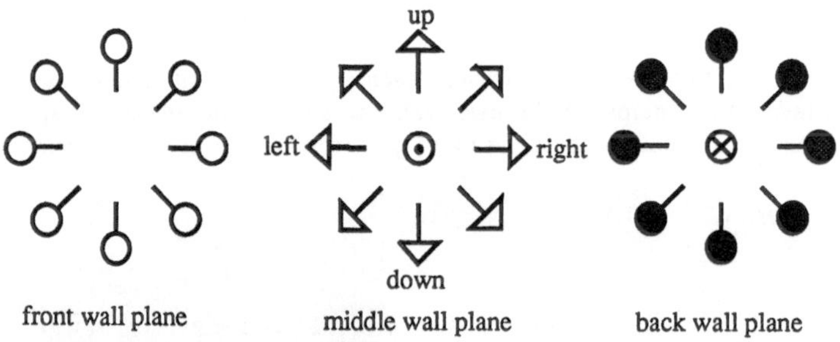

Fig. 7. Basic symbols of Handnotation

3.4 Notation Editor

Altering the scores is one of the most frequent and laborious tasks. This demand has precipitated the need for a simple, intelligent editor to enter, update and test the scores. The H-editor is specially designed for this purpose. Editing can be done interactively in command mode or in display mode.

In command mode, the H-editor reads command lines from the keyboard and processes it. It works by reading the score file on the command into an internal buffer, displaying and modifying the buffer contents by other commands, then writing all or part of the buffer to score files also on command. The format of a command to the H-editor is:

[frame [,frame]] operation [parameter]

The available operations are:

r *score*	read *score*
w *score*	write *score*
i	insert a frame
d	delete a frame
m	move frames
p	print frames
q	quit
l	set current stave
a *score*	test animation of *score*

The display mode editing is used mainly for modifying of symbols. In this mode, the score to be modified is displayed on a window. Within that window the user can move the mouse around to control where changes are to be made. By pressing the middle mouse on the window, the user can see the menu of the available symbols for the specified field. Then the user can make changes by selecting a symbol from the menu. When the user is uncertain of the symbol meaning, he can press the left mouse to read the explanation of each symbol.

By multi-windows, a user can view the animation and the score at the same time. The user can move back and forth between coding stage and animation stage to test and fix the score(Fig. 8).

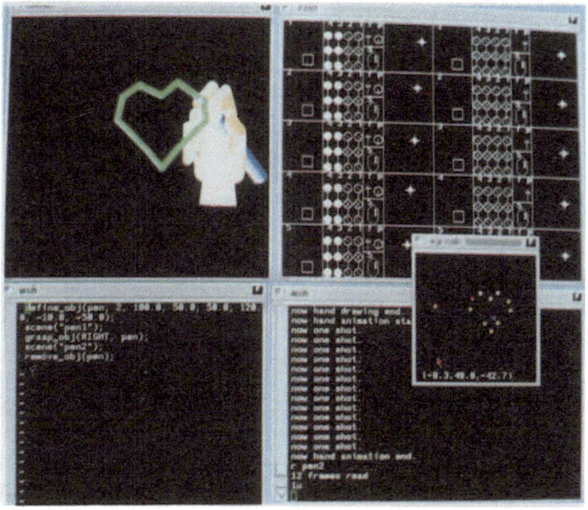

Fig. 8. Editing of Handnotation

3.5 Animation

The animation processor requires the information in the score to be translated in terms of geometric instructions. The information in the Handnotation is interpreted into geometric instructions through two steps of interpretation. A sequence of geometric instructions specifies the position and orientation of individual bone segments over a period of time.

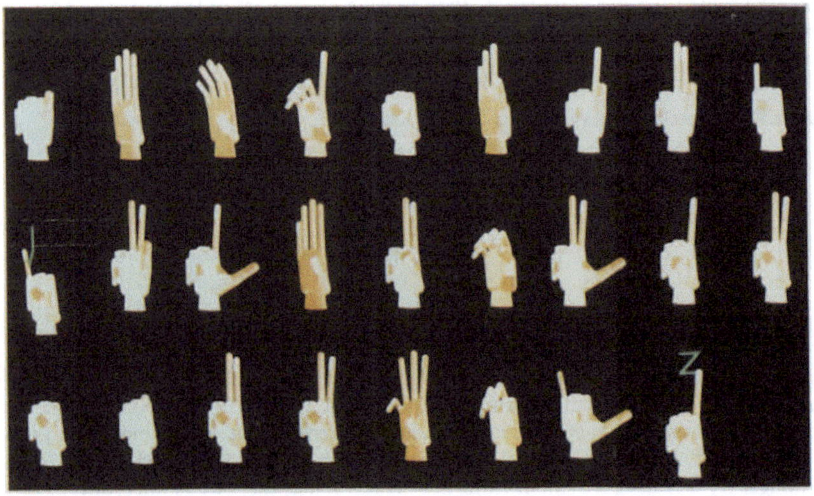

Fig. 9. Letters of alphabet described by finger spelling

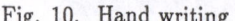

Fig. 10. Hand writing

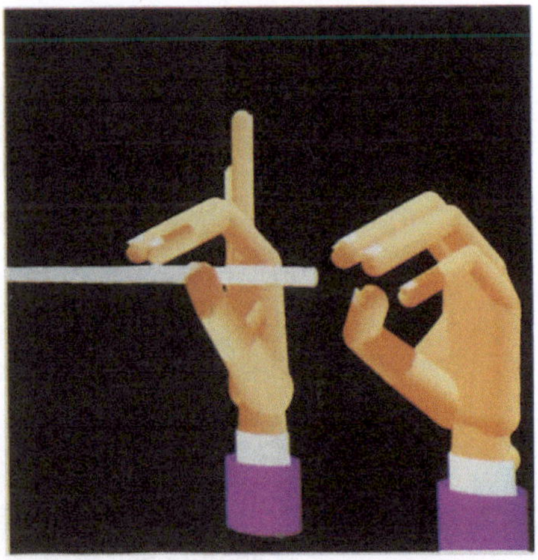

Fig. 11. Directing with a baton

Grasping or pinching requires solving the inverse kinematics problem. One approach to this problem is to find a closed-form solution by using algebra or geometry. Another approach is to find a numerical solution by some successive approximation algorithm. Although the former approach is generally more desirable in real-time control, it is not always possible to obtain closed-form solutions for animal limbs with more than six degrees of freedom(Yoshikawa 1990).

Instead of algebraic or geometric processes, a *heuristic search* is used for finding the joint angles. This is accomplished via the following algorithm:

1. Determine a goal
2. If *heuristic knowledge* contains the information for the goal then quit; else continue
3. Call *heuristic function* to find a feasible solution
4. If displacement has magnitude smaller than the threshold value or is no smaller than previous iteration then save the solution with goal in *heuristic knowledge* and quit; else repeat 3 to 4

This method is better than the simple dichotomous search since it makes use of empirical knowledge.

Once a structure of the skeleton is given, the covering routine creates the simplified surfaces on the skeleton automatically after calculating the necessary deformations. As high level notation gives only keyframe information, interpolated frames are calculated by an interpolation processor. The animator can interrupt the animation and change the view point or speed of animation. He can also switch between the hands or repeat the animation of some scenes for checking.

4. EXPERIMENT

Figure 9,10 and 11 show some results of experiments. Figure 9 shows the manual alphabet described by finger spelling. It can be specified simply by notation such as shown in figure 6. Figure 10 shows hand writing with a pen. The algorithm of hand grasping is explained in detail in the paper of Magnenat-Thalmann(Magnenat-Thalmann 1988). In hand writing, the pen has to move along with the hand after the pen is grasped. When the pen moves, it must leave an ink trace behind the pen. The user has to specify the contact point of the pen with the sheet from which the ink flows out. Programming is used with notation for object handling. Figure 11 shows hands that direct music with a baton. As the hands move in the same way repeatedly, it can be best specified by iterative statements in the score.

The implementation has been carried out on *Silicon Graphics Personal IRIS* graphics workstation. The program contains approximately 8,000 C code lines.

5. CONCLUSIONS

An efficient coding system is required to analyze 4D motion algorithm and refine it. The coding system should support users efficiently in their coding, refinement, and animation processes. The advantage of our hand motion coding system HAND include

- *Display of hand motion in notation.* This notational display enables viewing change of motion in context and simplifies reading and scanning the motion score.

- *Reduce learning time and editing time.* Seeing the symbols on the screen gives the user a clear sense of motion primitives, and mouse and graphical symbol menu provide natural means for editing a motion score. This is marked contrast with animation languages or commands, which require an operator to convert an idea into correct syntactic form and which may be difficult to learn, hard to recall, and a source of frustrating errors.

- *Immediate animation of the coded score.* When a command is sent to test the score, the results appear immediately on the window in animation.

No single system has all the attributes or design features that we admire - that may be impossible - but those described above have enough to win the enthusiatic support of many novice users. HAND is now being tested for the application in sign language translation.

ACKNOWLEDGEMENT

The authors wish to thank Dr. Deepa Krishnan, Dr. Myeong Won Lee and Ms. Karen Taniguchi for their valuable comments during the course of this work. Thanks are also extended to Dr. Shinagawa and members of Kunii Laboratory who supported this research.

REFERENCE

Badler NI and Morris MA (1982) Modelling Flexible Articulated Objects, *Proc Computer Graphics '82,Online Conf.* , pp.305-314.

Badler NI and Smoliar SW (1990) Digital Representations of Human Movement, *Computing Surveys*, Vol.11, No.1.

Badler NI, Barsky BA, Zeltzer D (1991) *Making them move: Mechanics, Control, and Animation of Articulated Figures*, Morgan Kaufmann Pub Inc. California.

Beaumont C (1969) The ballet called Giselle, Dance Horizons, New York.

Calvert TW and Chapman J (1978) Notation of Movement with Computer Assistance, *Proc. ACM Annual Conf.*, pp.727-730.

Calvert TW et al. (1991) Composition of multiple figure sequences for dance and animation, *The Visual Computer*, 7:114-121.

Catmull E (1972) A System for Computer-generated movies, *Proc ACM Annual Conf.*, pp.422-431.

Eshkol N and Wachmann A (1958) *Movement Notation*, Weidenfeld and Nicholson,London.

Hutchinson A (1970) *Labanotation*, Theatre Arts Books,New York.

Kapandji IA (1982) *The Physiology of the Joints*, Churchill Livingstone.

Kunii TL and Sun LN (1990) Dynamic Analysis-Based Human Animation, *Proc CG International '90*, pp.3-15.

Magnenat-Thalmann N and Thalmann D (1983) The use of high level 3-D graphical types in the Mira animation System, *IEEE Computer Graphics and Applications*, Vol.3, No.9, pp.9-16.

Magnenat-Thalmann N, Laperriere R and Thalmann D (1988) Joint-Dependent Local Deformations for Hand Animation and Object Grasping, *Proc. Graphics Interface '88*, Edmonton.

Magnenat-Thalmann N and Thalmann D (1990) *Computer Animation:Theory and Practice*, Springer,Tokyo.

Magnenat-Thalmann N, Thalmann D (1991) Complex Models for Animating Synthetic Actors, *IEEE Computer Graphics and Applications*, Vol.11, No.5, pp.32-44.

Reynolds CW (1981) Computer animation with scripts and actors, *Proc ACM SIGGRAPH, Computer Graphics*, Vol.16, No.3, pp.289-296.

Savage GT and Officer JM (1977) Choreo: An Interactive Computer Model for Choreography, *Proc. 5th Man-Machine Communication Conf.*, Calgary,Alberta.
Sturman D, Zeltzer D, Pieper S (1989) Hands-on interaction with virtual environments, *Proc. ACM SIGGRAPH Symposium on User Interface Software and Technology.*, Nov. 13-15, Williamsburg, Virginia, pp.19-24.
Watt AH (1989) *Fundamentals of three-dimensional computer graphics*, Addison-Wesley Pub Company Inc.
Yoshikawa T (1990) *Foundation of Robotics*, The MIT Press.
Zeltzer D (1985) Towards an integrated view of 3-D computer animation, *The Visual Computer*, 1:249-259.

Jintae Lee is currently a doctoral course graduate student of the Department of Information Science at the University of Tokyo. His research interests include computer animation, computer graphics, natural language processing and computer-aided translation. He received a BS in computer science and statistics from Seoul National University in 1981 and an MS in computer science from Korea Advanced Institute of Science and Technology in 1983. He is a member of IPSJ and KISS.

Address: Department of Information Science, Faculty of Science, the University of Tokyo, 7-3-1 Hongo, Bunkyo-ku, Tokyo, 113 Japan.

Tosiyasu L. Kunii is currently Professor of Information and Computer Science, the University of Tokyo.

He authored and edited more than 32 computer science books, and published more than 120 refereed academic/technical papers in computer science and applications areas.

Dr. Kunii is Founder of the Computer Graphics Society, Editor-in-Chief of *The Visual Computer: An International Journal of Computer Graphics* (Springer-Verlag), Associate Editor-in-Chief of *The Journal of Visualization and Computer Animation* (John Wiley & Sons) and on the Editorial Board of *IEEE Transactions on Knowledge and Data Engineering*, *VLDB Journal* and *IEEE Computer Graphics and Applications.* He is on the IFIP Modeling and Simulation Working Group, the IFIP Data Base Working Group and the IFIP Computer Graphics Working Group. He is on the board of directors of Japan Society of Sports Industry and also of Japan Society of Simulation and Gaming.

He received the B.Sc., M.Sc., and D.Sc. degrees in chemistry all from the University of Tokyo in 1962, 1964, and 1967, respectively. He is a fellow of IEEE and a member of ACM, BCS, IPSJ and IEICE.

Address: Department of Information Science, Faculty of Science, the University of Tokyo, 7-3-1 Hongo, Bunkyo-Ku,Tokyo, 113 Japan

Part III
Path Planning and Motion Control

Computer Animation of Robot Motion with Collision Free Path Planning

YONGCHENG LI, WEIMIN DU, ZESHENG TANG, and BO ZHANG

ABSTRACT

After given a brief introduction about known approaches for collision free path planning of robot motion, the outline of a topological Dimension Reduction Method is presented. In order to examine the correctness and efficiency of this method, a computer animation system is designed and implemented. The modeling of robot and its environment, the strategy of motion control are discussed. The key frames in animation are generated by specifying the appropriate set of parameter values, which are six joint angles of robot, the state of griper etc. The parameters are interpolated and images are finally and individually constructed from the interpolated parameters. The function of the animation system is described and some results are shown with a set of pictures.

Keywords: computer animation, robot motion, collision avoidance, path planning, parametric keyframe animation

1. INTRODUCTION

In the research and development of robotics and industrial automation, moving the robot among obstacles without collision is one of the key problems. The algorithms for motion planning with collision avoidance has been intensively explored in recent years. The motion planning problem, in its simplest form, is to find a path from a specified starting robot configuration to a specified goal configuration that avoids collision with a known set of stationary obstacles. One can view this problem not simply as part of robotics but rather as part of a discipline of object representation, design, editing, transformation and manipulation that is emerging from several areas including computational geometry, computer graphics, artificial intelligence, image processing and CAD/CAM as well as robotics per se.

Many approaches of motion planning are based on Configuration Space (C-Space) (Lozano 1983), which is actually the state-parameter space of the robot. For example, suppose a robotic arm has n degrees of freedom, then its C-Space will be $\Theta_1 \times \Theta_2 \times \cdots \times \Theta_n$, where Θ_i denotes the parameter of the i_th joint. With the mapping from the physical space corresponds to a point in the C-Space, a state of the robotic arm in physical space corresponds to a point in the C-Space; a physical obstacles corresponds to a C-Space-Obstacle, which means the obstacle is expressed with the C-Space coordinates. The findpath problem in physical space is equivalent to the investigation of C-Space.

Most known algorithms were concerning the problem in a two-dimensional plane with low degrees of freedom, e.g. moving a polygonal object among polygonal obstacles. There are several different approaches : VGRAPH (Lozano & Wesley 1979), Subdivision method (Brooks & Lozano 1983), "Freeway" method (Brooks 1983a), Topological approach (Cheng, Zhang & Zhang 1984; Schwartz & Sharir 1983), and Generalized Voronoi Diagram (GVD) algorithm (Takahashi & Schilling 1989). Among these methods, GVD algorithm shows great efficiency and generality for convex objects.

In need of planning path for a multi-joint robotic arm, we have to extend the method to solve the high-dimensional problem, which is difficult for some algorithms, such as VGRAPH, GVD algorithm, etc. Lozano (1987) developed a C-Space approach for different kinds of robotic arms in (Lozano 1987). Brooks still used "Freeway" method to plan the motion for a robotic arm (Brooks 1983b).

The "Freeway" algorithm described in (Brooks 1983b) has strong restrictions on the working space. The C-Space approach by Lozano (1987) uses slices projection method to transfer the problem from high dimension to low dimension. But the slices projection method partitions the C-Space equally, which does not take the distribution of the obstacles into account. So the contradiction between the efficiency and generality becomes a problem of the method.

The planning algorithm presented in this paper is mainly based on the topological method, which was early discussed in (Cheng, Zhang & Zhang 1984; Schwartz & Sharir 1983). Then Bo Zhang and Ling Zhang developed the Dimension Reduction Method (DRM) (Zhang & Zhang 1985; Zhang & Zhang 1989) which paves the way for solving high-dimensional problem using topological method. The DRM has the following features :

1) It solves the problem in point of a global view, just like man doing.

2) It makes the path planning , instead of continuously or numerically, topologically and then combinatorially. As a result, it gains efficiency.

3) It is an accurate, or complete, algorithm theoretically, which means it can find the path if and only if one exists.

4) Not only does it judge whether there exists a path but also gives a practical solution.

There are many advantages for using computer animation as a tool to do research on robot motion. It may be used to do research on different kinds of robots and different types of motion with a variety of planning approaches and control strategies whereas not restricted by real robot. It is much safe than using real robot which may be destroyed by collision with obstacles under erroneous planning. The techniques in computer animation of robot motion is also helpful for human animation (Magnenat & Thalmann 1988a; Magnenat & Thalmann 1988b; Tost & Pueyo 1988).

The computer animation system of robot motion should contain following functions :

- Construction of environment
- Specification of tasks
- Strategy selecting for carrying out a certain task
- Planning a collision free path
- Animation of robot motion

The rest of this paper is organized as follows. Section 2 describes an outline of our planning algorithm DRM. The details of animation for robot motion is discussed in section 3 which is followed by the description of the animation system in section 4. Some results of this computer animation system are shown in section 5.

2. THEORETICAL FOUNDATION OF FREE PATH PLANNING METHOD DRM

Because the mathematical proofs and deductions about DRM are very time-consuming and abstract, here we only outline the main idea of DRM.

In C-Space, the set made of points corresponding to collision free states of a moving object A among obstacles $\{B_i\}$ $(i = 1, \cdots, M)$ is called Free-C-Space (FCS), therefore the set of C-Space-Obstacles is C-Space / FCS, where / is the set difference.

Considering FCS as a graph in C-Space, the motion planning of A is equivalent to the connectivity investigation of FCS. Usually, FCS is a high-dimensional graph. For a 3-dimensional moving rigid object A among obstacles, if x represents the coordinates of a reference point P of A and θ represents the three Euler angles indicating the orientations of the reference axis PQ of A, then FCS $= G(F) = \{(x, F(x)) \mid x \in D(F)\}$, where $F : x \to 2^{\theta}$ (θ is the range of possible members of the Euler angles) is called the Rotation Mapping and $D(F)$ is the domain of F. $G(F)$ is a graph in C-Space $X \times \Theta$ and is called the Rotation Mapping Graph (RMG) and then $D(F) \subseteq X$. For a moving rigid object A among polyhedron obstacles, the Rotation Mapping F is always a Semi-Continuous multi-valued mapping.

Now we introduce DRM in the form of theorem :

Theorem : Assume C-Space is $X \times Y$, RMG is $\{x, F(x) \mid x \in D(F)\}$, where $F : X \to Y$ is a Semi-Continuous mapping, if $D(F)$ is connected, $F(x)$ is compact, and $\forall x \in D(F)$, $F(x)$ is a connected set on Y, then $G(F) = \{x, F(x) \mid x \in D(F)\}$ is a connected set on $X \times Y$.

This conclusion leads the connectivity investigation of high-dimensional space to that of lower-dimensional space. With the requirement of Semi-Continuous, the DRM can be extended to a general space $X = X_1 \times X_2 \times \cdots \times X_n$, where X_i $(i = 1, \cdots, n)$ is the sub-space of X. That means the connectivity investigation of X can be dissolved into those of X_i $(i = 1, \cdots, n)$.

The main procedures of the topology-based planning approach DRM is the following.

1) Partition of FCS

The first step we should do is to partition D into $\{D_i\}$ $(i = 1, \cdots, r)$ by r_growing boundaries, disappearance curves, disappearance planes and obstacle boundaries, where D is the domain of the free space.

For all D_i of $\{D_i\}$ we find the connected branches of $F(D_i)$ as follows.

$$F(D_i) = \sum_{j=1}^{n_i} F_j(D_i)$$

Thus

$$F(D) = \{D_i, F_j(D_i)\} \ (i = 1, \cdots, r;\ j = 1, \cdots, n_i)$$

2) Construction of Characteristic Network (CN)

Regarding each $(D_i, F(D_i))$ as a father-node (i) and each $(D_i, F_j(D_i))$ as a son-node (i, j) as its successor, we have a tree-like network called Characteristic Network (Fig. 1). In the Figure, $Layer_0$ represents the root node of the CN. $Layer_i$ denote the connected blocks on Θ_i $(i = 1, 2, 3)$. For example, node $(1, 1, 1)$ may have the simple form as $((\frac{\pi}{4}, \frac{3\pi}{4}), (0, \frac{\pi}{5}), (0, \frac{\pi}{2}))$, where $(\frac{\pi}{4}, \frac{3\pi}{4})$ is the free motion interval of TRUNK, $(0, \frac{\pi}{5})$ is the free motion interval of UPPER ARM, and $(0, \frac{\pi}{2})$ is the free motion interval of FORE ARM. A connectivity network ($Layer_4$ in Fig. 1) is constructed among these nodes. We can judge whether a state of robot is collision free by checking whether the state belongs to a node in CN.

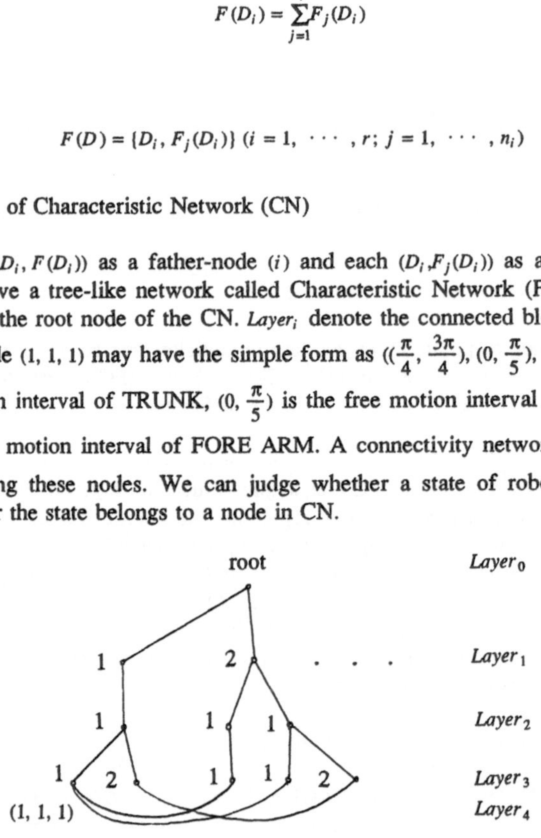

Fig. 1 Characteristic Network

3) Search for Path

Locating the initial and desired final configurations to nodes in CN, we can find a connected path in CN from the initial node to the goal node in the connectivity network ($Layer_4$). Then we have a corresponding collision free path of the moving object in physical space.

3. ANIMATION OF ROBOT MOTION

3.1 Modeling of Robot and Environment

In our computer animation system, the construction of robot model is based on the structure and shape of PUMA 560 which consists of a sequential rigid rods connected by joints as a chain (Fig. 2). One end of this chain is fixed on a supporting base. A gripper is assembled at another end of the chain. The motion of connected rod is dependent on the joint rotation. The robot has six degrees of freedom corresponding to six joint angles respectively. The TRUNK, UPPER ARM and FORE ARM are manipulated to fulfill the global movement, while the WRIST is for the local fine operations. Therefore, the robot can perform different kinds of tasks within its working range. In the model of robot, the TRUNK is represented by a cylinder, the UPPER ARM by an octahedron and the FORM ARM by a cuboid. The gripper is approximated by three planar polygons.

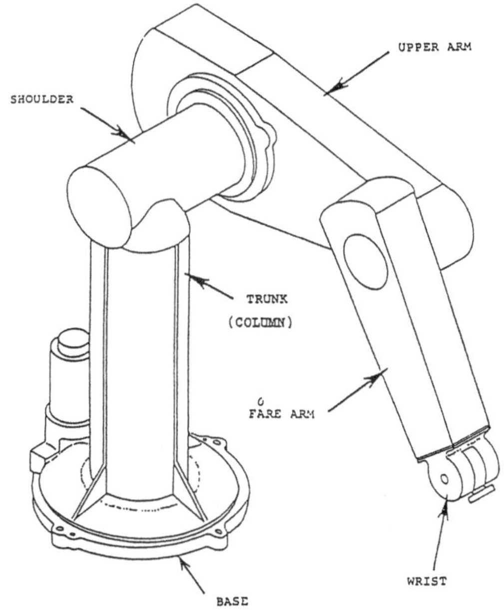

Fig. 2 Model of the robotic arm

When robot moves, each connect rod rotates around the joint. A local Euclian coordinate system is needed for each rod. The origin of this local coordinate system is located at the center of the joint and the axis around which the rod rotates is defined as z axis. The x axis and y axis are parallel and perpendicular with the longitudinal direction of the rod respectively.

Suppose the coordinate in which the supporting base is located in the world coordinate. The rotation angle of joint i in its local coordinate may be transformed to world coordinate by transformation matrix T_i. We have $T_i = A_{i-1,i} * T_{i-1}$. Here, T_{i-1} is the transformation matrix from coordinate of joint $i-1$ to world coordinate, $A_{i-1,i}$ is the transformation matrix from joint i to

$i-1$.

The environment of the robot workspace is made up of obstacles, such as pillars, walls etc., which are not limited in number, size and location. The obstacles are modeled by rectangular parallelepipeds, cylinders, and spheres. Also the object to be grasped by the robot is involved in the environment. Hence, the robot will perform such operations as picking up a certain object and put it down on the desired location while avoiding obstacles.

3.2 Motion Control

The input of the robot animation contains three parts.

* Robot parameters, such as length, rotation limits of each joint.

* Parameters of obstacles and their locations in environment.

* Tasks, e.g. grasp an object and put it down at a specified position.

There are several possible kinds of output codes in computer animation. Ours is the value of parameters (e.g. joint angles, gripper state) for certain keyframes. This allows the easy calculation of each frame by parametric interpolation.

To generate the motion corresponding to the task "pick-up the object A and put it on the location C", the planner must choose where to grasp A so that no collisions will result when grasping or moving them. Then grasp configurations should be chosen so that the grasped object is stable in the hand. Once the object is grasped, the system should generate the motions that will achieve the desired goal of the operations. A free motion should be synthetized; during this motion the principal goal is to reach the destination without collision, which implies obstacle avoidance. In this complex process, joint evolution is determined by kinematics and dynamics equations (Hegron, Palamidese & Thalmann 1989). In summary, the task-level system should integrate the following elements : path planning, obstacle avoidance, stability and contact determination, kinematics and dynamics. Due to the difficulties in the process, we have to divide our procedure into two parts : global planning and local planning, in order to generate the values of parameters for keyframes.

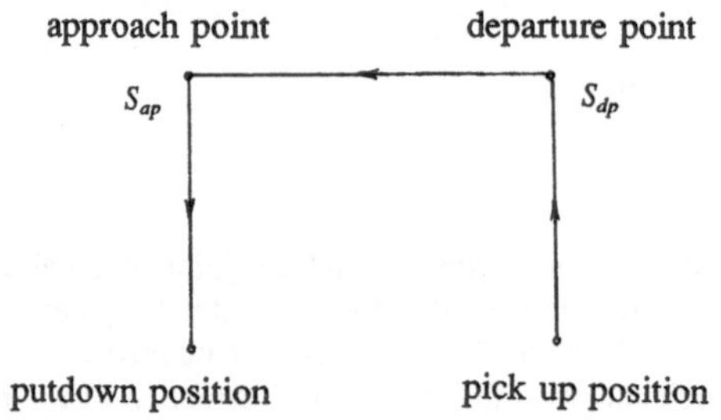

Fig. 3

We perform the global-planning in a relatively sparse environment by ignoring the configuration of the gripper. But when the robot approaches the grasping position, we have to consider the state of the gripper and plan a collision free path for both the gripper and the arm. As shown in Fig. 3, the general mode of the motion for the robot to fulfill a pick-and-place task is

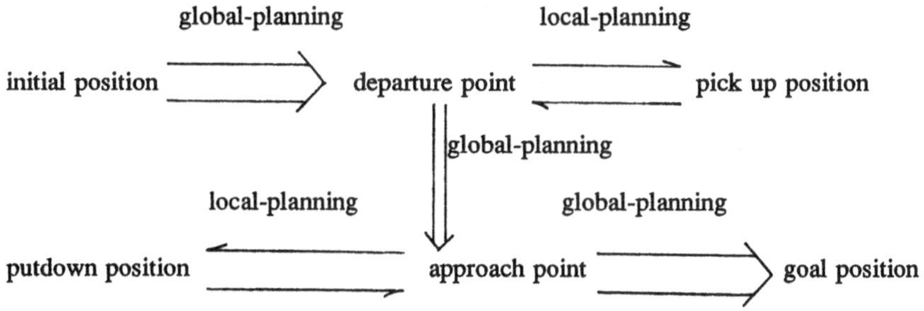

Global Planning

The global planning is the planning of a three-joint arm. There are two kinds of global plannings. One is called g_planning, where the gripper holding an object is replaced by a sphere with g, the length of the gripper including the object, as its radius and x, the center of the wrist, as its center (Fig. 4). The other is called 0_planning, where the gripper and the object are eliminated. Obviously, these two kinds of global planning are general three-joint arm motion planning which has been discussed in section 2. The only difference between these two global plannings is that the boundaries of the original obstacles in the g_planning must be grown by the size g before running the algorithm. Therefore, we have two characteristic networks, i.g. g_CN and 0_CN.

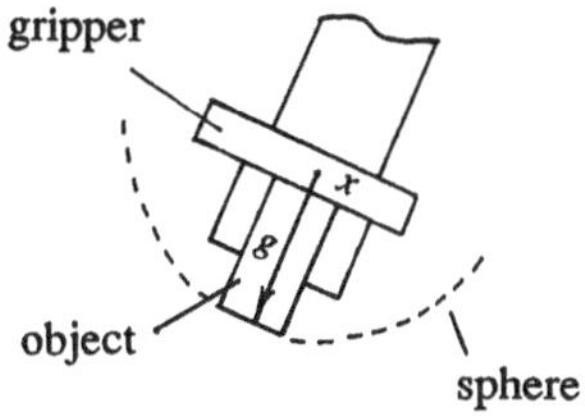

Fig. 4

In Fig. 3 the departure (approach) point should satisfy following constrains :

1) The corresponding state S_{dp} of the robot arm belongs to g_CN.

2) A collision free path exist for both the motions of the arm and the gripper from pick up (put down) position to departure (approach) point.

3) There is a connected path from initial (goal) position to departure (approach) point in g_CN.

4) There is a connected path from departure point to approach point in g_CN.

Local Planning

Based on the object to be grasped, several features of grasp is chosen. Then we have the position and orientation of the gripper. The corresponding state S_{pk} of the robot arm can be derived by inverse kinematics (Zelter 1985) calculation. In the case of a PUMA like_robot, there are altogether four possible solutions (therefore corresponding to four possible states of the robotic arm) to the inverse kinematics calculation. At least one state should belong to the 0_CN.

If the corresponding state S_{pk} of the robotic arm at pick up position belongs to a node in g_CN, we can regard the pick up position as a departure point. Otherwise, we have to select departure points discretely nearby pick up position. After a selection, the above four constraints are verified in turn. For the verification of constraint 2), we should first plan a local collision free path for the gripper from pick up position to departure point. Then, we have the orientation of the gripper and the cartesian trajectory of the center x of the wrist. The corresponding states of the robotic arm is calculated along the path by inverse kinematics. Certainly, these states must belong to some nodes of the 0_CN. The same is true of the local planning for the gripper from approach point to the putdown position.

In conclusion, we given an algorithmic description for the pick-and-place operation. Here S_I, S_G, S_{pk}, S_{pd}, S_{dp}, S_{ap} represent the states of the robotic arm at initial position, goal position, pick up position, putdown position, departure point, approach point respectively.

(1) If S_I, S_G, S_{pk}, S_{pd} belongs to nodes in g_CN, and a connected path exists ($S_I \rightarrow S_{pk} \rightarrow S_{pd} \rightarrow S_G$) in g_CN, then goto (4).

(2) Determine a departure (approach) point. If this step fails, then declare failure.

(3) Constraints checking

* local gripper planning
* robotic arm states checking
* global planning $S_I \rightarrow S_{dp}$, $S_{dp} \rightarrow S_{ap}$, $S_{ap} \rightarrow S_G$

If one of the above checking fails, goto (2).

(4) Give the keyframe parameter values.

Parametric Keyframe Animation

When above planning is finished, the animator creats keyframes by specifying the appropriate set of parameter values. The parameter values are six joint angles of the robot, the state of the gripper (close or open) and the position and orientation of a certain object which is grasped by the robot. Then parameters are interpolated and images are finally and individually constructed from the interpolated parameters. Since the state of the world is wholly controlled by the parameter values of the robot, the parametric keyframe animation we used here generates great efficiency and high animation quality.

4. DESCRIPTION OF COMPUTER ANIMATION FOR ROBOT MOTION

The Computer Animation System for Robot Motion has been developed with C language on the SUN workstation.

This system consists of the following functions : robot generation, environment allocation, model combination, path planning and motion display etc. These functions are organized and managed by hierarchical menus.

The menu system us as follows

- *Robot Generation*
- *Environment Allocation*
  - *Interactive Mode*
  - *Input Data File*
- *Model Combination*
- *Motion Display*
  - *Static Display*
    - *Initialization*
    - *View Point Specification*
    - *Three Views*
    - *Soaling*
    - *Realistic Image*
    - *Next Frame*
  - *Dynamic Display*
    - *Initialization*
    - *View Point Specification*
    - *Dynamic Display*
    - *Halt*
    - *Continue*
    - *Realistic Image*
- *Path Planning*

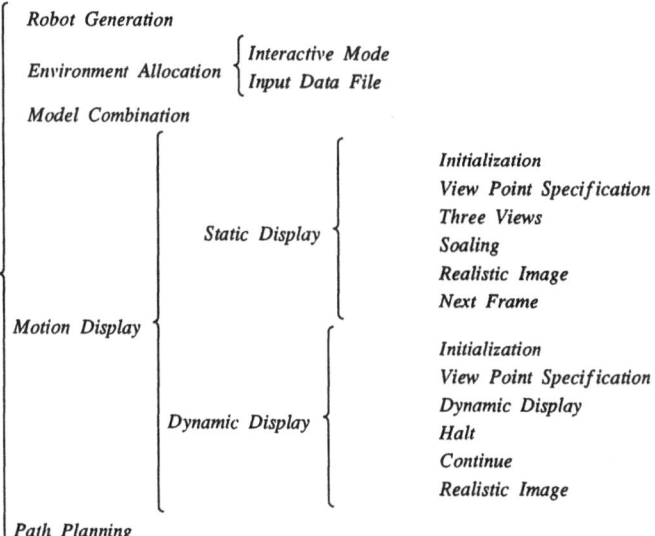

In this system, the model of robot is generated by predefined data. The objects which are the obstacles in environment may be created either from predefined data or interactively. The robot model and objects in environment may be combined together to check by the user if they are reasonably allocated. The robot model as well as the objects in environment may be modified or regenerated when it is needed. In static mode, the motion state is displayed frame by frame. The following operations such as view point specification, scaling and three views may be applied on each frame. In dynamic mode, the moving robot states are displayed continuously. It may be interrupted by mouse and switched to static mode. After careful examination of static picture of robot, the dynamic mode may be recovered by clicking "Continue" item in menu.

5. SOME RESULTS AND FUTURE WORK

Several typical examples have been tested. It shows that partition of FCS and construction of CN consume most of the time. The search-for-path procedure runs very fast. This implies that that animator has the ability to producing animation sequence quickly in the unchanged workspace for other different tasks. Fig. 5 to Fig. 12 shows some photographs of an example.

There is still some further work to be done in the following aspects :

* Performing more complicated tasks
* Coordinate motions of multi-robot
* Considering moving obstacles in the workspace
* Constructing a more lifelike model of the robot

The interest and research on computer animation of robot motion will both benefit robotics, computer animation and other relative areas.

Fig .5

Fig .7

Fig .6

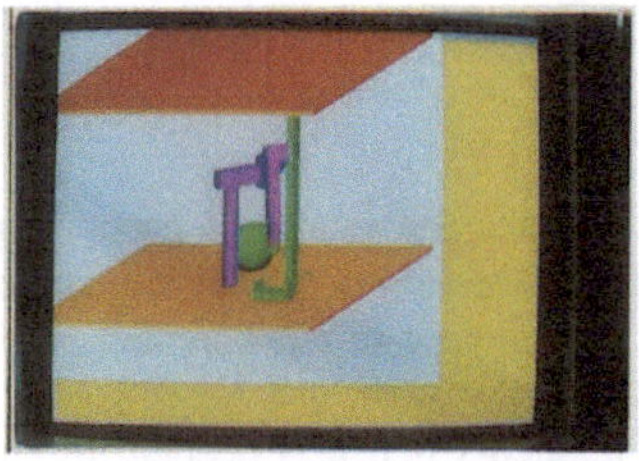

Fig .8

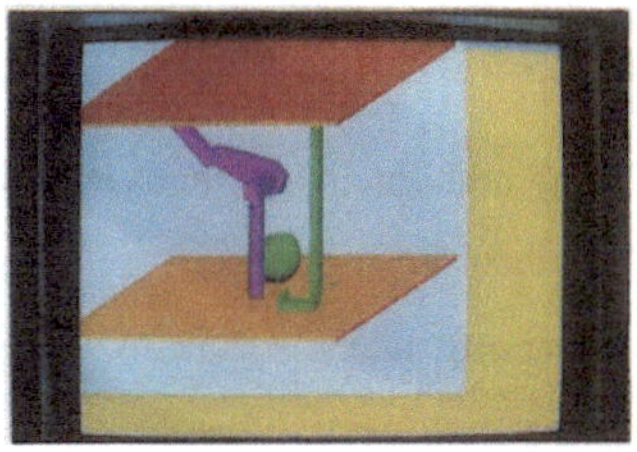

Fig .9

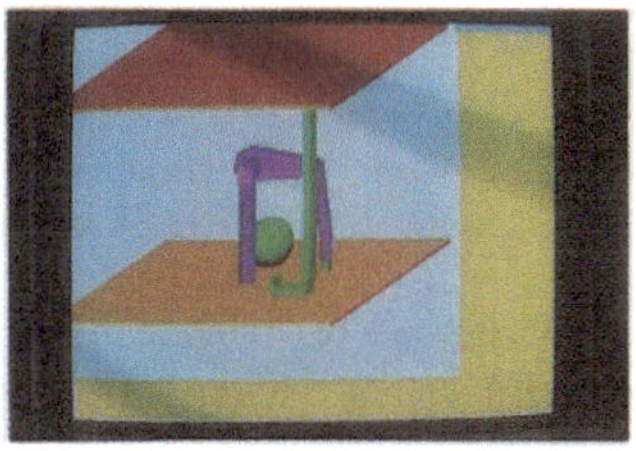

Fig .11

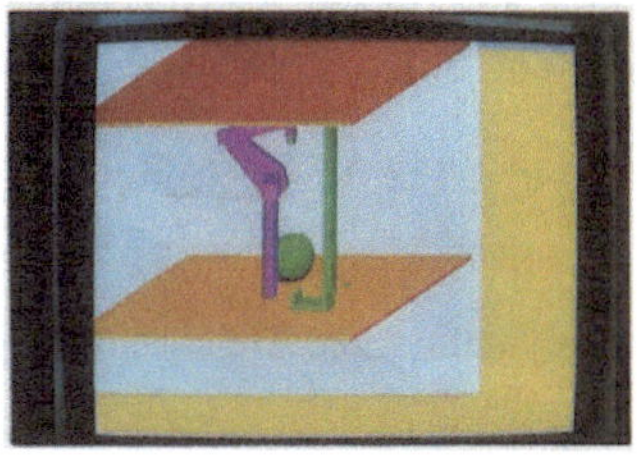

Fig .10

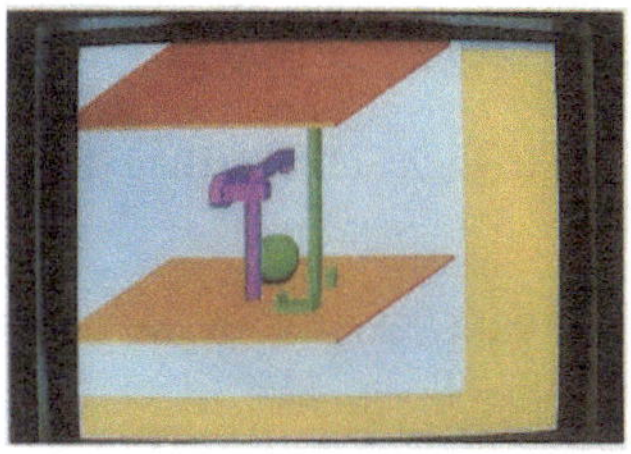

Fig .12

Reference

Brooks R.A. (1983a) Solving the find-path problem by good representation of free space. In Proc. 11th International Joint Conference on Artificial intelligence, 1029-1032

Brooks R.A. (1983b) Planning collision-free motions for pick and place operation. 1st International Symposium on Robotics Research, Bretton Woods, 1-37

Brooks R.A., Lozano-Pérez T. (1983) A subdivision algorithm in configuration space for findpath with rotation. In Proc. 8th International Joint Conference on Artificial intelligence, 799-806

Chien R.T., Zhang L., Zhang B. (1984) Planning collision free paths for robotic arm among obstacles. IEEE Trans. on Pattern Analysis and Machine Intelligence PAMI-6, 91-96

Hegron G., Palamidese P., Thalmann D. (1989) Motion Control in Animation, Simulation and Visualization. Computer Graphics Forum 8, 347-352

Lozano-Pérez T., Wesley M.A. (1979) An algorithm for planning collision-free paths among polyhedral obstacles. Commun. Ass. Comput. Mach., Vol. ACM 22, 560-570

Lozano-Pérez T. (1983a) Spatial planning : a configuration space approach. IEEE Trans. on Computers, V.C-32, 108-120

Lozano-Pérez T. (1987) A simple motion planning algorithm for general robot manipulator. IEEE Journal of Robotics and Automation, Vol. RA-3, No. 3

Magnenat-Thalmann N., Thalmann D. (1988) Task planning and intelligent activity for synthetic actors. SIGGAPH'88 Course Notes

Magnenat-Thalmann N., Thalmann D. (1988) Trajectory planning and obstacle avoidance for synthetic actors. SIGGAPH'88 Course Notes

Schwartz J.T., Sharir M. (1983a) On the piano movers' problem : I. The special case of rigid polygonal body moving amidst polygonal barriers. Comm. Pure Appl. Math., Vol. XXXVI, 345-398

Takahashi O., Schilling R.J. (1989) Motion planning in a plan using Generalized Voronoi Diagrams. IEEE Trans. on Robotics and Automation, Vol. 5, No. 2, 143-150

Tost D., Pueyo X. (1988) Human body animation : a survey. The Visual Computer 3, 254-264

ZelterD. (1985) Towards an integrated view of 3D computer animation. The Visual Computer 4, 249-259

Zhang B., Zhang L. (1985) Planning collision-free paths for 3-dimensional object with rotation. Report on ACADEMIA SINICA (China) and C.N.R. (France) Robotics Workshop

Zhang B., Zhang L., Zhang T. (1989) Motion planning of multi-joint robotic arm with topological Dimension Reduction Method. In Proc. 11th International Joint Conference on Artificial Intelligence, 1029-1032

Yongcheng Li is currently a Ph.D. candidate of Computer Science & Technology at Tsinghua University. He received his BSc, MSc in Computer Science & Technology from Tsinghua University in 1989, 1990. His current interests are in the areas of : Motion Planning, Robots Learning, and Theories of Action.

Weimin Du is a lecture of the University of Electronic Technology in Chengdu, China. He graduated from the Department of Mathematics in South-Western Normal University and got Bachelor Degree in 1985. Since then, he has been engaged in the University of Electronic Technology in Chengdu and has been the teaching assistant of the courses "Discrete Mathematics", "Assembly Language" and "Principles of Operating System". From Sept., 1990 to July, 1991, he was a visiting scholar in the Department of Computer Science and Technology of Tsinghua University and took part in the research work of computer Graphics and Computer Simulation of Robot Motion.

Zesheng Tang is a professor in the Department of Computer Science and Technology of Tsinghua University, Beijing, China. He is also the director of Computer Aided Design Technology Research Group of Tsinghua University. He graduated from the Department of Electrical Engineering of Tsinghua University in 1953. Since then, he has worked in this university in the area of Automation and Computer Science. From the beginning of the 1980s, Zesheng Tang and his colleagues started education and research work in the field of Computer Graphics. In 1985-1986, he visited the University of Michigan in Ann Arbor, U.S.A. and worked in Palo Alto Research Center of Xerox Corporation in California. His current research interest includes Geometric Modeling and its Application, Volume Visualization and Computational Geometry. He is also the instructor of course "Computational Geometry" for graduate students of Tsinghua University. Zesheng Tang is a council member and also the vice chairman of the CAD and Computer Graphics Society of China Computer Federation. He is a senior member and also the vice chairman of Computer Engineering and Application Society of China Electronic Institute. He was one of the co-chairman of Working Conference on Modeling in Computer Graphics which was held in Tokyo in April, 1991 and is also responsible for technical committee of the third International Conference on CAD and Computer Graphics. This conference is sponsored by China Computer Federation and Tsinghua University and will be held in August, 1993 in Beijing, China.

Bo Zhang is currently a professor of Computer Science & Technology at Tsinghua University. His research interests are robotics, artificial intelligence and computer applications. He has authored 3 computer science books and published 70 technical papers in computer science and artificial intelligence. He is now director of the National Lab. of Intelligent Technology & Systems.

Path Planning and Its Application to Human Animation System

Ryozo Takeuchi, Munetoshi Unuma, and Koji Amakawa

Abstract

This paper presents a human animation system with a path planning function. An animal moves towards its favorite things and flees from his enemies. These motions depend on instinct. This idea is applied to path planning by using 'attractiveness' to simulate these motions naturally. As examples the flight path of a butterfly, swiming pattern of a school of fish and human movements showing emotion are generated using the attractiveness.

Keywords: animation, path planning, human motion, butterfly, fish, attractiveness

1. Introduction

Motion is composed using a movement path and partial motion on individual partial paths. For generation of partial motion we have shown a motion generation method with emotion [Unuma 91]. This method gives variations of motion, but, it does not allow a motion path to be made. The motion path of an animal depends on its world which is composed of various things. For example, foods, rest-space and mates are favorite things which an animal wants to go to. On the other hand, it flees from enemies and dangerous things.

Automatic motion control has been studied in recent years. Investigation topics have included interpolation, script control, path planning, stimulus response, and so on [Wilhelms 87]. To achieve the aim of this paper, some kinds of automatic path planning and stimulus response are needed. An automatic motion control based on a script system [Reynolds 82] has many advantages and works well when an animator can describe patterns of an object's behavior in some programmed manner. However, it has some disadvantages. One is that there are some cases in which patterns of behavior cannot suitably be written out in any language. For example, a person's random walking through a store is hard to describe explicitly, since many vague, indefinite states exist. Another disadvantage is that the behavior of each kind of object must be described. For example, a school of small fish attacked by a large fish has been simulated [Uchiki 86]; but it was necessary to make and write out separate behavior models for each kind of simulated fish. So the greater the number of kinds of objects is, the more behavior models there are for the animator to describe. The aim of this paper is to present a method by which these disadvantages of automatic motion control, based on a script system, can be overcome to some extent. A new approach to automatic motion control is proposed which can create paths of various objects by a single program.

2. Basic Concept

The disadvantages of automatic motion control by a script are caused by the method in which one object perceives another object as to what it is, or what kind of object it is. Since patterns of moving objects' response to a certain kind of object vary, a different behavior model must be constructed for each kind of moving object. If a system creates motion based not on the kind but on a certain quantity of an object, and if that quantity is an essential and universal key to behavior of various kinds, it may be possible to make various behavior patterns by controlling the quantity. We have proposed the quantity of 'attractiveness' [Amakawa 88] which one object feels to another, psychologically and/or physically.

Suppose that an animal is freely moving among some objects. It will be most likely to approach the objects towards which it feels some attractiveness and to avoid those which it feels are dangerous or unattractive. This behavior pattern seems to be fundamental for many kinds of animals and can be applied to making various kinds of behaviors. For example, in the case of a school of fish A and another fish B attacking them, each fish A is attractive to fish B, and fish B tries to get any one of them, while every fish A of the school tries to get away from fish B when it approaches. Another example is that of persons randomly walking in a store while shopping. Some objects may be attractive to them and they are likely to approach the most attractive and examine it. When they find it no longer attractive, they move to another attractive thing or direction. In this way, many patterns of behaviors can be analysed into a changing value of attractiveness.

The attractiveness depends upon not only the object's nature but also the observer's perception and liking, since the nature of an object includes many aspects to be perceived and what is attractive to one observer may be unattractive to another. So the attractiveness can be regarded as some function of the perceived nature of an object and the liking of the observer. Attractiveness can be described in terms of four types of models: a model of the object's nature, a model of perception of the nature, a model of the observer's liking, and a model of the function which produces the attractiveness from the perceived nature and liking.

3. Model of Attractiveness

The model of attractiveness which we constructed and used to make some experimental animations is described here.

3.1 Model of Object's Nature

The nature of an object has many aspects or elements. For example, a flower has elements of color, fragrance, taste of the nectar, shape, size and so on. These elements should be expressed as a numerical value for calculation purposes. So nature is expressed in the form of a vector and each element stands for one component of the nature. Expression of a component of nature as a value may be a difficult problem. However, since the aim of this paper is not an exact simulation of natural objects, but easy motion control of animation, the problem of the value expression is not addressed here.

3.2 Model of Perception

Although perception itself is a complicated psychological phenomenon, a simple model of perception is needed for the purpose of animation. The concern is how to perceive the nature of an object. Since the nature model is a vector composed of some elements, the model of perception has to correspond to each element of the nature vector. For example, when a butterfly observes the nature of a flower, it may perceive the color element at a distance, but it needs to get nearer to perceive the fragrance element, and it has to touch the flower to perceive the taste element. It is reasonable to suppose that there are three kinds of regions around an object for each element of the nature respectively: the region where an observer does not perceive the element, the region where perception is vague, and the region where perception is exact. For simplicity, the model constructed has only two kinds of regions where an element is perceived as nothing, and as it is. Consequently, an object has as many perception regions as the number of elements of the nature vector plus one which corresponds to the region where no element is perceived. The shape of the perceived region then presents another problem. In the present method, it is approximated as a circle in 2D applications and a sphere in 3D ones.

3.3 Model of Observer's Liking

Liking for each component of the object's nature must also be expressed in a form appropriate for calculations. The liking model employs a vector approach like the nature model. Each element of the vector expresses in what direction and to what extent the observer likes the corresponding component of the nature, i.e., the sign of an element means in what direction or on which side, plus or minus, the liking is, and the absolute value of the element denotes the extent. For example, the liking vector $\mathbf{L}=(2,-3.7,5)$ means that this observer likes the plus side of the first nature element to the extent of '2', the minus side of the second nature element to the extent of '3.7', and the plus side of the third nature element to the extent of '5'.

3.4 Model of Function

The last model needed is that of the function which produces the attractiveness from the perceived nature of an object and the liking of the observer. The liking model has elements expressing the sign and the quantity of the liking to the corresponding elements of the nature, therefore multiplying the two corresponding elements of the liking and the perceived nature easily produces how attracted the observer is to the corresponding nature component. For example, when a liking element is '-2' and a perceived nature element is '-5', multiplying the two gives '+10' which is the object's attractiveness. The total attractiveness of an object can be simply defined as the total sum of the products of each liking element and perceived nature element, i.e., as the inner product of the liking vector and the perceived nature vector. For example, when the liking vector is $\mathbf{L}=(L1,L2,L3)$ and the perceived nature vector is $\mathbf{N}=(N1',N2',N3')$, the attractiveness $\mathbf{A}$ is calculated as the following:

$$\mathbf{A}=\mathbf{L}\cdot\mathbf{N}=L1\cdot N1'+L2\cdot N2'+L3\cdot N3'$$

Figure 1 shows a typical example of the model of attractiveness constructed as explained above. In this case, the number of elements of both the liking of the observing object and the nature of the observed object, i.e., the dimension of the liking vector and the nature vector, is two. The nature vector $\mathbf{No}$ is set as (N1,N2) and the perception regions corresponding to the elements N1 and N2 are set as shown. The liking vector $\mathbf{L}$ is set as (L1,L2) where the elements express the liking to the corresponding nature elements. The attractiveness $\mathbf{A}$ is defined as the inner product of the liking vector $\mathbf{L}$ and the perceived nature vector $\mathbf{N}$. As a result, the perceived nature vector $\mathbf{N}$ and the attractiveness change depending on which region the observing object is in. This is shown in the table of Fig.1.

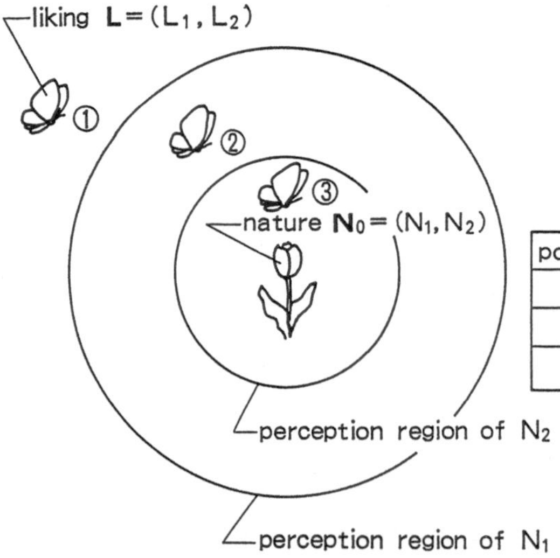

attractiveness $A = \mathbf{L} \cdot \mathbf{N}$

N : perceived nature

position	**N**	A
1	(O, O)	O
2	(N_1, O)	L_1N_1
3	(N_1, N_2)	$L_1N_1 + L_2N_2$

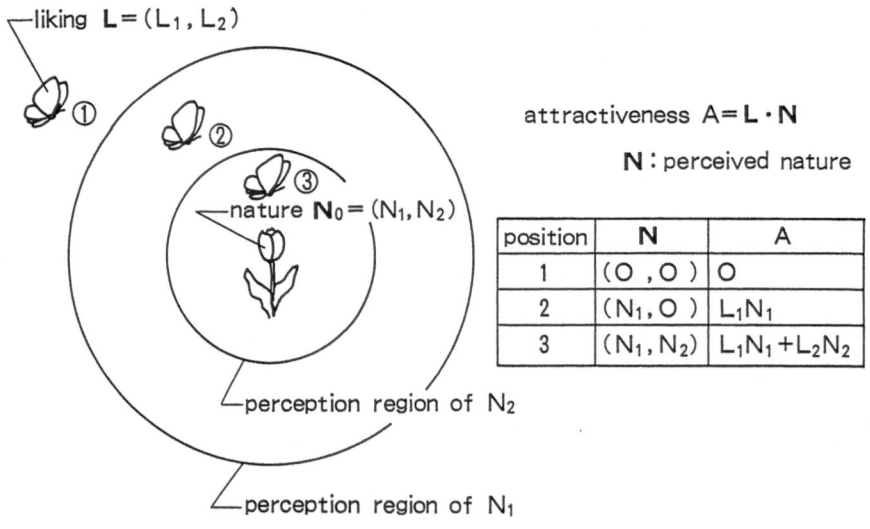

Fig.1 The model of attractiveness

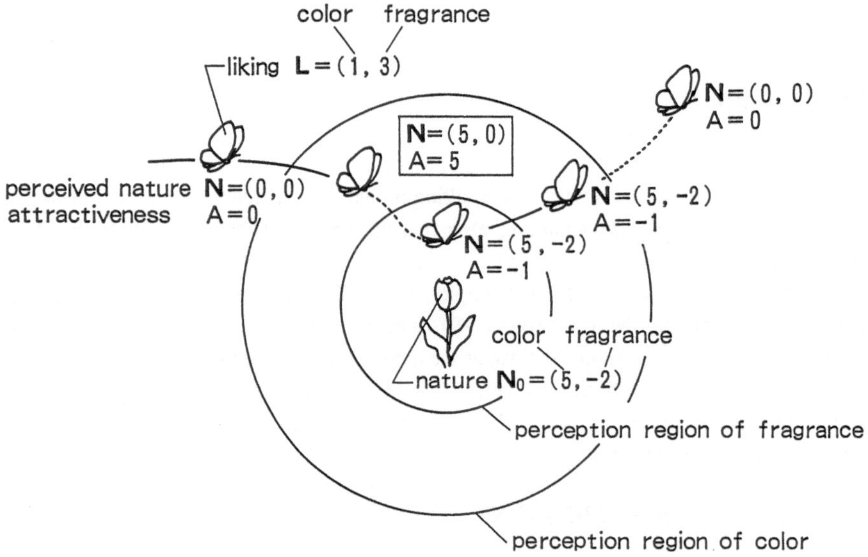

Fig.2 An example of the attractiveness model

Fig.2 is a concrete example of the attractiveness model. Let the observing object be a butterfly and the other object a flower. The nature of the flower is expressed in values of the elements of color and fragrance. The butterfly's liking is set as shown. First, the butterfly does not perceive anything about the flower, so the attractiveness of the flower is zero. When the butterfly chances to enter a perception region, it perceives the element of the nature and is attracted according to the attractiveness value. In this particular case, the attractiveness becomes negative after the butterfly learns the nature of the flower exactly, and it moves away from the flower. The memory of the butterfly may then be set to remember the perceived nature so that whenever it is within the perception region of this flower, a repeated approach is prevented.

4. Motion Control by Attractiveness

After the attractiveness of each object is calculated, it has to be converted to motion of the observing object in some way. The conversion depends upon the kind of the observing object, the type of motion the animator wants, and other conditions. The easiest conversion is probably that for making an object's path. Because the attractiveness expresses how much attraction the observing object feels to another object, in a simple model the observer is just attracted physically according to the attractiveness value. So we let a force proportional to the attractiveness be exerted on the observer in the direction toward the corresponding object. The motion calculation is done according to Newton's laws of motion with the given mass of the observer, so that acceleration and velocity are produced. This means that the model here is a kind of force field model. The case in which the observer perceives more than one object is rather hard to simulate exactly, but it can be done simply by exerting the force which is the sum of all force vectors. With this vector-adding method, undecisive behavior of the observer which wants all attractive objects is approximately created.

Fig.3 shows simple motion control by attractiveness. The observing object feels the attractiveness of object 1 as negative, and that of object 2 as positive. Forces F1 and F2 are exerted on the observer toward each direction according to each respective attractiveness value. As a result, the added force vector **F** is exerted which changes the velocity vector **V**. In many cases, a velocity limit should be set to give some cruising speed in order to make the motion natural.

5. Experiments

Using the attractiveness method shown above, some experiments were done.

5.1 Two Dimensional Experiment of Making Paths

Fig.4 shows the calculated paths of the experiment in which the method was two-dimensionally implemented and tested. The thick curve represents the path of the observing object. The center of the concentric circles represents the observed object. Each circle represents the perception region of a nature element of the object. There are two concentric circles for each object, because the nature is expressed by two elements. The numbers shown are the attractiveness values which the observer feels if it enters the corresponding perception region. Figs.4(a)-(c) are results obtained for the same set of conditions, except for the positions and extents of the perception regions of the objects. The observer sometimes went directly to one object without knowing the other was there as in (a), or it found an object unattractive and moved to the other to be satisfied as in (b), or had some trouble finding the best object as in (c). Fig.4(d) presents a case with three objects. The number of objects did not make any fundamental difference. These results verified the essential applicability of the attractiveness model to making paths for various behaviors.

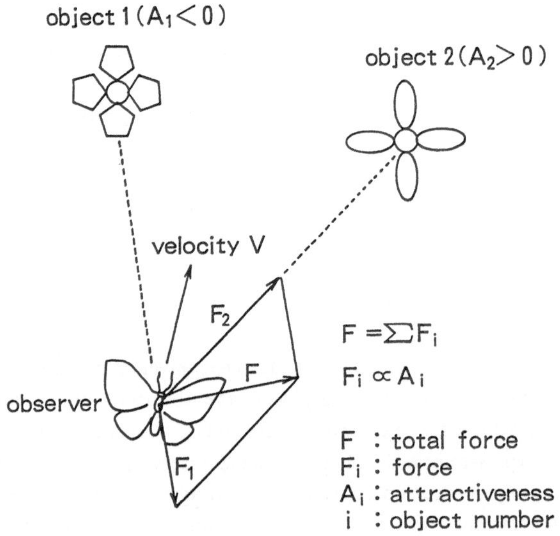

Fig.3 An example of motion control by attractiveness

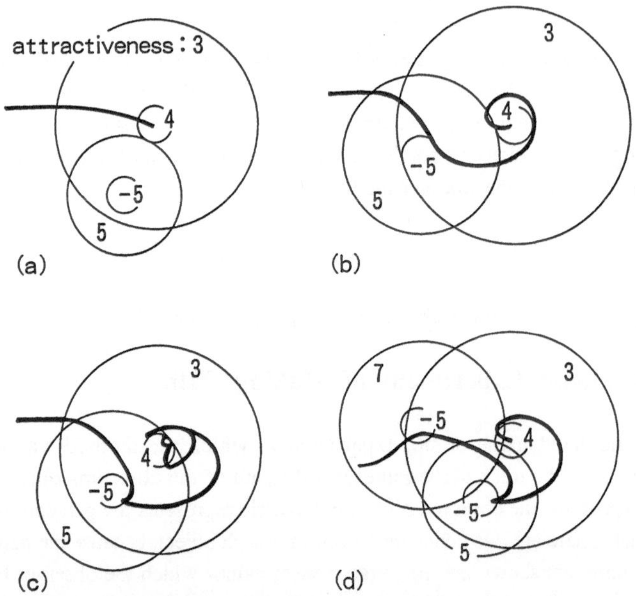

Fig.4 Paths calculated by the presented method

5.2 Three Dimensional Application to Animation

The method was applied to making an experimental three dimensional animation of a butterfly. Fig.5 shows a wireframed butterfly flying among some flowers. The basic path was calculated by the attractiveness method, and some randomness was added to it to produce a final more natural path. The flapping and gliding motions of the butterfly were programmed and added to the path. This three dimensional implementation of the method produced essentially the same results as the two dimensional one.

Fig.6 shows an example rendered scene of the animation. The behavior of the butterfly, searching for a better or more attractive flower, was created automatically. It looked natural, and the experimental animation was considered successful.

5.3 Application to Group Behavior

Some experiments were made simulating group behavior. Fig.7 shows an example simulating a school of small fish attacked by a large fish of another kind. The conditions were set so that each small fish had a positive attractiveness to both the large fish and the other small ones, the large fish had a highly negative attractiveness to each small one, and the mass and the velocity limit of a small fish were smaller than those of the large one. The program used was the same as for the butterfly animation, except that the concept of territory was implemented and added. The territory model used for the experiment shown in Fig.7 was a very simple one in which the sign of the attractiveness of an object was made negative when it entered the territory of the observer. This territory model was too simple at times and made the observer vibrate because of discontinuity of the attractiveness value between the inside and outside of the territory. It should be made more sophisticated, similar to the model in which the repulsion force is inversely proportional to the square of the distance [Reynolds 87]. Although the territory model was not complete, the simulation results were satisfactory. The method produced natural behavior as the small fish fled from the large fish attacking them. Therefore it was proved that various behaviors could be made with the proposed method without scripting any behavior model for each kind of object.

6. Applied to Human Motion Generation

Human motion is composed of path planning and partial motion on each partial path. Path planning by using 'attractiveness' is applied to human motion generation. Fig.8 shows a motion generation system for humans. At first, the field conditions are set. Field conditions include nature of each object, perception area of each object, liking of each observer, evaluation function and the initial velocity of each moving object. Attractiveness is calculated for each video frame. Then the movement path is calculated using it. Partial motion with emotion and personality is selected using the attractiveness. For example, if it is plus and a big value, there are some favorite things near the observer and he/she is very pleasant and brisk. So he/she briskly walks or runs. On the other hand, if attractiveness is minus and a big value, as when there are some enemies or dangerous things near the observer, he/she feels terrible as he/she escapes. Finally human motion with emotion and personality is generated from each partial motion on each moving path.

Figs. 9 and 10 show examples of generated motion. The first involves a favorite object. The observer walks fast and briskly when the object found. He/she runs pleasantly when the object is liked. Walking becomes normal after getting it. The second case shows a disliked object. At first, he/she walks to the object to find out what it is, but walking becomes dejected after identifying it. These examples show

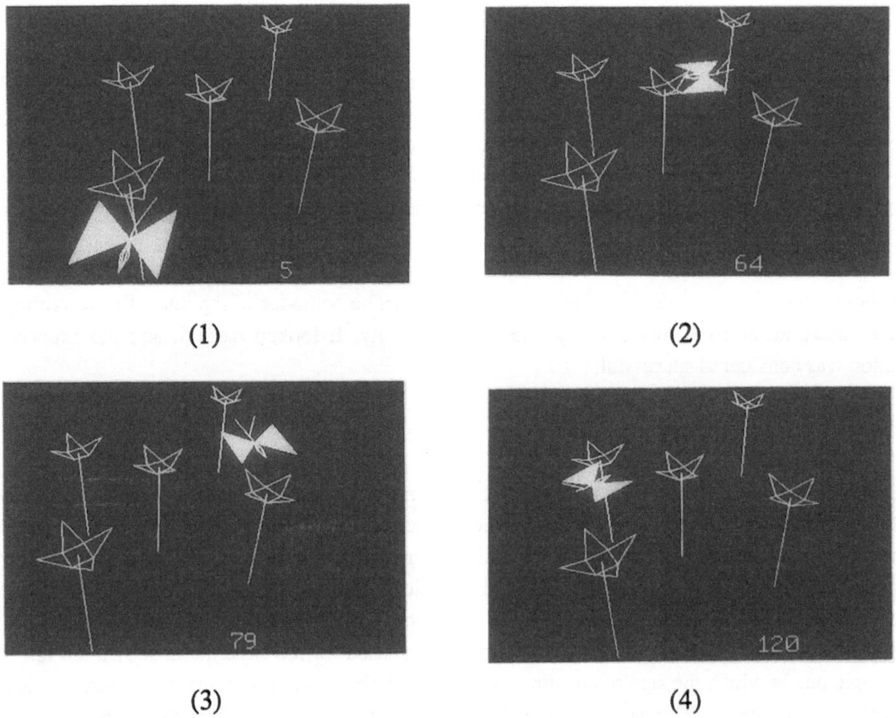

Fig.5 Application to animation of a butterfly

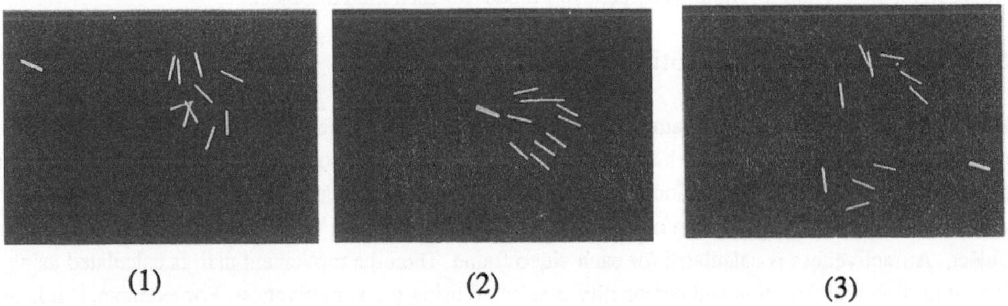

Fig.7 Example simulating a school of small fish attacked by a large fish of another kind

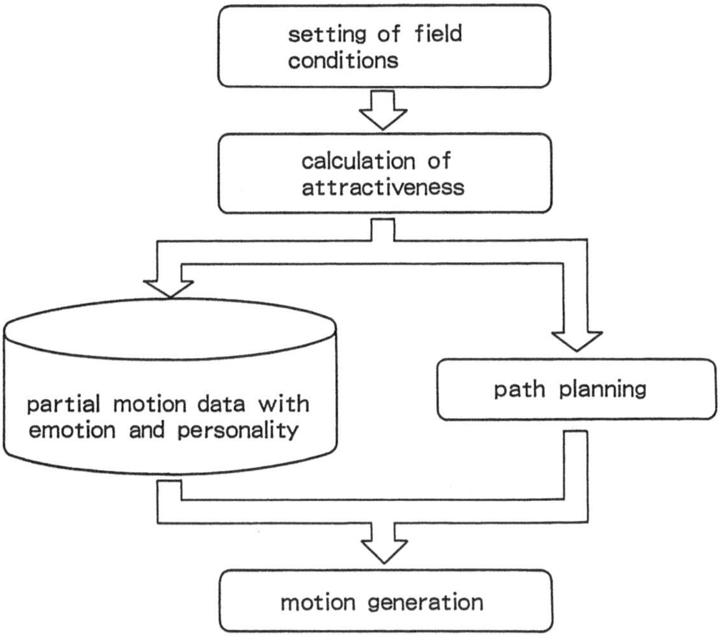

Fig.8 Human animation system with the attractiveness

attractiveness is effective for generating human motion.

Fig.11 shows an another example of generated human motion. Here, a car is suddenly driven into a crowd. As persons perceive the car, they run away from it. This scene is the same as that of the school of small fish shown in Fig.7.

7. Conclusions

We have proposed a path planning method using 'attractiveness'. The method is based on the nature of animals. Motion of an animal depends upon what objects there are and how it likes them. It goes to favorite things, while it flees its enemies and dangerous things. Attractiveness is composed of an object's nature, perception area, observer's liking and an evaluating function. The motion path of animals is simulated by using attractiveness. As examples the flight path of a butterfly in a flower garden was simulated naturally, and a school of small fish attacked by a large fish was also simulated. The small fish moved about as if sprayed from a water fountain. When a human motion system was combined with the attractiveness, human motion, with emotion and personality, was easily generated.

8. Acknowledgments

We would like to thank Messers. Ken-ichi Anjyo, Yoshiaki Usami, Tsuneya Kurihara and Kiyoshi Arai for suggestions and discussions.

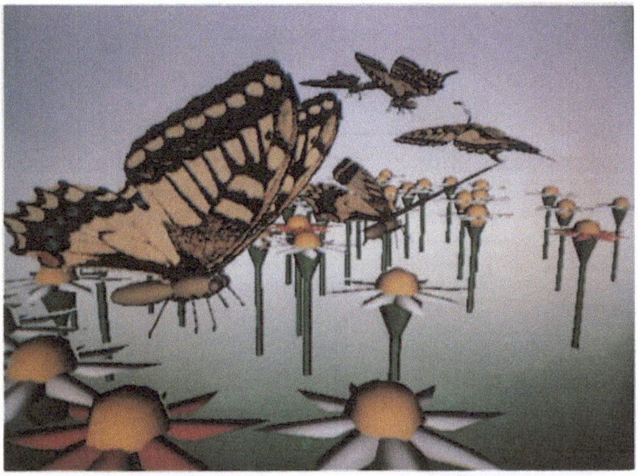

Fig.6 Rendered scene of the butterfly animation

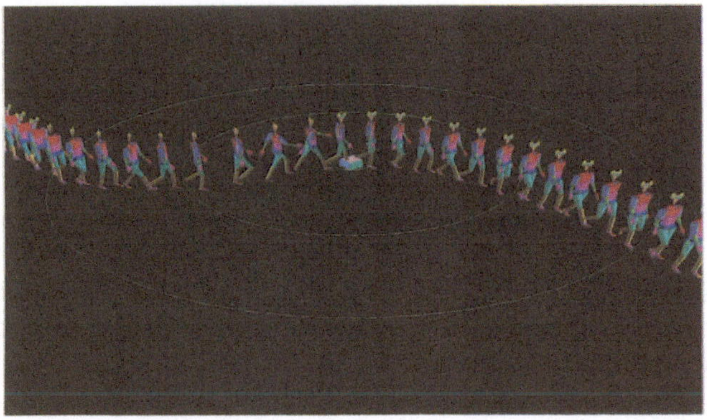

Fig.9 Sample of generated human motion in the case of a favorite object

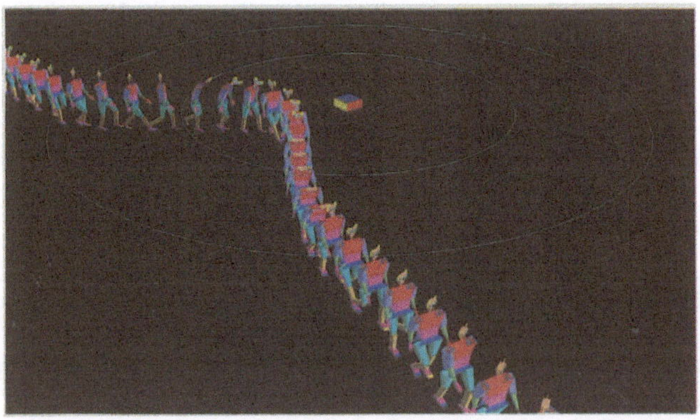

Fig.10 Sample of generated human motion in the case of a disliked object

(1)

(2)

(3)

(4)

(5)

(6)

Fig.11 Sample of generated human motion in the case of a car being driven into a crowd

9. References

[Unuma 91] Unuma M. and Takeuchi R., "Generation of Human Motion with Emotion" Computer Animation '91, pp.77-88,1991

[Wilhelms 87] Wilhelms J., "Toward Automatic Motion Control", IEEE CG&A, pp.11-22, 1987

[Reynolds 82] Reynolds C.W., "Computer Animation with Scripts and Actors", Computer Graphics, pp.289-296, 1982

[Uchiki 86] Uchiki T., Maruichi T. and Tokoro M., "A Method for Generating Animation Using Active Character", Proceedings of the Second NICOGRAPH Paper Contest, pp.197-206, 1986 (in Japanese)

[Amakawa 88] Amakawa K. and Takeuchi R., "A Method of Motion Control for Computer Animation", Proceedings of the Fourth NICOGRAPH Paper Contest, pp.98-103, 1988 (in Japanese)

[Reynolds 87] Reynolds C.W., "Flocks, Herds, and Schools: A Distributed Behavioral Model", Computer Graphics, pp.25-34, 1987

Ryozo Takeuchi received a BA in 1968 and an MA in 1970, both from Nagoya University, Japan. He first joined the Electrical Insulation Research Section in Hitachi Research Laboratory, Hitachi, Ltd., Japan in 1970, and later, in 1982 the Data Terminal Section where he engaged in the development of full-color document scanners and full-color image printers. He has been a senior researcher in the Computer Graphics Section since 1987, and he is now engaged in research on basic computer graphics technologies.

Mr. Takeuchi is a member of the Institute of Electrical and Electronics Engineers, and the Institute of Electronics, Information and Communication Engineers of Japan. He received an Outstanding Papers Award from the IEEE CES in 1977.

address: The 10th Department, Hitachi Research Laboratory, Hitachi, Ltd.,
4026 Kuji-cho, Hitachi-shi, Ibaraki-ken 319-12 Japan
e-mail: takeuchi@hrl.hitachi.co.jp

Munetoshi Unuma received a BA in 1983 and an MS in 1985, both from Ibaraki University, Japan. Then he joined the Data Terminal Section in Hitachi Research Laboratory, Hitachi, Ltd., Japan, where he was engaged in the development of coders/decoders for facsimile, based on the error diffusion method. He is currently a researcher of the Computer Graphics Section. His interest is human motion simulation.

Mr. Unuma is a member of the Electronics, Information and Communication Engineers of Japan.

address: same as above
e-mail: unuma@hrl.hitachi.co.jp

Koji Amakawa is a graduate student of computer and information sciences at the University of California, Santa Cruz. He received a BS in mechanical engineering, an MS in energy conversion engineering, both from Kyushu University, Japan, in 1980 and 1982, and an MS in computer and information sciences from the University of California, Santa Cruz in 1991. He was previously a researcher at Hitachi Research Laboratory, Hitachi, Ltd., Japan. His interests lie in machine learning, non-linear system simulation, and computer graphics.

address: Baskin Center for Computer Engineering and Information Sciences, 225 Applied Sciences Building, University of California, Santa Cruz, CA95064, U.S.A.
e-mail: koji@cis.ucsc.edu

Automating Virtual Camera Control for Computer Animation

Tsukasa Noma and Naoyuki Okada

ABSTRACT

This paper presents an approach to automating the control of virtual cameras in computer animation. The best view direction is determined based on the *view direction unsuitability functions* of actors and actors' weights, and the camera is then positioned. To keep the order of actors on the screen, a BSP-based rule is also proposed.
Key words: computer animation, virtual camera, automatic camera control, viewing

1 INTRODUCTION

Computer animation has already had a considerable impact on many aspects of computer use, and its popularity is growing in science, engineering and art. Over the next few years, we can expect a vast increase in the range of computer animation applications. Even now, however, the production of computer animation is still costly, and the heavy dependence on man power might be a serious obstacle to the wider use of computer animation.

This paper presents an approach to automating the control of virtual cameras in computer animation. In this approach, the direction of a virtual camera is determined by actors' *view direction unsuitability function* (VDUF) with their weights, and the camera position is then calculated based on the locations of actors. The generated view function, which is composed of the camera position and direction, does not surprise viewers, as is often the case with commercial CG films, but the view function is natural and suitable for explaining the situation from a cinematic commonsense point of view. This approach, then, promises saving much time in the production of computer animation.

In the next section, we overview the background of our work and discuss the requirements for automatic virtual camera control. Section 3 presents our approach to automating the control of virtual cameras with some examples. Finally, Section 4 concludes this paper with some comments on future research directions.

2 BACKGROUND AND REQUIREMENTS

2.1 Background

In 1990, we started a research project called MULTRAN (MULtimedia TRANslator), the aim of which is to develop a system for understanding, generation, and translation through multimedia (Okada 1992). In this project, the mutual translation between natural language and image is particularly important, and computer animation is adopted as an output medium on the image side.

Now let us suppose that an animation is to be produced from a story written in natural language. To make a translation, (1) global and rough scenario, (2) local and detailed motion of actors, and (3) viewing functions should be determined *automatically*. In most of the existing animation systems, however, these three are specified interactively and/or with animation language.

Concerning scenario and motion, there has been some published work. Takashima et al. (1987) made a scenario from a story written in natural language, and then produced an animation. Badler et al. (1991) also made an animation from a sequence of natural language instructions. For the automatic motion control of actors, Magnenat-Thalmann and Thalmann (1990) introduces some techniques including task-level specifications (Zeltzer 1985) and the use of dynamics (Bruderlin 1989).

Next, let us overview the previous work about viewing functions and virtual cameras. Magnenat-Thalmann and Thalmann (1985) extended the notion of virtual cameras and realized some special effects including wipe effects. Ware et al. (1990) discussed how to specify viewpoint in virtual environments and made a comparison among three metaphors. Mackinlay et al. (1990) also proposed *logarithmic motion* for controlling a viewpoint in a virtual world. In addition, Turner et al. (1991) discussed the use of dynamics for virtual camera control. Although these made some contributions to the enhancement of the power of virtual cameras, no attempt is made to *automate* virtual camera control.

An example of automatic virtual camera control is found in (Shinagawa 1990), where view function generation is automated for walk-through animation. Its purpose is, however, to walk through the object reproduced from the cross sectional data for medical imaging, and hence the techniques are not applicable to *natural* camera positioning for story-based animation. Phillips et al. (1992) also proposed automatic viewing control method, but it is for 3D direct manipulation. Summing up the above, there has been no work on automatic virtual camera control for computer animation in a general situation.

2.2 Requirements for Automatic Virtual Camera

A virtual camera has seven degrees of freedom — three for camera position, two for line of sight, one for twist angle, and the other for zooming. These seven degrees of freedom have been fully used in computer animation, since the visual impact of complicated camera motions has been the basis for much of the commercial computer animations produced (Turner 1991).

Reviewing the camera work in ordinary movie films, however, there are few cases where stimulating camera motion is used. This is partially because the motion of a real camera is physically restricted, but it is fact that we need not and *must not* make full use of the seven degrees of freedom of a camera to tell a story. Otherwise, the viewer would be confused.

Just as Lasseter (1987) pointed out the importance of the principles of traditional animation, we assert that we should pay special attention to the principles of camera work in films (Arijon 1976). The twisting of camera is rarely used in ordinary films. Except for expressing emotions, upward and downward camera angle cannot be found so often. If we fix the zoom parameter of a camera, that is, the focal length of the lens, then all the degrees of freedom we have to treat is only 3. The initial problem thus comes down to how to determine the position and direction of a virtual camera *on a two-dimensional plane.* In addition, we decided to deal with only *fixed* virtual cameras. With *cutback techniques*, fixed cameras have their sufficient power of expression. In what follows, we will discuss with the above-mentioned restrictions.

Now we present the requirements for automating virtual camera control in computer animation. The requirements are listed below:

1. *The rule should be general and all-inclusive.*
   As is often the case with art, cinematic camera work is usually explained based on specific cases, some of which might contradict each other (Arijon 1976). To automate the decision in computer, however, the rule should be applicable to any case.
2. *In the rule, the camera angle should be influenced by the direction of actors.*
   The direction of actors as well as their position is an important factor of deciding camera position and direction. Furthermore, the rule should take some actors into consideration simultaneously.
3. *The rule should cover cutback techniques.*
   Cutback is the most fundamental and general method giving variety to camera work, and thus indispensable to the rule for general-purpose camera control.
4. *The rule should not be contradictory to Triangle Principle.*
   Triangle Principle (Arijon 1976) is the rule that the view point should always be on one side of the line between main actors. The advantage of this principle is that the order of actors on the screen is never changed. Otherwise, it would be difficult for the viewer to understand who one is.

3 AUTOMATING VIRTUAL CAMERA CONTROL

This section introduces our approach to automating the control of virtual cameras. This approach, which is an extension of that in (Noma 1991), is summarized as follows: For a set of actors A, the view direction to A is calculated based on the *view direction unsuitability functions* of all the elements of A. After the decision of the view direction, the camera position is determined considering the view direction and the actors' position. In the following subsections, each step is discussed in detail.

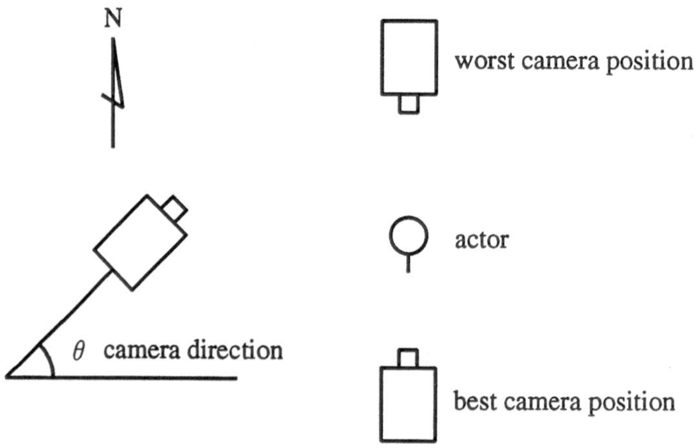

Figure 1: An actor facing to the south.

3.1 View Direction Unsuitability Function

The view direction unsuitability function (VDUF) f of an actor is a function that represents its unsuitability degree of any view direction. Formally, it is defined as:

$$f : [0, 2\pi) \rightarrow [0, \infty). \tag{1}$$

Typically, f has the minimum value for the front direction and the maximum for the back direction.

For example, in Fig. 1, an actor faces to the south. To view a scene of the actor, the best view direction is from south to north ($\frac{\pi}{2}$), and the worst is from north to south ($\frac{3}{2}\pi$). An example VDUF f for the actor is given as:

$$f(\theta) = k(\theta - \frac{\pi}{2})^2, \tag{2}$$

and its graph is shown in Fig. 2. Note that θ is circular at 0 and 2π, and the view direction in Fig. 2 is in degree.

3.2 Determining View Direction

Unless all the actors have the similar VDUFs, informally speaking, except for the case where they set their face to the same direction, there is no single suitable view direction for every actor. Thus, to calculate the view direction for the set of actors, we have to consider the *importance* of each actor, which is represented by its *weight*.

Let A be a set of actors, $a_1, a_2, \ldots, a_n$ be the elements of A, f_i be the VDUF of a_i, and w_i be the *weight* of a_i. The VDUF F of A is defined as:

$$F(\theta) = \frac{\sum_{i=1}^{n} w_i f_i(\theta)}{\sum_{i=1}^{n} w_i} \tag{3}$$

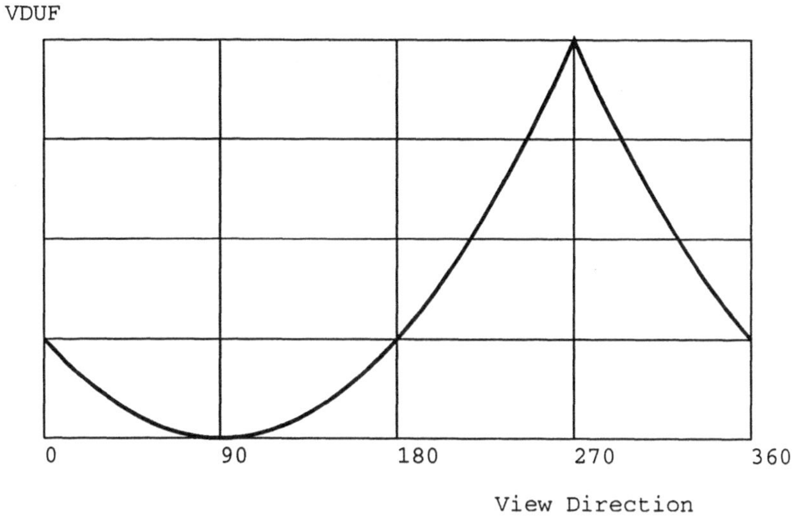

Figure 2: An example VDUF for the actor.

The denominator of (3) is for the normalization of VDUF, which enables us to use any set of actors as an element of larger set of actors. This kind of recursiveness is of much use in case of dealing with a group of actors. Then the most suitable view direction of A is obtained as the value θ giving the minimum $F(\theta)$.

w_i and f_i are also the function of time, and they change as the story unfolds. For example, if we adopt the rule that the weight of a speaker should be more than others', then the face of the speaker can be seen at any time (cutback). In Sections 3.5 and 3.6, the change of actor's VDUF and weight is discussed in further detail.

3.3 Determining Camera Position

Although it is difficult to determine the *real* best camera position according to a situation, we suppose that the best camera position is the position from which all the actors are covered by the visual field of the camera in the best view direction determined as shown in the previous subsection.

Let θ_0 be the best view direction for a set of actors A and 2φ be the angle of field of the camera. The best camera position for A is the intersection point of two lines tangent to the convex hull of A: one's angle is $\theta_0 + \varphi$ and the other's is $\theta_0 - \varphi$ (Fig. 3).

If an actor turns to a different direction, and his VDUF is subsequently changed, the camera position should be recalculated. The same should be done in case of actor's motion and/or the change of speaker. The model described here does not consider side margins on a screen. By giving appropriate margins, the scene becomes more natural.

Figure 4 shows a sample situation where three actors a_1(Red), a_2(Green), and a_3(Blue) are talking

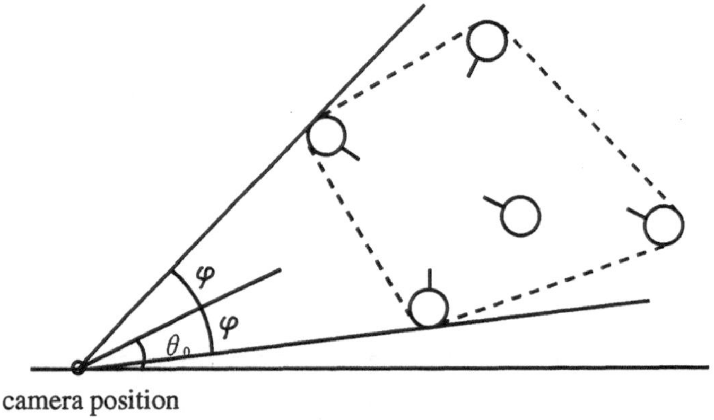

Figure 3: The best camera position as the intersection point of two tangential lines of A's convex hull.

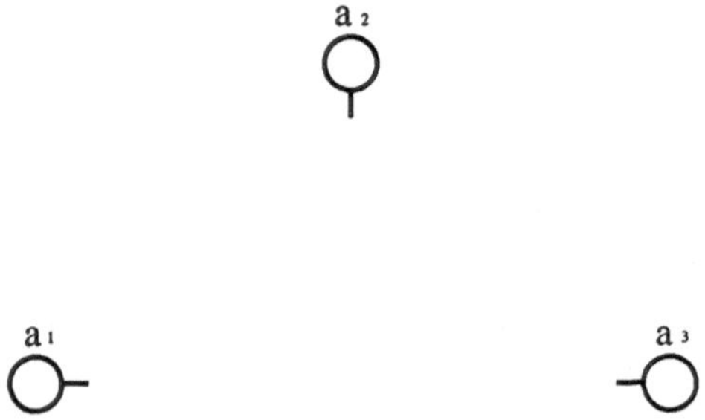

Figure 4: The position and direction of three actors talking with each other.

with each other, and Fig. 5 is three scenes of the situation: a_1 is speaking in (a), a_3 is speaking in (b), and a_2 is speaking in (c). Their camera position and direction is determined by giving weight 2.5 to a speaker and 1 to a non-speaker.

3.4 Triangle Principle by BSP

The camera positioning described in the previous subsection fulfills Requirements 1, 2 and 3 in Section 2.2. Depending on the VDUFs and weights of actors, however, Requirement 4 is not necessarily satisfied. A counter example is shown in Fig. 6. In this scene, the position and VDUF of each actor are the same as those in Fig. 5. The weight of a_1 is, however, extremely large.

To keep the order of two actors a_1 and a_2 on the screen, it is sufficient for the camera to be on one side of the line between a_1 and a_2. In other words, the camera should always exist on the half-plane. We thus propose another rule using BSP (Binary Space Partitioning).

(a) a_1 is speaking.

(b) a_3 is speaking.

(c) a_2 is speaking.

Figure 5: Three scenes of the situation.

Figure 6: The scene giving extremely large weight to a_1.

Let B be a subset of A. The elements of B, denoted by $a_{i_1}, a_{i_2}, ..., a_{i_m}$, are assumed to be so important that their order on the screen should be kept. The proposed rule is that the camera should always exist in the following area S:

$$S = \bigcap_{1 \leq j < k \leq m} h(a_{i_j}, a_{i_k}) \tag{4}$$

where $h(a_{i_j}, a_{i_k})$ is the half-plane from which a_{i_j} is seen on the left-hand side and a_{i_k} is on the right-hand side.

In Fig. 7, S is hatched in the situation of Fig. 4.

If the recalculated camera position is outside S, the view direction should be modified so that the camera position does not go out of S. Obviously, this rule ensures that the order of the actors would be kept.

3.5 Dynamic Scenes

The above-mentioned decision rule of camera position and direction works well for the case where actors are almost still, for example, in conversational situations. In case of dynamic scenes where actors move, however, the most suitable camera position and direction always change. Although it is possible to move the camera with repetitive calculations per frame, this would cause the vibration of camera motion because of actors' slight motion.

Hence we propose the use of the fixed camera covering the scene in a fixed interval of time. For the time interval between t_1 and t_2 ($t_1 < t_2$), the *interval-based view direction unsuitability function* (IVDUF) $\tilde{F}$ of a set of actors A including $a_1, \ldots, a_n$ is a function that represents A's view direction unsuitability degree *for the interval*, and $\tilde{F}$ is defined as:

$$\tilde{F}(\theta) = \frac{\sum_{i=1}^{n} \int_{t_1}^{t_2} w_i(t) f_i(\theta, t) dt}{\sum_{i=1}^{n} \int_{t_1}^{t_2} w_i(t) dt} \tag{5}$$

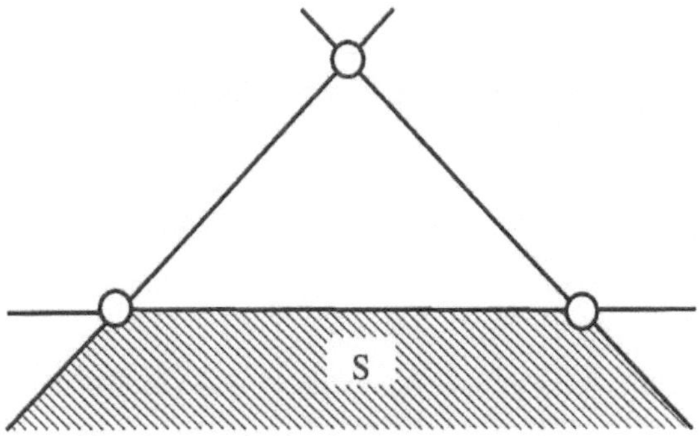

Figure 7: S is represented as hatched area.

On a similar line as VDUF, the most suitable view direction of A in the interval is the θ giving the minimum $\tilde{F}(\theta)$. The camera position is subsequently obtained as the intersection point of the two lines tangent to the convex hull of the trajectories (loci) of the actors.

3.6 Determining Weight

With the discussion in the previous subsections, the problem of virtual camera control came down to the problem of giving weight to actors. This subsection is thus devoted to determining actors' weight.

To automate weight determination, there are two approaches. One is deciding an actor's weight based on the task he is doing. An example is giving more weight to a speaker, as shown in Section 3.2. This approach can easily be realized in a task-oriented animation system (Zeltzer 1985).

The other approach is directly extracting weight information from script or natural language text. The natural language processing group of our project is now trying to decide each actor's *degree of sympathy* implicitly appeared in the text, and it would be able to be used as actor's weight.

4 CONCLUSION

An approach to automating virtual camera control is presented. It is general and all-inclusive (Requirement 1), the camera angle is based on the actors' direction (Requirement 2), and cutback techniques are covered (Requirement 3). Combining with the BSP-based rule, the approach is not contradictory to Triangle Principle (Requirement 4).

Future work includes two topics: One is the extension of our automatic camera model. Dynamic camera motion is of much concern. The other is the development of an interactive camera control system where the output of our model is used as *default* and animators can easily modify the camera work.

REFERENCES

Arijon D (1976) *Grammar of the Film Language.* Focal Press, London

Badler NI, Webber BL, Kalita J, Esakov J (1991) Animation from Instructions. In: Badler NI, Barsky BA, Zeltzer D (eds) *Making Them Move: Mechanics, Control, and Animation of Articulated Figures.* Morgan-Kaufmann, San Mateo, CA, pp 51–93

Bruderlin A, Calvert TW (1989) Goal-Directed, Dynamic Animation of Human Walking. *ACM SIGGRAPH Comput. Graph.* 23(3): 233–242

Lasseter J (1987) Principles of Traditional Animation Applied to 3D Computer Animation. *ACM SIGGRAPH Comput. Graph.* 21(4): 35–44

Mackinlay JD, Card SK, Robertson GG (1990) Rapid Controlled Movement Through a Virtual 3D Workspace. *ACM SIGGRAPH Comput. Graph.* 24(4): 171–176

Magnenat-Thalmann N, Thalmann D (1985) Single and Multiple Virtual Movie Cameras for Special Cinematographic Effects. In: Kunii TL (ed), *Computer Graphics: Visual Technology and Art*, Springer-Verlag, Tokyo Berlin Heidelberg New York, pp 271–283

Magnenat-Thalmann N, Thalmann D (1990) *Computer Animation: Theory and Practice.* 2nd rev ed, Springer-Verlag, Tokyo Berlin Heidelberg New York

Noma T, Okada N (1991) Automatic Viewing for Computer Animation (in Japanese). *Proc. 42th Annual Convention IPS Japan*, pp (2)367–368

Okada N, Endo T (1992) Story Generation Based on Dynamics of Mind. *Computational Intelligence* 8(1), To appear

Phillips CB, Badler NI, Granieri J (1992) Automatic Viewing Control for 3D Direct Manipulation. *Proc. 1992 Symposium on Interactive 3D Graphics*, To appear

Shinagawa Y, Kunii TL, Nomura Y, Okuno T, Young Y (1990) Automating View Function Generation for Walk-through Animation Using a Reeb Graph. In: Magnenat-Thalmann N, Thalmann D (eds) *Computer Animation '90.* Springer-Verlag, Tokyo Berlin Heidelberg New York, pp 227–237

Takashima Y, Shimazu H, Tomono M (1987) Story Driven Animation. *Proc. CHI+GI '87*, pp 149–153

Turner R, Balaguer F, Gobbetti E, Thalmann D (1991) Physically-Based Interactive Camera Motion Control Using 3D Input Devices. In: Patrikalakis NM (ed) *Scientific Visualization of Physical Phenomena.* Springer-Verlag, Tokyo Berlin Heidelberg New York, pp 135–145

Ware C, Osborne S (1990) Exploration and Virtual Camera Control in Virtual Three Dimensional Environments, *ACM SIGGRAPH Comput. Graph.* 24(2): 175–183

Zeltzer D (1985) Toward an Integrated View of 3-D Computer Animation. *The Visual Computer* 1(4): 249–259

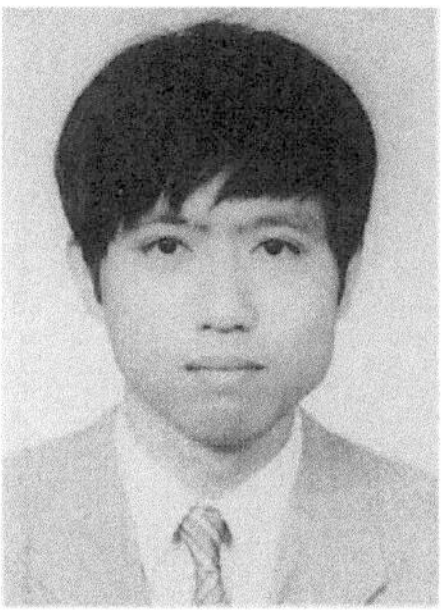

Tsukasa Noma is currently an associate professor in the Department of Artificial Intelligence at Kyushu Institute of Technology. His research interests include computer graphics and artificial intelligence. He received the BSc degree in mathematics in 1984 from Waseda University, and the MSc and DSc in information science from the University of Tokyo in 1986 and 1989. He is a member of ACM, IEEE, Information Processing Society of Japan, Computer Graphics Society, and Japanese Society for Artificial Intelligence.

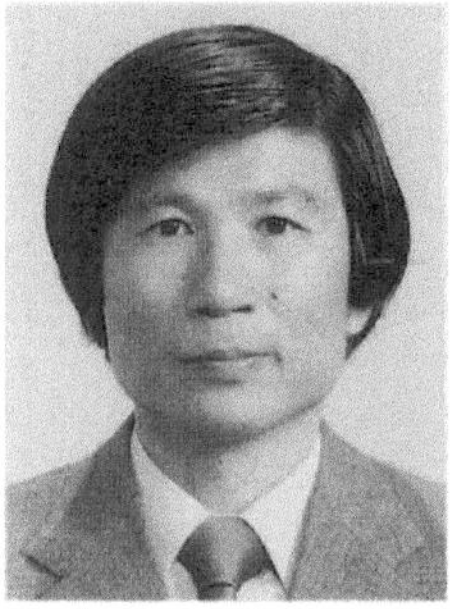

Naoyuki Okada is currently a professor in the Department of Artificial Intelligence at Kyushu Institute of Technology. He has been active in integrated semantic processings of language and vision. He received the BEng degree in applied science in 1964 from Tokai University, the MEng in electronic engineering from Kyushu University in 1966, and the DEng in computer science from Kyushu University in 1976. He is a member of Information Processing Society of Japan, Institute of Electronics, Information, and Communication Engineers of Japan, Japanese Society for Artificial Intelligence, and Japanese Cognitive Science Community.

Address: Department of Artificial Intelligence, Faculty of Computer Science and Systems Engineering, Kyushu Institute of Technology, 680-4 Kawazu, Iizuka, Fukuoka, 820 JAPAN.
E-mail: {noma,okada}@ai.kyutech.ac.jp

Part IV
Geometric Models

Algorithmic Animation of Constructing Surfaces from Cells

Tosiyasu L. Kunii, Yoshihisa Shinagawa, and Shigeo Takahashi

ABSTRACT

The expressive capability of object shapes in CAD systems so far have been limited to polyhedra or combinations of primitive shapes such as cubes, cylinders and balls. The surface coding method based on Morse theory, however, enabled us to code and construct complex shapes of objects that are smooth using primitives called "cells." It constructs object surfaces by pasting cells. For users to better understand the construction procedure, computer animation that shows the construction procedure is useful. This paper presents the algorithm animation of the surface construction and the transformation of the constructed surface. First, a user specifies the skeleton of the object called the Reeb graph. Surface coding is then automatically carried out. Finally, the animation of constructing the object from top to bottom is generated. The surface of a human cochlea is constructed as an example of the algorithm animation.
Key Words and Phrases: Morse theory, 3D reconstruction, cell, algorithmic animation

INTRODUCTION

3-dimensional (3D) objects handled by Computer-Aided Design (CAD) systems up to now have been restricted to simple shapes such as polyhedra in the case of Boundary Representation (B-rep) systems and the combinations of primitives in the case of Constructive Solid Geometry (CSG) systems such as cubes, cylinders and balls. Although contemporary CAD systems encompass representations of smooth surfaces, they were limited to parametric surfaces such as B-spline surfaces and swept surfaces (the terminologies used above can be found, for example, in (Farin 1990)). The surface coding method based on Morse theory (Shinagawa, Kergosien and Kunii 1991) enabled us to code complex shapes of objects such as human organs. Using the codes, a method was proposed to form smooth surfaces by pasting primitives called "cells" (Shinagawa 1991). To decide the sequence of pasting cells, a user specifies the skeleton of the object called the Reeb graph (Reeb 1946) using the icons defined in (Shinagawa, Kergosien and Kunii 1991). For users to better understand how to construct surfaces using the cells, the system provides computer animation that shows the construction procedure; i.e., the surface is constructed from top to bottom pasting the cells.

OUTLINE OF THE SURFACE CONSTRUCTION SYSTEM

In the system, we use three kinds of cells: 1D, 2D and 3D cells. They are called a 1-cell, 2-cell and 3-cell respectively. Simply speaking, a 0-cell is a point, a 1-cell is a chip of a string and a 2-cell is a patch of a surface. Fig. 1 shows how the cells are pasted to form the surface of a torus. According to Morse theory, there is one-to-one correspondence between a cell and a non-degenerate singular point of a Morse function defined on the object surface that is a C^2 2-manifold. In our system, we use the height function that gives the height of a point on the object surface embedded in $\boldsymbol{R}^3$ (Shinagawa,

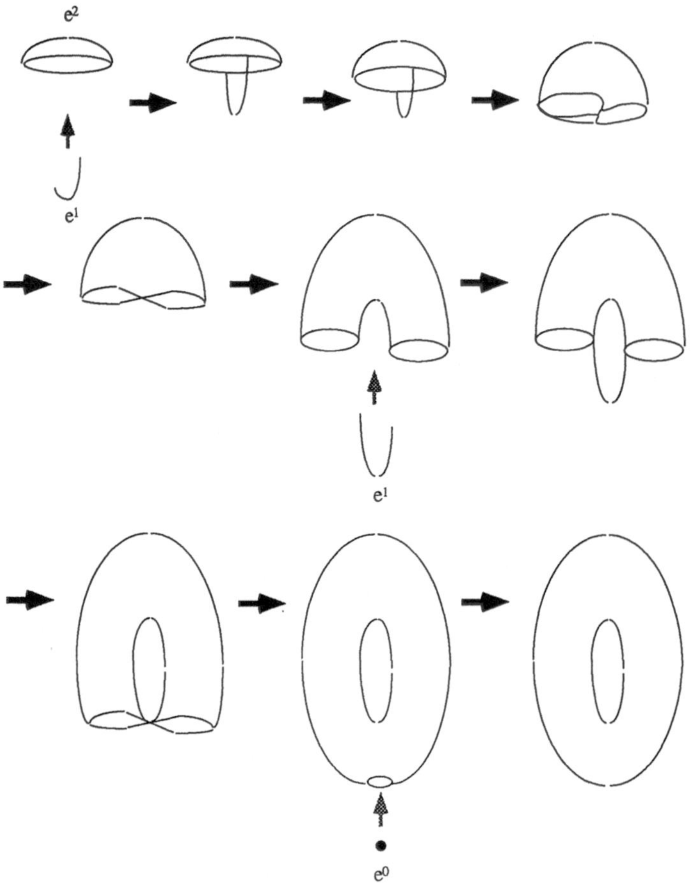

Fig. 1 Surface Construction of a torus

Kergosien and Kunii 1991). In this case, there are three kinds of non-degenerate singular points: peaks, saddle points and pits (see Fig. 2a). A peak corresponds to a 2-cell, a saddle point to a 1-cell and a pit to a 0-cell. (Description of Morse theory can be found, for example, in (Milnor 1963).) Scanning from top to bottom, codes are generated by listing the operations of attaching cells that correspond to the singular points. There are four kinds of operators: *put_e2*, *put_e1_divide*, *put_e1_merge* and *put_e0* (k-cell is abbreviated to *ek* above). Each operator has several parameters. For attaching a 1-cell, there are two operators: one for dividing a contour and the other for merging two contours.

To specify the sequence of attaching cells, the Reeb graph (Reeb 1946) is used. The Reeb graph of the height function is obtained by considering the cross sectional contours of the object (see Fig. 2b). A cross sectional contour is represented by a point in the Reeb graph as shown in Fig. 2c. Users define the Reeb graph using the icons shown in Fig. 3a. The icon representation of a torus is illustrated in Fig. 3b. The operations can be directly obtained from the icon representation.

After pasting a cell, the surface that a cell is attached to is transformed like a clay model as shown in Fig. 1. The surface is reconstructed by associating geometric information with the cells such as the locations of the cells and the way each contour is transformed. The transformation is represented by generating cross sectional contours slice by slice from top to bottom. Surface patches are generated

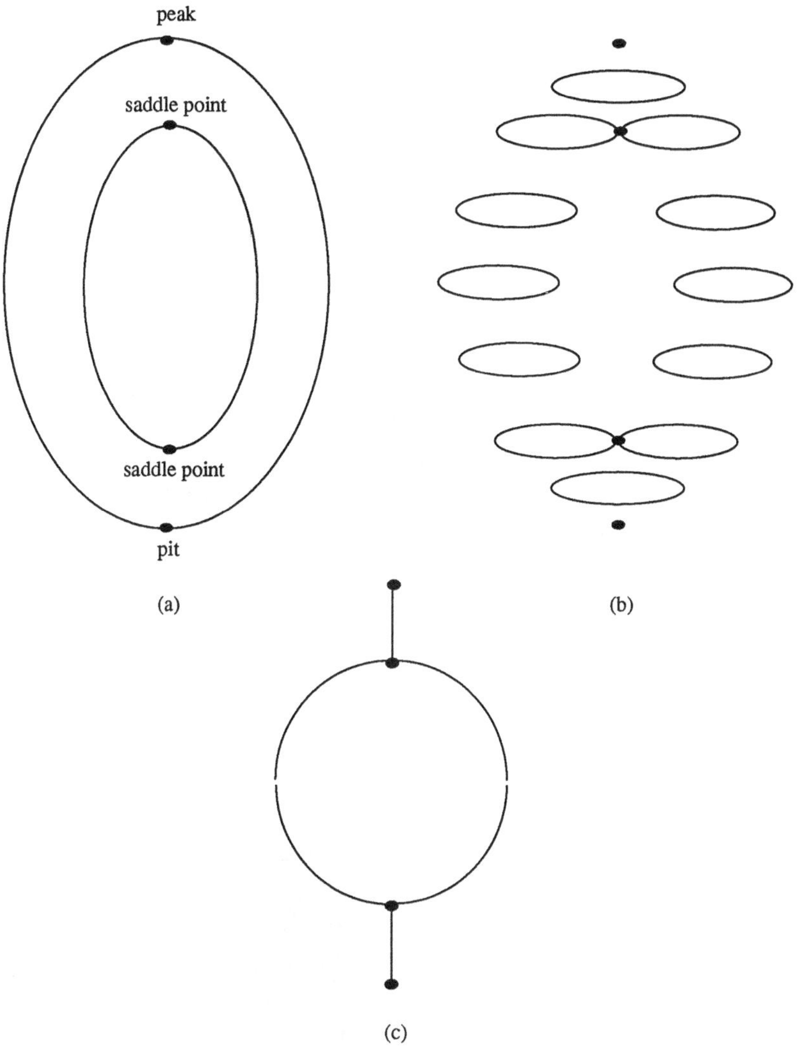

Fig. 2 (a) A torus, (b) its cross sections and (c) its Reeb graph (Shinagawa et al. 1991)

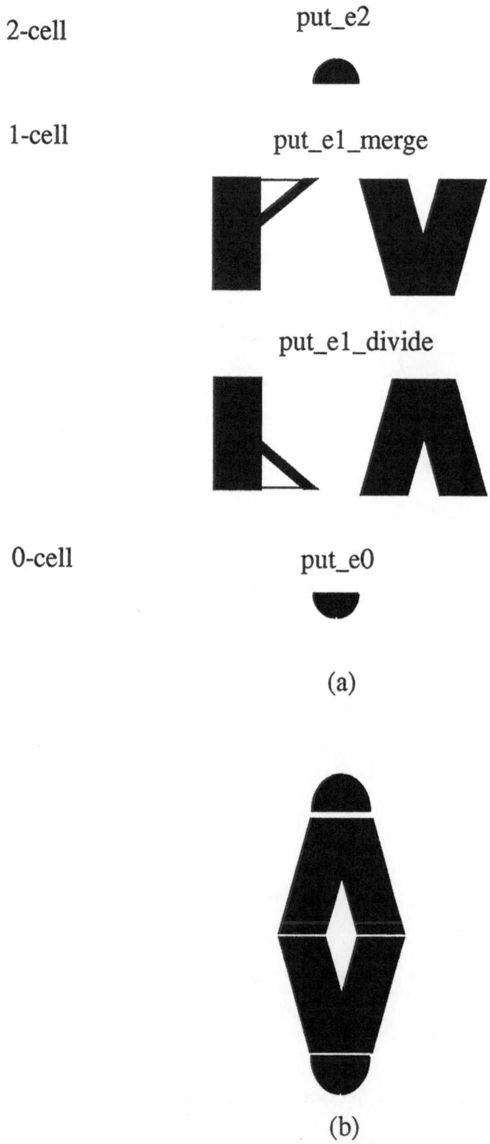

Fig. 3 Icons for the Reeb graph

between contours on the adjacent cross sections. Users specify how a contour is transformed as the cross sectional plane scans the object. The transformation of a contour is specified by interpolation functions or guiding curves along which the control points of the contour move. As with a 1-cell, its path is specified.

ALGORITHM ANIMATION OF THE CONSTRUCTION PROCEDURE

The generated surface may have multiple layers as is often seen in natural objects such as human organs and the contours are merged and divided as the object is scanned from top to bottom. The multiple layers are represented by a nested structure of cross sectional contours using a tree. It is not easy for users to understand the complex structures at a glance even semi-transparent representation (Kaneda, Harada, Nakamae, Yauda and Sato 1987; Mao, Fujishiro and Kunii 1990) is used. For this reason, we used the fourth dimension: time. The procedure of reconstructing the surface from top to bottom is envisaged as the computer animation. This animation is a kind of algorithm animation that visualizes the surface construction algorithm using cells. Although the system does not provide general purpose algorithm animation such as described in (Stasko 1990; Brown 1988; London and Duisberg 1985), it explains the construction procedure visually. In our system, the computer animation that shows the construction algorithm is the best representation for understanding the structure of the object.

TRANSFORMATION ANIMATION OF CONSTRUCTED SURFACES

The object shape thus constructed can be transformed by changing the locations of the contours. The process of transformation can be recorded as computer animation. The users choose the 'key' contour to be moved. Key contours are the ones with which users associate the geometric information when creating the object surfaces. Intermediate contours are also moved according to the movement of the key contours because their locations are obtained as the interpolation of key contours. When guiding curves are used for the interpolation, the curves also move when the contours they are attached to move.

Display Examples

Fig. 4 shows a scene from the surface construction animation. Fig. 5 shows the reconstructed object: a human cochlea.

CONCLUSIONS AND FUTURE WORK

The algorithm animation of the surface construction using cells and the transformation of the constructed surface has been presented. The transformation method presented in this paper is limited to the cases where the structure of the Reeb graph does not change. The extension of the transformation to the cases where the Reeb graph changes is left as future research.

ACKNOWLEDGMENTS

We wish to express our gratitude to Dr. Kansei Iwata, the president of Graphica Co., Ltd. and Mr. Norimasa Koyama, the executive director of Cadtech Inc. for offering the drum scanner, G-225C,

Yokogawa Hewlet Packard Co., Ltd. for HP9000 model 550 and Silicon Graphics Co., Ltd. for IRIS 4D/70GT. Special thanks are extended to Dr. Yannick L. Kergosien of Mathématiques, Université de Paris-Sud for information on the Reeb graph and his precious comments to our papers.

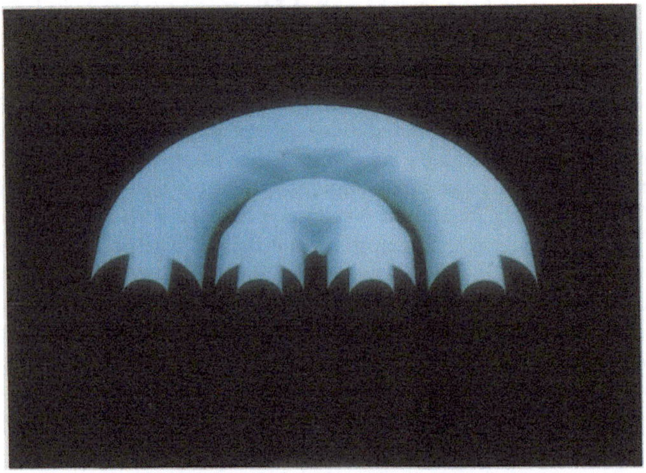

Fig. 4 A scene from the construction animation

Fig. 5 Constructed object: a human cochlea

REFERENCES

Brown MH (1988) Exploring Algorithms Using Balsa-II. *IEEE Computer*, Vol.21, No.5, pp. 14–36

Farin GE (1990) *Curves and Surfaces for Computer Aided Geometric Design; A Practical Guide.* 2nd ed, Academic Press

Kaneda K, Harada K, Nakamae E, Yasuda M, Sato AG (1987) Reconstruction and Semi-Transparent Display Method for Observing Inner Structure of an Object Consisting of Multiple Surfaces. *The Visual Computer*, Vol.3, No.3, pp.137–144

London RL, Duisberg RA (1985) Animating Programs Using Smalltalk. *IEEE Computer*, Vol.18, No.8, pp. 61–71

Mao X, Fujishiro I, Kunii TL (1990) A translucent Display Algorithm for G-octree Represented Grey-Scale Images. *The Journal of Visualization and Computer Animation*, Vol.1, No.1, pp.22–25

Miln63 Milnor J (1963) *Morse Theory.* Princeton University Press, New Jersey

Reeb G (1946) Sur les points singuliers d'une forme de Pfaff completement integrable ou d'une fonction numerique. *Comptes Rendus Acad. Sciences Paris* Vol.222, pp. 847–849

Shinagawa Y, Kergosien YL and Kunii TL (1991) Surface Coding Based on Morse Theory. *IEEE Computer Graphics and Applications*, Vol.11, No.5, pp. 66–78

Shinagawa Y (1991) *A Study of a Surface Construction System Based on Morse Theory and Reeb Graph.* Dissertation Submitted to the Department of Information Science, Faculty of Science, the University of Tokyo

Stasko JT (1990) Tango: A Framework and System for Algorithm Animation. *IEEE Computer*, Vol.23, No.9, pp. 27–39

BIOGRAPHIES

Tosiyasu L. Kunii is currently Professor of Information and Computer Science, the University of Tokyo.
He authored and edited more than 32 computer science books, and published more than 120 refereed academic/technical papers in computer science and applications areas.
Dr. Kunii is Founder of the Computer Graphics Society, Editor-in-Chief of *The Visual Computer: An International Journal of Computer Graphics* (Springer-Verlag), Associate Editor-in-Chief of *The Journal of Visualization and Computer Animation* (John Wiley & Sons) and on the Editorial Board of *IEEE Transactions on Knowledge and Data Engineering*, *VLDB Journal* and *IEEE Computer Graphics and Applications*. He is on the IFIP Modeling and Simulation Working Group, the IFIP Data Base Working Group and the IFIP Computer Graphics Working Group. He is on the board of directors of Japan Society of Sports Industry and also of Japan Society of Simulation and Gaming. He received the B.Sc., M.Sc., and D.Sc. degrees in chemistry all from the University of Tokyo in 1962, 1964, and 1967, respectively. He is a fellow of IEEE and a member of ACM, BCS, IPSJ and IEICE.

Yoshihisa Shinagawa is currently a Research Associate of the Department of Information Science of the University of Tokyo. His research interests include computer graphics and its applications. He received the B.Sc. and M.Sc. degrees in information science from the University of Tokyo in 1987 and 1990 respectively. He is a member of the IEEE Computer Society, ACM, IPSJ and IEICE.

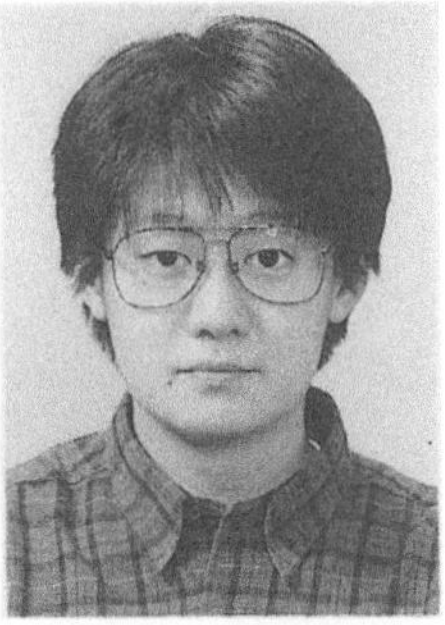

Shigeo Takahashi is currently a master course graduate student of information science at the University of Tokyo. His research interests include computer graphics, topology and computer aided geometric design. He received his B.Sc. degree in information science from the University of Tokyo in 1992.

address: Department of Information Science, Faculty of Science, University of Tokyo, 7-3-1 Hongo, Bunkyo-Ku, Tokyo, 113 Japan

Controlling the Architectural Geometry of a Plant's Growth – Application to the *Begonia* Genus

RENÉ LECOUSTRE, PHILIPPE DE REFFYE, MARC JAEGER, and PIERRE DINOUARD

ABSTRACT

During growth, a plant makes use of an architecture whose characteristics are continually modified with time. The orientation of the axes, the leaves, and the flowers must be dynamically controlled in the creation of realistic 3-D computer graphic animations of the plant development. Practical solutions adapted to botanical principles are proposed in this document. The solutions allow for modification in relation to time, scale, position and orientation of the organs, all of which are calculated from the plant's architectural fundamentals (the branching, the phyllotaxy, the length of the internodes, etc.)

Keywords: botany, growth simulation, modeling, 3-D coputer graphics, realism

INTRODUCTION

The fundamentals in modeling the growth and architecture of plants necessary in reading this article were outlined in de REFFYE et al. (1988,1990). A complete knowledge of the qualitative and quantitative laws observable in plant growth is important in this modeling, as the chosen approach is purely experimental. Other theories using these specific algorithms have been developed in the generation of trees (Aono 1984; Eyrolles 1986; Prusinkiewicz 1988; Reeves 1985; Smith 1984). These methods, whose purpose is not botanical precision, have given interesting results in computer graphics, although their biological content is weak or non-existant.

In this presentation, we will specify certain dynamic aspects in the geometry of the plant. These details should be considered throughout the growth simulation in order to increase the realism.

Refer to the previously cited articles for all that concerns general techniques in the modeling presented here. The case of *Begonias*, in particular brings together most of the difficulties met with plants. We will thus use them as an illustration.

We were asked by the center for the preservation of *Begonias* in the city of Rochefort to produce computer graphics pictures that would promote this magnificent family of plants so rich in variability.

1. SUMMARY OF THE PARAMETERS USED IN THE SIMULATION OF A PLANT

The necessary parameters in the control of plant growth exist in three types.

1.1 Topological parameters

These parameters concern the aspects of production inherent in plants: for example, the number of leaves per node (one for the Horsechesnut, two for the coffee tree, and three for the Oleander), or the number of pre-formed organs in the buds (one for the coffee tree, and a variable number for the apricot tree). These ontological parameters are only slightly sensitive to the environment.

1.2 The parameters in the functioning of buds

These parameters concern the laws of growth, death, and branching processes in buds, which are modeled with stochastic processes. The bud sends out internodes somewhat regularly that create a foliate axis step by step. The parameters of this process are sensitive to the position of the buds in the tree's architecture, the duration of functioning in the buds, and their interaction with the environment. The growth of a plant is diagramed in Fig. 1.

1.3 Geometrical parameters

The geometrical parameters are those most often studied by the creators of the algorithmic theories cited above. The phyllotaxy, the branching angles and the length of the internodes are used most often. Some are only slightly sensible to the action of the environment and others vary according to the influence of different factors:

1. The strength of the plant will affect the scale of the different organs (length of internodes, size of the leaves) according to the nutritional conditions

2. The physiological age of the apical buds will provoke a progressive metamorphosis of the leaves into floral elements while also affecting the phyllotaxy of the stem and the size of the organs

3. The tropisms will modify the direction of the axes and the increase in leaf area

4. Time controls the unfolding of the organs in space and modifies the position of the axes (sagging of the branches)

During the development of a plant, all of these factors are involved. In order to achieve a certain realism, the positioning of the plant's organs in space must be progressively corrected by the simulation program. We propose several empirical solutions to these purely geometric problems. The images of *Begonias* proposed in this work are the result of simulation by AMAP Software developed at CIRAD/GERDAT, either in wire frame or filled polygones from Silicon Graphics work station.

At regular time intervals, the meristem's activity is a function of three processes quantified by statistical laws. The different processes are illustrated by the following figures.

- GROWTH PROCESS : determines whether the meristem is lengthening or is resting.
- BRANCHING PROCESS : determines whether new axes are appearing or not.
- DEATH PROCESS : determines whether the meristem is dying or not.

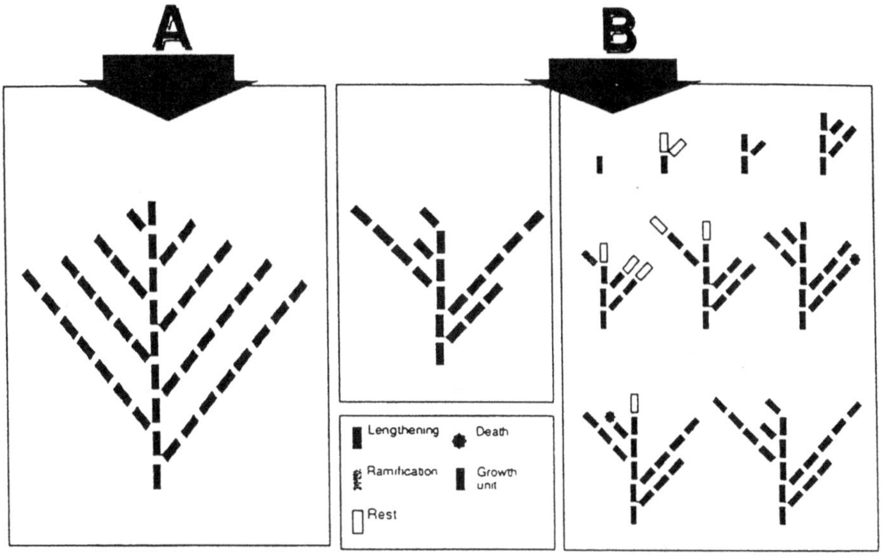

Figure A shows the whole possible tree realized if all the clock cycles give birth to an internode.

Thus growth, branching and death can be modelized.

Figure B shows, according to a succession of stages, the realisation of different growth tests on the apical and axillary meristems.
In this example, it is considered that each signal of the clock is annual (the G. U. is restricted to a single internode)
We notice a first lengthening at one year, two rests at 2 years, then two lengthenings, one of wich is making a ramification at 3 years (since it is a new axis) . The growth of this tree ends at nine years.

Fig. 1. Simulation of the growth mathematical model functioning

2. BASICS IN THE MORPHOLOGY OF *BEGONIAS*

Plants of the *Begonias* genus are quite complex. The foliate axes are alternatively symmetrical, thus there are two types of leaves: the left leaves and the right leaves. The nodes carry stipules, as shown in Fig.2

Fig. 2. *Begonia cubensis*

The foliate axes have their own strategy of growth (Hallé [8]). They send out inflorescences that are veritable trees within the tree and that have their own growth models. These inflorescences have simple organs, bracts and complex flowers that can be male or female, as shown in Fig. 3.

Fig. 3. *Begonia coralina*

There are two extremes in *Begonias* - those with erect stems (bamboo-like or shrub-like) and those with succulent creeping stems (rhizomatus). Naturally, all other possibilities fall between these two main types.

The positioning of all other organs is coordinated in time and is simulated step by step by the AMAP growth engine created in the laboratory.

3. MODELING OF FOLIATE AND FLORAL ORGANS

The leaves and flowers are, by some standards, sorts of trees. The leaf will be defined by its branching nerves which support the limb. The flower will be defined as an axis bearing different floral organs: sepals, petals, stamens. We have thus simplified the principal program in order to create a sub-program capable of generating calculated *Begonia* leaves and flowers. This approach is purely geometrical. Figure 4 shows the stages in the construction of a *Begonia corallina* leaf.

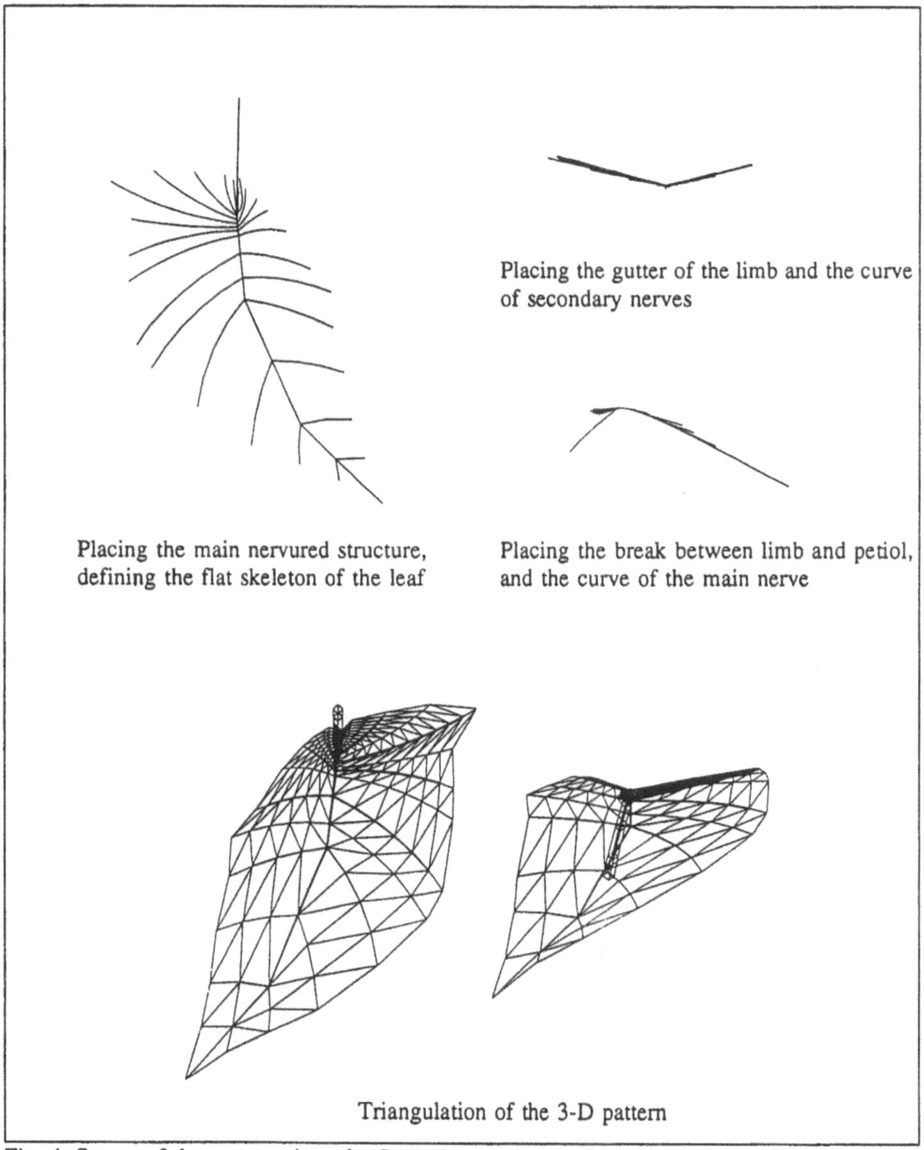

Placing the gutter of the limb and the curve of secondary nerves
Placing the main nervured structure, defining the flat skeleton of the leaf
Placing the break between limb and petiol, and the curve of the main nerve
Triangulation of the 3-D pattern

Fig. 4. Stages of the construction of a *Begonia corallina* leaf

The parameter file of a leaf contains the crude geometrical instructions (length of internodes, branching angles, curvature of nerves) necessary in the construction of the leaf. The alternate leaf will thus be constructed symmetrically.

Once the nerve branches are constructed, a triangulation algorithm is used in order to construct the limb between them.

Certain leaves are composate and require a supplementary assembly, as shown in Fig. 5. This sub-program can generate various leaves. The construction of flowers is also done procedurally. Each elementary floral part (sepal, petal, stamen) is modeled by our single leaves modeler. It is assembled automatically at the time of the flower's generation from the positioning of the ovary. While considering the rotations resulting from the presence of the whorl and from the phyllotaxy, we will distinguish female flowers and male flowers. This sub-program can simulate a large variety of flowers, as shown in Fig. 6, including, of course, the *Begonia* flowers.

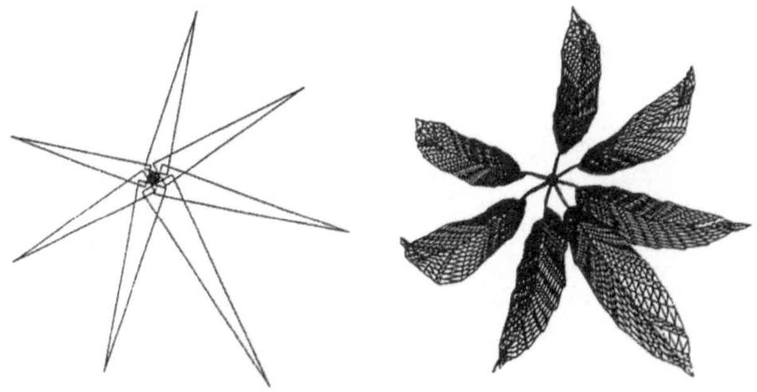

Fig. 5. Construction of a *Begonia coralineifolia* leaf

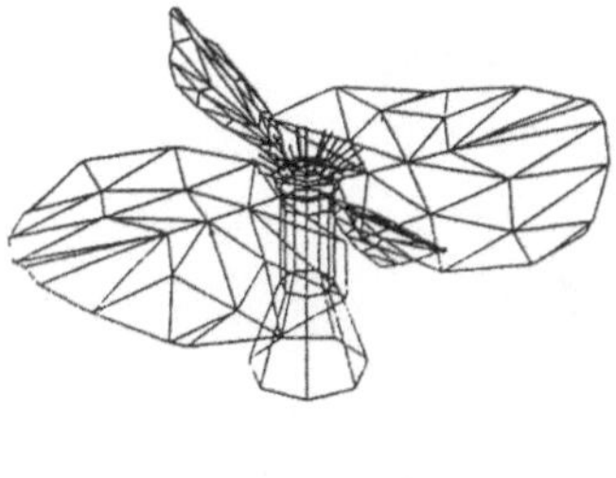

Begonia verschafeltiana
Male flower

Begonia 'Corbeille de feu'
Female flower

Fig. 6. Simulation of Begonia flowers

4. MODELING OF PHOTOTROPISM

Begonia leaves seek light. It is helpful not only to arrange them according to the rules of phyllotaxy, but also to orient the limb surface correctly. A leaf can be defined by first approximation as a surface programmed with a principal direction given by the petiole and with a normal at the limb's surface.

Minimizing the difference in the direction of the light and the leaf's normal permits a correct result, as shown in Fig. 7. Visually, the leaf orients itself towards the light.

Fig. 7 Phototropism simulation
Main axis inclinated between 5 à 85° in relation to vertical axis

5. MODELING OF THE STEM'S BEARING

Begonia stems bend more or less under the effect of gravity. The modeling of growth is based on the elasticity theory. Given an embedded stem with a section, a point of application of a force, and a module of elasticity, one can calcultate the curve resulting from the equilibrium. Following the values of the parameters, erect bearings, as shown in Fig. 8, or weak bearings, as shown in Fig. 9, will be obtained.

Fig. 8. *Begonia* 'Sachsen'

Fig. 9. *Begonia radicans*

6. MODELING OF THE BEARING OF INFLORESCENCES

The same theory allows for control of the bearing of inflorescences. They can be erect on the rhizomous, as shown in Fig. 10, or positioned at the top of the stems, as shown in Fig. 3.

Fig. 10. *Begonia macdougalli*

7. SIMULATION OF APICAL GROWTH

During apical growth, the terminal meristem unfolds new leaves and lengthens the internodes. At the same time, the leave's scale, the branching angle, the length and diameter of the internode that bears it must be dynamically controlled.

The leaf also deviates the following internode creating a caracteristical zig-zag, as shown in Fig. 11.

Fig. 11. *Begonia* 'Richmondensis'

In order to simplify, it is supposed that the leaf dilates. In fact, in the initial stage, it is rolled up or somewhat shriveled. The internodes and the leave's scales are controlled by the classic function of growth in Biology

$$d = d_0 (1 - e^{-at})$$

The branching angles evolve linearly from an initial angle to a final angle depending on the number of internodes. The diameter of the stem evolves progressively as well. Finally, the stem's zig-zag gradually disappears. All of this permits a correct simulation of the spontaneous geometry of a stem during apical growth. It is helpful also to model the growth of inflorescences on the stem. These structures have their own internal dynamics, as shown in Fig. 12.

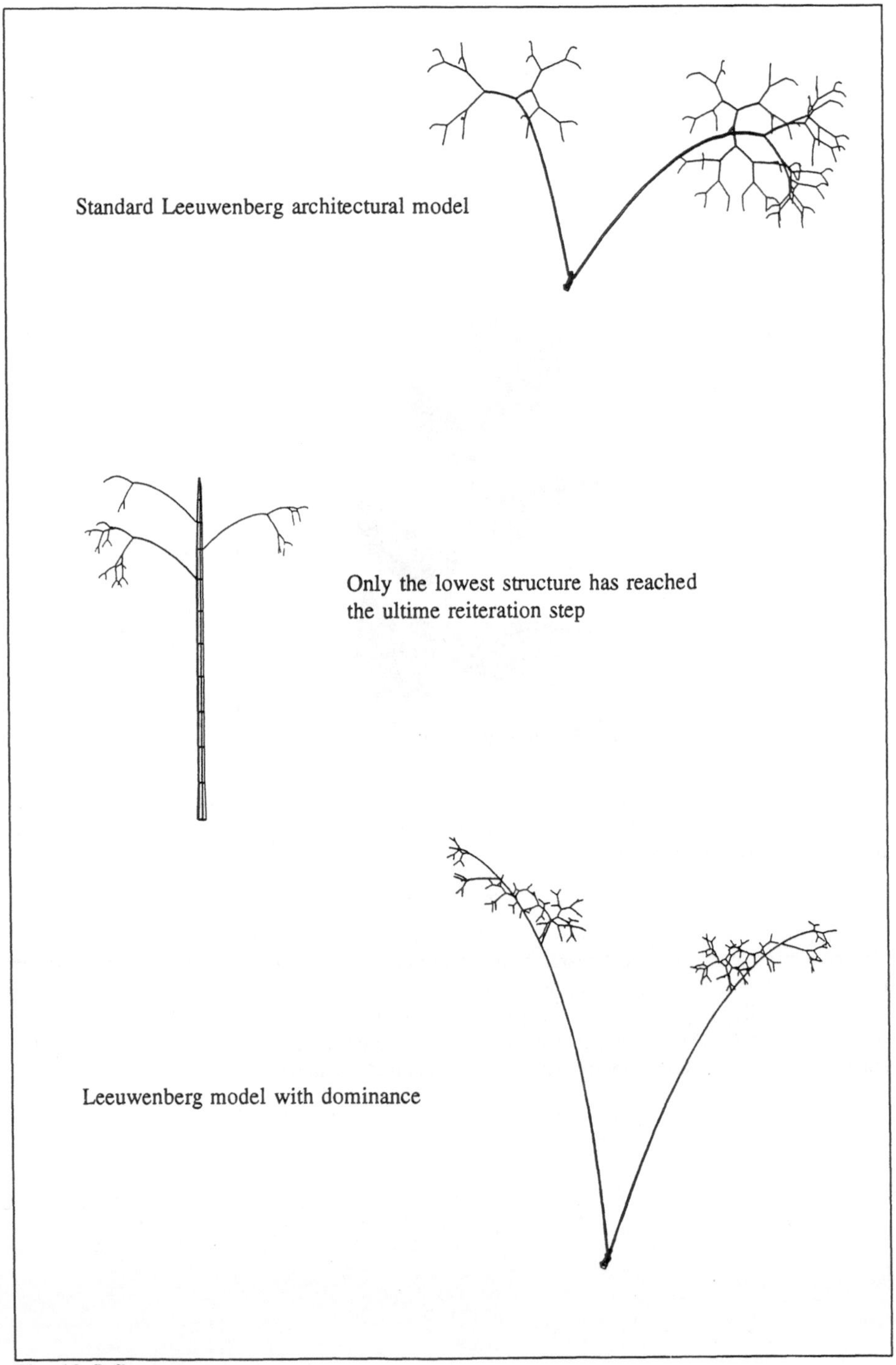
Standard Leeuwenberg architectural model
Only the lowest structure has reached the ultime reiteration step
Leeuwenberg model with dominance

Fig. 12. Inflorescences

Fig. 13. Five steps of *Begonia corallina* growth

Fig. 14. Realistic simulation of *Begonias* in a greenhouse

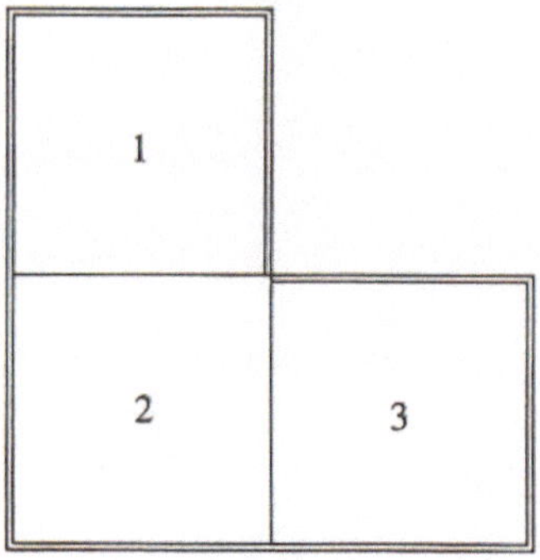

1: *Begonia radicans*
2: *Begonia luxurians*
3: *Begonia compta*

8. COMPUTER ANIMATION OF PLANT GROWTH

Now that all of these details are taken care of and once the biological paramaters have been measured, one can procede to a simulation of the plant's growth with the AMAP Software developed at CIRAD/GERDAT. This software permits a realistic rendering and computer animations. Figure 13 represents *Begonia corallina* corresponding to different ages.

9. VISUALIZATION OF *BEGONIA* IN A GREENHOUSE ENVIRONMENT

The rapid rendering of AMAP Software is particularly well-adapted to plant scenaries which can contain millions of polygones. It uses the maximum number of hardware processors available with Silicon Graphics work station.

The shadows and fog-effect are processed with Z-buffer techniques. Figure 14 shows botanical simulation faithful to three species of *Begonia* in their greenhouse environment.

CONCLUSION

Only the strict observation of plants allows for the identification of the parameters that control their geometry and their growth dynamics. The study of a plant genus, like that of the *Begonia*, is particularly rich in information since one can observe the characteristical variations in parameters and their internal correlations. The recent studies at Rochefort and at CIRAD that involve this genus should allow the comprehension of parental phenotypes. Our modeling will permit the prediction of cross-breeding results and will become an efficient tool for horticulture. It is, at least, our goal.

Special thanks to Jennifer L. Plunkett, translator, and to Marie-Hélène Lafond, document editor.

REFERENCES

Aono M, Kunii TL (1984) Botanical tree image generation. IEEE Computer Graphics and Applications 4(5): 10-33

Eyrolles G, Françon J, Viennot G (1986) Combinatoire pour la synthèse d'images realistes de plantes. Actes du Deuxième Colloque Image, CESTA, pp 648-652

Hallé F, Oldeman RAA, Tomlinson PB (1978) Tropical trees and forest: an architectural analysis. Springer-Verlag, Berlin Heidelberg New York

Pusinkiewicz P, et al. (1988) Development models of herbaceous plants for computer imagery purposes. Computer Graphics 22(4): 141-150

Reeves WT, Blau R (1985) Approximate and probabilistic algorithms for shading and rendering. Computer Graphics 19(3): 313-322

Reffye Ph de, Edelin C, Françon J, Jaeger M, Puech C (1988) Plant models faithful to botanical structure and development. Computer Graphics 22(4): 151-158

Reffye Ph de, Dinouard P, Jaeger M (1990) Basic concepts of computer plant growth simulation. In: NICOGRAPH'90 Computer Graphics:"Where do we go now that we've arrived?", Tokyo, nov 90, pp 219-234

Smith AR (1984) Plants, fractals and formal languages. Computer Graphics 18(3): 1-10

René Lecoustre is currently responsible for landscape applications and creation of the AMAP (Atelier de modélisation de l'architecture des plantes) plant database at CIRAD (Centre de cooperation internationale en recherche agronomique pour le développement), Montpellier. He was entomologist at IRFA (Institut de recherche sur les fruits et les agrumes) on Palm-Tree in Mauritania. Then, he was entomologist at IRHO (Institut de recherche pour les huiles et les oléagineux) in Côte d'Ivoire (Africa) where he studied biological control on Oil Palm. From 1983 to 1986, he was responsible for the coordination of modeling and biometry works at IRHO in Côte d'Ivoire. Then, he became deputy director at the CIRAD's modeling unit on the AMAP program. In 1987, he became doctor engineer in population biology at the University of Montpellier. His thesis subject was on biological control with 3 antagonists.

Philippe de Reffye is currently the Director of the Modeling Laboratory at CIRAD (Centre de cooperation internationale en recherche agronomique pour le développement), Montpellier. He was genetician at IRCC (institut de recherche du café, du cacao et autres plantes stimulantes) on Coffee tree and Cocoa in Côte d'Ivoire (Africa). He is Doctor ès Sciences for plants improvement, University de Paris-Sud, 1979. His thesis subject was on modeling and simulation of tree growth and architecture.

Intersection and Minimal Distance of 3D-Object

FRANK KLINGSPOR, DIETMAR LUHOFER, and THOMAS ROTTKE

Abstract

The major problem in three-dimensional geometric applications such as the computation of arbitrary polyhedra intersections is the great diversity of possible configurations of geometric objects. Thus, even seemingly straightforward operations often require an enormous number of floating-point computations. This problem can be alleviated by an appropriate preprocessing of the objects involved. For this purpose, we suggest tetrahedronizing geometric objects and organizing the tetrahedra in a *topological B*-Tree*. The topological B*-Tree can function both as an index and as an object data structure and is thus ideally suited for a wide spectrum of geometric applications. Furthermore, it can easily be used to support parallel algorithms. Parallel search algorithms can only be efficient if the data is very evenly distributed among the available parallel resources. For this purpose, we have developed a geometric hashing method extended by a special control mechanism. As demonstrated for the intersection of non-convex polyhedra, using the topological B*-Tree to support preprocessing of geometric objects leads to a significant reduction in the number of required floating-point operations and therefore in execution time as well.

Keywords:

geometric searching, parallel topological B^*-Trees, data distribution, polyhedra intersections, minimal distance

1 Introduction

Non-standard data bases for non-point geometric objects are used, among others, in the fields of process animation, image processing, graphical data processing and computer aided design. Many applications in which geometric objects are stored in a database require not only an index structure that supports geometric queries (e.g., point queries, line queries, polygon queries, volume queries and closest pair or nearest neighbour queries), but also an object data structure that supports geometric operations such as detection or computation of intersections, distance computations, etc. However, selecting geometric objects can be quite expensive. There are essentially two reasons for this:

- A great deal of data is required to describe geometric objects (such as polygons or polyhedrons). Therefore, access to secondary memory can become a bottleneck to the system.
- Complicated floating point computations (e.g., polygon or polyhedron intersections) are required in order to decide whether a specific object is to be selected. As a result, the processor can also become a bottleneck.

Fast access to geometric objects can only be achieved by the application of parallel resources (both processor and memory).

We will first introduce our basic data structure the topological B*-Tree and its parallel variant followed by a short excursion into the problem of data distribution of parallel discs. The rest of the paper is dedicated to polyhedra computations, concentrating mainly on the problem of polyhedra intersections. However, in the course of this discussion, it will become clear that the data structure (topological B^*-Tree) and algorithmic approach proposed here can basically be used for any geometric operation on complex objects (e.g., polyhedra). Finally, we will close with some brief comments on related topics of further research, in particular the use of parallelism in connection with geometric algorithms using the topological B*-Tree.

2 Related Works

There are numerous proposals for geometric index structures and object data structures, respectively, in the relevant literature. Specifically, for 3d-objects, the most frequently recommended structures are octrees [11], BSP trees [2] and variants of these. The most common index structures are R-trees [3], grid files [7] and hash tables [6]. The structure of an R-tree is dependent on the order in which objects are inserted. This can adversely affect the efficiency of query processing. On the other hand, for certain object configurations, the directory of a grid file can grow more than linearly with data size [10]. Efficient hashing methods usually require advance knowledge of the data distribution in question. However, for most applications, such advance knowledge is not available. Especially for parallel processing of indexes, a structure such as a B*-tree, which is more robust in these respects, would be desirable. BSP trees have the drawback that too much redundant information is stored, as there are normally multiple references to objects. This results in higher memory requirements than are absolutely necessary. This is not always acceptable, especially if the structure is also to be stored in external memory, as is usually the case. Furthermore, octrees and BSP trees can degenerate in a similar manner to ordinary binary trees.

3 Topological B^*-Trees

B^*-Trees have proved to be particularly well suited as index data structures for data with scalar keys in data base applications [1]. In particular, because of their well structured nature (balanced, linear ordering, all nodes with the exception of the root at least half full) B^*-Trees are independent of data distribution and the order in which objects are inserted. In order to preserve as many as possible of the desirable characteristics of the B^*-Tree for representing geometric Indexes while at the same time obtaining a data structure that can be used for parallel processing in a transputer network [4] [5], we have expanded the classical B^*-Tree to a *topological B^*-Tree*[9]. The keys of the topological B^*-Tree correspond to axis-aligned subspaces of a universal space. The differences of the topological B^*-Tree as compared to the classical B^*-Tree are a result of the geometric interpretation of this key (axis-aligned rectangles). The method of always splitting a node relative to the median key value - as in the case of the classical B^*-Tree - is not well suited for use with geometric objects. The main problem is that there are configurations of objects such that the objects cannot be disjointly separated by a split relative to a single key value. For instance, the planar region shown in Figure 1 can not be split according to a unique coordinate value such that the objects contained therein are assigned to unique subregions. On the other hand, if one permits subregions to overlap the tree becomes susceptible to the order of insertion of objects. The solution we have chosen is to define an additional, non-geometric and universally applicable criterion according to which objects are separated in such cases. To this end, we define a key to consist of two parts:

- Domain (the rectangular region in which objects may be located) and
- Range (the rectangular region in which objects are located).

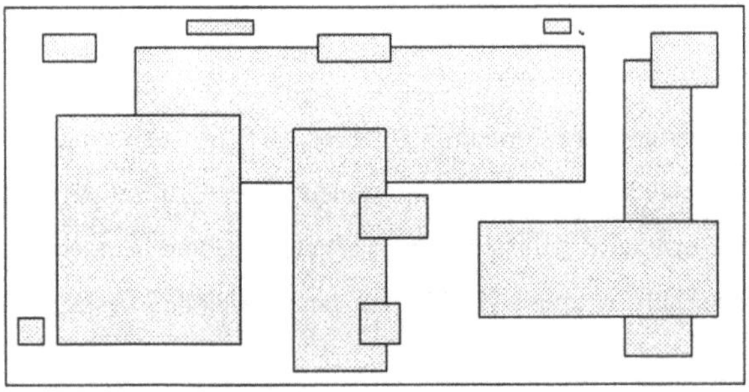

Figure 1: Objects in a geometric region

Domain and range both consist of a rectangular subregion parallel to the coordinate axes of the universal space and a volume interval: an object must be located in the subregion determined by the value of its key, and its volume must lie within the volume interval given in the key (see Figure 2).

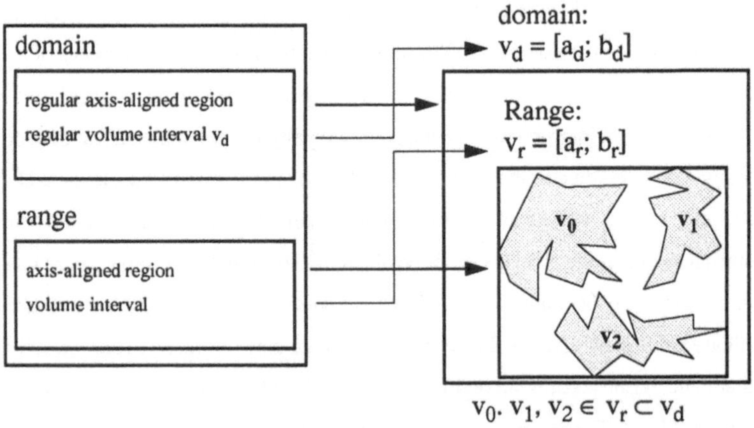

Figure 2: structure of key

Using this key, objects that cannot be separated according to geometric location are separated according to volume. As a further advantage, objects can be linearly ordered in the tree according to their volume, thereby retaining most of the characteristics of the classical B^*-Tree. While arbitrary (axis-aligned) rectangular regions may be used for the range, it is sufficient to use only regular rectangles, i.e. rectangular regions that come about by repeatedly splitting regions in half. In any case, the range is always a subset of the corresponding domain.

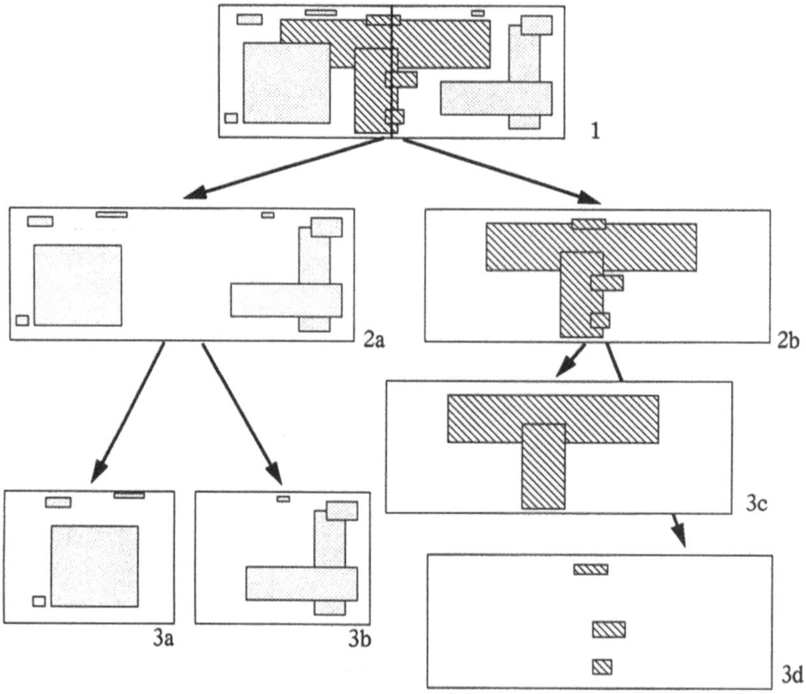

Figure 3: split process

An entry of the tree is split according to the following scheme: First, the median line of the domain is determined, and the objects are separated according to whether they intersect the median line or not (*normal split*, see Figure 3, region 1). The former objects make up a new entry in which all objects lie either to one or the other side of the median line. Should a split of this entry later become necessary, it can therefore simply be split along this median line (*area split*, see Figure 3, region 2a). Parts 3a and 3b show the two new subregions produced by such an area split. Those objects that intersect the median line can be further separated according to their volume (*volume split*, see Figure 3, region 2b). Parts 3c and 3d show the two new subregions that result from a volume split of the subregion IIb. Geometric objects are inserted into the topological B^*-Tree according to their bounding box and their volume.

A search query is processed in two steps as follows: First, all objects whose bounding box intersect the search region are selected. The second step, then, consists of deciding whether these objects actually lie within the search region. Note that the intersection of an object with the search region does not necessarily follow from the intersection of its bounding box with that region.

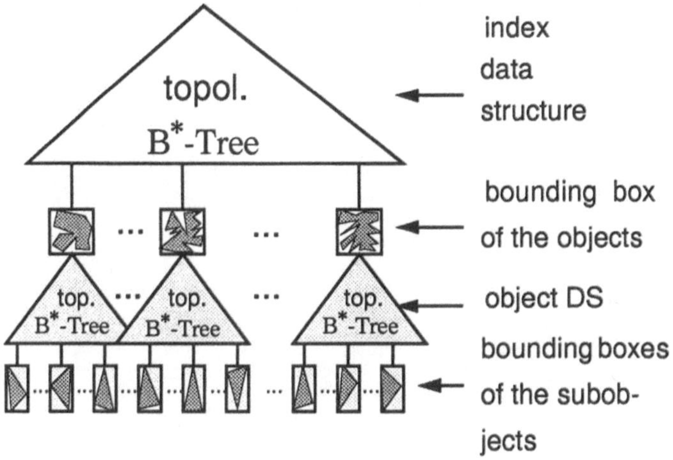

Figure 4: topological B-Tree for complex objects*

If objects are composed of a large number of atomic sub-objects (e.g., polygon composed of triangles, polyhedron composed of tetrahedra) then these objects themselves can be represented in the form of a topological B^*-Tree by storing their atomic components in such a tree (see Figure 4).

4 Nearest Neighbour Heuristic

Although the topological B^*-Tree, as described above, already offers good performance when compared to the optimal attainable clustering (generated bottom-up by way of dynamic pro-

gramming), this performance can be further improved by using the special *nearest neighbour heuristic* described in the following. Figure 5 shows a configuration of objects in which the two objects ob_1 and ob_2 would be separated by an area split, although they lie close together.
In this case, it would be better to treat ob_1 and ob_2 as a single object ob_3 (shown dashed in Figure 5). Accordingly, the nearest neighbour heuristic clusters objects which are located close together. In contrast to the normal topological B^*-Tree, when using the nearest neighbour heuristic, objects *must* be stored in buckets.

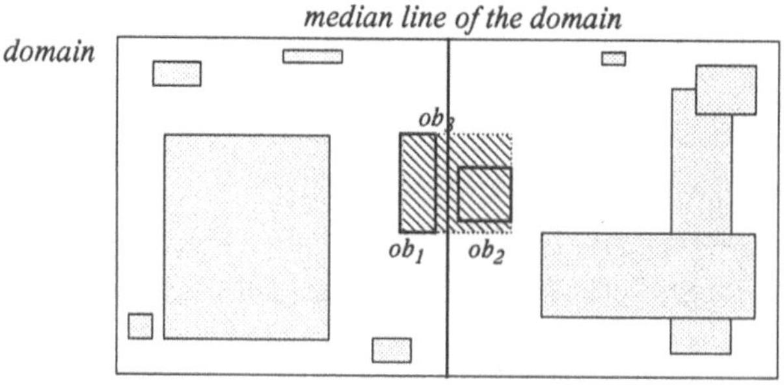

Figure 5: close objects separated by a split

We define

$$d(x,y) = \sqrt{\sum_{i=1}^{dim}\left[\frac{|x_{low}(i) - y_{low}(i)| + |x_{high}(i) - y_{high}(i)|}{2}\right]^2}$$

to be the distance between two axis-aligned rectangles (It is sufficient to regard only axis-aligned rectangles, as the index structure partitions the universal space in the same manner as an orthogonal grid. An arbitrary geometric object intersects a grid if and only if its bounding box does so.).

The first step of this method consists of using the index structure to locate the bucket containing the nearest neighbour ob_N of the object ob_I which is to be inserted. This is the bucket in which ob_I must be inserted. If this insertion causes the range of this bucket to exceed its domain, the corresponding entry of the index is removed and re-inserted in the classical manner as described in Section 2. Using the nearest neighbour heuristic one achieves a clustering of objects with similar bounding boxes. Figure 6 illustrates how objects are clustered at bucket level.

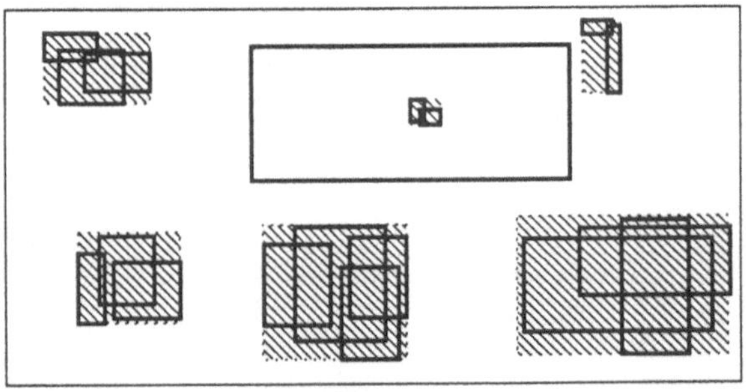

Figure 6: Clustering at bucket level

For our tests we inserted 8192 objects into 3 different data structures: the topological B^*-Tree, the topological B^*-Tree with nearest neighbour heuristic and an optimal Tree generated by

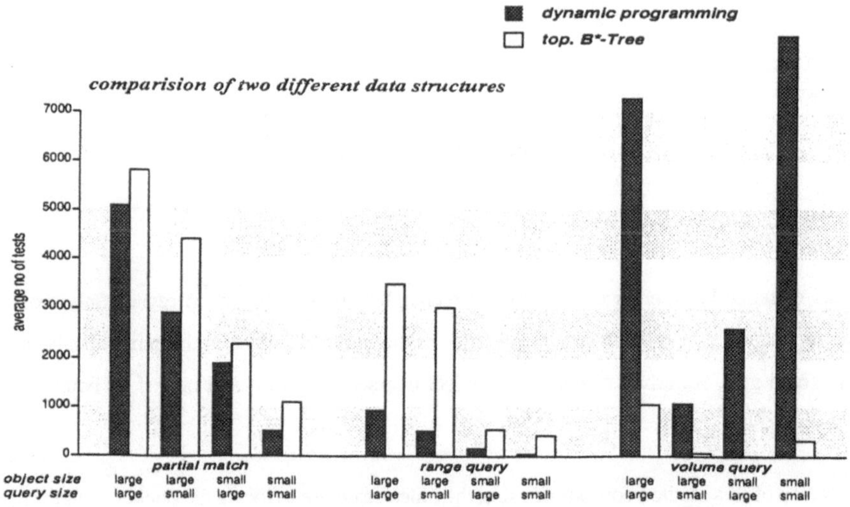

Figure 7: average number of tests required per query

dynamic programming. The number of each entry of the Figure 7 shows the average number of tests needed to find the objects specified by the query.

For large objects, the volume reached up to 1/4 of the volume of the universal space. Small objects had at most 1/512 of the volume of the universal space. Large query regions covered up to 1/8 of the universal space, small query regions at most 1/128.
It turns out that topological B^*-Trees provide good average performance and outperform optimal clustering in volume queries.

5 Parallel topological B^*-Trees

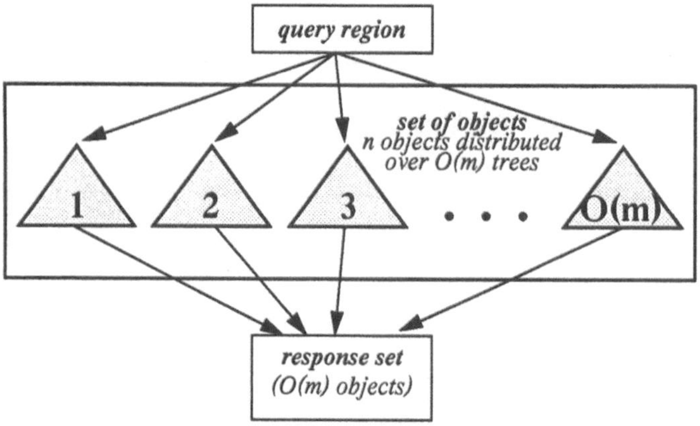

Figure 8: Array parallel topological B-Tree*

There are two ways to use topological B^*-Trees for parallel searching:

One partitions the data (n geometric objects) into disjoint subsets of equal size and constructs a topological B^*-Tree for each data subset (array parallelism, see Figure 8). Provided all data subsets require approximately the same amount of processing time, the speed-up attained by this sort of partitioning is linear. The degree of partitioning should therefore linearly depend on the expected size (or, in the case of real time applications, on the worst case size) of the response set (set of objects selected by a given query). To this end, one tree is created for every expected element of the response set. If the data is very evenly distributed (i.e., same distribution density in all partitions) one can expect one response per tree and query. Under these conditions, all O(m) responses to a query on O(m) trees are found in expected time of O(log n). In comparison, the sequential variant of the topological B^*-Tree requires O(log n) time for each object of the response set, resulting in a total of O(m log n) time for O(m) objects in the worst case. Therefore, parallelism by partitioning is the optimal solution given a homogenous distribution density in all partitions.

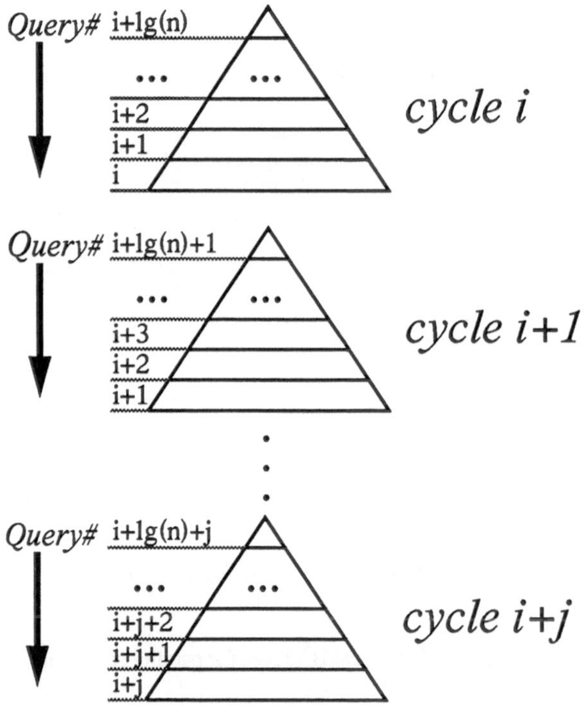

Figure 9: Pipeline-structured parallel topological B-Tree*

- Parallelism is achieved by superimposing a pipeline structure on the topological B^*-Tree (see Figure 9). This type of parallelism only makes sense if continuous search queries are to be expected. Each node of the tree is then assigned its own process which during a given time slice searches all entries of this node in response to at most one query. For the next time slice, the query is passed on to the processes corresponding to descendant nodes determined by the relevant entries of the previous time slice. In this way, q queries can be processed in O(q+log n) time. If q is very large with respect to n then an average time of O(1) per query is required.

6 Data Distribution

It is particularly important to have as even a distribution as possible among the various parallel trees or parallel disks. Three ways to achieve this are:

- geometric clustering,
- hashing,
- random assignment of data to a partition.

The results of our research have led us to the conclusion that two factors are of particular importance in choosing a distribution method:

- Data distribution should be as homogenous as possible across partitions.

- The partitions should be of nearly equal size, as even slight differences in size can lead to significant differences in the number of accesses per partition.

Typical results of our performance tests for queries of types partial match, range query and volume query are summarized in the table of Figure 10. For the sake of simplicity, we have only listed the results for very large and very small objects and queries respectively. The test results for non-extreme (i.e., neither very small nor very large) sizes of objects or queries respectively are monotonically dependant on object and query size.

For our tests, the objects were distributed among 16 parallel disks. We executed 1024 queries of each query type and counted the resulting number of accesses to each disk. The upper number of each entry of the table shows the average difference in the number of accesses as compared to the average number of accesses per partition during a query. The lower number (in bold italic print) shows the corresponding standard deviation. The set of objects used consisted of 8192 polygons which were made up of an average of 384 points each.

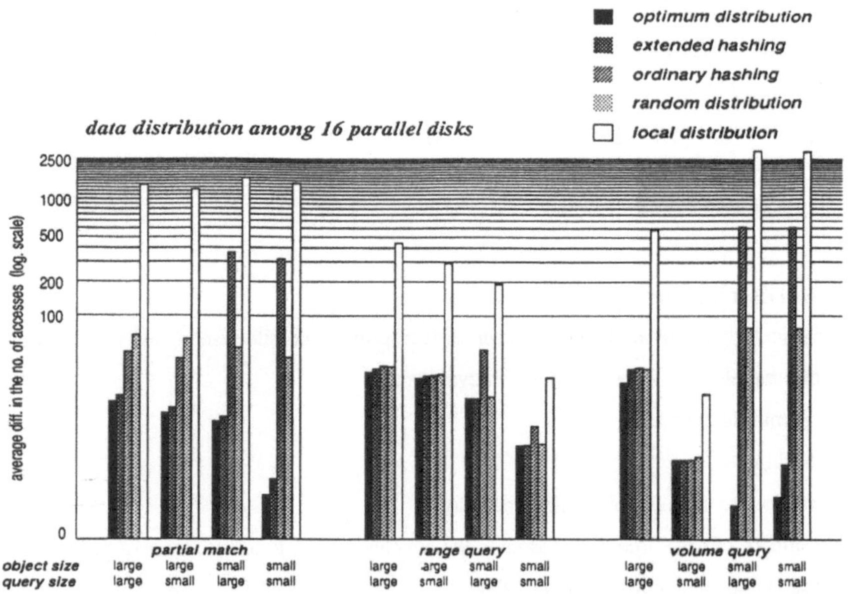

Figure 10: Test results for distribution on parallel disks.

For large objects, the volume of the bounding box of a polygon reached up to 1/4 of the volume of the universal space. Small objects contained polygons whose bounding box had at most 1/512 of the volume of the universal space. Large query regions covered up to 1/8 of the universal space, small query regions at most 1/128.

It turns out that geometric clustering is not suited at all as a partitioning method; neither are the partitions of nearly equal size nor is data distribution homogenous. It can occur that only one tree is active during a search query. Random partitioning does lead to more or less homogenous data distribution. However, there are still differences in partition size, which can lead to significant differences in required processing time. The same can be said for hashing. To distribute geometric objects, we used an extended hashing method (hashing according to the bounding box and volume of an object) with a control mechanism to ensure that the difference between partition sizes does not exceed a certain value. This method proved to be very nearly optimal.

7 Polyhedra Intersections

Computing the intersection of non-convex polyhedra is one of the more time-consuming operations in the field of geometric computation. This is due not only to the asymptotic time complexity of the operation itself, but also to the large number of floating-point computations involved. Nonetheless, in many applications in which such an operation is needed, it is also a requirement that the execution time stay below a given limit.

```
function intersect_polyhedra(TList1, TList2: TetrahedraList):
                                        IntersectionList;

var    Tetra1, Tetra2: Tetrahedron;
       TetraIntersectionList: IntersectionList;
       TetraIntersection: Intersection;
begin
  TetraIntersectionList:= empty;
  reset_list(TList1);
  while not end_of_list(TList1) do
  begin
    Tetra1 = read_next_element(TList1);
    reset_list(TList2);
    while not end_of_list(TList2) do
      begin
      Tetra2 = read_next_element(TList2);
      TetraIntersection:= intersect_tetrahedra(Tetra1, Tetra2);
      if TetraIntersection ≠ empty then
        insert(TetraIntersectionList, TetraIntersection);
    end;       (* while *)
  end;         (* while *)
  join_partial_intersections(TetraIntersectionList);
end;           (* intersect_polyhedra *)
```

Figure 11: brute force function intersect_polyhedra

For the intersection of convex polyhedra one can achieve an asymptotic time complexity of O(n log n), as is shown in [8]. However, as in the two-dimensional case, computing the intersection of non-convex polyhedra gives rise to several additional problems which increase the lower bound of complexity to $O(n^2)$. Notably, the intersection of non-convex polyhedra can consist of up to n^2 disjoint (possibly non-convex) polyhedra. The techniques developed to intersect convex polyhedra are, by themselves, entirely inadequate to efficiently deal with such problems. Given that the polyhedra in question are already available in tetrahedronized form (i.e., as a list of tetrahedra), a combinatorial approach is more appropriate: In the simplest form, one first computes the intersection of each tetrahedron of one polyhedron with each tetrahedron of the other and then joins together the appropriate partial intersections.

This brute force approach is illustrated by the function "intersect_polyhedra" listed in Figure 11. Within the two nested while-loops (lines 8 - 18 and 12 - 17, respectively) the intersection of each pair of tetrahedra of the two input polyhedra is computed. If a pair of tetrahedra intersect, the resulting polyhedron is inserted into the output list "IntersectionList". After computing all possible tetrahedra intersections, corresponding tetrahedra intersections are joined by the procedure call of line 20.

Assuming that both polyhedra consist of n tetrahedra, this "brute force method" always requires the computation of n^2 (often empty) tetrahedron/tetrahedron intersections with all the floating-point operations that this involves. An optimal intersection algorithm based on tetrahedronized polyhedra, however, should only compute the non-empty tetrahedra intersections. To achieve this, an efficient method of accessing only those pairs of tetrahedra which actually intersect is required. Here, the topological B*-Tree can be put to good use.

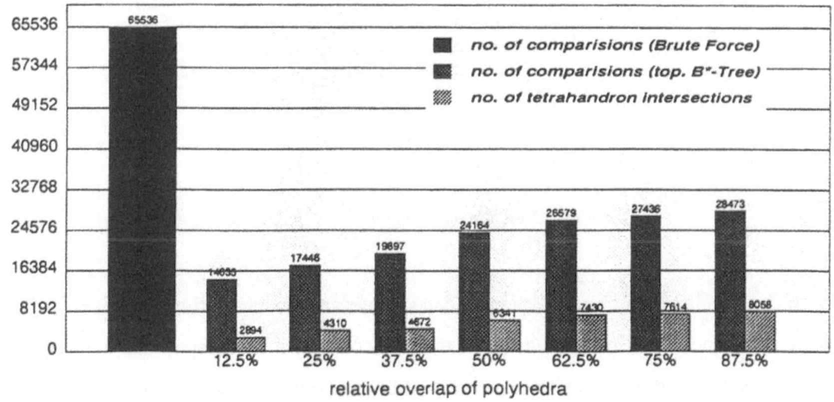

Figure 12: Performance comparison for polyhedra intersection methods: Brute Force vs. topol. B-Tree*

Using simple range queries to the topological B*-Tree, only those tetrahedra of both polyhedra are examined which lie within the intersection of the bounding boxes of the two polyhedra. Furthermore, for each tetrahedron of the first polyhedron thus selected, only those tetrahedra of the other polyhedra are examined whose bounding boxes intersect its own bounding box. In this way, most pairs of non-intersecting tetrahedra can be quickly eliminated from further consideration without time-consuming floating-point computations. Figure 12 summarizes an average performance comparison of the brute force method and the method using the topological B*-Tree for polyhedra made up of 256 tetrahedra each and with various degrees of overlap. We define the degree of overlap of two polyhedra as the ratio of the volume of the bounding box intersection to the volume of the union of the bounding boxes of two polyhedra. For each overlap value chosen 64 polyhedra pairs were randomly generated as test data. As one sees, using the topological B*-Tree pays off especially well for polyhedra that only overlap to a slight extent. However, there is an appreciable gain for polyhedra with a large degree of overlap as well.

8 Minimal Distance

Computing the minimal euclidean distance between two arbitrary non-convex polyhedra poses similar problems to the computation of polyhedra intersections discussed in the previous section. One must principally examine all pairs of elements of the two polyhedra (i.e., either tetrahedra pairs or point pairs, edge pairs, etc.). This requires $O(n^2)$ time, presuming both polyhedra have n vertices. As in the previous section, we propose using tetrahedronized polyhedra and topological B^*-Trees to eliminate as many of these pairs as possible without actually computing their minimal distance. Our proposed method is described briefly below and assumes non-intersecting polyhedra.

In a first step, the spatial clustering of tetrahedra induced by storage in a topological B^*-Tree is used to heuristically find an initial pair of tetrahedra that lie intuitively "close" together. The minimal distance of this pair determines an upper limit for the minimal distance of bounding boxes of tetrahedra still to be examined. One polyhedron is then determined as reference polyhedron. For each tetrahedron of the reference polyhedron, the topological B^*-Tree of the other polyhedron is visited to find those tetrahedra whose bounding box lies closer to the current reference tetrahedron than the current upper limit. The minimal distance of each such pair is computed as it is found and the upper limit revised downward as closer tetrahedra pairs are encountered. After completing this procedure for every tetrahedron of the reference polyhedron the current upper limit is equal to the minimal distance between the two polyhedra. Because of the successive reduction of the current upper limit, the number of tetrahedra that need to be examined in each traversal of the tree become, on the average, continuously fewer.

We have implemented the method described using various heuristics and criteria to find the initial, intuitively close pair of tetrahedra in the first step. The average time complexity of the described procedure is to a large extent dependent on the choice of this heuristic. First empirical results indicate that by an appropriate choice of this heuristic an average case complexity of O(n log n) is attainable.

Figure 13 summarizes a performance comparison for various polyhedra sizes (64 test cases each) of our implementation of the method described above to a brute force method implemented for non-tetrahedronized polyhedra given in form of a doubly connected edge list as described in [8]. We chose the number of edge/edge and point /facet distance computations as comparison criteria, since these basic operations directly reflect the time complexity the respect to problem size (number of polyhedron vertices). A significant performance improvement is evident even for small polyhedra and this effect increases with problem size.

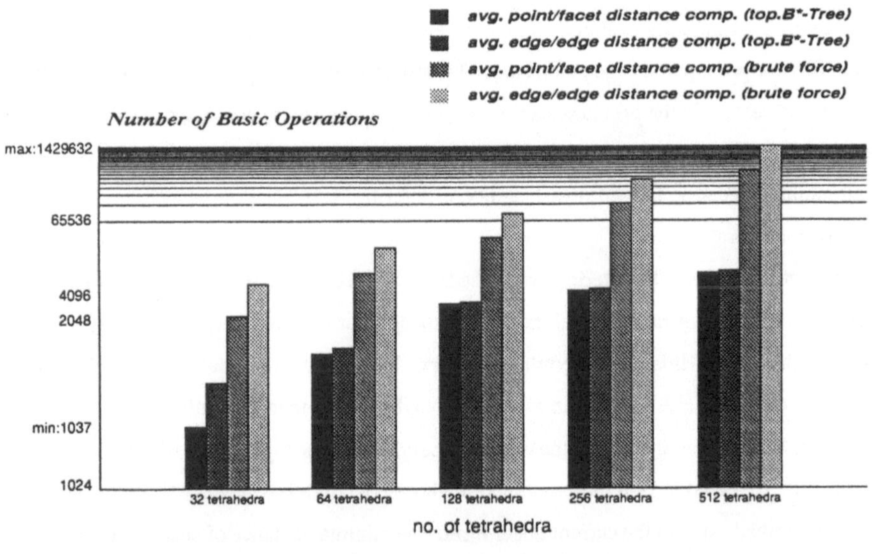

Figure 13: Performance comparison for minimal distance methods: Brute Force vs. topol. B-Tree*

9 Conclusions

Using parallel topological B^*-Trees as recommended here, access times for complex geometric objects can be significantly reduced and one can dramatically reduce the execution time required for geometric algorithms operating on such objects as well. In summary, the main advantages are:

- The topological B^*-Tree is well suited for parallel processing, i.e., all parallel resources are evenly used.
- Index and object data structures are homogenous, which leads to simpler algorithms.
- Parallel access to external data
- With the help of large, distributed internal memory, a large number of objects can be buffered internally.
- The parallel index can be adapted to different data distributions and query profiles by adopting an appropriate node size as well as an appropriate degree of partitioning.
- A well structured representation of complex objects leads to a saving of processor time (e.g., for the computation of geometric intersections).
- A substantial speed-up can be attained for sequential algorithms such as polyhedra intersections.
- Topological B*-Trees were specifically developed to support parallel processing of geometric data. As such, they can easily be used to support parallel geometric algorithms. In the case of polyhedra intersections, an obvious way to achieve this would be to parallelly compute the intersection of each tetrahedron of one polyhedron with the complete other polyhedron, joining the resulting tetrahedron/tetrahedron-intersections on the fly. This reduces the time complexity from $O(n^2)$ in the sequential case to $O(n)$ with the use of $O(n)$ parallel processors.
- Furthermore, the basic approach described for polyhedra intersections can also be used for such algorithms as computing the minimal distance between two arbitrary polyhedra: Using the topological B*-Tree, one can find the closest of n tetrahedra of one polyhedron to a given tetrahedron in time $O(\log n)$. Therefore, the time complexity for computing the minimal distance between two polyhedra is $O(n \log n)$. Using appropriate parallelism can further reduce this.

References

[1] Bayer, R. and McCreight, E., *Organization and maintenance of large ordered indexes,* Acta Informatica, 1 (1972), pp. 173 - 189.

[2] Fuchs, T., *On visible surface generation by a priori tree structures*, Computer Graphics, 14 (1980), pp. 124-133.

[3]Guttman, A., R-trees: *A dynamic data structure for spatial searching*, ACM SIGMOD, (1984), pp. 47 - 57.

[4] Klingspor, F. and Rottke, T., *Realzeitzugriff auf ausgedehnte geometrische Objekte in einem Transputernetz*, Proc. of the TAT '91, Informatik-Fachberichte, Springer, (1991).

[5] Klingspor, F.and Rottke, T., *Realzeitzugriff auf ausgedehnte geometrische Objekte mit parallelen topologischen B^*-Bäumen*, Proc. of the PEARL 91, Informatik-Fachberichte, Springer, (1991).

[6]Kriegel, H.P., Seeger, B., *PLOP-Hashing: A Grid File without Directory*, Proc. 4th Int. Conf. on Data Engineering, (1988), pp. 369 - 376.

[7]Nievergelt, J.H. et al., *The grid file: An adaptable, symmetric multikey file structure*, ACM TODS 9 (1984), pp. 38 - 71.

[8]Preparata, F.P. and Shamos, M.I., *Computational Geometry*. An Introduction, Springer, NewYork (1985).

[9]Rottke, T., *Parallele Suchprozesse in der geometrischen Datenverarbeitung*, Technischer Bericht, Fachbereich Informatik, FernUniversität Hagen, to appear.

[10]Rottke, T. et al., *On the Analysis of Grid Structures for Spatial Objects of Non-Zero Size*, Graph-Theoretic Concepts in Computer Science (1987).

[11]Samet, H., *The Quadtree and Related Hierarchical Data Structures*, ACM Computing Surveys (1984), pp. 187 - 260.

Thomas Rottke is a doctorate candidate at the department of computer science at the university of Hagen, Germany, since 1988. He is currently writing his doctoral thesis on parallel geometric searching. His research interests include parallel and real time programming, computer graphics and software engineering. Rottke received his diplomas in mathematics and computer science at the university of Hagen in 1985 and 1988 respectively. From 1985 to 1988 he worked in the area of research and development.
Address: Praktische Informatik III, Post Box 940, W-5800 Hagen, Germany.

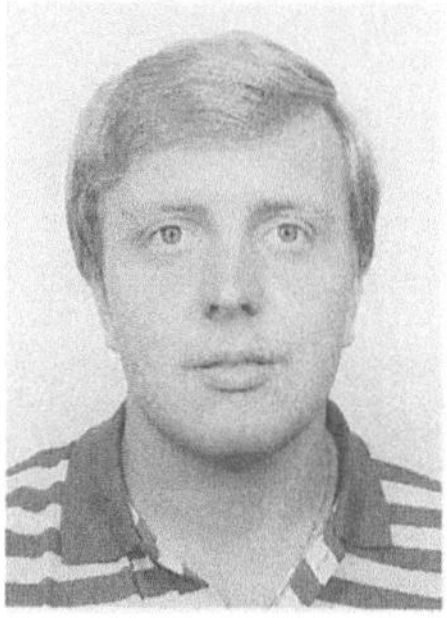

Frank Klingspor is a student of computer science at the university of Dortmund, Germany. He is currently writing his diploma thesis on parallel geometric index structures.
Address: Praktische Informatik III, Post Box 940, W-5800 Hagen, Germany.

Dietmar Luhofer is a student of computer science at the university of Hagen, Germany. He is currently writing his diploma thesis on algorithms and data structures for non-convex. 3D-objects.
Address: Praktische Informatik III, Post Box 940, W-5800 Hagen, Germany.

Part V
Languages and Systems

Hierarchy, Labels and Motion Description

GEOFF WYVILL, ANN WITBROCK, and ANDREW TROTMAN

Abstract

When we use a hierarchical model, we have to provide a means for the animator to refer to the individual parts. A labelling system is described for doing this. The idea is applied in an experimental system for controlling a simple human model performing acrobatics.

key words: Computer animation, hierarchy, scripts, kinematics

1. Introduction and context

In this paper we examine the labelling of parts in a hierarchy in the context of *scripted* animation of synthetic actors in three dimensions.

In traditional animation, every aspect of every frame is individually controlled. An automated animation system aims to provide the artist with detailed control at less cost. There have been many ways proposed to do this, ranging from a crude inbetweening of keyframes via parametric interpolation to rule-based kinematic algorithms and dynamic systems using physical laws. In describing these techniques, the emphasis has, quite reasonably, been on how each motion is described. In this paper, we address a related problem: how should motion description be related to the parts of a complicated model?

For the purpose of this discussion, we assume that both the modelling and animation are done by means of a *script*. That is, a set of instructions that can be laid out in text form. This is not meant to suggest that we recommend animating this way. When the basic tools for describing motion of characters have been established, the script elements may well be entered using an interactive interface. The use of a script is a device for discussing these elements.

Ideally, we should give directions to a synthetic actor as we would to a human actor. For example: "Walk to the desk and pick up the telephone." Of course, instructions at this level, leave out a great deal of detail. We expect the human actor to use a lot of knowledge: to recognise the desk with the telephone on it; to avoid other actors on the stage; to pick up the receiver, not the whole telephone; and probably, to hold the appropriate part of the instrument to her ear.

At the low-level of our scripts, we are more concerned with such problems as making sure that all the arms and legs move with the actor and that the hand that picks up the telephone arrives in the right place and is still connected to the actor's arm when the contact is made.

All the experiments in this research have been conducted using the *Katachi* system at the University of Otago. *Katachi* is an experimental system for modelling, animation and rendering. It has no user interface and everything is done by scripts represented by "C" programs, or data files. *Katachi* uses CSG models and everything in a scene is represented by a hierarchy of components. Thus our concern is how to access and control this hierarchy in a way that an animator can understand.

2. Background

We make no attempt to summarize the mass of literature on human animation. Norman Badler (1986) has done that very well. Here we mention only work that is relevant to the question: "What can an animation script include?"

Dynamics can generate motion that is guaranteed to be natural because it follows physical laws. The work of Baraff (1990) demonstrates this with colliding falling objects. But for human animation, we do not know what forces are being applied to all the joints. Wilhelms and Barsky (1985) give a detailed formalisation to the problem of applying dynamics to an articulated body and Wilhelms (1986) discusses a practical way to specify the motion kinematically while using the results of dynamics. Various forms of an approximate and/or hybrid approach have been suggested, see Armstrong (1985, 1986), Wilhelms (1988), Isaacs (1988), Boulic (1990) and van Overveld (1990, 1991).

The idea of using a script for building objects comes from PDL-2 (Wyvill 1975). PDL-2 is a language for defining 2D pictures composed of lines only but it features labels. ASAS (Reynolds 1982) uses scripts with a LISP syntax, and describes 3D models and their animation. Maiocchi and Pernici (1990) describe how to use a library of recorded human motion to generate natural movement in artificial figures. Their approach is object oriented and uses the script concept. Similarly CINEMIRA (Thalmann 1990) animates from a script. In its simplest form, a script is kinematic in nature, but it doesn't have to be. David Zeltzer (1982) used functional control elements in the form of local programs to control parts of a motion. Ideally, we would like our script to operate at every level from a truly goal directed instruction (Drewery 1986) through remembered actions, dynamics or procedures to create default or usual motion, to detailed kinematics where the user is given absolute control, but must pay for it by having to keep track of all the details.

3. Problems inherent in hierarchy

The advantages of hierarchy in modelling are so obvious that we are rarely directed to the problems. A simple, humanoid actor is described as a tree structure of components as suggested in Fig. 1. Within the computer system, each component can be represented by a record containing pointers to its sub-components. With each pointer is associated information telling us where the sub-component is and in what rotation. This information is conveniently encoded in transformation matrices and by traversing the tree, we can generate the absolute position of each part, by systematically concatenating the transformations of its ancestors in the structure.

This means that the animator can move the actor knowing that all the parts will move together. She knows that the arms will move with the body and the hands will move with the arms. She knows where the hands are: at the ends of the arms. She knows where the arms are: attached to the shoulders. There is no need to know where the hands are in global space, until the actor is required to pick something up: with a hand.

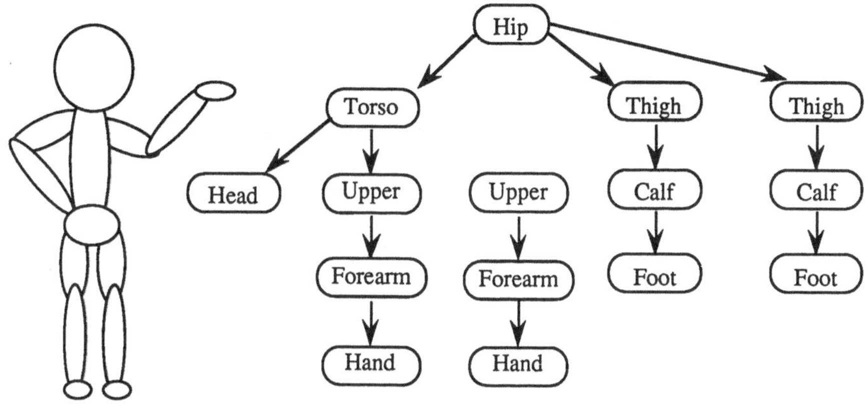

Fig. 1. Eve: a simple humanoid figure and tree structure.

At this point, we need to know where the hand is. More than that, we need to make sure that the whole body motion has not made it impossible for the hand to reach its target position. This defines our first problem: how does the animator identify, position and orient a given component in the hierarchy?

Suppose our first actor, Eve, presents the second, Adam, with an apple. To ensure that the apple moves with and remains in Eve's hand, it is attached to the hierarchy that defines Eve. At some point, it has to be transferred to the hierarchy that defines Adam. How is this to be specified?

The third problem concerns the control of a virtual camera in the scene. We would like to display Eve's view of Adam as he walks towards her. The camera is located at Eve's head and is to be kept pointing at Adam as they both move.

4. Labels in the hierarchy

Labelling the nodes of a hierarchy is not a new idea. Almost every computer file directory does exactly that. Labels were used in the PDL-2 language (Wyvill 1975) much as they are in the Katachi system for building models except that PDL-2 was strictly 2D and was not used for animation.

Objects in Katachi are represented by nodes that have two kinds of pointer, horizontal and vertical. A collection of nodes linked by horizontal pointers represent immediate components of the same object. A vertical pointer defines the object which is the component, Fig. 2.

Each node contains transformation matrices to say where the component is in the current object. Thus, in Fig. 2, the transformation of "right_arm" also applies to "upper", "forearm" and "hand". A label is a text field that may be added to any node. It labels that node and its associated local coordinate system. Thus the label "right_arm" in Fig. 2, labels the coordinate system into which "upper", "forearm" and "hand" are transformed.

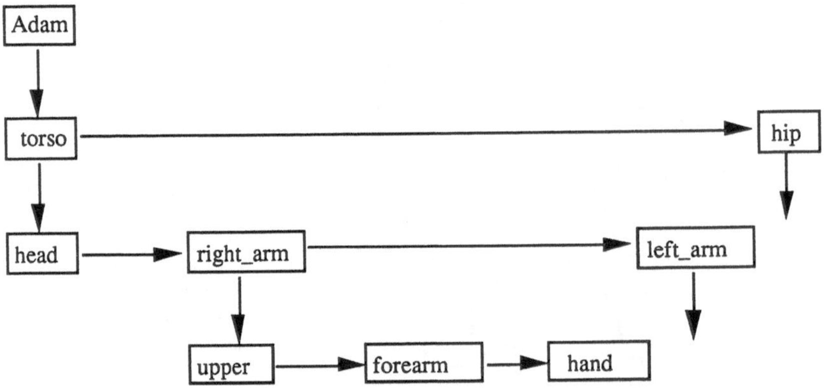

Fig. 2. Katachi structure.

The basic operation on labels is to identify the position of a label within an object. This 'position' is actually represented by a pair of transformation matrices, fore and aft, that represent instructions to transform a point from or to the coordinate system of the labelled component. We represent this by the function find:

```
int find(label, ob, fore, aft)
char *label;
object ob;
matrix fore, aft;
```

Find returns as its value, the number of occurrences of the label. The matrices fore and aft have their values set to represent the first occurrence.

Duplication of labels is permitted because parts in the hierarchy are duplicated. It would be unnatural to prevent the left hand from having a label "index_finger" because that label had already been used in the right hand. When we find a label, we avoid ambiguity by specifying an additional label as an ancestor of the target, e.g:

```
find( "right_arm/index_finger", Adam, fore, aft)
```

first finds the label "right_arm" and then searches the sub-structure for the label "index_finger". Notice that it is not necessary to describe the full path name which could be "right_arm/hand/index_finger", it is sufficient to specify the desired label and enough ancestors to avoid ambiguity.

5. Shared components

In engineering design applications, it is reasonable for the hierarchy to include shared components. This reduces the size of the data structure and maintains the principle that one data item is stored in only one place. If we are representing the design of a car, it is reasonable to keep only one copy of the wheel design and refer to it four times in the structure. Should we modify the wheel, all four wheels will change together.

For animation, this is no longer appropriate. The right and left hands may share a basic structure, but they will have different shapes at different times. One hand may be open when the other is closed. In a purely constructive system, we would build two hands with different structure to reflect their different shapes. This implies rebuilding the hierarchy for each frame of the animation. We prefer to regard the hierarchy as something that can be modified. So we build a right arm and duplicate it to make the left arm. (The positioning of the left arm will include a reflection.) Thus in pseudocode we may build:

```
hand = palm(...)        + digit("index_finger", where1)
                        + digit("middle_finger", where2)
                        + digit("ring_finger", where3)
                        + digit("little_finger", where4)
                        + digit("thumb", where5);
forearm = limb(...)     + transform(hand, where6);
right_arm = limb(...) + transform(forearm, where7);
left_arm = transform(duplicate(right_arm), where8);
```

Palm, digit and limb are routines that build those parts. Digit, by implication, has two arguments: the label and some position information encapsulated in the arguments where1, where2 etc.

6. Nested coordinate systems

Every object in the hierarchy has its own coordinate system. The coordinate system of a whole scene corresponds to the root of the hierarchy and is sometimes called "world space", but it is no different from any of the other systems. If our camera is positioned within a component, then our viewing system is, conceptually, in the coordinate system of that component.

A pointer into the hierarchy gives us direct access to the definition of a component in its own space. Thus in the example above, the variable hand points directly to the right hand.

find("index_finger", hand, fore, aft)

gives us the position of "index_finger" in the local space of hand whereas

find("index_finger", left_arm, fore, aft)

finds the "index_finger" of the left hand in the coordinate system of the left arm.

Having simultaneous access to these spaces means that we can change the position of the finger in the hand-space to close the hand and instantly find the position and rotation of the finger in the arm-space.

7. Application of labels

The labels immediately offer solutions to the problems of Section 3. The first problem, "where is Eve's right hand?" becomes trivial:

find("right_arm/hand", Eve, fore, aft);

tells us all we need to know.

In the second problem, Eve gives an apple to Adam; to which hierarchy is it attached? We don't attach the apple to Eve's hand directly. The apple belongs to the scene rather than to the component that is Eve.

```
scene = Eve + Adam + Apple;
find("Eve/right_arm/hand", scene, apple.fore, apple.aft);
```

gives the apple the same transformations as Eve's right hand. Later, we can use:

find("Adam/right_arm/hand", scene, apple.fore, apple.aft);

to put it into Adam's hand. Of course, in practice, the apple will not be placed where the hand is, but close to it, so this is a simplification.

The third problem was to place a camera for tracking. A camera has a position, a view angle, a point of attention and an 'up vector'. Each of these attributes can be set separately using the labels. We place the camera using:

find("head", Eve, fore, aft)

extracting the position data alone from fore and aft. The point of attention is gained from:

find("head", Adam, fore, aft)

and the 'up vector' can be fixed in relation to the scene. In our present system, we have to 'find' the camera for each frame. It might be better to define find as a function attached to the hierarchy so the camera move would follow the motion of Adam and Eve automatically, but, at present, our hierarchy does not include functions.

8. Building a body

It is not difficult to construct an articulated body with the CSG hierarchy alone but for the animation script we need more information about each body-part. This could be built into the CSG hierarchy but that would turn it into a specialised system for articulated bodies. Instead, the additional information is kept in an auxiliary structure. The basic unit is a list structure that mirrors the CSG structure. Horizontal pointers link items to a common root and vertical pointers refer to sub-groups.

Each node of this body-structure contains the following additional information:

- a path name to link to the actual part in the CSG tree,
- a path name to say which part it is linked to in the body,
- a mass and centre of gravity -- (Other information for dynamic calculations could be added here.)
- the position of the point of attachment in local coordinates,
- the position of the place in the parent component where it is attached,
- a list of rotation instructions for the animation.

This information can be created algorithmically or read from a file. Either way it is effectively constructed from a script after the manner of Reynolds (1982). The following is a fragment of the file for creating a person:

chest	partname
torso	part attached to
solid_sphere	rigid part description
0.7, 0.4, 0.7	scale(X,Y,Z)
brown plain	colour texture (repeated values for complex objects)
0.0, 0.0, 1.0	centre to joint
0.0, 0.0, 0.6	joint to parent's joint
0.13	proportion of mass
YZ	default plane of rotation
n	any initial rotation?
...	various rotation specifications

This creates a part called chest connected to torso. Each of these parts is made from a solid sphere stretched into an ellipsoid. Then follow colour and texture information and the attachment coordinates.

An important feature of this approach is that the components can be specified in any order because the linkage is given explicitly.

The spheres are already available as CSG primitives. If a more complicated, rigid shape is required, it can be built using the underlying CSG system, given a name and then asked for in the script just like the primitive shapes. Mary-Lou's head (Figs. 3 and 4) was constructed like that.

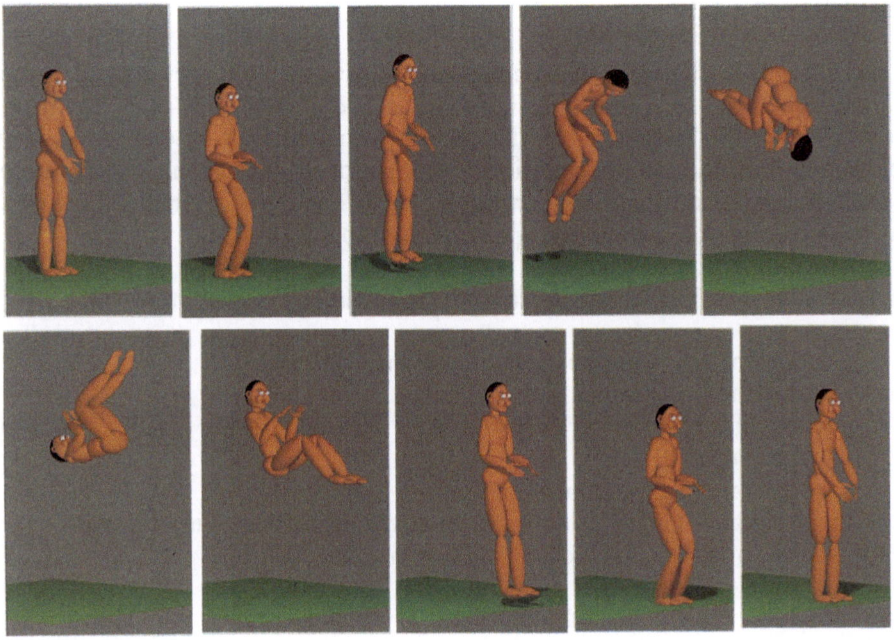

Fig. 3. Frames showing Mary-Lou performing a somersault.

9. Motion scripts

The whole idea of this structure is that we can mix dynamics, constraints and direct kinematic instructions to control our figures. The simplest example is fully kinematic. We provide lists of rotations for components to take place during specific time intervals. The following file fragment describes the action of Mary-Lou's left leg during the somersault, Fig 3.

```
lfoot
0.0,0.25 ZY 30.0 0.5 0.5
lfoot
0.25,0.3 YZ 30.0 0.5 0.5
lcalf
0.0,0.25 YZ 60.0 0.5 0.5
lcalf
0.25,0.3 ZY 60.0 0.5 0.5
lthigh
0.0,0.25 ZY 30.0 0.5 0.5
```

The first entry reads: during the time 0.0 to 0.25 rotate the left foot (lfoot) from Z to Y in local coordinates, by 30 degrees with uniform acceleration for half the time and uniform deceleration for the second half.

But the somersault motion is not quite that simple. During the first part of the motion, Mary-Lou's toes are bound to the ground plane. This means that all the angular changes cause the body to drop and rise again. At a pre-determined time, the toes are released and Mary-Lou's body is free to rise.

At this point, it would be appropriate to switch to a dynamic model. In fact we continue with a script that takes the whole body up and down with uniform acceleration and spins it with uniform accleration/deceleration. As Mary-Lou's toes contact the ground, we switch back to control her from joint angles again.

10. Reaching

A feature of the structure with labels is that there is no implication that a body is placed where the root node is. We can find such things as the centre of gravity or the position of the left toe and fix the relative motion from there. We would like to be able to ask the question "Can Mary-Lou reach the ball from where she is standing?" This implies two fixed points and asks us to deduce something about the linkage of the body to be able to reach both. We have implemented a very simple algorithm to do this based on the idea of the effective length of a chain of joints. In effect, we first ask if Mary-Lou can touch the ball with her hand. This she can do if the wrist is near enough. Otherwise, we look at the hand plus forearm and see if the pair of joints can make the right distance from the shoulder. If not, we look at other joints to see if the shoulder can be made nearer, and so on.

Figure 4 shows an example of this algorithm working as expected. Mary-Lou extends her arm and touches the ball. Figure 5 shows the algorithm working correctly, but not as expected. The ball is placed near the viewer, half an arm's length from Mary-Lou. Since she cannot reach the ball with her hand, Mary-Lou moves her forearm, to put the hand nearer the ball. She still needs more distance and gets it by extending from the shoulder and bending forward. Although she can reach the ball by this method, a more natural solution would be to twist the body and lean forward or to turn and take a step towards the ball first.

11. Conclusion

We have implemented a simple hierarchy to represent geometric models and provide a system of labels on selected components. Use of the labels solves some of the classical problems of hierarchy and gives us a base on which to build animation rules. So far, we have kept to simple scripts augmented by a minimal reaching algorithm. The structure gives us an environment for the implementation of more complicated algorithms and constraints.

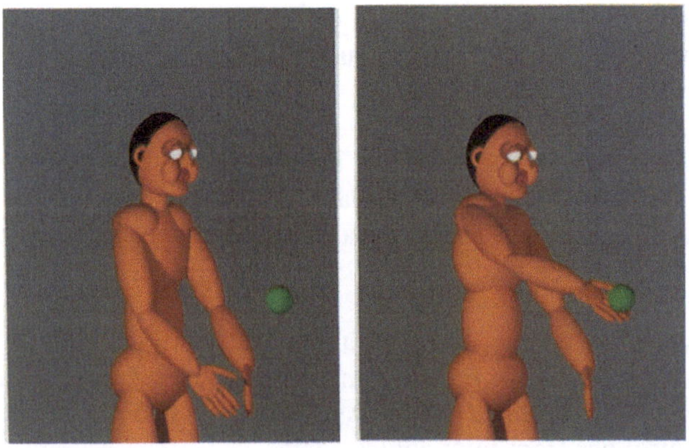

Fig. 4. Mary-Lou performs a simple reach.

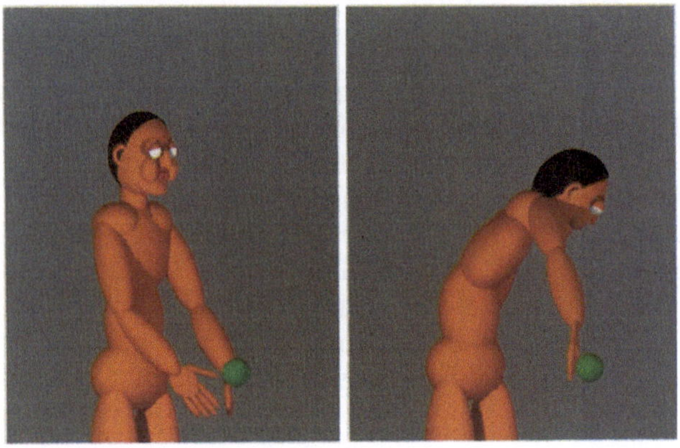

Fig. 5. Mary-Lou contorts herself in an effective if unusual reach.

12. References

Armstrong WW, Green M, Lake R(1986) Near-Real-Time Control of Human Figure Models, Proceedings of Graphics Interface '86:147-151

Armstrong WW, Green MW (1985) The dynamics of articulated rigid bodies for purposes of animation, *The Visual Computer* 1(4): 231-240

Badler NI (1986) Animating Human Figures: Perspectives and Directions, Proceedings of Graphics Interface '86: 115-120

Baraff D (1990) Curved surfaces and coherence for non-penetrating rigid body simulation, *Computer Graphics,* SIGGRAPH '90 Proceedings 24(4): 19-28

Barzel R, Barr AH (1988) A Modeling System Based on Dynamic Constraints, *Computer Graphics,* SIGGRAPH '88 Proceedings, 22(4): 179-188

Boisvert D, Magnenat-Thalmann N, Thalmann D (1989) An Integrated Control View of Synthetic Actors, *New Advances in Computer Graphics,* Proc. CG International '89, Springer, 277-288

Boulic R, Magnenat Thalmann N, Thalmann D (1990) A global human walking model with real-time kinematic personification *The Visual Computer* 6(6): 344-358

Bruderlin A, Calvert TW (1989) Goal-Directed, Dynamic Animation of Human Walking *Computer Graphics,* SIGGRAPH '89 Proceedings, 23,(3): 233-242.

Drewery K, Tsotsos J (1986) Goal Directed Animation using English Motion Commands, Proceedings of Graphics Interface '86: 131-135.

Getto P, Breen D (1990) An object-oriented architecture for a computer animation system, *The Visual Computer,* 6(2): 79-92

Isaacs P M, Cohen M F (1988) Mixed methods for complex kinematic constraints in dynamic figure animation, *The Visual Computer,* 4(6): 296-305

Maiocchi R, Pernici B (1990) Directing an animated scene with autonomous actors, *The Visual Computer,* 6(6): 359-371

Reynolds C (1988) Computer Animation with Scripts and Actors *Computer Graphics,* SIGGRAPH '82 Proceedings, 16(3): 289-296.

Magnenat Thalmann N, Thalmann D (1990) *Computer Animation Theory and Practice,* Second Edition Springer-Verlag

van Overveld CWAM (1990) A Technique for Motion Specification in Computer Animation, *The Visual Computer,* (6): 106-116

van Overveld CWAM (1991) An iterative approach to dynamic simulation of 3-d rigid-body motions for real-time interactive computer animation, *The Visual Computer,* 7(1): 29-38.

Wilhelms J P, Barsky B A (1985) Using dynamic analysis to animate articulated bodies such as humans and robots, *Computer-generated images: The state of the art,* Proceedings of Graphics Interface '85: 209-229

Wilhelms J (1986) VIRYA - A Motion Control Editor for Kinematic and Dynamic Animation, Proceedings of Graphics Interface '86:141-146.

Wilhelms J, Moore M, Skinner R (1988) Dynamic animation: interaction and control, *The Visual Computer,* 4(6): 283-295

Geoff Wyvill (1975) Pictorial Description Language, *Interactive Systems,* Proceedings of Eurocomp: 511-526

Zeltzer D (1982) Motor Control Techniques for Figure Animation, *IEEE CG&A* 2(9): 53-59

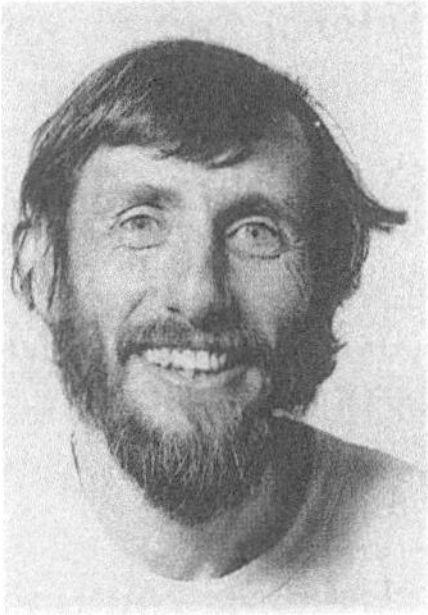

Geoff Wyvill received a BA from Oxford University, MSc and PhD degrees from the University of Bradford. He worked as a research physicist for the British Petroleum Company and lectured in computer science at the University of Bradford from 1969 to 1979. Since then he has been at the University of Otago where he runs the computer graphics laboratory. He is currently on sabbatical leave at EPFL, Lausanne, Switzerland. His main research interests are in geometric modelling and animation. He is best known for his work in CSG and implicit surface modelling. He is on the editorial boards of The Visual Computer and Visualization and Computer Animation and a member of SIGGRAPH, ACM, CGS and NZCS.

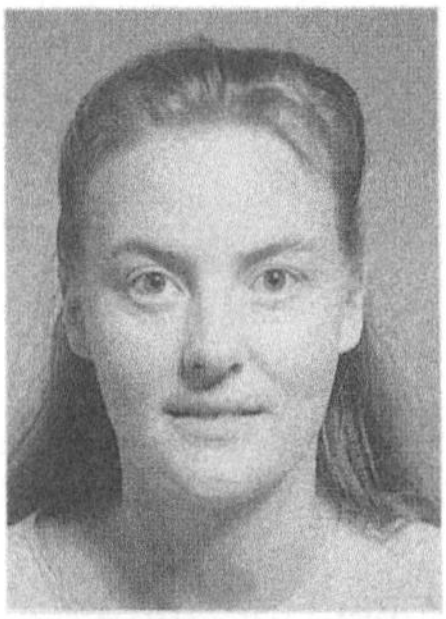

Ann Witbrock is a graduate student at the University of Otago. Before entering Computer Science, Ann trained as a dancer for 12 years. She completed her NZCE in Electronics and Computer Technology at Christchurch Polytechnic in 1986 and her BSc at the University of Canterbury in 1989. Her current research interests include Hierarchical Animation, Motion Definition, Dance, and CSG.

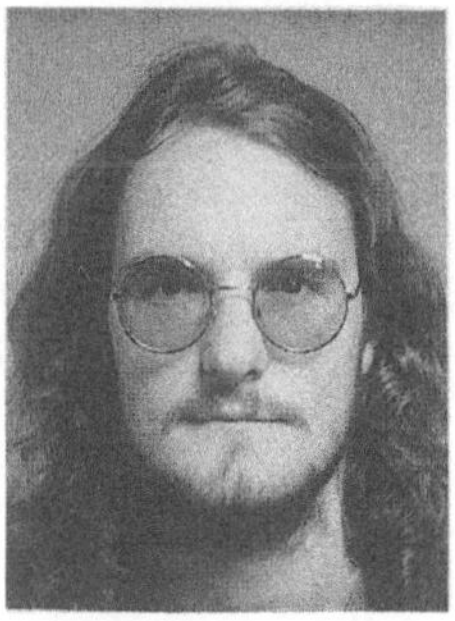

Andrew Trotman is a graduate student at the University of Otago. He completed his BA in Computer Science during 1988. Andrew's research interests include CSG, Ray Tracing, Implicit Surfaces, algorithmic efficiency and algorithmic correctness. Andrew is a member of SIGGRAPH and ACM.

A Language for Animating Scene Descriptions

SCOTT HOPWOOD, IAIN SINCLAIR, and KEVIN G. SUFFERN

ABSTRACT

We present a methodology that permits any scene description to be non-interactively animated. Using a simple, powerful language, Swish, a scene description can be augmented with an imbedded time description. The time description details the changes in terms of the scene description language itself; thus, the time description language can be used with a variety of renderers. Swish accepts files containing imbedded Swish commands and parses them to produce representations of scenes at specific time instances.

Key Words : animation, scene descriptions, embedded time descriptions

1 INTRODUCTION

To animate means "to bring to life". We present a language Swish which allows "dead" three-dimensional scene descriptions to be animated. We define a *scene description* (also known as a display list, viewing specification or input file) to be any database of elements which has a consistent text representation. Scene descriptions are a portable, straightforward way of specifying geometric and non-geometric objects. While this representation is used by a large number of traditional graphics packages, it has been pointed out (Zeleznik *et al.*, 1991) that it does not incorporate any explicit notion of time.

A *time description* is any systematic extension to a scene description which outlines how the elements will change over time. Swish is an explicit imbedded animation control language where all time-varying transformations are modelled with a small and powerful set of commands imbedded in a scene description. An interpreter parses the scene description files with imbedded Swish commands and uses this information to produce scene descriptions at specific instances of time. Because the contents of the scene description are irrelevant to the interpreter, Swish can be used with a variety of renderers.

We have used Swish with the public domain ray tracer *Rayshade* (Kolb, 1991).

Our approach differs from other animation languages that have sought to control entities with procedural control (Reeves and Blau, 1985), constraint-based and object-oriented techniques, rotoscoping (Ginsberg and Maxwell, 1983), and numerous types of physically-based models (Barr, 1989).

2 THE TIME DESCRIPTION LANGUAGE AND INTERPRETER

We discuss here several simple examples to illustrate the use of some of the Swish commands. A simple scene may consist of a viewing point, a point being looked at, a single light source and a sphere. One specific scene description for these objects looks like this:

```
#define ON    1
#define OFF   0

eyep          -5 3 -5
lookp         0 0 0

sphere        1             // radius
              0 0 0         // x y z

light point   ON            // brightness (real)
              3 10 3        // x y z
```

All time description augmentations are enclosed within separators such as the { } braces. (These and other symbols can be easily changed if they are found to conflict with the scene description language.)

The general format of a time description is:

```
time_description  =

    {instruction [parameters] [: scene_description_text ]}
```

The basic time unit is the *frame*, an arbitrary, discrete interval which is used to describe all changes over time. The simplest form of time description uses `at` (abbreviated as `@`) to specify frames; "at these frames, the following text holds".

As an example, to describe a light turning on and off twice over a twenty-frame interval, we substitute the parameters which vary over time (in this case, the brightness of the light) with a time description. In plain language, it says: "for the following frame numbers : the beginning frame to `4`, `10` to `14`, and `20` to the last frame (denoted as `$`) – `ON` will be used at this point in the scene description. At frame numbers `5` to `9` and `15` to `19`, `OFF` will be used at this point in the scene description".

```
light point {@ 0-4, 10-14, 20-$: ON}
            {@ 5-9, 15-19: OFF}
            3 10 3
```

Note that *what* changes over time – the `ON` and the `OFF` – is described in terms of the scene description language itself; the time description specifies *how* the scene will change over time. Thus, the time description is independent of any particular scene description language. The scene description text following the colon is passed out by Swish's interpreter to the scene description file.

Using an iterative construct, we can describe the same time-varying transformation more succinctly. The time description language provides the `loop` directive for this:

```
light point {loop 0-20:
               {@ 0-4: ON} {@ 5-9: OFF} }
             3 10 3
```

Note from this example that time description commands can be nested.

Swish can also be used to gradually increase the brightness of the light :

```
//   Increase the brightness during the first 32 frames, then leave it
//   steady

light point  {@ ^-32: {frame}*0.02}
             {@ 33-$: ON }}
```

Swish provides variables to access the absolute frame number (`frame`) and the absolute elapsed time (in seconds) (`time`). There are variables that return the *relative* frame number and time – the frame number and time within the scope of the current expression (`rframe` and `rtime` respectively). In addition, variables representing the first and last frame number (^ and $ respectively) may be set and referenced.

In computer animation, it is important for objects and textures to move and transform smoothly. Swish provides the `hermite` directive to perform Hermite curve interpolation. This directive operates on an arbitrarily long list of number-lists (each number-list having a uniform number of elements, and an optional control vector). For example,

```
sphere 1 {hermite 0: 0 0 0  (0 0 1)
                 10: 1 20 17
                 20: 15 25 30}
```

We can specify the technique used to render a given portion of a scene over a given portion of time. The `method` directive associates executable files with a scene description, allowing Swish's interpreter to send off sequences of frames to specific renderers.

```
//    Use ray tracing for the first 32 frames and use diffuse
//    interreflection for the rest

{@^-32: {method "/usr/local/bin/rayshade"} }
{@33-$: {method "/usr/local/bin/radiance"} }
```

If a particular scene description language permits the inclusion of other scene descriptions, we can use the time description to include frames that were generated by other animation systems. For example,

```
{@ 0-48: #include hand{frame}.scn}
{@ 49-$: #include walk{ ({frame}-48)}.scn}
```

Part of the Swish system is interpreter which can animate scene descriptions enhanced with imbedded time description commands. The interpreter acts like a preprocessor, taking the enhanced scene description as input and producing multiple frames (directly renderable scene descriptions) as output.

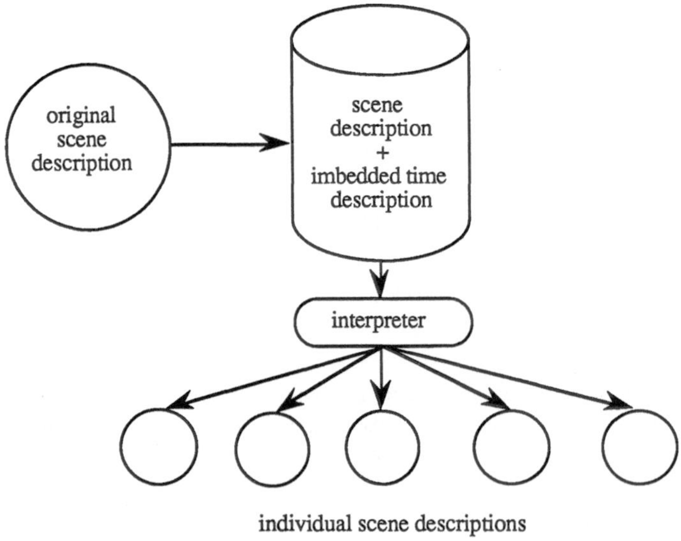

Fig. 1 An interpreter that parses an imbedded time description.

3 APPLICATIONS

3.1 Intended Use

The low-end nature of our time description system – simple, small, easy to learn, use and implement – makes it especially suited for educational use. It demonstrates elementary animation concepts and suffices for an example of a functional animation system. In addition, students can be encouraged to extend the system to model specific phenomena, or to use it in testing their own renderers.

The simplicity and readability of a time description language means that it can be used by people from a non-technical background. Researchers can also use it as a non-interactive visualization tool; because of its power and terseness, it is a suitable output language for many varieties of animation systems.

There is no particular class of "animation problem" to which a time description is especially suited – it doesn't model interaction, and there are no "objects" to speak of (apart from the `scene_description_text` to which the time description is applied).

3.2 Examples

We used Swish to add support for motion-blur facilities to Kolb's public-domain raytracer, *Rayshade*. Swish also produced parametrised expressions which could be used for real-time previewing. *Rayshade* has its own animation language support, but it is inadequate for many applications; Swish is therefore used to change camera positions and texture characteristics, and to coordinate the animation of large groups of objects.

Time descriptions were added to two *Rayshade* scenes in order to animate them. In the first example, a model of a city was embellished with a time description to provide a smooth flyby (Fig. 2). The position of the camera was changed with the `hermite` instruction; note how the buildings are motion-blurred. The time description was also used to move the position of light sources and alter the characteristics of the fog.

Fig. 2 A flyby of some skyscrapers above fog (with motion blur).

In the second example, a gift shop (Fig. 3), the regular movements of the clocks' mechanisms were simulated using `loop` in conjunction with simple expressions that involved the relative `time` variable. The clock's mechanisms are also motion blurred.

Fig. 3 Animated objects in a gift shop with motion blurr.

Both animations were recorded with the system described in Van Domselaar *et al.* (1992).

4 EXTENSIONS

Swish could be extended to perform some kind of modeling. However, this would require a precise definition of an object and its state – something that varies greatly between scene description languages – thereby removing the genericity of the time description language. However, a specific time description language could perform operations on lists of objects, giving the animator limited power to describe particle systems (Reeves, 1983), Lindenmayer systems (Lindenmayer, 1968), etc., without having to resort to writing code or using other animation packages.

Other extensions to Swish could allow the addition of types, as in the CINEMIRA-2 language (Magnetat-Thalmann and Thalmann, 1987). Functions other than `hermite`, such as ASAS' (Reynolds, 1982) `newton` number-sequence function, could also be invoked.

There are many other ways to animate a time-enhanced scene description besides the Swish system. Output frames could be directly farmed off to remote machines for networked processing. Alternatively, the time description language could be directly coded into the renderer (allowing "cels" to be incorporated, so that the renderer wouldn't have to calculate pixels for the areas in the frame on which the "cel" was superimposed).

An application could permit time-enhanced scene descriptions to be repeatedly edited, interpreted, previewed in real-time, and then sent off to be rendered when the animator is satisfied. The language could be extended to allow specification of the rendering technique, for scene descriptions which are readable by different renderers.

5 SUMMARY

We have described Swish, a simple, powerful language and interpreter that permits low-level animation of scene descriptions. It can be used to describe a diverse range of non-interactive, time-varying transformations for any scene description language. Its virtues are simplicity, readability, portability, power and practicality. It is well-suited for use in educational and research environments, and has been used to produce a number of complex animations with a minimum of time and effort.

ACKNOWLEDGEMENTS

We thank Stephen Boyd Gowing for his input in the "scribbling ideas" phase of this work. We also warmly thank Craig Kolb for producing and maintaining *Rayshade*, a superb piece of public-domain rendering software which was used in conjunction with Swish to produce the animations for this paper.

APPENDIX

This appendix contains the context free grammar for Swish.

```
input          : [text] [swishcommand] [input]

text           : [Tchar text]

swishcommand
   : Tdelimstart swishoption Tdelimend  // delimiters default to '{' and '}'

swishoption
   : Ttime                            // seconds passed from start
   | Trtime                           // seconds passed from last delimiter
   | Tloop  framerange ':' section    // looping mechanism
   | Tmethod path                     // use a particular renderer
   | Tframe                           // frames passed from start
   | Trframe                          // frames passed from last delimiter
   | Tblur ':' section                // produce motion blur for this section
   | Tnoblur ':' section              // produce no motion blur for this section
   | Tat timeframes ':' section       // during the following times do this section
   | Thermite splinedef               // produce a spline for the current Trtime
   | Tdelimeters symbol symbol        // change the delimeters to some other symbol

section        : input                // allows nested time description commands

path           : symbol

symbol         : Tquote chars Tquote

chars          : char [chars]

timeframes     :  framerange  [',' timeframes]

framerange     : frame '-' frame

frame          : ['!'] frameval       // '!' to make the following number absolute,
                                      // not relative

frameval       : Tnum                 // the current frame number
               | '^'                  // the first frame
               | '$'                  // the last frame

splinedef      : frame ':' splinepts ['(' contolvals ')'] [',' splinedef]

                                      // the frame number for the spline value,
                                      // the value,
                                      // any control values

numlist        : Treal [numlist]
```

```
// symbols

Ttime          : 'time'
Trtime         : 'rtime'
Tframe         : 'frame'
Trframe        : 'rframe'
Tblur          : 'blur'
Tnoblur        : 'noblur'
Tat            : 'at'
               | '@'
Thermite       : 'hermite'
Tdelimiters    : 'delimiters'
Tquote         : ' " '
Tloop          : 'loop'
Tmethod        : 'method'
```

REFERENCES

Barr AH (1989) Topics in Physically Based Modelling. Addison-Wesley, New York.

Ginsberg CM and Maxwell D (1983) Graphical marionette. Proceedings of the SIGGRAPH/SIGART Interdisciplinary Workshop on Motion : Representation and Perception, Toronto, April 4-6, 172-179.

Kolb CE (1991) Rayshade User's Guide and Reference Manual, available on UNIX networks.

Lindenmayer A (1968) Mathematical Models for Cellular Interactions in Development, Parts I and II, J. Theor. Biol., **18**, 280-315.

Magnetat-Thalmann N and Thalmann D (1987) Image Synthesis Theory and Practice, Springer-Verlag, Tokyo, New York.

Reeves WT (1983) Particle Systems - A Technique for Modelling a Class of Fuzzy Objects. ACM Transactions on Graphics, **2**, Number 2, 91-108.

Reeves WT and Blau R (1985) Approximate and Probabilistic Algorithms for Shading and Rendering article Systems, Proceedings SIGGRAPH 85, 313-322.

Reynolds CW (1982) Computer Animation with Scripts and Actors, Proceedings SIGGRAPH 82, 289-296.

Van Domselaar N, Suffern KG, and Sinclair I, A Video Editor for Teaching and Research in Computer Animation (1992) These proceedings.

Zeleznik RC, Brookshire Conner D, Wloka MM, Aliaga DG, Huang NT, Hubbard PM, Knep B, Kaufman H, Hughes J, van Dam A (1991) An Object-Oriented Framework for the Integration of Interactive Animation Techniques, Proceedings SIGGRAPH 91, 105-111.

Scott Hopwood is an undergraduate student at the University of Technology, Sydney. His research interests include computer graphics, languages, and visualization.

Address : School of Computing Sciences, University of Technology, Sydney, PO Box 123, Broadway, NSW, AUSTRALIA.

E-mail : @shopwood.socs.uts.edu.au

Iain Sinclair is an undergraduate student at the University of Technology, Sydney. His interests include computer animation, computer art, and human-computer interaction.

Address : School of Computing Sciences, University of Technology, Sydney, PO Box 123, Broadway, NSW, AUSTRALIA.

E-mail : axolotl@socs.uts.edu.au

Kevin Suffern received an M.Sc. from Cornell University in Astronomy in 1973 and a Ph.D. in Applied Mathematics from the University of Sydney in 1978. From 1979 to 1981 he worked in the School of Mathematics and Physics at Macquarie University in Sydney, before joining the School of Computing Sciences at the University of Technology, Sydney, where he is currently a Senior Lecturer. In 1986 he was a Visiting Research Scientist in The Center for Interactive Computer Graphics, Rensselaer Polytechnic Institute, and in 1990 he was a Visiting Associate Professor in the Rensselaer Design Research Center, Rensselaer Polytechnic Institute. His main interests are computer graphics, computer aided geometric design, and computer art. He is a member of ACS, ACM, and SIGGRAPH.

Address : School of Computing Sciences, University of Technology, Sydney, PO Box 123, Broadway, NSW, AUSTRALIA.

E-mail : kevin@socs.uts.edu.au

Risk and QFD Guided Prototyping of Graphical Animation Software

MARKO HEIKKINEN, RAINO LINTULAMPI, and PETRI PULLI

ABSTRACT

We present early experiences of using a new approach for development of graphical computer aided software engineering (CASE) tools with model execution and animation capabilities. The spiral model for software development process, Quality Function Deployment (QFD) and prototyping form the backbone of our approach. Main characteristics of our approach are advanced risk-driven and QFD supported decision making enabling efficient teamwork on animation tool development. We present two concrete examples of our approach in the context of a graphical animation tool for object oriented software designs.

Keywords: animation, prototyping, risk analysis, spiral model, quality function deployment.

1 INTRODUCTION

1.1 Scope

Graphical animation tools are software intensive systems, where the application domain concepts are given operational semantics by means of graphical animation. The development of such animation tools involves both high-speed, high-precision graphics animation software development, and high-level, interactive visualisation software that forms the semantic framework for animation. In this paper we deal with the latter kind of software development.

1.2 Contribution and Substance

We present preliminary experiences of using a new approach for development of graphical computer aided software engineering (CASE) tools. The spiral model for software development process [5], Quality Function Deployment (QFD) [24], [17], [2] and prototyping form the backbone of the approach. The spiral model guides the development towards the most difficult and risk-prone parts as early in the project as possible. By using prototypes it is possible to check the feasibility of the difficult parts before implementing less difficult features. QFD is used in capturing and ranking user needs and technical features of the system. It is also used in comparing and ranking various implementation alternatives. The combination of the spiral model, QFD and prototyping was found to be efficient in this kind of development work. It helped us to pay attention to the most difficult and most desirable features. It also prevented us from developing fancy features that nobody wants.

1.3 Application Domain

Graphical software specification and design languages are becoming an important part of systems development process. This is especially true for real-time embedded computer systems due to their increasing complexity and development risks. Ward&Mellor [21] and Hatley&Pirbhai

[14] extensions for Structured Analysis, Statecharts [13], OOSD [22], [23] and HOOD [16] are examples of these languages. In this paper we concentrate on the Wassermann OOSD notation[1]. The objective of our research work has been to extend an existing graphical animation tool with features that would enable us to execute SA/SD structure charts and object oriented designs.

2 BOEHM'S SPIRAL MODEL

In the last few years more and more attention has been paid to alternative software development models that could both overcome deficiencies [1] of the traditional waterfall model [4] and accommodate activities such as prototyping, reuse, and automatic coding as part of the process. The spiral model proposed by Boehm [5] is a major step into this direction. The main distinguishing feature of the spiral model is that it creates a risk-driven approach to the software process rather than a primarily document-driven or code- driven process.

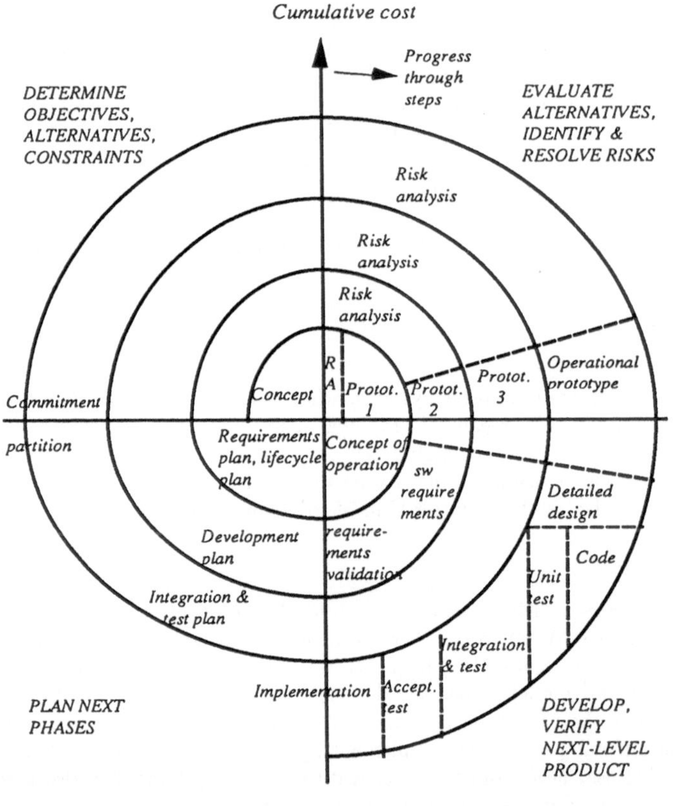

Figure 1: Boehm's spiral model for software development process. The radial dimension represents the cumulative cost, and the angular dimension represents the progress made in completing each cycle of the spiral.

The spiral model views the development process in polar coordinates, Figure 1. The radial dimension of the graph represents cumulative project cost, the angular dimension represents progress of the project through various steps. A cycle of the model is an increase of 360 degrees in angular coordinates. The plane is divided into four quadrants that represent different kinds of activities, as follows:

[1] An earlier version of this paper [15] describes our experiments with SA/SD structure charts.

Quadrant 1	Determination of objectives, alternatives and constraints
Quadrant 2	Evaluation of alternatives; identification and resolution of risks
Quadrant 3	Development activities
Quadrant 4	Review and planning for future cycles

In addition, the boundary between quadrants I and IV represents a commitment to carry the project through another cycle. Note that the angular coordinate does not progress evenly with time. Some cycles of the spiral may require months to complete, while others require only days or even hours. Similarly, although increasing angular dimension denotes progress within a cycle, it does not necessarily denote progress towards project completion [20].

2.1 Risk Management

The spiral model guides a developer to postpone detailed elaboration of low-risk software elements and to avoid going too deep in their design until the high-risk elements of the design are stabilised. Risk management requires appropriate attention to early risk resolution techniques such as early prototyping and simulation. The spiral model may incorporate prototyping as a risk reduction option at any stage of development and explicitly calls for a suitable risk assessment and risk control activities throughout major portions of the development process.

Risk management involves the following steps [7]:

- Risk assessment techniques
  - Risk identification produces lists of the project specific risk items likely to compromise a project's success.
  - Risk analysis quantifies the loss probability and loss magnitude for each identified risk item, and it assesses compound risks in risk item interactions.
  - Risk priorisation produces a ranked list of risk items according to their severity.
- Risk control techniques
  - Risk management planning helps prepare you to address each risk item. It also includes the coordination of the individual risk item plans with each other and with the overall project plan.
  - Risk resolution produces a situation in which the risk items are eliminated or otherwise resolved.
  - Risk monitoring involves tracking of the project's progress towards resolving its risk items and taking corrective action where appropriate.

2.2 Concurrent Threads of Activities

The spiral model allows concurrent threads of development activities that may traverse the traditional progression of software product phases in a loosely synchronised manner. The concurrent threads may be organised around levels of risk [5]. Figure 2 gives an example of concurrent development threads [20].

In Figure 2, the horizontal axis represents elapsed time. The vertical axis represents the level of abstraction at which a representation or understanding of the system is being developed. The development process is depicted by three traces through the two dimensional space. Each trace corresponds a thread of engineering activities. In general, moving downwards represents progress. A highly jagged trace represents an activity thread in which much iteration (prototyping) takes place. This is seen in Figure 2 during the third spiral when the high-risk thread develops an architectural prototype, which is analysed and thrown away. Based on the lessons

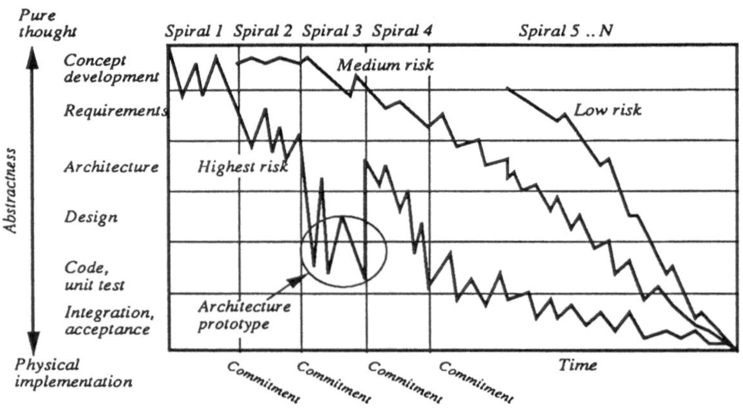

Figure 2: Level of abstraction vs. time under the spiral model.

learned from the architectural prototype, the high-risk thread enters full-scale design and implementation during Spiral 4. Concurrent with the third and fourth spirals the medium-risk elements are being specified. During the fifth and later spirals the high-, medium- and low-risk threads progress concurrently, leading to incremental integration, installation, and use. The spiral model is a generic model, so it does not explicitly define the milestones to be produced for each cycle. The spiral has to be customised on a company or project basis.

2.3 Spiral Description Tables

Use of spiral description tables is one of the supporting techniques that we have adopted for customising the spiral model for project specific needs. We describe the work to be carried out during each spiral (cycle) by using tables with fixed slots for information. Each table is associated with one spiral. Spirals are numbered from 0 up, the innermost being 0. The use of tables is necessary because it is impossible to incorporate all the necessary information into a graphic spiral.

Both [5] and [20] use tables for describing the example spirals. However they differ slightly according to which slots are used. We have chosen to use tables similar to [5] extended with an additional slots "status", "version", "work description", and "validation", which we feel necessary for our purpose. Examples of spiral tables will be presented in subsequent chapters.

3 QUALITY FUNCTION DEPLOYMENT

Quality Function Deployment (QFD) [24], [17], [2] was developed in Japan as an integrated set of quality tools and techniques. It is used for market research and product design purposes to make explicit the "voice of the customer" throughout the product design process. Basic to the application of QFD is the use of variety of matrices to examine in detail the interaction of various dimensions, such as function, cost, customer demands, raw materials, etc. We used a QFD variant modified especially for software development [24]. Our QFD process consisted of user/stakeholder identification, user need analysis, technical requirement identification & analysis and alternative comparison.

We expect to gain the following advantages by using QFD:

- QFD makes it possible to show links between objectives, alternatives and risks.
- QFD allows quantifying identified links.
- Quantification enables ranking of alternatives how well they meet objectives.
- Explicit links and quantification enables open discussion and review before starting to prototype and making commitments.

On the other hand we expect to encounter the following difficulties when using QFD:

- Weak links may be difficult to identify.
- Quantifying links is dependent on the experience of the designer.
- Techniques must be developed for identification and quantification of risk, and connecting this data to QFD matrices.
- Matrices must be kept compact and suited for tool support.

4 DEVELOPMENT EXAMPLE

4.1 Graphical Animation Tool Overview

As a concrete example of our approach we present an extension to a graphical animation tool that makes it possible to execute SA/SD structure charts and object oriented designs. Appendix A shows one animator window that contains one piece of a C++ application described using OOSD notation.

The tool is implemented in the Smalltalk-80 programming environment [11] and it is a direct descendant of the SPECS [9] and Espex [18] tools. The Specs/Espex platform contains a window-based menu driven graph editor and an integrated graph simulator with animation support. Animation means that the movements of data items and signals between transformations are made visible on a workstation display.

Animation of both logical and physical models is possible. It is even possible to execute a heterogeneous model [19] where some sections of the system are described as a logical model and some other sections as a detailed physical model. The animation covers both control aspects and computations performed on data. The computations can be described using either Smalltalk-80 or the C language. Execution of the graphs is based on the object oriented Petri net formalism [9], developed at ETH, Zürich. This graphically executable formalism is a combination of channel/instance nets, predicate/transition nets [10] and the object oriented Smalltalk-80 programming language [12].

4.2 Initial Risk Assessment

We started our development activities with an initial risk analysis as part of the project planning. The initial risk assessment is a step of determining the common and special risks that are a threat to successful outcome for the planned project. The initial risk assessment consists of risk identification, risk analysis, and priorisation. This initial risk assessment does not remove the need later in the project to periodically assess if new risks have surfaced.

4.2.1 Risk Identification

By using checklists [5], [25], [8] the following risk items[2] may touch[3] the project.

[2] The list is unordered.

[3] Software developers are not used to openly discussing risks. Admitting that there is a risk is usually understood that something is wrong with the project or with the developers.

- Personnel shortfalls
- Unrealistic schedule and budget
- Developing the wrong software functions
- Developing the wrong user interface
- Gold Plating: Object oriented features
- Shortfalls in externally furnished components: Smalltalk-80 version upgrade from 2.5 to 4.0
- Real-time performance shortfalls
- Straining computer science capabilities: human-machine performance.
- Tools availability: Graphic workstation

4.2.2 Risk Analysis and Priorisation

We found it rather difficult to quantify an individual risk item's probability. This is clearly subject to further study. However we were able to rank them subjectively in three groups according to probability.

- Frequent
  - Developing the wrong software functions
  - Developing the wrong user interface
  - Unrealistic schedule and budget
- Probable
  - Shortfalls in externally furnished components: Smalltalk-80 version upgrade from 2.5 to 4.0
  - Tools availability: Graphic workstation
  - Straining computer science capabilities: human-machine performance.
- Improbable
  - Personnel shortfalls
  - Gold Plating: OOD features
  - Real-time performance shortfalls

The loss associated with each of the risk items seems to be about equal in this case. Each risk may cause an unsatisfactory outcome jeopardizing the task.

4.3 Initial Risk Control

Initial risk control consists of risk management planning. Later in the project, risk resolution and risk monitoring takes place according to the plan if necessary.

4.3.1 Risk Management Planning

One of the basic ideas of the spiral model is that the risk management plan can be combined with the project plan and expressed in the same customised spiral model. Therefore the initial risk management plan has a major effect of what form the project specific spiral model takes.

The following activities[4] were planned to bring the identified risks under control.

- Early use of QFD to select COM notation
  - Developing the wrong user interface
  - Straining computer science capabilities: human-machine performance.
- Early use of QFD to rank software functions
  - Developing the wrong software functions
  - Developing the wrong user interface
- Prototyping
  - Straining computer science capabilities: human-machine performance.
  - Gold Plating: OOD features
  - Real-time performance shortfalls
- Design-to-cost and design-to-schedule [6]
  - Unrealistic schedule and budget
- Acquire and freeze tools: Postpone Smalltalk-80 version upgrade until task finished, negotiate a high performance Sun 4 workstation
  - Shortfalls in externally furnished components: Smalltalk-80 version upgrade from 2.5 to 4.0
  - Tools availability: Graphic workstation
- Parallel development: Have a student install the prototyping platform (Espex tools) on the Sun 4 workstation after delivery. Carry out development on existing Sun 3 until Sun 4 tools are installed and in order.
  - Personnel shortfalls
  - Shortfalls in externally furnished components: Smalltalk-80 version upgrade from 2.5 to 4.0
  - Tools availability: Graphic workstation

4.4 Customised Spiral Model

The development activities were organized into four spirals. Only the first two spirals are described here. The final two spirals are less detailed and are to be fine-tuned during the work in Spiral 1 Quadrant 4.

Spiral: Spiral 0: Notation and Features

Version: 1.0

Status: Draft

[4] The list of planned actions is not exhaustive and is somewhat simplified for the purpose of clarity.

Objectives: Capture the basic features of COM animation. This includes selection of the notation to be used and a rough description of desirable features. Find out if COM animation work has been carried out elsewhere and if there are reusable results.

Constraints: Sun/Unix/Smalltalk-80 environment, the features to be created must be compatible with the existing Espex tools and its forthcoming extensions. Time schedule estimate 1 man-month. Many notations are language dependent (Ada).

Alternatives: Wassermann notation, MachineCharts, HOOD notation, SA structure chart. Some other notation or subset/combination of these or other notations.

Risks: Neither OOD notations nor development methods are stabilised. US originated notations may not be well-known in Europe.

Risk resolution: Literature search & study for existing systems. Evaluation of existing CASE tools to find out if there are any existing implementations of features supporting the COM animation. QFD comparison of notations.

Risk resolution results:

Work description:

Validation: Audit of the notation comparison & selection document and the feature list within the project group Other expert reviewers may also be used.

Plan for next phase:

Commitment:

Spiral: Spiral 1: Preliminary User's Manual.

Version: 1.0

Status: Draft

Objectives: Capture the features of the Code Organisation Model Animation. These include features of COM animation, support for OOD graphics & animation and interface of animation with existing C code Produce preliminary user's manual for the features.

Constraints: Notation selected during Cycle 0. Time schedule and effort of the task: 1.5 man-months.

Alternatives: Smalltalk-80 version 2.5 or version 4.0 can be used.

Risks: The interface to C has not been experimented with the Espex environment before. Additional risks may arise during Spiral 0.

Risk resolution: A document describing the desired features. Tests of their feasibility using prototypes for animation, OOD graphics and C interface. Reusing & modification of existing Espex code Possible QFD analysis of the features to be selected for Spiral 2.

Risk resolution results:

Work description:

Validation: Evaluation of the prototypes and the feature description document.

Plan for next phase:

Commitment:

. . .

Spiral: Spiral 3: Navigator.

Version: 1.0

Status: Draft

Objectives: Proper implementation and refinement of the model navigation tool. Updatings to User's manual and tool descriptions.

Constraints: Status of COM animation tool after spiral 2. Schedule and effort estimate 1 man-month.

Alternatives: Graphical tree representation, dynamic hierarchical menu.

Risks: . Performance, when model is changed and the display is updated. Resolution for large models, especially for node names.

Risk resolution: Prototyping the risky parts.

Risk resolution results: Graphical tree.

Work description: Smalltalk-80 implementation by creating a new subclass for Net Editor and NetEditorView classes.

Validation: Evaluation of the prototype tool by an example model. CEC review in Madrid Jan 92. Internal audit for User's manual documentation.

Plan for next phase:

Commitment:

4.5 Experiences

4.5.1 Notation Alternatives

Figure 3 summarises the notation alternatives that were considered for the COM animation tool. The basic requirement for the notation was that it could be used to to represent the module structure and call hierarchy of program modules. Possibility to represent object oriented design and compatibility with the existing tool were also important requirements.

FEATURES / NOTATION	Developer	Type	Tool support
OOSD	Wassermann, Pircher & Muller	Structure charts + OOD, graphics	Software Through Pictures
Machine Charts	R. Buhr	ADA oriented OOD, graphics + text	TimeBench
HOOD	CISI Ingenierie, MATRA Espace,CRI	ADA oriented OOD, graphics + text	HOOD-SF
SA Structure Chart	Yourdon & Constantine	Structure charts, graphics	CodeLink & many others
Booch notation	G. Booch	ADA oriented OOA, OOD, graphics	not available
Taylor notation	D. Taylor, A. Hecht	OO structure charts, graphics	not available

Figure 3: Notation alternatives and their tool support for the COM animation tool.

4.5.2 QFD for Ranking the Alternatives

The QFD process for software development starts from identifying the potential users and stakeholders of the software. There may be frequent and infrequent users - or some that do not themselves use the software but will recommend where it will be used. The stakeholders are people or organisations that must participate, review, approve and cooperate in order for a software to be constructed and delivered - their needs and concerns must also be understood correctly [24]. The QFD technique allows users to modify the matrices for their own purposes. It is also possible to create totally new non-standard matrices if needed [17], [2].

We follow the QFD matrix naming convention proposed by [17] (Figure 4). We use Z0 matrix (Appendix B) for identifying users and their characteristics. The purpose of Z0 matrix is to derive priorities to all stakeholders of the system. Z1 matrix (Appendix C) is used for analysing and giving priorities to user needs and requirements. These matrices produce weighed values of user needs that can further be used in the matrix A1. This matrix contains the user needs and plausible technical features of the software fulfilling the needs. As a result it produces information that help to choose the technical features that produce the greatest user satisfaction.

For choosing the most suitable notation for the graphical animation tool we used the matrix F2 (Appendix D). It contains the (weighed) technical features and different alternatives for implementing the features. As a result each alternative gets a weight that can be used as a guideline in the implementation. The F2 matrix is a derived matrix that was specially created for our purposes.

Before the evaluation we had an intuition that the Wassermann (OOSD) notation would best suit for our purposes. During the QFD process this proved to be correct. The strong SA features

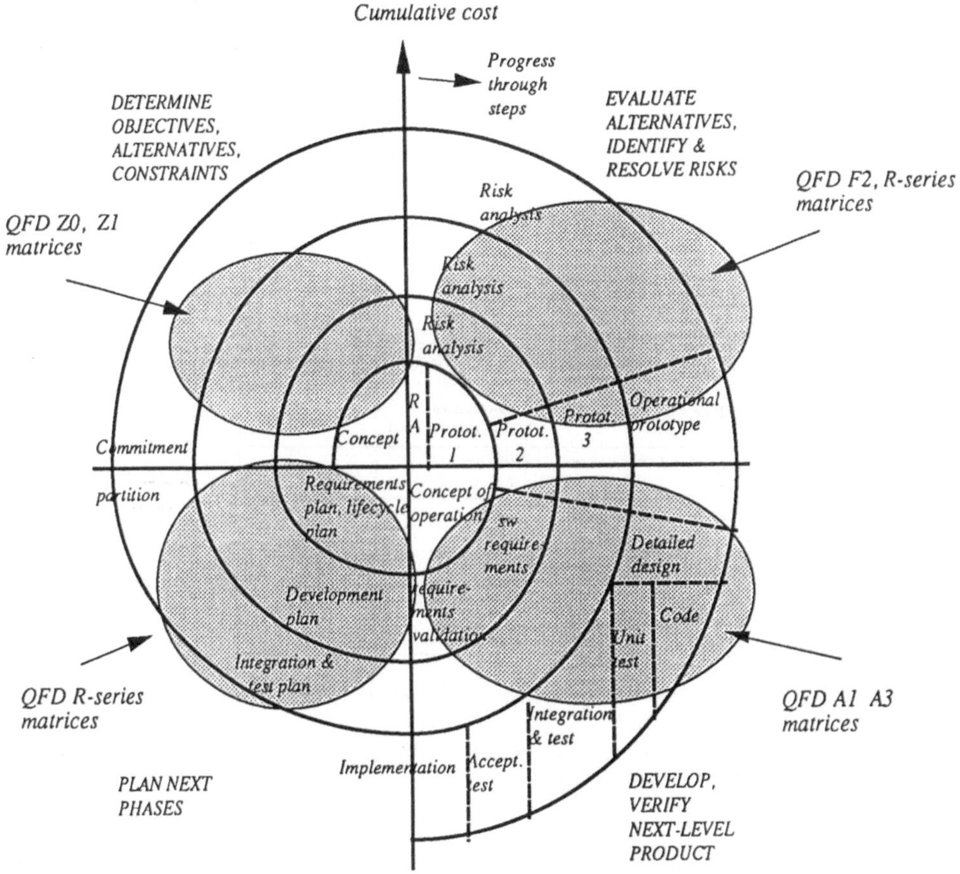

Figure 4: Possibilities of applying QFD in the spiral process.

in the COM notation, good OOD features, and ease of integration to the current notation used in Espex were the strongest reasons for the selection of OOSD.

The QFD matrices were created and maintained with the ReQueX research tool [3] developed at VTT Computer Technology Laboratory.

4.6 Navigator

The purpose of the Navigator is to make traversing along the model hierarchy easier. The navigator provides a quick way to move from one place to another in the model by skipping the hierarchy boundaries.

The window contains the hierarchical structure of the model as a tree representation, Appendix E. Each node of the tree represents one diagram (= editor or simulator window) of the model. By moving cursor on top of the desired node and clicking the mouse button the corresponding diagram is opened/activated. The navigator remembers from where it was activated and opens diagram based on that information. If diagram window of a node is open, the node is coloured black, otherwise white.

Navigator window size is adjustable. If you shrink it enough, (there are threshold values for both width and height) the names of the nodes are not visible to prevent the window becoming too blurred. When you increase the window size, the names will come back again.

5 CONCLUSIONS

The spiral model makes it possible to plan in advance the prototyping and risk management steps necessary when developing graphical animation applications. Initial risk assessment and risk control study may help determine the nature of the project and may help in defining the phasing of the work into spirals and their contents. We have found it necessary to use tables to describe the contents of individual spirals. We have found it convenient to use QFD as a decision making techniques supporting teamwork and concurrent engineering. Further study is needed on risk analysis techniques, especially on quantifying the risk item probabilities and their loss effects, and connecting this data to QFD matrices. Promising area of development is foreseen in developing QFD matrices for risk analysis and priorisation.

ACKNOWLEDGEMENTS

The work presented in this paper has been carried out in the IPTES project. The objective of the IPTES (Incremental Prototyping Technology for Embedded Real-Time Systems) project is to develop methodologies, tools and theoretical results on distributed prototyping of real-time systems. IPTES is partially funded by the European Communities under the ESPRIT programme, project no. EP5570 and Technical Development Centre of Finland, TEKES.

The IPTES consortium is formed by IFAD (Denmark), VTT (Finland), MARI (UK), CEA/LETI (France), ENEA (Italy), Synergie (France), Universidad Politécnica de Madrid (Spain) Telefónica I+D (Spain), and Politecnico di Milano (Italy).

REFERENCES

[1] Agresti, W. (editor). New Paradigms for Software Development. IEEE Computer Society Press, 1986.

[2] Akao, Y. Quality Function Deployment. Integrating Customer Requirements into Product Design. Productivity Press, Cambridge, Massachusetts, 1990. Originally published as *Hinshitukenai katuyou no jissai* by Japan Standards Association.

[3] Auer, A., Ala-Siuru, P., Puustinen, H. Adopting QFD Techniques to Real-Time Systems Design: First Results. Proceedings of the 35th EOQC Annual Conference June 17-21, 1991, Prague, Czechoslovakia, pp. 229-234.

[4] Boehm, B. Software Engineering Economics, Prentice-Hall, 1981.

[5] Boehm, B. A Spiral Model of Software Development and Enhancement. IEEE Computer, 21(5), pp. 61-72, 1988.

[6] Boehm B. Tutorial: Software Risk Management. IEEE Computer Society, 1989. 496 p.

[7] Boehm, B. Software Risk Management: Principles and Practices. IEEE Software, January 1991, pp. 32-41, 1991.

[8] Charette, R.N., Software Engineering Risk Analysis and Management. McGraw-Hill, New York, 1989. 325 p.

[9] Dähler, J., Gerber, B., Gisiger, H-P., Kündig, A. A Graphical Tool for the Design and Prototyping of Distributed Systems. ACM Software Engineering Notes, 12(1987)7, pp. 25-36.

[10] Genrich, H., Lautenbach, K. System Modelling with High-Level Petri Nets. Theoretical Computer Science 13(1981), North Holland, 1981.

[11] Goldberg, A. Smalltalk-80: The Interactive Programming Environment. Addison Wesley, Reading Massachusetts, 1984.

[12] Goldberg, A., Robson, D. Smalltalk-80: The Language and its implementation. Addison Wesley, Reading Massachusetts, 1985.

[13] Harel, D. Statecharts: A Visual Formalism for Complex Systems. Science of Computer Programming 8(1987), pp. 231-274.

[14] Hatley, D.J., Pirbhai, I.M. Strategies for Real-Time System Specification, Dorset House, 1987.

[15] Heikkinen, M. Employing Spiral Model, Prototyping and QFD in Graphical Case Tool Development. In: Encernacao, J., (Ed), Eurographics Technical Report Series. Vol. EG91GR&D. ISSN 1017-4656. Pp. 53-66.

[16] Anon. HOOD Reference Manual. European Space Agency, Noordwijk, The Netherlands, 1989.

[17] King, B. Better Designs in Half the Time: Implementing QFD Quality Function Deployment in America. Goal/QPC, Methuen, Massachusetts, 1989.

[18] Lintulampi, R., Pulli, P. Graphical Prototyping of Tasking Behaviour. To appear in the Proceedings of the 8th IEEE Workshop on Real-Time Operating Systems and Software, May 15-17, 1991, Atlanta, Georgia. Pergamon Press, 1991.

[19] Pulli, P. An Interpreter for Heterogeneous Prototypes of Embedded Software. Technical Research Centre of Finland, Publications 79. Espoo 1991. 46 p + app. 76 p.

[20] Marmor-Squires, A. (Principal investigator). Process Model for High Performance Trusted Systems in Ada. Technical Report, TRW Systems Division, Fairfax, Virginia, August 1989.

[21] Ward, P.T., Mellor, S.J. Structured Development for Real-Time Systems, Vol 1-3. Yourdon Press, New York, 1985-1986.

[22] Wassermann, A.I., Pircher, P.A., Muller, R.J. An Object-Oriented Structured Design Method for Code Generation. ACM Software Engineering Notes, 14(1989)1, pp. 32-55.

[23] Wassermann, A.I., Pircher, P.A., Muller, R.J. The Object-Oriented Structured Design Notation for Software Design Representation. IEEE Computer, 23(1990)3, pp. 50-63.

[24] Zultner, R.E. Software Quality [Function] Deployment - Applying QFD to Software. 13th Rocky Mountain Quality Conference, 1989.

[25] Anon. AFSC/AFLC Pamphlet 800-45: Software Risk Abatement. Reprinted in Boehm, B., Tutorial: Software Risk Management, IEEE Computer Society Press, 1989, pp. 148-171.

APPENDIX A: OOSD ANIMATION

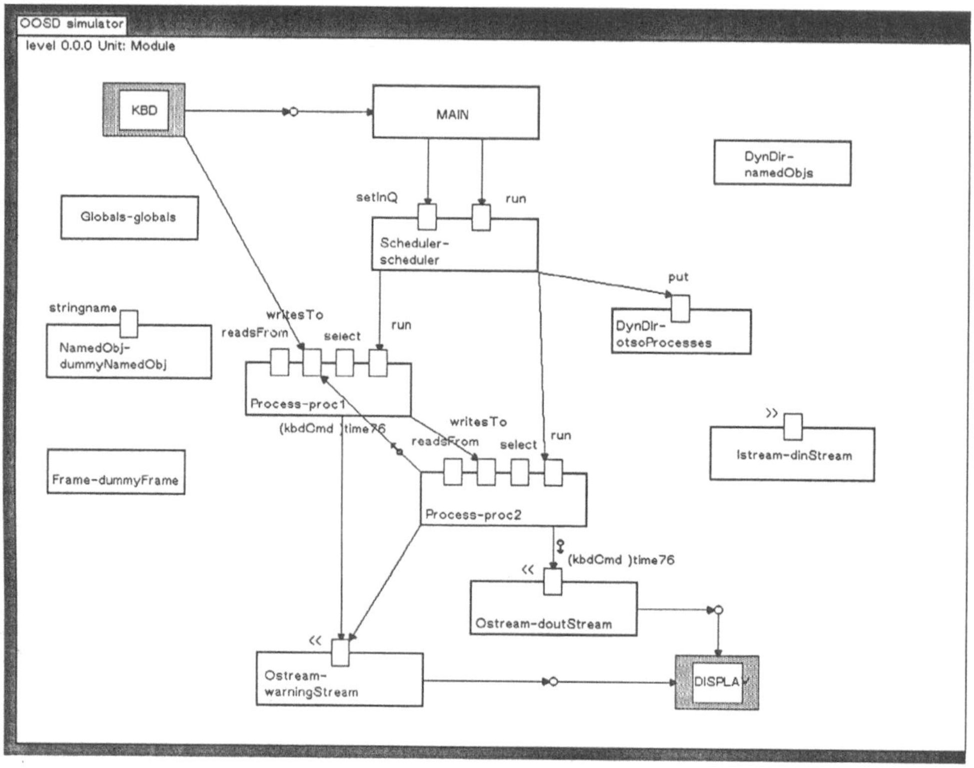

APPENDIX B: QFD MATRIX Z0

ReQueX
VTT **Comp Tech Lab**

Author:	MPH
Date:	4.4.91
Version:	1.0
Status:	accepted
Project:	IPTES

Z-0 matrix **User identification/market segmentation**

User characteristics

	Users GROUP R	GROUP I	GROUP D	GROUP U	GROUP E	
Number of employees	+	++	+++	+	+	
Annual turnover	+	+++	++	+	+	
Creative input	+++	++	+	+++	+	
Role in review procedure	+	+	+++	+	+++	
Dissemination power	+	+++	+	+++	+++	
Role in utilization	+	+++	++	+	+	
Publicity	++	+	+	+++	+	
no	10	15	13	13	11	62
weight %	16,129	24,194	20,968	20,968	17,742	

no. = any number

APPENDIX C: QFD MATRIX Z1

ReQueX

VTT Comp Tech Lab

Author:	MPH
Date:	4.4.91
Version:	1.0
Status:	accepted
Project:	IPTES

Z-1 matrix Mapping users to user needs

Users

User needs	GROUP R	GROUP I	GROUP D	GROUP U	GROUP E	total	adj. priority
Performance	4 / 65	4 / 97	9 / 189	0 / 0	1 / 18	368	4
Extendability	4 / 65	9 / 218	4 / 84	9 / 189	9 / 160	715	8
Portability	1 / 16	9 / 218	4 / 84	0 / 0	1 / 18	335	4
Safety	1 / 16	9 / 218	9 / 189	1 / 21	4 / 71	515	6
Readability of documentation	4 / 65	4 / 97	9 / 189	1 / 21	1 / 18	389	4
Consistency of documentation	1 / 16	4 / 97	9 / 189	1 / 21	1 / 18	340	4
Completeness of documentation	1 / 16	4 / 97	9 / 189	1 / 21	1 / 18	340	4
User support	0 / 0	1 / 24	9 / 189	0 / 0	0 / 0	213	2
Ease of usage	4 / 65	1 / 24	9 / 189	0 / 0	0 / 0	277	3
Ease of installation	9 / 145	4 / 97	9 / 189	0 / 0	0 / 0	431	5
Visual appearance and good user interface	9 / 145	9 / 218	4 / 84	1 / 21	9 / 160	627	7
Support for a practical specification method	4 / 65	9 / 218	9 / 189	1 / 21	4 / 71	563	6
Support for real-time issues	9 / 145	1 / 24	9 / 189	9 / 189	1 / 18	565	6
Verification and validation	4 / 65	1 / 24	9 / 189	9 / 189	1 / 18	484	5
Model building facilities	9 / 145	1 / 24	9 / 189	1 / 21	1 / 18	397	4
Scientific background	4 / 65	1 / 24	1 / 21	9 / 189	4 / 71	369	4
Support for research goals	9 / 145	1 / 24	1 / 21	9 / 189	9 / 160	539	6
Publicity	4 / 65	0 / 0	0 / 0	9 / 189	4 / 71	324	4
Support for graduate studies	4 / 65	0 / 0	0 / 0	9 / 189	0 / 0	253	3
Future commercial exploitation of results	1 / 16	9 / 218	4 / 84	0 / 0	9 / 160	477	5
Exploitation of earlier research results	9 / 145	4 / 97	1 / 21	9 / 189	4 / 71	523	6
weight %	16,129	24,194	20,968	20,968	17,742		

Correlations

9 strong contribution

4 moderate contribution

1 weak contribution

0 no correlation

APPENDIX D: QFD MATRIX F2

ReQueX
VTT Comp Technology Lab

F2 matrix **Value analysis**

Author:	MPH
Date:	9.4.91
Version:	1.0
Status:	accepted
Project:	IPTES

Variations

Technical requirements

	weight	Taylor	OOSD	MachChar	Hood	SA St.Ch.	Booch
Notational strength for COM animation	5	2 10	4 21	2 10	2 10	4 21	2 10
Notational strength for data structure animation	2	3 6	4 9	3 6	4 9	4 9	2 4
Notational strength for object class animation	4	4 15	2 7	0 0	0 0	0 0	4 15
Notational strength for object instance animation	5	2 10	4 21	4 21	4 21	0 0	4 21
Notation compatible with current Espex graphs	5	1 5	4 20	1 5	0 0	4 20	0 0
Notation suitable for graphical execution	5	2 10	4 19	4 19	3 15	4 19	2 10
Purely graphical notation	4	4 18	4 18	3 13	0 0	4 18	4 18
Notation easy to learn	2	3 7	3 7	3 7	3 7	4 9	2 5
European-originated notation	3	0 0	0 0	0 0	4 12	0 0	0 0
Notation not tied to an implementation language	4	3 12	3 12	1 4	1 4	2 8	2 8
Notation shows object instantiation	4	0 0	3 13	0 0	3 13	0 0	4 18
Notation shows object interfaces	4	3 12	3 12	3 12	3 12	0 0	3 12
Notation shows parameter values of messages	3	2 6	4 12	4 12	3 9	4 12	3 9
Notation shows inheritance	2	3 6	1 2	0 0	0 0	0 0	3 6
Notation shows program modularity	8	4 32	4 32	3 24	2 16	4 32	3 24
Notation shows timing aspects	2	0 0	1 2	4 10	4 10	0 0	0 0
Model navigator	4	0 0	0 0	0 0	0 0	0 0	0 0
Inscription editor	3	2 6	4 13	3 10	3 10	4 13	2 6
C-support as minispec	5	3 14	3 14	2 9	2 9	3 14	2 9
Token appearance	3	3 10	3 10	2 7	2 7	3 10	0 0
Visual token matching	3	1 3	4 11	3 8	3 8	4 11	1 3
Training for users	3	0 0	0 0	0 0	0 0	0 0	0 0
User's manual	3	0 0	0 0	0 0	0 0	0 0	0 0
Experience report	4	0 0	0 0	0 0	0 0	0 0	0 0
* Textual specification	4	0 0	0 0	0 0	0 0	0 0	0 0
	Weight	183	255	177	170	196	177
	%	16	22	15	15	17	15

Linear value
0 for unsatisfactory
1 for tolerable
2 for sufficient
3 for good
4 for ideal

APPENDIX E: NAVIGATOR

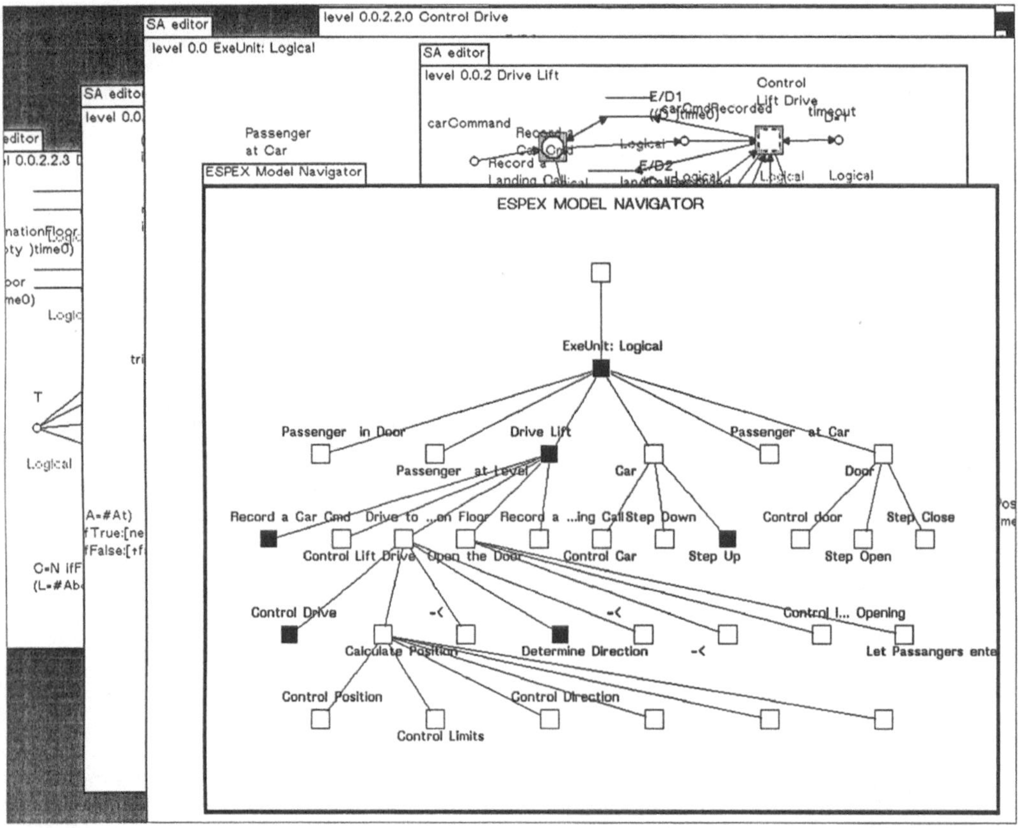

AUTHORS' BIOGRAPHIES

Marko Heikkinen is currently a research scientist at Technical Research Centre of Finland, Computer Technology Laboratory, Oulu, Finland. His interests include computer graphics, QFD, and computer aided software engineering tools. He received his M.Sc. in University of Oulu in 1990.

Raino Lintulampi is currently a research scientist at Technical Research Centre of Finland, Computer Technology Laboratory, Oulu, Finland. His interests include real-time systems development and concurrent engineering techniques. He received his M.Sc. in University of Oulu in 1985.

Petri Pulli is currently a senior research scientist at Technical Research Centre of Finland, Computer Technology Laboratory, Oulu, Finland. His interests include hard real-time systems, prototyping, scheduling and risk analysis. He received his M.Sc. and Ph.D. in University of Oulu in 1981 and 1991.

Address: Technical Research Centre of Finland (VTT), Computer Technology Laboratory, Box 201, SF-90571 Oulu, Finland. Tel. + 358 81 551 2111. Fax. +358 81 551 2320.

A Video Editor for Teaching and Research in Computer Animation

NEIL VAN DOMSELAAR, KEVIN G. SUFFERN, and IAIN D. SINCLAIR

ABSTRACT

A simple video editor has been developed for use in a teaching and research environment. It allows sequences of computer generated animation frames to be recorded on video tape using stop frame techniques, without the users having to know anything about how the video recording process works. The editor is in use for teaching and research in computer graphics animation at the University of Technology, Sydney.

Key Words : video recording, stop frame animation, computer graphics education.

1. INTRODUCTION

The School of Computing Sciences teaches two undergraduate elective subjects in computer graphics, *Introduction to Computer Graphics* in Autumn Semester to approximately 100 students, and *Topics in Computer Graphics* in Spring Semester to approximately 40 students. The objectives of the latter subject are to teach image synthesis techniques and computer animation.

The School has seven Silicon Graphics Personal Iris workstations to support the teaching of *Topics in Computer Graphics*. Three of these are equipped with 24 bit planes, and these machines are also equipped with Z-buffers which allow hidden surface removal to be performed in hardware. The other four workstations are equipped with eight bit planes and do not have Z-buffers. All Personal Irises are equipped with special hardware which performs three dimensional transformations and the perspective projection. This hardware gives the Personal Irises impressive abilities for real time animation, which include the ability to display approximately 5000 small polygons per second with hidden surface removal and shading with up to seven point light sources.

The image synthesis techniques covered in *Topics in Computer Graphics* include the Phong illumination model, incremental shading techniques for polygons, ray tracing, texture mapping, and radiosity. Other topics covered which support the rendering process include object modelling techniques : polygons, curved surfaces, fractals, particle systems, modelling hierarchical objects, aliasing and antialiasing, and colour theory.

In teaching the above techniques the students are given two programming assignments which involve both modelling and rendering. One exercise involves fractals, particularly the modelling and rendering of fractal landscapes, and the other is to implement a simple ray tracer.

With this experience behind them, the students are taught the principles of computer animation. The topics covered include key frame systems, kinematic specification of motion control for objects and cameras, scripting systems, and physically based modelling (Barr, 1989).

As a final assignment, each student produces a short three dimensional animation sequence of up to 30 seconds duration on a topic chosen by the student. In the past all the animations have been real time, and have relied upon the Iris's animation abilities discussed above to provide smooth animation. Popular animation topics have been particle systems and the motion of simple polygonal and wire-frame objects. These do not tax the ability of the Irises to display real time animation, but just as importantly, the calculation time per frame is short enough that the animations are not slowed down. The animations are recorded on video tape to provide a permanent record of the student's work, and allow them to be reviewed for assessment purposes. The system used for the recording was described in Suffern and Murray (1990).

In order to display real time animation, the Irises must be able to perform the calculations for each frame as well as render it, in a 30th of a second. If this is not possible, the display rate drops to 15 frames per second, 8 frames per second, etc depending on the scene complexity and the amount of calculations required. Real time animation of ray tracing and other realistic image generation techniques is not possible, because the rendering time for each frame can be arbitrary long, perhaps taking hours for ray tracing complex scenes, or performing radiosity calculations. The only way such animations can be viewed in real time is to record them on a storage medium such as video tape or film, and play them back in real time. The system we developed to perform this process consists of hardware and software, and is described in the following sections.

2. DESCRIPTION OF THE EQUIPMENT

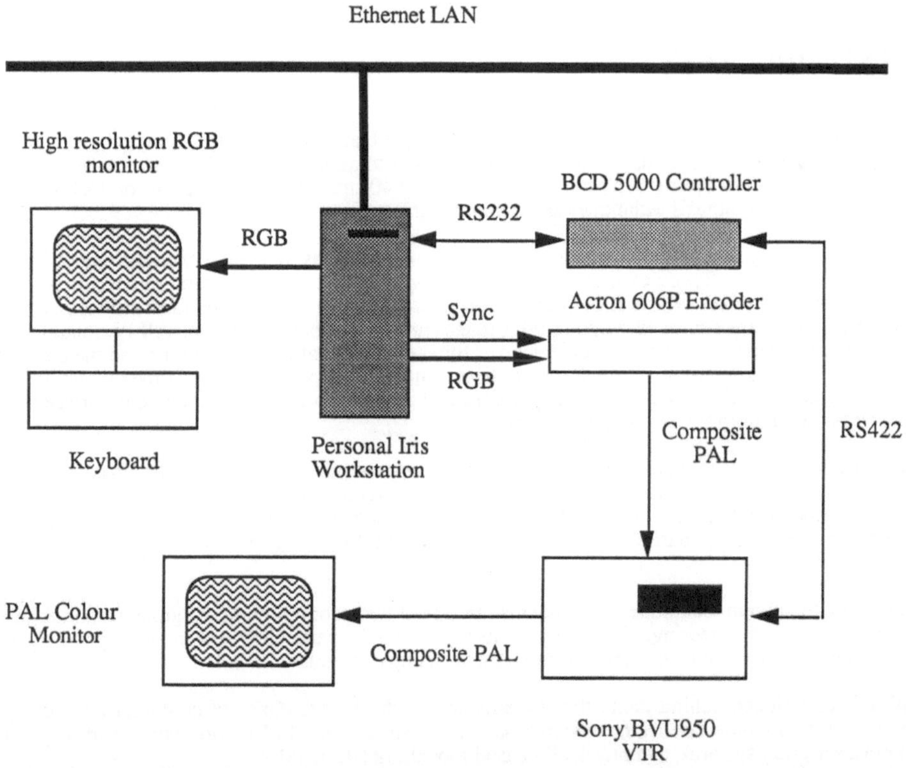

Fig. 1. The animation system

The hardware parts of the system, shown schematically in Fig. 1, consist of an Iris 4D/25 workstation equipped with a Video Genlock board that allows RGB output at the PAL resolution of 780x576 pixels, an Acron 606P Encoder for converting the RGB signals to composite PAL video, a BCD 5000 Animation Controller, and a frame accurate Sony BVU 950 U-matic video tape recorder. The BVU 950 is equipped with a Time Code Generator/Reader for generating and reading EBU longitudinal time code signals.

Getting the system to work was not a simple task for a number of reasons. First, each piece of equipment was from a different manufactor, and they all had to work together. Second, no member of staff had a video background, which was necessary to understand the video jargon in the equipment manuals. We had to obtain frequent phone advice from the equipment retailers, and at one stage the retailer of the Acron Encoder had to send a video technician around with testing equipment to diagnose and fix some problems. Third, all the equipment originated in the US and Japan, which would have made direct contact with the manufactors expensive. These counties also use NTSC as the TV broadcast standard instead of PAL and use SMTE time code signals instead of EBU.

3. THE VIDEO EDITOR SOFTWARE

There are two problems associated with the frame by frame recording process.

The first problem concerns the way the Personal Iris workstations work. The Iris video generator can only generate RGB signals at two resolutions : 1280 x 1024 pixels for driving the computer screen, and (when equipped with a Video Genlock board), PAL resolution at 780x576 pixels. Only one of these resolutions is operative at any time, and when in PAL mode, the computer screen is unusable. This is because the monitor is only designed for the high resolution signals. The contents of the PAL window, the lower left 780x576 pixels on the screen, can be seen in the attached PAL monitor shown in Fig. 1. This monitor is also used for viewing the tape. As a result, the Iris cannot be used directly for anything else while a program is generating frames and recording them on tape.

The second problem concerns the technical details of the recording process itself. To record an animation using frame by frame recording, a knowledge of how to program the BCD controller is necessary, as is some knowledge of how the Sony tape recorder works. In addition, during the recording process, some frames are sometimes not recorded properly. If this happens the frame (or sequence of frames) must be replaced on the tape. This is not a trivial exercise, particularly for students (and staff members!) who are usually not familiar with video terminology and operations.

The Video Editor described here was designed to overcome these two problems, and a schematic view of the system appears in Fig. 2. The software consists of a number of functions which can be called from an application C program. It provides the following functions:

(1) An application program such as a ray tracer, which generates a sequence of frames to be animated, can easily store the frames in separate files on the the Iris hard disk. The frames are stored in compressed form using the UNIX *compress* command, and individually numbered in sequence. This helps overcome the first problem discussed above because the application program, or multiple application programs, can generate and store frames in the background while the Iris is used for other tasks. In fact, since no special equipment is required for this, the application programs can run on any of the Iris workstations on the network, as well as other workstations.

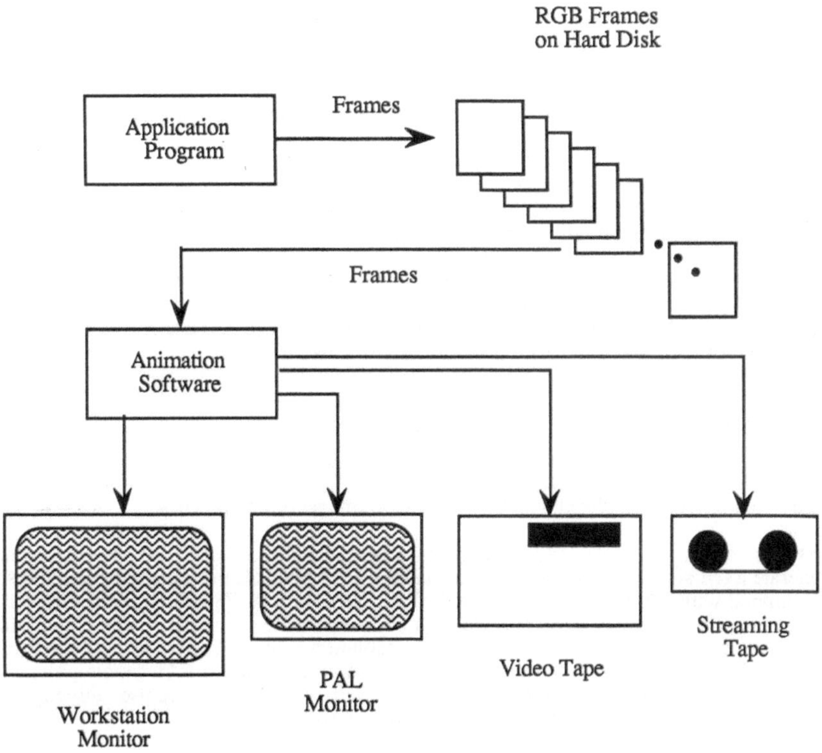

Fig. 2 Schematic illustration of the animation recording system

To store the frames on disk, the user only has to insert a few statements in the application program, as indicated in the following pseudo code :

```
char  filename [255] ;
int   i ;

i = 1 ;
while (more frames to generate)
{
   Generate a frame
   sprintf (filename,".rgb.%d",i++) ;
   grab (filename) ;
}
```

The function *grab*, which is part of the animation software, stores the frame on disk in compressed form.

(2) Sequences of frames which form an animation sequence can be displayed on the Iris screen. Because of data transfer rates, this is slower than real time animation, but gives the user the opportunity to preview the animation. The user can specify which frames are to be displayed, for example every 5th frame, instead of every frame. If some of the frames need to be rendered again, they can be easily stored on disk again with the correct numbers.

(3) Sequences of frames can be recorded on video tape using frame by frame recording by entering a simple command. The user can specify where on the tape the recording is to start, how many frames are to be recorded, and which frames on the hard disk are to be recorded.

(4) Sequences of frames on the video tape can be played in real time, or the frames can be stepped through slowly. Individual frames can also be displayed. Frames from the video tape are displayed on the PAL video monitor in Figs. 1 and 2.

(5) A single frame, or a sequence of frames on the tape can be replaced with the same number of new frames.

(6) Frames on the hard disk can be archived on streaming tape in *tar* format, and retrieved from the tape. This is useful for permanent storage of the frames in RGB format and for transporting images from one site to another.

The Editor not only provides a simple means for frames to be stored on the hard disk, but removes a lot of the tedium from the user in having to program the BCD animation controller or the Sony tape recorder. It is the controller that sends instructions to the tape recorder, and the Editor provides a simple set of commands for sending instructions to the controller. At the user level the commands specify the tasks the tape recorder is to perform, and make no direct reference to the controller commands. A summary of the Editor commands is given in the Appendix.

4. USE OF THE VIDEO EDITOR

The Editor was used for the first time in *Topics in Computer Graphics* in Spring Semester 1991, and it was very successful. It is a valuable tool for teaching animation techniques because it allows computationally intense calculations to be animated. In ray tracing for example, animated sequences are an excellent way to illustrate some of the effects associated with the refraction of light through transparent media. The system is also being used for some research projects.

The main problem associated with its use was one of disk storage capacity for the images before they are recorded to video tape. Even using compression techniques, the School does not have the capacity during semester time to store the frames for more than a few animation sequences. Fortunately the system allows sections of animations to be generated (one second for example) and then recorded. Using this technique, it is not necessary to store all the frames on disk at one time. The use of more efficient image compression techniques in the future such as JPEG and MPEG will alleviate this problem.

Figure 3 shows a frame from a 40 second ray traced animation *Through the Looking Glass* produced by Phillip Drury, a student in *Topics in Computer Graphics.* As each frame for this animation took up to 2 hours to generate on an Iris, and Mr. Drury wrote a distributed ray tracer which used up to forty workstations in the School (Silicon Graphics and Suns) to render the frames. Figure 4 shows a frame from an animation sequence which involves fractal mountains. This was produced by Mr Steve Davies, another student in *Topics in Computer Graphics.*

Fig. 3 A frame from *Through the Looking Glass* by Phillip Drury.

Fig. 4 Fractal mountain animation by Steve Davies.

5. FUTURE DIRECTIONS

The system is presently being modified to use the JPEG compression algorithm, and in future will also use the MPEG algorithm.

At present, titling sequences have to be generated by the application programs, and a useful addition would be software for the production of title and credit sequences that could be pre-pended and appended to the RGB sequences.

The Editor works in the normal UNIX command line interface, and its ease of use would be enhanced if it used the Iris's windowing system to provide a graphical user interface.

There are no facilities for adding sound tracks to the recordings at present, and this would also be a useful addition to the system.

Although the system is written specifically for the equipment used in the School of Computing Sciences, the particular combination of equipment we use is quite common. The system could be modified without difficulty to work with other equipment. For example, the BCD 5000 controller works with over 30 different VTR's and laser disk players, and a single command specifies which machine. The most extensive changes would be required if a different controller was used. The software is all written in C and there is very little that is specific to the Iris.

Copies of the software can be obtained free of charge from Kevin Suffern.

ACKNOWLEDGEMENTS

We thank Michael Murray who wrote some of the initial code and provided advice on the design of the Editor.

APPENDIX

Summary of Video Editor commands

Notation :

Two types of frame numbers are used in the commands listed below. The first are frame numbers of the RGB images on the hard disk; images are named with the format **stem.rgb.framenumber**, where **stem** is the name of the sequence, **rgb** indicates the frame is in RGB format, and **framenumber** is an integer. Example : **test.rgb.1, test.rgb.2...test.rgb.1000**.

The second type of frame numbers refer to frames on the video tape, and these can be expressed in two formats. The first is an absolute frame number, where each frame is numbered consecutively from the start of the tape, for example 10029 is the 10029th frame from the beginning of the tape. The other format is EBU which is the form : hour:minute:second:frame, where there are 25 frames per second. For example, the absolute frame number 10029 is 00:06:41:04 in EBU, that is, 6 minutes, 41 seconds, and 4 frames. Commands which take video frame numbers will accept either format.

Entries enclosed in square brackets [ ] are optional

list [dir]
List all frame sequences in the specified directory. Default is the current directory.

display name.rgb
display stem fromFrm toFrm step
Display the specified frame or sequences of frames on the hard disk.
Example **display test 1 1000 1,** displays every frame from 1 to 1000.

record name.rgb [frm]
Record the single frame at the specified frame number **frm** on the video tape. The default is the current frame number.

record stem first last step [frm]
Record the sequence of frames from the **stem** sequence starting at **first** and ending at **last**. The recording starts at the specified video frame on the tape. The default is the current frame. The argument **step** specifies which frames on the disk are to be recorded. For example, **step** = 1 means every frame. Sometimes a quick preview of the animation may be desired, in which case **step** > 1 can be used.
Example **record test 1 1000**

goto frm
Go to the specified frame on the video tape.

Examples	**goto 10029**	(Absolute frame number)
	goto :00:06:41:04	(EBU frame number)

play fromFrm toFrm
Play the specified sequence of frames on the video tape in real time (25 frames per second).

step [+ [n] | – [n]]
Step forwards or backwards the specified number of frames on the video tape. The default is one frame forward, the vertical bar is logical conjunction.

startgenlock
Put the Iris display into PAL mode.

endgenlock
Restore the high resolution Iris RGB mode.

open
Open the connection between the Iris and the BCD controller.

Close
Close the connection between the Iris and the BCD controller.

putarchive directoryname
Store the contents of **directoryname** on streaming tape in tar format.

getarchive directoryname
Restore the tar archive from streaming tape to **directoryname**.

help
Displays all the commands and their usage.

REFERENCES

Barr AH (1989) Topics in Physically Based Modelling, Addison-Wesley, New York.

Suffern KG and Murray MJ (1990), A System for Teaching Rendering and Animation Techniques in Computer Graphics, Computers in Education, McDougall A and Dowling C (Editors), Elsevier Science Publishers, 305-310.

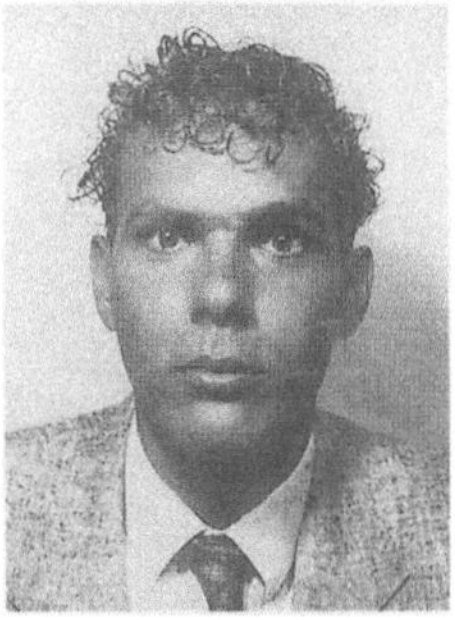

Neil Van Domselaar is currently employed at Security Domain Pty. Ltd. in Sydney, Australia. His research interests include computer graphics and operating systems. He completed a Bachelor of Applied Science Degree in Computing Science at the University of Technology, Sydney in 1991.

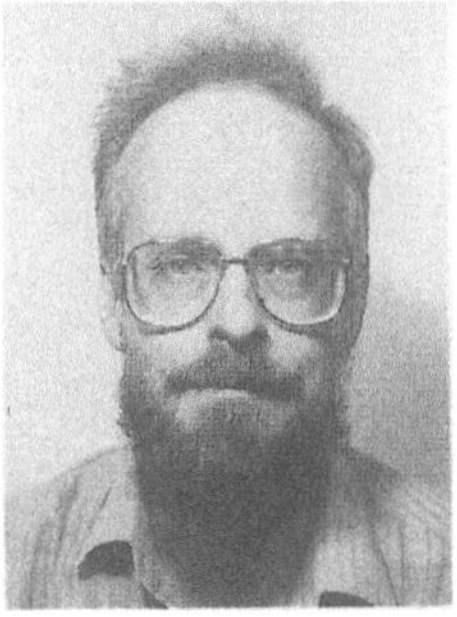

Kevin Suffern received an M.Sc. from Cornell University in Astronomy in 1973 and a Ph.D. in Applied Mathematics from the University of Sydney in 1978. From 1979 to 1981 he worked in the School of Mathematics and Physics at Macquarie University in Sydney, before joining the School of Computing Sciences at the University of Technology, Sydney, where he is currently a Senior Lecturer. In 1986 he was a Visiting Research Scientist in The Center for Interactive Computer Graphics, Rensselaer Polytechnic Institute, and in 1990 he was a Visiting Associate Professor in the Rensselaer Design Research Center, Rensselaer Polytechnic Institute. His main interests are computer graphics, computer aided geometric design, and computer art. He is a member of ACS, ACM, and SIGGRAPH.

Address : School of Computing Sciences, University of Technology, Sydney, PO Box 123, Broadway, NSW, AUSTRALIA

E-mail : kevin@socs.uts.edu.au

Iain Sinclair is an undergraduate student at the University ofTechnology, Sydney. His interests include computer animation, computer art and human-computer interaction.

Address : School of Computing Sciences, University of Technology, Sydney, PO Box 123, Broadway, NSW, AUSTRALIA.

E-mail : axolotl@socs.uts.edu.au

Author Index

Keyword Index